Traces of History

Patrick Wolfe is a writer and historian who lives and works in Wurundjeri country near Healesville, Australia. His books include *Settler Colonialism and the Transformation of Anthropology*. He has worked at universities in Australia and the United States and is currently in the History Programme at La Trobe University.

Traces of History

Elementary Structures of Race

PATRICK WOLFE

VERSO
London • New York

First published by Verso 2016
© Patrick Wolfe 2016

Cover Image: Arthur Boyd, *Persecuted lovers* (1957–58), Melbourne oil, tempera on composition board, 137.2 × 182.9 cm 141.5 × 187.0 × 7.0 cm (frame). A.R.Ragless Bequest Fund 1964 Art Gallery of South Australia, Adelaide

3 5 7 9 10 8 6 4

Verso
UK: 6 Meard Street, London W1F 0EG
US: 20 Jay Street, Suite 1010, Brooklyn, NY 11201
www.versobooks.com

Verso is the imprint of New Left Books
ISBN-13: 978-1-78168-917-2 (PB)
ISBN-13: 978-1-78168-916-5 (HC)
eISBN-13: 978-1-78168-919-6 (US)
eISBN-13: 978-1-78168-918-9 (UK)

British Library Cataloguing in Publication Data
A catalogue record for this book is available from the British Library

Library of Congress Cataloging-in-Publication Data
A catalog record for this book is available from the Library of Congress

Typeset in Galliard by MJ&N Gavan, Truro, Cornwall
Printed in the US by Maple Press

For my brother Mike and in loving memory of our sister Mary,
whose endless strength will always be an inspiration.

Mary Wolfe, 1952–2014
Londoner, lesbian, teacher, cyclist, author,
activist, friend, auntie, sister

Contents

Contents

Introduction

Teaching Aboriginal History at an Australian university brought me into unexpected contact with race politics in the United States. A disproportionate number of my students were from the USA, exchange students looking for something they could not study at their home universities. When asked what sparked their interest in the history of Aboriginal peoples' experience of White Australia, these students were almost unanimous:

'I've studied race issues back home, from slavery to civil rights, and I'd like to know how Black people have fared in Australia.'

'Well,' I would respond, 'Aboriginal people here are indeed called "Black", only they're Indigenous. Their ancestors weren't bought and sold in slave markets. They were dispossessed. Indians are Aboriginal people's closest counterparts in the United States, not Black people.'

With few exceptions, this reply would elicit surprise, or sometimes a polite indifference. Some students, by no means only African American ones, would respond: 'Maybe; but for me race is about colour. That's what leads to discrimination. When you say "colored" in the United States, you generally mean Black. That's why I'm interested in the Aborigines. They're Black, too.'

The few Aboriginal students tended not to reciprocate this sentiment. They generally took well to the US students, but without selecting for colour. They simply preferred them to the White Australians, whose innocence was all too familiar. Mention Native Americans, however, and the response of Aboriginal students was immediate and positive, as it was to the mention of Maoris, Palestinians, Sami, West Papuans or Native Hawaiians. In each case, Aboriginal students responded with a confidence they rarely displayed within the White university, a confidence that declared them to be speaking of their own. The community these students shared with other Indigenous people is deeper than colour, and more specific than discrimination. It is a common history: one of invasion, of loss of land, of elimination, of resistance, of survival and the hazards of renaissance. The role that colonialism has assigned to Indigenous people is to disappear. By contrast, though slavery meant the giving up of Africa, Black Americans were primarily colonised for their labour rather than for their land. These basic historical differences live on in settler popular culture, where representations of Black Australians and Red Americans distinctly resemble each other, while each contrasts sharply with representations of Black Americans. While Aboriginal people are called Black, for instance, they are not popularly credited with the natural sense of rhythm that still signifies fitness for labour on the part of those whose ancestors were enslaved. Conversely, unlike Aborigines, Black Americans have not been routinely stereotyped as a dying race. This convenient condition has instead been assigned to Native Americans.

Racialised distinctions such as these bespeak different histories, of different forms of expropriation – in one case of labour, in another of land. Moreover, such differences are site-specific. Whereas the enslavement of Africans in the United States produced the most rigorously polarised regime of race, the enslavement of Africans in Brazil produced a variegated continuum of colour classifications. To recuperate the distinct histories that fall together under the common heading of 'race', this book will trace some of the ways in which regimes of race have reflected and reproduced different forms of colonialism. Race, I shall argue, is a trace of history: colonised populations continue to be racialised in specific ways that mark out and reproduce the unequal relationships into which Europeans have co-opted these populations. This argument will be exemplified with reference to the diversity distinguishing racial discourses obtaining in Australia, the USA, Brazil, central Europe, and Palestine/Israel.

The chapters to come will explore a range of racial constructs, each instantiating a particular colonial relationship: in Australia and in the USA, White authorities have generally accepted – even targeted – Indigenous people's physical substance, synecdochically represented as 'blood', for assimilation into their own stock. When it has come to African American people's physical substance, however, it has only been in the past few decades that US authorities have dispensed with the most rigorously exclusionary procedures for insulating the dominant stock, the 'one-drop rule' having assigned a hyperpotency to African heredity that recalls the ineradicability of Jewishness in European anti-semitism.[1] By contrast, Brazil's policy of 'racial democracy' has sought to whiten the African Brazilian population by means of a combination

---

1 Following Hannah Arendt, I spell antisemitism with a lower-case 's' on the ground that there is no such thing as Semitism.

of White immigration and officially sanctioned miscegenation intended to lighten the prevailing phenotype. Strategically, Brazil's project of deracinating lower-order African Brazilians with a view to constructing a uniformly European nation resembles Israel's project of deracinating lower-order Arab-Jews with a view to constructing a uniformly Jewish nation. In these last two cases, as we shall see, race works through *de*-racination.

There are no grounds for assuming that such striking disparities represent the uniform workings of a discursive monolith called 'race'. Rather, this book will stress the diversity distinguishing the regimes of difference with which colonisers have sought to manage subject populations. These distinctions are very important. They entail different, and not always harmonious, strategies of anticolonial resistance. For instance, when Black people in the USA campaigned for equal rights in the mid-twentieth century, much of their political programme centred on the demand that they be treated equally with Whites. At the same time, however, treating Indians the same as Whites – which is to say, assimilating them into mainstream society – was a settler-colonial strategy that the Native American political movement, in common with the Aboriginal political movement in Australia, was striving to resist. The mathematics of the head-count is inimical to Native sovereignty. A focus on colour (or non-Whiteness) obscures such historically produced differences – in this case, between a history of bodily exploitation and one of territorial dispossession. A relationship premised on the exploitation of enslaved labour requires the continual reproduction of its human providers. By contrast, a relationship premised on the evacuation of Native people's territory requires that the peoples who originally occupied it should never be allowed back.

A mutuality between these otherwise antithetical relationships was sealed in the White man's discourse of property. As John Locke provided, in texts that would profoundly influence Euroamerican colonial ideology, private property accrued from the admixture of labour and land.[2] As this formula was colour-coded on the colonial ground, Blacks provided the former and Indians the latter, the application of Black people's labour to Red people's land producing the White man's property – a primitive accumulation if ever there was one. The two societies, Native and enslaved, were of antithetical but complementary value to White society. Whereas Black people were valuable commodities, Indians obstructed the expansion of settlement. Though juridically excluded, therefore, enslaved people were demographically fostered, to the extent that their numbers continued to grow even after slave imports into the USA were

---

2 John Locke, *Two Treatises of Government* (Cambridge: Cambridge UP, 1963 [1698]).

finally halted in 1808.[3] In the Indian case, by contrast, no effort was spared to eliminate them, in ways that have varied according to context. The expansion and consolidation of US settler society conjoined and depended on both these historical relationships, along with others. To be effective, anti-racist solidarities should conjoin as wide a range of historical relationships as colonialism itself has created.

Traces of History

In the sound-bite vocabulary of race, the three points of Eric Williams's Atlantic triangle,[4] Africa, America, and Europe, became embodied as Black, Red, and White: a chromatic taxonomy that continues to register the historical relationships that gave rise to it. Thus it is no accident that the most durable names that have been applied to the two colonised populations, Black (or Negro) and Indian, refer to a bodily characteristic and a territorial designation respectively. Racially, Black people's value as labour was registered in a regime whereby no amount of amalgamation (miscegenation, as it came to be called after the Civil War) would affect a person's status as a slave – and, in its fully racialised post-emancipation form, as a Black person.[5]

The founding logic of this calculus is brutally obvious: it maximised the reproduction of slaves. As such, it contrasts with the logic informing the racialisation of Indians, whereby – as in the case of Indigenous people in Australia – non-White blood figured as highly unstable rather than as inexhaustibly resistant to admixture. In both the USA and Australia, White blood has been credited with a cuckoo-like capacity to breed Nativeness out, a biogenetic extension of frontier homicide that contrasts diametrically with the one-drop rule that applied to the formerly enslaved. In the contemporary USA, blood quantum regulations, which exclude Indians with non-Indian ancestry from tribal reckoning, constitute a post-frontier analogue to the Vanishing Indian. In Australia, light

---

3 'The endurance and even expansion of United States slavery, without any substantial additions from importation, is unique in the world history of slavery.' Carl N. Degler, *Neither Black nor White: Slavery and Race Relations in Brazil and the United States* (New York: Macmillan, 1971), 61.

4 Eric Williams, *Capitalism & Slavery* (Chapel Hill: North Carolina UP, 1994 [1944]), 51–107.

5 F. James Davis, *Who Is Black? One Nation's Definition* (University Park: Pennsylvania State UP, 1991). Contemporary sources remain highly informative. See, e.g., A. E. Jenks, 'The Legal Status of Negro-White Amalgamation in the United States', *American Journal of Sociology* vol. 9 (1915–16), 666–78; Charles S. Mangum, Jr., *The Legal Status of the Negro* (Chapel Hill: North Carolina UP, 1940). Some counterexamples and regional variations to Davis's generally reliable account can be found in Pauli Murray (comp. and ed.), *States' Laws on Race and Color* (Athens, GA: Women's Division of Christian Service, 1951).

skin has rendered Aboriginal children liable to official abduction into White society.[6]

Thus there is nothing stable or essential about being Black, since Black people in Australia were targeted for biocultural elimination in a manner antithetical to the racial targeting of Black people in the USA. On the other hand, as will be shown in more detail below, Indigenous people in both countries, whether classified Red or Black, have been racialised in remarkably similar ways. What matters, then, is not phenotypical endowment. It is not as if social processes come to operate on a naturally present set of bodily attributes that are already given prior to history. Rather, racial identities are constructed in and through the very process of their enactment. In other words, just as, for Durkheim, religion was society speaking,[7] so, I shall argue, race is colonialism speaking, in idioms whose diversity reflects the variety of unequal relationships into which Europeans have co-opted conquered populations.

Given the variety of historical experiences that underlie different regimes of race, a plural formula might be more rigorous, if less felicitous: races are traces of histories. As Matthew Jacobson and others have shown, the demographic hothouse that was US society in the expansive nineteenth century engendered classificatory convolutions as White authorities strove to preserve Anglo-Protestant hegemony in the face of the ever-shifting balance of populations deriving from large-scale immigration. At various stages, the boundaries of Whiteness were stretched to accommodate 'Hindus', and even – despite the steady exclusion of the Chinese – some Japanese (though not, of course, for long).[8] According to David Roediger and Noel Ignatieff, those particularly unlikely Blacks, the Irish, were rendered White sometime around the middle of the nineteenth century.[9] Correspondingly, in the wake of slave emancipation (state by state in the North), the exclusion of Black ancestry was intensified, the racial category 'mulatto' being abandoned along with the juridical category 'free Black'.[10]

---

6 *Bringing Them Home: Report of the National Inquiry into the Separation of Aboriginal and Torres Strait Islander Children and Their Families* (Canberra: Human Rights and Equal Opportunity Commission, 1997); Anna Haebich, *Broken Circles: Fragmenting Indigenous Families, 1800–2000* (Fremantle: Fremantle Arts Centre Press, 2000).

7 Emile Durkheim, *The Elementary Forms of the Religious Life* (J. W. Swain, trans., London: Geo. Allen & Unwin, 1915 [1912]).

8 Matthew Frye Jacobson, *Whiteness of a Different Color: European Immigrants and the Alchemy of Race* (Cambridge, MA: Harvard UP, 1999).

9 David R. Roediger, *Working Toward Whiteness: How America's Immigrants Became White. The Strange Journey from Ellis Island to the Suburbs* (New York: Basic Books, 2005); Noel Ignatieff, *How the Irish Became White* (New York: Routledge, 1995).

10 David Theo Goldberg, *Racial Subjects: Writing on Race in America* (New York: Routledge, 1997), 35–42; Paul R. Spickard, *Mixed Blood: Intermarriage and Ethnic Identity in Twentieth-Century America* (Madison: Wisconsin UP, 1989), 433, n. 27;

By contrast, in the Native case, the end of the US frontier ushered in a new mode of programmatic whitening in the form of the blood quantum regime that initially attended the Dawes-era allotting of reservation land.[11] Comparably, across generations, Aboriginal children in Australia were stolen for Whiteness, while, in Palestine/Israel, in the wake of the 1948 Nakba, Mizrahi Jews, some of them Palestinian, were obliged to relinquish their Arabness and become second-class Jews, rendering the residual 'Arab' population – Palestinians – a minority.[12] In view of this diversity, it is apparent that, useful though it may once have been for denaturalising race, the well-worn piety that race is a social construct does not get us very far. Rather than a conclusion, this general premise founds a set of questions: how are races constructed, under what circumstances, and in whose interests? This book addresses these questions.

Ideology

As the foregoing illustrates, racial constructs emerge at different times as well as in different places. Thus it is reasonable to question the grounds for treating these multifarious differentiating practices under the one rubric. In view of their heterogeneity, do they share enough in common to be grouped together under the collective heading of 'race', in the singular? A reference shared by each of these varied constructs, a common language in which they are all couched, is ideological: the distinctive notion of race that emerged in Enlightenment discourse on both sides of the north Atlantic in the second half of the eighteenth century. This is not to suggest that Europeans failed to recognise and act on observable phenotypical differences until the 1780s. Precursors, 'blackamores' and their ilk, are legion.[13] Nor is it to pretend that an overland journey from,

---

Gilbert Thomas Stephenson, *Race Distinctions in American Law* (London: D. Appleton & Co., 1910), 13.

11 T. J. Morgan, 'What Is an Indian?', in Commissioner of Indian Affairs, *Sixty-First Annual Report* (Washington, 1892), 34; Paul Spruhan, 'A Legal History of Blood Quantum in Federal Indian Law to 1935', *South Dakota Law Review* 51 (2006), 32; Kent Carter, 'Snakes & Scribes: The Dawes Commission and the Enrollment of the Creeks', *Prologue Magazine* (US National Archives) 29, no. 1 (Spring 1997). See archives.gov/publications.

12 Ella Shohat, 'Sephardim in Israel: Zionism from the Standpoint of Its Jewish Victims', *Social Text* 19/20 (1988); Shohat, *Taboo Memories, Diasporic Voices* (Durham: Duke University Press, 2006); Yehouda Shenhav, *The Arab Jews: A Postcolonial Reading of Nationalism, Religion, and Ethnicity* (Stanford: Stanford University Press, 2006); Sami Shalom Chetrit, *Intra-Jewish Conflict in Israel: White Jews, Black Jews* (London: Routledge, 2010). *Nakba* is an Arabic term meaning 'catastrophe'. Palestinians and others use it to refer to the ethnic cleansing that accompanied the establishment of the state of Israel in 1948.

13 From an extensive, and all too often conceptually unsystematic, literature, see, e.g., Winthrop D. Jordan, *White over Black: American Attitudes Toward the Negro,*

say, Botswana to Finland would fail to disclose a significant degree of anatomico-geographical correlation. The point is, rather, that the mere fact that people have differentiated between human collectivities does not mean that they have been imbued with the discursive formation that today we call 'race'.

Indeed, the unexamined assumption that other forms of collective differentiation necessarily presuppose racial thinking is a prime example of the ideological process whereby race has been naturalised in Western culture. European xenophobic traditions such as Judaeophobia, Islamophobia or Negrophobia are considerably older than race. Though most if not all of its ingredients can be found in earlier classifications, race itself is a distinctive configuration of ideological elements that we do not find configured in this way before the late eighteenth century, but that we do find so configured, and mutually reinforcing, from that time on.[14] Moreover, this configuration is a specifically European (or Eurocolonial) invention. While other societies have invaded, colonised, and settled – albeit on a smaller scale than Europe – the discourse of race is a distinctly European phenomenon, one among any number of cultural typologies – that we may term xenologies – for differentiating between human collectivities. Accordingly, interesting though comparative information relating to non-European colonial discourses would be, this book confines itself to European (extending to Western) colonialism.

As it emerges in the late eighteenth century, race is a classificatory concept with two general characteristics. First, it is hierarchical. Difference is not neutral: to vary is to be defective, in concert with the degree of variation alleged to obtain. Second, it links physical characteristics to cognitive, cultural, and moral ones, encompassing the concrete and the abstract, the animal and the human, the somatic and the semiotic.[15] Thus race is not a negotiable condition but a destiny, one whose principal outward sign is the body. In systematically harnessing social hierarchies to natural essences and recruiting physical characteristics to underwrite the scheme, race constitutes an ideology in the purest of senses.[16]

1550–1812 (Chapel Hill: North Carolina UP/Institute of Early American History and Culture, 1968).

14   See, e.g., Ian Hannaford, *Race: The History of an Idea in the West* (Baltimore: Johns Hopkins UP, 1996); George L. Mosse, *Toward the Final Solution: A History of European Racism* (Madison: Wisconsin UP, 1985).

15   This formula is my own distillation from the very large literature on race. 'The search for the *Leitmotiv*, for the rhythm of the thought as it develops, should be more important than that for single casual affirmations and isolated aphorisms.' Antonio Gramsci, *Selections from the Prison Notebooks* (Quintin Hoare and Geoffrey Nowell Smith, trans. and eds, London: Lawrence and Wishart, 1971), 383–4.

16   As used by Marx and Engels, who did not define the concept formally, ideologies represent ruling groups' dominance as given in nature rather than as historically imposed and contingent. Attributing suzerainty to natural processes is a particularly

Historically, the emergence of the ideology of race accords with the shift from mercantilism to an industrial economy, which transformed colonial social organisation in the century following the Enlightenment. Upon industrialisation, the colonial system that had centred on the trading-post gave way to a set of global social relations in which, both at home and abroad, production and consumption were reconstituted to suit the requirements of metropolitan factories.[17] This system, which was much more invasive than mercantilism's trading at the borders, dispensed with the Native middleman and introduced the logic of production into the heart of Native societies, requiring either their removal or their transformation. Disciplinary innovations of the type that we associate with Michel Foucault were integral to this shift.

By comparison, mercantile relationships such as those that had characterised the North American fur trade had been relatively unintrusive. Around the Great Lakes, for instance, in the intercultural middle ground that Richard White has magisterially narrated, with its assorted boundary-straddlers, *coureurs de bois*, mixed marriages, Métis and related hybridities, the fur trade had produced dependency but not – at least, not on a general scale – direct exploitation.[18] Industrialisation cut out the middle ground, taking much of the Native population with it. On this basis, the classificatory shift that Ann Stoler has identified – from generic alterities such as colour and religion that had circulated in early forms of European colonialism, to the consolidation of race as the 'organizing grammar' of the nineteenth-century colonial system[19] – can be seen as key to the increasingly intrusive regimentation that the shift to an industrial economy involved.

To turn to race's thematic content, I wish to propose that what sets race apart from other ideological constructs – and definitively embeds it in the late eighteenth century – is its merger of two central but otherwise distinct elements of Enlightenment discourse. Race reconciled the great taxonomies of natural science with the political rhetoric of the rights of man. The political optimism infusing the belief in improvement sat awkwardly with the immutable categories of philosophical realism, opposing the hierarchical structuring of natural-scientific

powerful mode of legitimation, since it renders the situation seemingly eternal and unchangeable. See, e.g., Karl Marx and Friedrich Engels, *The German Ideology* (New York: International Press, 1970), 64–5.

17   For a clear and concise summary of this much-discussed shift, see Peter Burnham, 'Capitalism, state, political economy', in Iain McLean and A. McMillan (eds), *The Oxford Concise Dictionary of Politics* (Oxford: Oxford UP, 2003).

18   Richard White, *The Middle Ground: Indians, Empires, and Republics in the Great Lakes Region, 1650–1815* (New York: Cambridge UP, 1991).

19   Ann Laura Stoler, *Race and the Education of Desire: Foucault's* History of Sexuality *and the Colonial Order of Things* (Durham: Duke UP, 1995), 27.

classifications to the formal equality that constituted citizenship in liberal-democratic theory.[20] As a taxonomy par excellence, however, race provided categorical boundaries within genus *homo* that ensured the exclusiveness of the bearers of the rights of man.

This Jeffersonian fusion of bourgeois political ideology with classificatory natural science, of power with knowledge, gave race its singular epistemic purchase on post-Enlightenment thought. Thus the point is not only that the prestige of science afforded an authoritative warrant to the categorical cleavage within humanity that the concept of race ordained. It is rather (or also) that race reconciled and unified two of the most formative – perhaps the two most formative – components of Enlightenment discourse, resolving the tension between improvement and fixity by allocating them differentially. In this regard, race naturalised the theological narrative that was being substantially secularised in Enlightenment political ideology. Whereas the Rousseauan vision of improvability through education recast the Christian possibility of grace (in the case of Jews, of conversion), race could also endow debasement with the fixity of a curse. Race, in short, was endemic to modernity.

The ambivalent tension between these bedrock themes of Enlightenment thinking – taxonomy/fixity versus mutability/improvement – equipped race with a strategic versatility that enabled subject populations to be differentially racialised. Depending on which tendency prevailed, the same progressive hierarchy that could be used to show how colonised people's deficits were anchored in their physiognomy could also be used to show the occurrence of evolutionary progress up the hierarchy.[21] On the basis of the former alternative – savages were degraded and it showed in their bones – massacres and removals could be justified by reference to Natives' inbuilt incorrigibility. There was no reforming them. On the basis of the latter alternative, however – the option of progress – Natives were improvable, even assimilable, and, accordingly, fit for the attentions of missionaries and reformers. Hence some of the most significant opposition to Indian Removal in the Jackson-era USA came from missionaries who did not want their charges to be taken beyond their reach.[22] At the

---

20 The suggestion is only that there was tension between these two strands of Enlightenment discourse, not that they were contradictory. In promoting personal observation over orthodoxies received from the fathers, empiricism was inherently democratic.

21 A paradigm case of these hierarchies is Petrus Camper's craniometry. See Ann Thompson, 'Issues at Stake in Eighteenth-Century Racial Classification', *Cromohs* 8 (2003), 1–20. Human skulls were first divided (according to the *norma verticalis*, or view from above) into the familiar hierarchy of five varieties (Caucasian, Mongolian, Ethiopian or Negroid, American, Malay) by Johann Friedrich Blumenbach in the third edition (not the 1775 first edition that is customarily cited) of his *De Generis Humani Varietate Nativa Liber* (Göttingen, 1795).

22 Theda Perdue, 'Race and Culture: Writing the Ethnohistory of the Early South',

same time, however, and on the basis of the same scale of improvability, Africans became irretrievably destined for slavery.

Race's adaptability was sufficient to accommodate the complexity of imperialism's far-flung network of unequal social relations. For every articulation – relations of slavery, of indenture, of dispossession, of compradorship, of (inter)mediation, of commercial exchange – a corresponding racial category could be nominated. This versatility is the key to race's heterogeneity, enabling the diverse range of applied constructs that we shall survey to be expressed in a common, genetically phrased idiom of hierarchy and deficit.

Racialisation

Ideology is, therefore, only part of the story, albeit an important one. In addition to noting race's development as an organised narrative or doctrine, we need to observe it in operation, as a set of classificatory regimes that seek to order subject populations differentially in pursuit of particular historical agendas. To this extent, the term 'racism' seems redundant, since race already is an 'ism'. As performed and contested on the ground, which is this book's focus, race emerges not as singular or unified but as a fertile, Hydra-headed assortment of local practices. To express this applied versatility, we may distinguish between race as doctrine, which is of a piece with Enlightenment thinking and has a measure of discursive coherence, and racialisation as an assortment of local attempts to impose classificatory grids on a variety of colonised populations, to particular though coordinated ends. This book is about racialisation, race in action, which is prior to and not limited to racial doctrine. It argues that different racialising practices seek to maintain population-specific modes of colonial domination through time. This is the sense in which I argue that race constitutes a trace of history. In historical practice, the ideology of race is intrinsically performative, in the sense classically espoused by J. L. Austin and John Searle: rather than simply describing human groups, it brings them into being as inter-relating social categories with behavioural prescriptions to match.[23] Racialisation refers to this active productivity of race, whereby colonialism refashions its human terrain.

It is important to note the priority of practice. Before the eighteenth

---

Ethnohistory vol. 51 (2004), 711; Mary E. Young, *Redskins, Ruffleshirts, and Rednecks: Indian Allotments in Alabama and Mississippi, 1830–1860* (Norman: Oklahoma UP, 1961), 28.

23 Performative utterances act on the world rather than merely describing it. Their force is illocutionary rather than propositional, constitutive rather than constative or declaratory. See J. L. Austin, *How to Do Things with Words* (Cambridge: Cambridge UP, 1975); John R. Searle, *Expression and Meaning: Studies in the Theory of Speech Acts* (Cambridge: Cambridge UP, 1979).

century, Europeans had not needed the doctrine of race to discriminate against subjugated populations.[24] Dispossession, slavery, expulsion, confinement, massacre and other xenophobic practices had been carried on in terms organic to the era concerned, with Christianity typically furnishing an exegetical warrant. Even doctrinally, many of the traits that would become associated with race had already been incorporated into colonial practice. As many scholars have observed, European traditions provided a demonology of themes and images (the wild man, witches, anthropophagy, nomadism, etc.) that were presupposed within colonialism and displaced onto newly discovered peoples.[25] In Shakespeare alone, the modern populations whose respective racialisations will be analysed below – Black people (Othello), Jews (Shylock) and Native Americans (Caliban) – had already been typified, only not in the language of race.[26] As race emerged in late-eighteenth-century Europe, however, it was the other way round: the discourse presupposed colonialism.

In particular, Jews were initially conspicuous by their absence from the ascending scales of skulls that marked the progression from simian depths up to the West European ideal type, often represented by Winckelman's Apollo Belvedere (who, comically enough, being a statue, did not actually boast a skull). Between the apes and Apollo, these charts placed Africans (or 'Kalmyks') below cranial images that could include ostensibly East Asian and Native American types but not Jews (See Fig. 1).[27] True, Jews could be said to have had an absent presence, with the lone eminence of Apollo struggling to exclude the Hebrew component from the Hebrew-Hellenic synthesis underlying Pauline Christian culture; but the Jewish element in these early racial hierarchies was at most tacit, in stark contrast to the prominence that representations of Jews would attain in later nineteenth-century racial discourse. As we shall see when we come to consider European antisemitism, it was not just that colonialism exported

---

24 Thus the distinction between racial doctrine and racialisation does not map onto that between langue and parole, since the practice precedes and is not regulated by the doctrine.

25 Well-known examples include Roger Bartra, *Wild Men in the Looking Glass: The Mythic Origins of European Otherness* (Carl Berrisford, trans., Ann Arbor: Michigan UP, 1994); Michael Taussig, *Shamanism, Colonialism, and the Wild Man: A Study in Terror and Healing* (Chicago: Chicago UP, 1987); Hayden White, 'The Forms of Wildness: Archaeology of an Idea', in White, *Tropics of Discourse: Essays in Cultural Criticism* (Baltimore: Johns Hopkins UP, 1978), 150–82. For some of the imagery, see Ambroise Paré, *On Monsters and Marvels* (Janis L. Pallister, trans., Chicago: Chicago UP, 1982 [1573]).

26 Shakespeare could not have heard of Australian Aborigines but it seems a safe bet that, had he been aware of their existence, a travestied Shakespearean Aboriginal would have become part of modern-Western legend.

27 Peter (Petrus) Camper, *Dissertation sur les Variétés de l'Espece Humaine* (Paris and the Hague, 1791), Table 3. Note how Apollo's implausibly robust marble hair enables his brow to figure as loftier than the others.

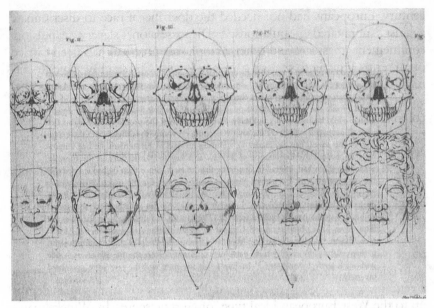

Fig. 1

stereotypes from the legendary traditions of Europe. Reciprocally, colonialism subsequently came to furnish a racialised mythology that could be
displaced back onto stigmatised minorities within Europe itself.

In other words, Jews came relatively late to race – or, rather, race came
late to Jews. Through colonial practice, a doctrine devised to rank subjugated peoples from outside Europe became discursively available to
be redirected inwards, onto emancipated European Jews, refurbishing
their theoretically outmoded exteriority. At that point Judaeophobia,
an age-old European practice, took on the distinctive features of racial
antisemitism, a post-Enlightenment discourse which, as Hannah Arendt
pointed out, had been significantly prefigured in the colonial world.[28]

There is a further reason for focusing on practice rather than merely
doctrine. No account of race that fails to address its emotive virulence can
be adequate. Fear, hatred, rapine, violence, callousness, and cruelty are of
the essence of race, and any discussion of the phenomenon that overlooks
or understates these core features can only miss the point. A comparable problem is raised by accounts of race and racism that try to reduce
this pathology of modernity to a rational calculus of interests, so that,
to cite but one well-known instance, it was once seen as progressive to
attribute the efflorescence of lynching in the southern states of the USA

28 Hannah Arendt, 'Race-Thinking Before Racism', *Review of Politics* 6 (1944),
revised in Arendt, *The Origins of Totalitarianism* (San Diego: Harvest/Harcourt, 1966),
158–84.

to the depression of the 1890s and to White people's perception that Blacks were rivals for their jobs.[29] While this perceived rivalry may well account for all sorts of ruthless tactics to eliminate Black people from the job market, tactics that would no doubt extend to homicide – especially since the discontinuation of slavery had removed the constraint on killing Black people that their status as valuable property had previously entailed – it fails to account for the demonic redundancy, the step so far over the line that it had to surpass itself, that characterised the surfeit of public violence and cruelty that lynching all of a sudden began to manifest from around the turn of the 1890s.

What kind of rational interest motivates individuals to wrench the teeth, nails and hair, peel the skin, gouge the eyes, castrate, and burn alive someone who is exclaiming in agony? Even harder to explain, how did such practices take place in public, in full daylight, and secure widespread popular endorsement – to the extent that an open trade in commemorative postcards and souvenir body parts developed?[30] How could it happen that, after Sam Hose had been slowly burned and mutilated to death in public in Atlanta, Georgia, in 1892, his knuckles should be placed on display in the window of a grocer's shop in Mitchell Street?[31] I leave the disturbing examples at that, but they could be multiplied at length. I cite them in order to stress that no rational calculus of interests can account for such redundant elaborations. Without some sense of the visceral force of race's appeal, we cannot begin to account for it, let alone do anything about it.

As a bodily attribute, race is not so much a concept as a sensation, mobilising the most immediate of nervous responses. Hence it exceeds

29 'The lynching of Black men and women was one of the extra-legal terrorist devices used to secure and maintain ruling class hegemony', Bettina Aptheker, in her (ed.), *Lynching and Rape: An Exchange of Views by Jane Addams and Ida B. Wells* (The American Institute for Marxist Studies, Occasional paper no. 25, New York: AIMS, 1977), 9.

30 To cite rather than recommend, since this reading is indescribably horrible: James Allen (ed.), *Without Sanctuary: Lynching Photography in America* (Santa Fe: Twin Palms Publishers, 2000); W. Fitzhugh Brundage, *Lynching in the New South: Georgia and Virginia, 1880–1930* (Urbana: Illinois UP, 1993); Philip Dray, *At the Hands of Persons Unknown: The Lynching of Black America* (New York: Random House, 2002); Jacqueline Dowd Hall, '"The Mind that Burns in Each Body": Women, Rape, and Racial Violence', in Ann Snitow, Christine Stansell and Sharon Thompson (eds), *Powers of Desire: The Politics of Sexuality* (New York: Monthly Review Press, 1983), 328–49.

31 The public sadism displayed in the all-White murder of Sam Hose (whose real name was Samuel Wilkes, may he rest in peace) became a cause célèbre among anti-lynching campaigners. See especially Ida B. Wells-Barnett's pamphlet, *Lynch Law in Georgia: A Six-Weeks' Record in the Center of Southern Civilization, as Faithfully Chronicled by the 'Atlanta Journal' and the 'Atlanta Constitution'* (Chicago: Chicago Colored Citizens, 20 June 1899), 7–10, accessed at memory.loc.gov/cgi-bin. For a defence of the behaviour of Hose's murderers in a respectable national journal, see Thomas Nelson Page, 'The Lynching of Negroes – Its Cause and Its Prevention', *North American Review* vol. 178 (1904), 33–48.

rational calculation – as Arendt put it, race has survived libraries of refutation.[32] On the day-to-day level, race penetrates the most mundane moments in life, acquiring recognition and reinforcement at the flick of an eye, a self-policing microphysics of biopower that incessantly implicates and re-implicates all parties to the encounter, as in some gigantic hall of mirrors ('Look, a Negro!').[33] Through such quotidian interchanges, race recruits biology to install the international division of labour at the level of individuals' own sensory experience, soliciting reflex allegiance to the otherwise disenchanting categories made available in capitalism's secular set of social relations. Offsetting the theoretically unrestricted social mobility that the 'free' market introduced, race provided a stable zone of ascribed and continuing identities, binding social reproduction to biological reproduction. Hence the fraught atmosphere of miscegenation discourse, in which sexual and social relations meet on the surface of the human body. In its vulnerability, promulgating absolute boundaries that could not be relied on to exist, miscegenation discourse was never far from the surpassing barbarities of lynching.

Under what circumstances, then, does racialisation occur? When, to put it bluntly, does race kick in? In this book, I argue that racialisation represents a response to the crisis occasioned when colonisers are threatened with the requirement to share social space with the colonised. In the Indigenous case, this threat arises in the wake of the frontier, when Natives become physically contained within settler societies. As we shall see, in both Australia and the USA, racial discourse intensified in the post-frontier era, with Indigenous people becoming subject to the divisive elaborations of blood quantum discourse. Alternatively, where the enslaved or the internally colonised are concerned, as in the cases of the American[34] slaves and the European Jews whose experiences we shall be considering, racial discourse has intensified in the wake of emancipation, which removes a juridical barrier that had previously set them apart from the dominant society as decisively as the physical frontier distanced Natives. In the context of this challenge, race's role as a by-product of democracy becomes particularly apparent in its retrieval of the inequities that the extension of citizenship has theoretically abolished.[35] As Vann Woodward observed of segregation in the US South:

32   Arendt, 'Race-Thinking Before Racism', 39.
33   The allusion is, of course, to Frantz Fanon, *Black Skin, White Masks* (Charles Lam Markmann, trans, New York: Grove Press, 1967), 109.
34   'American' here referring both to African Brazilians and to Black people in the USA. Except for quotations, the term 'American' has a continental reference in this book.
35   Kiernan Malik, *The Meaning of Race: Race, History and Culture in Western Society* (London: Macmillan, 1996) has explored the connections between race and democracy. With specific reference to the USA, see Edmund S. Morgan's pioneering *American*

The barriers of racial discrimination mounted in direct ratio with the tide of political democracy among whites. In fact, an increase of Jim Crow laws upon the statute books of a state is almost an accurate index of the decline of the reactionary regimes of the Redeemers and the triumph of white democratic movements.[36]

Race enabled universality to presuppose distinction.

It is important to make clear that the difference between these two occasions for racialisation – emancipation and territorial engulfment – is not the Cartesian opposition between, on the one hand, a social factor (emancipation) and, on the other, a pre-social or environmental one (territorial engulfment). Both are social factors. The governing settler-colonial imperative being the acquisition and retention of territory, its transfer from Native ownership requires the mobilisation of technologies of violence together with the social relations that underpin their deployment. Moreover, once engulfment has taken place – on the ending of the frontier – the obstruction that Natives present to the development of settler society ceases to be primarily physical, as in the frontier balance of violence, and persists as an exotically constituted set of alternative – and, even more inconveniently, prior – sovereignties, an intrinsically social condition. Under these circumstances, exclusion does not eliminate the Native counterclaim to the territory that settlers have transferred from their possession. Rather, exclusion merely preserves Native sovereignty in a separate realm that continues in parallel to the settler one.

This consideration does not apply in the case of imported populations, who are held to have surrendered their sovereignties before arrival; a formula that cannot be applied to people who were there before the settlers themselves arrived. Assimilation – the non-homicidal, or not necessarily homicidal, dissolution of Native difference into the settler mainstream – is a characteristically post-frontier attempt to eliminate the obstruction presented by the persistence of Native sovereignties along with their attendant territorial counterclaim. This process is no less social than emancipation. Both social goals – exclusion and assimilation – are pursued by means of race; exclusion being sought through eternalised constructs that rely on the theme of fixity in Enlightenment scientific realism, while assimilation is sought through permeable constructs that rely on the ethic of improvement in Enlightenment political discourse.

Slavery, American Freedom: The Ordeal of Colonial Virginia (New York: Norton, 1975), as taken up by David Brion Davis, *The Problem of Slavery in the Age of Revolution* (Ithaca: Cornell UP, 1975). More recently, Aziz Rana has treated the theme with reference to the dispossession of Native Americans. Rana, *The Two Faces of American Freedom* (Cambridge, MA: Harvard UP, 2010).

36 C. Vann Woodward, *A History of the South, Volume 9: Origins of the New South, 1877–1913*, Baton Rouge: Louisiana State UP/Littlefield Fund, 1951), 211.

It is crucial to note that the mutability of Native bloodlines is just as positively constructed as the fixity ascribed to the excluded. The propensity to vanish is no less essentialised than the propensity not to. Thus, accounts of race in the USA that marginalise the unstable racialisation of Indigenous people in comparison to the ineradicability ascribed to Black heredity are participating in the very phenomenon that they purport to analyse. This is also the case where race itself is depicted as only encompassing one of its variants – the one involving fixity – at the expense of assimilationism's soluble constructs. Significantly, this scholarly deficiency is less of a problem in Australia, where, with the notable exception of Pacific labourers indentured into the Queensland sugar industry, the economic counterparts to enslaved people in the USA – convicts and indenturees – were overwhelmingly White, the racialisation of Indigenous people being correspondingly less overshadowed in recent Australian scholarship.

Whether presented juridically or geographically, therefore, the threat to social space is no mere metaphor. Rather, in the most concrete of both practical and geographical senses, and often simultaneously, race and place are inextricable. The simplest definition of Indigenous people, obviously enough, is that they are the only ones who have not come from somewhere else. In US cities, these transnational somewhere-elses find approximate reconfiguration in the ethnic zoning of residential neighbourhoods, where locality recapitulates the myriad historical migrations whose convergence makes up the settler present, patchily reconfiguring imperialism's global complexity at the local level. No less concretely, in the US South, the defining feature of an 'uppity black' – which is to say, a candidate for lynching – was a failure to know their place, while the thoroughly racialised figure of the 'wetback' signifies a history of crossing over. In Australia, the settler euphemism of choice for the massacring of Aboriginal people, 'dispersal', was as inherently spatial as was its material outcome.[37] In antisemitic parlance, Jews somehow managed to combine confinement to the Pale of Settlement – or, locally, to the ghetto – with universal wandering. As apartheid-era South African Prime Minister B. J. Vorster said: 'If I were to wake up one morning and find myself a black man, the only major difference would be geographical.'[38]

---

37   Classic accounts include James Boyce, *Van Diemen's Land* (Collingwood: Black Inc., 2008); Bruce Elder, *Blood on the Wattle: Massacres and Maltreatment of Australian Aborigines since 1788* (Sydney: Child and Associates, 1988); Roger Milliss, *Waterloo Creek: The Australia Day Massacre of 1838. George Gipps and the British Conquest of New South Wales* (Ringwood, Australia: McPhee Gribble/Penguin, 1992).

38   Quoted in Ben Silverstein and Patrick Wolfe, 'Ideology', in Philippa Levine and John Marriott (eds), *The Ashgate Research Companion to Modern Imperial Histories* (Burlington: Ashgate, 2012), 484 (I would love to claim this find but, alas, it's one of Ben's).

Thus we should extend Mary Douglas's timeless insight that dirt is matter out of place to the human domain: race denotes certain peoples as being out of place, rendering the subordinate populations concerned inherently dirty, as we see in the ubiquitous linkage of race and hygiene.[39] The primal threat posed by contamination sheds some light on the barbarity characterising colonisers' treatment of subject populations. To contaminate is to invade. Race's deep anatomical moorings bring together geographical and physiological mappings so that a people in the wrong place is experienced as an assault on the body, summoning a reflex response which, though collectively enacted, is personally experienced at a powerfully intimate level. As Douglas also noted, cleansing is a response to danger, to the existential threat that dirt poses to purity.[40] The remedy for a people being out of place, after all, is ethnic cleansing.

Race would have been redundant in the mediaeval ghetto. When everyone, or practically everyone, was either Jewish – and, accordingly, inside – or Gentile – and, accordingly, outside – there was little to distinguish who you were from where you were. The algebra of inequality – inclusion versus exclusion, exploitation versus privilege, purity versus danger – was built into the landscape. As such, knowledge was local, in the most literal sense, a capacity to place each other that paired anonymity with anomaly. In being renowned for wandering – a distinctive accomplishment, born of expulsion – 'the Jew' gathered the insecurity of enclosure unto himself. When it confronts modernity, local knowledge struggles to maintain its anchorage in the consensual foundations of a situated community. The first time he attended a segregated theatre, Gustave de Beaumont, Alexis de Tocqueville's travelling companion in 'Jacksonian America', found his eye drawn to a dazzling beauty seated in the mulatto section, whose complexion was perfectly white. With precocious ethnographic decorum, he entered, as he put it, into the prejudices of his neighbour:

> I asked him how a woman of English origin could be so lacking in shame as to seat herself among the Africans.
> 'That woman', he replied, 'is colored.'
> 'What? Colored? She is whiter than a lily!'
> 'She is colored,' he repeated coldly; 'local tradition has established her ancestry, and everyone knows that she had a mulatto among her forebears.'[41]

---

39   Mary Douglas, *Purity and Danger: An Analysis of the Concepts of Pollution and Taboo* (New York: Praeger, 1966).

40   This is summed up in her title. Douglas, *Purity and Danger*. Andrea Smith has made a similar connection in her *Conquest: Sexual Violence and American Indian Genocide* (Boston: South End Press, 2005), 120.

41   Gustave de Beaumont, *Marie or, Slavery in the United States: A Novel of Jacksonian America* (Barbara Chapman, trans., Baltimore: Johns Hopkins UP, 1999 [1835]), 5.

In the absence of local knowledge, race restores place, compensating for anonymity. In the contemporary United States, to be the wrong colour is to live on the wrong side of the tracks. Beaumont happened on a revealingly transitional moment. Had he returned a decade or two later, the beauty's mulatto status could as well have depended on the perceived shading of her inner wrist. In the fluid spaces of urban modernity, as Malinda Lowery has remarked, 'where a black person's inferior economic status could not be assumed', race made the difference.[42]

Regimes of Race

The applied focus on race as practice does not mean that its doctrinal formulation is unimportant. Rather, racial doctrine is one among a number of resources that a given regime of race coordinates and mobilises, others being economic, political, moral, mythic, legal, institutional, sexual, and aesthetic – the whole gamut of social discourse.[43] I use the term 'regime' to express this comprehensiveness. Conceptually, the idea of a regime is indebted to Marcel Mauss's 'total social fact'.[44] Semantically, however, the unwieldiness of Mauss's term aside, the word 'fact' is too static and too politically neutral for what I want to express, which, apart from being mobile and active (race being high-maintenance), is quintessentially political, race being an instrument of overlordship.

Hence my preference for the term 'regime', which combines active direction and political dominance with an implication of accompanying contestation and resistance. The structures are not inert. They require constant maintenance and refurbishment, a contestatory process that, as we shall see, causes regimes of race to shift across time, taking on transformed modalities that bear the traces of anticolonial practice. Race, it cannot be stressed strongly enough, is a process, not an ontology, its varying modalities so many dialectical symptoms of the ever-shifting hegemonic balance between those with a will to colonise and those with a will to be free, severally racialised in relation to each other. Race registers the state of colonial hostilities. The common factor is Whiteness. Amidst all the differences distinguishing the various regimes of race that we shall examine, the overriding goal is White supremacy.

Throughout this book, therefore, regimes of race do not figure as faits accomplis, as transcending history, but as ever-incomplete projects whereby colonisers repetitively seek to impose and maintain White

---

42 Malinda Maynor Lowery, *Lumbee Indians in the Jim Crow South: Race, Identity, and the Making of a Nation* (Chapel Hill: North Carolina UP, 2010), 122.

43 Accounts such as Mosse's *Toward the Final Solution: A History of European Racism* only address the doctrinal component of racism as a whole.

44 Marcel Mauss, *The Gift: Forms and Functions of Exchange in Archaic Societies* (Ian Cunnison, trans., London: Cohen & West, 1966 [1925]), 76–7.

supremacy. There is nothing stable about race, nothing unchallengeable. Even in the heart of the metropolis, even where the basic distinctions of East and West, European and Arab, were concerned, as Saree Makdisi has recently brought to light:

> It took time for these kinds of constructs to develop in a self-sustaining way ... and for that to happen both population and space had to be configured and reconfigured, managed and manipulated, in order to eventually allow the self/other opposition to work on a large – racial or civilizational or even simply national – scale.[45]

Race's gathering together of the full range of social discourse is observable everywhere. Being central to colonialism, a system that appropriates and exploits land and labour, race's economic and political dimensions are obvious enough, as is its legal function of marking the uneven distribution of juridical statuses and rights between communities. Morally, race warrants uneven standards of treatment for different human groups, so it is only to be expected that social institutions from the domestic realm (the family) through to the most public of arenas (government) should be profoundly marked by race. Discursively, racialised groups are typically also gendered, as in the feminised 'Asiatic' male, while racial aesthetics are closely bound up with standards of beauty and ugliness, the quality of darkness falling on the wrong side of one of the deepest archetypical polarities in Western mythology.

Moreover, being so closely tied to biological reproduction, a heterosexual charge attaches to race that precipitates extreme sanctions and behaviours. Race's intimate neurophysiological anchorage – to share a race is to share a body – makes for a cathected mode of belonging that partakes of the emotional intensity of family ties, whose sexual insulation warrants the most extreme of sanctions. Thus it is no accident that the pre-eminent metaphor to be applied in twentieth-century racial discourse should be that of blood, the very quantity that, in being thicker than water, sacralises family relations, setting them apart from the generality of moral norms. As some of the following chapters will illustrate, this particularly applies to miscegenation discourse, which can provide a vantage point for comparing different regimes of race.

Preaccumulation

In addition to its synchronic gathering together of colonialism's coexistent social discourses, race compresses colonialism's cumulative history.

---

45 Saree Makdisi, *Making England Western: Occidentalism, Race & Imperial Culture* (Chicago: Chicago UP, 2014), 3.

Colonisers – at least, the successful ones – arrive already vested with a multitude of historical preconditions that equip them to prevail in their encounters with local populations. These preconditions, a kind of historical capital, bring together a range of economic, technological, military, cultural, and moral attributes that combine centuries of Eurocolonial history. Moreover, in any given case, this cumulative historical plenitude confronts an independently accumulated Indigenous plenitude with composite outcomes that are unique to each particular situation. I shall refer to both the historical endowment that colonisers bring with them and to Natives' countervailing historical plenitudes as preaccumulation. While derived from Karl Marx's concept of primitive accumulation, itself an adaptation of Adam Smith's 'previous' accumulation, preaccumulation departs from such predecessors in being externally activated, coming into play in the presence of a countervailing plenitude.[46] Colonialism did not impress its will on a blank slate.

Once established, European colonialism acquired global reach, a characteristic that endowed the project with an effectively unlimited capacity to reproduce itself. In settler colonies, this near inexhaustibility opposed itself to the relative fixity of the Native stock, by which I mean the finite aggregate of material assets that remains locally available for Native societies to reproduce themselves over the long term.

The disparity is crucial. In demographic terms, for instance, it meant that, whereas invasion rendered the Native population subject to extreme reproductive constraints, there were always more settlers where the first ones had come from – which, in the final analysis, meant anywhere else, the settler population being augmentable not only by further cognate settlers but, in addition, by any number of coerced subordinates imported from other sites of exploitation. Economically, Native societies were reduced to generating subsistence from an ever-shrinking repository that, even within territory that remained unconquered, became subject to the depredations of an advance guard of settlement made up of frontier irregulars (with or without auxiliary subordinates), imported livestock, exotic predators, and more besides. The technological and military capacities that settlers inherited from Europe's expansive history are also well known, as is Europeans' acquired immunity to the diseases they imported with them.

On occasion, the advantages could change hands. Thus the horses that facilitated Spanish conquests in the Americas subsequently helped Plains Indians hold off Euroamerican domination until the second half of the nineteenth century, while Maoris adopted the introduced potato, itself

---

46   Karl Marx, *Capital: A Critique of Political Economy* (vol. 1, Frederick Engels, ed., Samuel Moore and Edward Aveling, trans., Moscow: Progress Publishers, 1954), 667–715; Adam Smith, *An Inquiry into the Nature and Causes of the Wealth of Nations* (Edwin Cannan, ed., New York: Modern Library, 1937), 259–60.

a re-exported colonial import, to advantage. In Brazil, runaway slaves escaped on railways built to ship the very coffee they were supposed to be producing.[47]

On the whole, however, settlers brought with them a conquering inheritance that had been forged through centuries of colonial expansion and associated class struggle on an increasingly global scale. The two were inseparable, the cotton that the industrial proletariat made up in Manchester's dark mills being sourced from colonised labour put to work in Egypt, India, and the US Deep South, the two sources of labour further providing an expanding market for the products of their involuntary collaboration.

It is important to understand preaccumulation culturally as well as materially, as a historical endowment of consciousness. Colonisers brought with them historically specific ideologies of race, class, gender and nation that had participated decisively in collective subjugations at home and abroad. As Barbara Fields has observed:

> When English servants entered the ring in [colonial] Virginia, they did not enter alone. Instead, they entered in company with the generations who had preceded them in the struggle; and the outcome of those earlier struggles established the terms and conditions for the latest one. But Africans and Afro-West Indians did enter the ring alone.[48]

Unlike enslaved Africans in the Americas, Natives did not enter the ring alone. Their reinforcements were not oceans away. Nevertheless, their histories had equipped them with resources that were not tailored to the unequal confrontation that settlers' endless renewability set in train. Natives' finite local stock was no match for imperialism's global elasticity. Rather, they were reduced to relying on a shrinking pool of indigenous resources whose reproduction had been severely hampered by settler encroachments. The disparity was quantitative not qualitative, a matter of material renewability rather than of cultural aptitudes, the shrinkage of Natives' locally bounded subsistence stocks occurring in concert with, and being part of, the expansion of imperialism's global networks. Moreover, this aggregated historical disparity was telescoped at individual sites of confrontation. In contrast to the cumulative, centuries-long development of industrial capitalism and its global

---

47 'The very railways that had made the extension of coffee agriculture possible now served the slave.' Richard Graham, 'Action and Ideas in the Abolitionist Movement in Brazil', in Magnus Mörner (ed.), *Race and Class in Latin America* (New York: Columbia UP, 1970), 64. For the Maoris' adoption of the potato, see James Belich, *Making Peoples: A History of New Zealanders. From Polynesian Settlement to the End of the Nineteenth Century* (Honolulu: Hawai'i UP, 1996), 145–6, 159.

48 Barbara Jeanne Fields, 'Slavery, Race and Ideology in the United States of America', *New Left Review* 181 (1990), 104.

network of social relations, Eurocolonial society arrived in Native country *ex nihilo* (or perhaps *ex machina*) and ready-made, condensing the power and expansive violence of the long run. This pre-formedness, a plenitude that is relatively resistant to local determinations, is colonialism's primary competitive advantage.

There is a crucial difference between preaccumulation and the European experience of primitive accumulation that has figured so prominently in Marxist historiography. This is even apart from a certain Eurocentrism in established Marxist history-writing, which tends to emphasise the final stages of the production process – industrial technologies and the domestic process of class formation that accompanied their development – at the expense of earlier stages of primary production that were often conducted overseas, by subordinated labour not necessarily motivated by the lash of wages. Apart from the metropolitan parochialism of this narrative, whereby many of the raw materials of industrial production figure as somehow miraculously (or, at least, internally) conceived, the crucial difference is that, when Europe was piecing together its imperial-industrial-capitalist hegemony, there was no prior Europe already riding on its back. Arriving in Native country, on the other hand, capitalism already contained its own global preaccumulations – including, Russian-doll-like, capitalism itself – along with strategic resources such as the enslavement of Africans.

True, there were rival civilisational conglomerates, in particular the Islamic world, but these proved to be no match once the Atlantic had become a West-European sea.[49] Moreover, Native preaccumulations could themselves facilitate colonial expansion. In the Americas, for example, Natives taught Europeans to grow subsistence crops such as corn and potatoes. In early-colonial Australia, invading colonisers regularly marvelled at the local environment's park-like aspect, counting themselves multiply blessed that 'nature' (including divine providence) should have come to furnish them with ready-made grazing runs. In fact, the Australian landscape's benign aspect was the cumulative consequence of millennia of Indigenous management, in particular the use of fire to reduce undergrowth and to contain spontaneous conflagrations within local limits. Within a few years of Europeans taking over the country and discontinuing Native fire-management practices, the current cycle of massive bushfire disasters was set in train.[50] The land that settlers

---

49   This sea was, of course, actively populated by many different groups. Paul Gilroy, *The Black Atlantic: Modernity and Double Consciousness* (London: Verso, 1993) remains the classic source. My point concerns the ultimate overlordship of this densely transacted zone.

50   Tom Griffiths, *Forests of Ash: An Environmental History* (Cambridge: Cambridge UP, 2001); D. M. J. S. Bowman, *Australian Rainforests: Islands of Green in a Land of Fire* (Cambridge: Cambridge UP, 2000), 218–49. For a master-work on this and related

seize is already value-added. There is no such thing as wilderness, only depopulation.[51]

In replacing Indigenous agency with that of the cosmos, the concept of nature enabled improvements effected by Natives to figure as serendipity. This is an enduring settler theme. As Robert Kenny has recently observed in relation to the romantic strand in contemporary conservation discourse, 'to suggest that pre-settlement Australia was "pristine" is to place Aboriginal Australians in the category nature, and thus deny them humanity.'[52] Marx himself participated in this erasure, depicting capitalism in the Americas as being of the purest historical type, unalloyed by feudal survivals – without Europe, there could be no meaningful history.[53]

In this cutting-out of the Native middleman, *terra nullius* and market economics fuse inseparably, connecting settler capital directly to a landscape miraculously emptied of the accumulated human labour, male and female, that has made it what it is. In the outcome, all the ostensibly self-sustaining actors in liberalism's individualist drama – the entrepreneur, the labourer, the investor, the citizen – turn out to be collectively reliant on the continuing violence of colonial expansion. As Manu Vimalassery has pointed out, the very nations whose wealth was Adam Smith's central concern 'were in fact empires'.[54] Imperialism is not the latest stage of capitalism but its foundational warrant. To make the liberal an individual took a cast of thousands, most of them in the wings.

Ideologically, then, colonialism's preaccumulated inheritance consists not only in explicitly xenophobic discourses of human alterity such as scientific racism or the white man's burden. In all sorts of unspecific ways, colonised peoples could be assimilated to nature, placing them on the receiving end of Cartesian dualism and, accordingly, as in need of control.

---

topics, see Bill Gammage, *The Biggest Estate on Earth: How Aborigines Made Australia* (Sydney: Allen & Unwin, 2011).

51 See also Marcia Langton, 'What Do We Mean by Wilderness?: Wilderness and *Terra nullius* in Australian Art', *The Sydney Papers* (Sydney: Sydney Institution, summer 1996).

52 Robert Kenny, *Gardens of Fire: An investigative memoir* (Perth: Western Australia UP, 2013), 145.

53 In one of his panoramic asides, Marx characterised 'North America' as 'a country where bourgeois society did not develop on the foundation of the feudal system, but developed rather from itself; where this society appears not as the surviving result of a centuries-old movement, but rather as the starting-point of a new movement ... In England [by contrast], bourgeois society does not exist in pure form, not corresponding to its concept, not adequate to itself.' Karl Marx, *Grundrisse: Foundations of the Critique of Political Economy (Rough Draft)* (Martin Nicolaus, trans., London: Penguin/New Left Review, 1993), 884–5.

54 Manu Vimalassery, 'The Wealth of the Natives: Toward a Critique of Settler Colonial Political Economy', forthcoming in Patrick Wolfe (ed.), *The Settler Complex: Recuperating Binarism in Colonial Studies* (UCLA Indian Studies Center Press, 2015).

Ultimately, for instance, the expansionist master-narrative that historians have glossed as *terra nullius* relied on this assimilation. On the basis of a vernacular Lockeanism whereby property rights were seen as accruing from the admixture of one's labour with the soil – an entitlement evidenced by agriculture, irrigation, enclosure, centralised governance and a range of other qualifications that Natives were declared to lack – colonisers claimed entitlement to Native territory on the ground that Europeans alone had the purposive rationality required to render land more efficient (that is, capable of sustaining a higher population) than in its natural state, which was the condition in which it would languish if left in Native hands.[55] In contrast to Europeans, Natives had failed to disembed themselves from nature. They remained enchanted, in the most demeaning of senses.

In this wider cultural context, therefore, nature is not the only value that Kenny's latter-day conservationists preserve. Along with nature, they are equipping *terra nullius* with a twenty-first-century style of discursive sustainability. Moreover, in colonialism's Cartesian thematics, the corollary to being assimilated to nature is being inassimilable to culture. In this respect, the unassimilated Native contrasts maximally with *homo economicus* himself, whose formal contractual rationality – mechanical, impersonal, and, above all, context-neutral – rendered him free of historical accretions and, accordingly, maximally adaptable to a society in the making.

The need to accommodate a fractious convergence of settler populations, often bringing long-established metropolitan enmities with them, renders new-world societies susceptible to democratic ideologies that exchange immigrants' historical baggage for the abstract equivalence of egalitarian individualism. As Max Weber seemed to recognise in setting so much of his analysis of the emergence of the capitalist ethic in the USA, though without spelling this out: the unmarked means-end optimiser of the capitalist market place was simultaneously the ideal settler-coloniser, *homo assimilans*.[56]

Relations of Invasion

As observed, in concert with the ideological constructions that it gathers together, colonialism is a pre-eminently material set of institutions and

---

55   For the term '*terra nullius*', which was not in vogue in the eighteenth century, see Andrew Fitzmaurice, 'The Genealogy of *Terra Nullius*', *Australian Historical Studies* 129 (2007), 1–15.

56   Weber went back to his original 1905 publication to add material dealing specifically with the USA, in particular the essay 'The Protestant Sects and the Spirit of Capitalism'. See the expanded, Weber-authorised, 1920 version of his celebrated analysis, Max Weber, *The Protestant Ethic and the Spirit of Capitalism* (Stephen Kalberg, trans., Los Angeles: Roxbury Publishing, 2002), 127–48.

practices. Capital and labour from diverse locations converge on the cheap expropriated land that settler invasion makes available. This global elasticity ensures that the local contest is recurrently and ever-augmentably weighted against the Native's finite stock, reinforcing the settler advantage across time. Where regimes of race are concerned, the salient feature of this elasticity is demographic. Considering the emphasis that settlers place on individual diligence, the extent to which they rely on the efforts of others is striking.

When colonists first arrive, they generally try to persuade the Natives to work for them. With the exception of some industries, however (such as Andean mining for the Spanish, Aboriginal labour in the Australian cattle industry, and, of course, sexual servitude), this option is typically abandoned before very long. In principle, it is not good policy to incur reliance on a population that one is simultaneously seeking to eliminate, nor to promote the survival of the bearers of sovereignties that exceed the settler import. In practice, the possibilities for escape are favourable for Natives whose coercion is taking place in the midst of a surrounding network of support systems. Moreover, unlike Africans, whose proximity to Europe meant that they had shared Europe's diseases for centuries, Natives succumbed in large numbers to the exotic pestilences that settlers introduced.[57] For reasons such as these, Natives were generally held unsuitable for colonial labour, duly becoming lazy, dishonest and unreliable in the settler scheme of things.[58]

Significantly, this putative incapacity for work did not actually reside in qualities inherent in Natives themselves. Rather, it was geographic. Natives were deemed unsuitable for work to the extent that they remained in their own country. Move them somewhere else, and they could become good workers on the spot, as in the case of the 'blackbirded' Fijians whose stringent exploitation has been recounted by Tracey Banivanua Mar.[59] Disparaged at home as irredeemable cannibals who needed to be replaced by indentured South Asians, these Natives turned out to be well suited for labour on Queensland sugar plantations, where they were transported – and appropriately re-racialised – so that settlers could avoid reliance on local Aboriginal people. Analogously, Jean-Baptiste Le Moyne de Bienville, founder of New Orleans, advised the French crown to exchange local Natives for Africans enslaved on

---

57   David E. Stannard, *American Holocaust: The Conquest of the New World* (New York: Oxford UP, 1992), 57–146; Russell Thornton, *American Indian Holocaust and Survival: A population history since 1492* (Norman: Oklahoma UP, 1987).

58   See Syed Hussein Alatas, *The Myth of the Lazy Native: A Study of the Images of the Malays, Filipinos and Javanese from the 16th to the 20th Century and Its* [sic] *Function in the Ideology of Colonial Capitalism* (London: Frank Cass, 1977).

59   Tracey Banivanua Mar, *Violence and Colonial Dialogue: The Australia-Pacific Labor Trade* (Honolulu: Hawai'i UP, 2007).

Caribbean plantations, his reason being that, while the Indians could hardly run away from the islands, once the Africans had arrived in Louisiana their propensity to escape would be countered by fear of the surrounding Indians.[60] The capacity or incapacity for colonial labour is site-specific.

Ubiquitously, therefore, settlers bring their labour with them, usually already coerced, whether as slaves, convicts, indenturees, *Mizrahim*, or other subordinated categories (in some times and places, being Irish would do). The upshot is a plurality that reflects imperialism's global interconnectedness, the goal of settler dominion being pursued by means of a protean range of suppressive and divisive strategies that are typically framed in the idiom of race. Given its intimate anatomical moorings, race is a particularly powerful way to encourage discord between subjugated populations. Again, therefore, at the same time as stressing the differences that regimes of race engender, it is crucial to stress their complementarity, the mutuality with which they together sustain the common end of colonial domination.

We have already noted the tension between African American and Native American orientations to the US civil rights movement. As observed, that tension reflected, as it continues to reflect, the respective historical experiences of chattel slavery and territorial dispossession.[61] Yet the mutuality between the two is complete. As Ronald Takaki needed no more than a sentence to explain: 'In order to make way for White settlement and the expansion of both cotton cultivation and the market, some 70,000 Choctaws, Creeks, Cherokees, Seminoles, and Chickasaws were uprooted and deprived of their lands, and hundreds of thousands of Blacks were moved into the Southwest to work the soil as slaves.'[62]

Analogously, in Hawai'i, the suppression of Kanaka Maoli governance and land tenure was a precondition for the importation of indentured Pacific labourers onto US-owned plantations. That suppression remains directly continuous with current attempts even further to erode Kanaka Maoli entitlement to the Ceded (or, as they are bitterly dubbed, Seized) Lands.[63] Through the combination of two distinct colonial relationships

60 Joe Gray Taylor, *Negro Slavery in Louisiana* (New York: Greenwood, 1977), 5. For comparable examples from British North America, see A. Leon Higginbotham, Jr., *In the Matter of Color: Race and the American Legal Process. The Colonial Period* (New York: Oxford UP, 1978).

61 Cherokee activist Pamela Kingfisher stated to African American delegates at the UN Conference against Racism in 2000: 'You can have the mule; but the forty acres are ours.' For quotation and apposite discussion, see Andrea Smith, *Conquest*, 47–51.

62 Ronald T. Takaki, *Iron Cages: Race and Culture in Nineteenth-Century America* (New York: Knopf, 1979).

79 'Southwest' because, in the 1830s – though increasingly less so – the nation's western boundary was effectively the Mississippi.

63 See, for example, the Conklin website: bigfiles90.angelfire.com. For the Ceded

of inequality – applying immigrants' labour to Natives' land – colonial surplus value is generated. Imperialism reconfigures global histories at the local level.

On this basis, when it comes to the racialisation of any particular social group, the following analysis will be twofold: on the one hand, it will trace the shifting contested ways in which a particular group becomes racialised after its initial co-optation by Europeans, noting the continuities and the differences in the forms that its racialisation (or would-be racialisation) subsequently takes over time; on the other hand, it will delineate the particular contribution that the racialisation of any one group has made to the overall maintenance of the colonial system, with particular reference to the ways in which the specific racialisations applied to different groups are coordinated at the level of the whole.

The approach is, therefore, avowedly historical, tracing racial regimes forwards in time from conquered groups' initial co-optation into the colonial system while also making the earlier, preaccumulated histories that Natives and Europeans respectively brought to their initial confrontation an important part of the analysis. For example, as observed, there are considerable differences between the racialisation (or, as we shall see, non-racialisation) of people descended from Africans enslaved in Brazil and the racialisation of people descended from Africans enslaved in North America. A major factor in this difference, or so I shall argue, is the fact that, when Portugal embarked on its career of transatlantic slavery, it was already a maritime empire with characteristics that were quite different from British imperialism, and these differences fed through into the different racial regimes that have been imposed and contested in the two countries ever since. Race is not a static ontology. As its name suggests, it is an ongoing, ever-shifting contest.

Complex Solidarities

A major implication for anti-racist collaboration is the need to recognise the shared provenance of such differences in the White man's imposition of the colonial rule of private property. Yes, some Indians were involved in Black slavery, and, yes, some Blacks participated in Indian dispossession, but neither Indians nor Blacks were the originators and collective beneficiaries of these systemic crimes. Rather, both were caught up in a system that had been created and was being maintained by others. As we shall note in a number of contexts, the outcomes of colonialism cannot be reduced to voluntarism. The liberal discomfort occasioned by the occurrence of tensions between Indians and Blacks reflects a universalism

Lands, see John M. Van Dyke, *Who Owns the Crown Land of Hawaii?* (Honolulu: Hawai'i UP, 2008).

that takes for granted a pastiche of differences – colours, races, minorities, ethnicities – on a multicultural canvas that levels the varied histories that produced these differences in the first place. Historically analysed, these apparent conflicts of sectional interest emerge as traces of the complementary roles into which different conquered populations have been coerced by colonial settlers.

These distinct modes of coercion together subtend the overarching system of Euroamerican colonialism, so solidarities should be framed at this more encompassing level. Solidarity is not assimilation. To conjoin is not to dissolve. To work together, differences have to be integrated rather than levelled. Correspondingly, the promotion of racialised identities from below does not necessarily further the interests of the colonised. When insurgent classifications misguidedly seek to promote unworkable solidarities through obfuscating or homogenising away the different historical experiences that underlie ethno-racial specificity, they recapitulate assimilationism (which, after all, is an erasure of difference). Understandable though its motivation is, therefore – and quite apart from its questionable reliance on phenotype – the 'people of colour' classification can risk incurring this problem. Whatever their motivations, when inattentive to history, undifferentiated categories risk encouraging discord rather than solidarity. Paradoxical as it may seem, to homogenise is to divide – which leaves White people doing the ruling.

In stressing the different historical experiences that underlie particular regimes of race at the same time as it stresses their systemic complementarity, this book seeks to make a contribution to the struggle against race and the colonial relations of inequality that it sustains. In order for something to be resisted, it must first be understood. To this end, we will approach differentiation by way of its negation, focusing on the points at which racial classifications most conspicuously come undone.

For such classifications, in common with other cultural boundaries, operate most visibly where they are vulnerable, at the points where the divisions that they proclaim break down. In the case of emancipated Jews in central Europe, as we shall see, their difference from Gentile society was so tenuous that they were condemned for their similarity – being charged, in bourgeois society, with the possession of bourgeois traits. In some of the other cases that we shall consider, racial boundaries have been so ubiquitously transgressed by sexuality that a cross-cultural survey of discourses of miscegenation provides a way to approach systems of colonial domination comparatively. In these cases, the object of concern is not, therefore, sexual relations in themselves. Rather, colonial authorities' attempts to police racial categories are significant for the light they cast on that which they seek to protect.

Nonetheless, in addition to revealing the historical contingency of regimes of race, and tracing the different forms of colonial coercion that they respectively encode, a focus on miscegenation discourse underscores the profoundly gendered fact that, along with immigration (though more constantly across time), women's bodies are the key site for the reproduction of colonialism's unequally related populations. 'From our point of view,' as Eduardo de Oliveira e Oliveira observed of the Brazilian context – in which, as we shall see, miscegenation has been claimed to testify to a relatively benign form of slavery – 'the Portuguese tendency to miscegenation does not necessarily indicate tolerance, much more the reverse: miscegenation necessarily indicates an extreme form of exploitation and degradation of the Black woman.'[64]

This book is about the systemic logics in which that exploitation participates. As we shall see through the examples to come, colonialism presumes to prescribe whether the child a woman bears in her womb becomes one of her own people or one of her oppressors.[65]

Thus the key factor in colonial and 'post'-colonial race relations is not, as some once argued, simple demographic numbers,[66] since populations have to be differentiated before they can be counted. Difference, it cannot be stressed enough, is not simply given. It is the outcome of differentiation, which is an intensely conflictual process. If a one-drop rule applied in Australia, for instance, the Aboriginal population would escalate overnight. Hence the incendiary effect of a Queensland bumper sticker, the display of which was truly for none but the brave, which proclaimed an 'Aboriginal family reunion – invite your white relatives'.[67] Rather than simple counting, demography involves the most complex and tortuous contestation, as in Virginian Natives' century-long struggle to refuse categorisation as 'colored', a struggle that was waged, as Jack Forbes remarked, 'with uneven success and ... which served to poison African-American/Indian relations as well as to split communities, churches, and even families.'[68] Miscegenation discourse is about holding the line when it comes to power, privilege, and access to resources. As such, it is at the material core of identity politics, which culminate and reproduce colonial subordination into the present.

On this basis, in the hope of contributing to anti-racist solidarities, this book will explore a range of racial regimes with a view to

---

64 Eduardo de Oliveira e Oliveira, 'O mulato, um obstáculo epistemológico', *Argumento* 1, no. 3 (1974), 70.

65 Or even, in the less frequent case of the offspring of a slaveholding White woman and a Black man, one of her family's slaves.

66 William A. Green, *British Slave Emancipation: The Sugar Colonies and the Great Experiment, 1830–1865* (Oxford: Oxford UP, 1976).

67 I owe this anecdote to Jeremy Beckett.

68 Jack D. Forbes, *Black Africans and Native Americans: Color, Race and Caste in the Evolution of Red-Black Peoples* (2nd ed., Urbana: Illinois UP, 1993), 258.

highlighting both the foundations on which Europeans have established racial supremacy and the changing ways in which they have sought to maintain it. The opening two chapters will compare the different racialisations of two peoples who are both called Black: Indigenous people in Australia and African Americans in the USA. As already indicated, the regimes of race that Europeans have sought to impose on these two populations have been practically antithetical. Black people in Australia have been subjected to a set of inclusive discourses intended to bring about their assimilation into White Australian society, while Black people in the USA have been subjected to a rigidly exclusive regime whose ostensible object has been the preservation of White racial purity.

In chapters three and four, which complete the first half of the book, it will be seen that, in some significant regards, the racialisation of Jews in post-emancipation central Europe resembles the racialisation of Black people in the USA, especially in the post-emancipation era, while the racialisation of both Black people and Indians in Brazil will emerge as distinctly different from the racialisation of Black people in either Australia or the USA. In all these cases, the particular regimes of race that have been imposed on the populations concerned reflect and reproduce the manner of their incorporation into European social systems. Moreover, as will emerge, a feature common to all these situations is a complex interplay between discourses of assimilation and of exclusion, the local outcomes of this interplay being varied and mobile.

With much of the conceptual groundwork by this stage established, the four chapters in the second half of the book focus on the interplay between assimilation and exclusion, presenting more extensive case studies from two settler colonies, the USA and Palestine/Israel. In different but related ways, and under different but related circumstances, US and Israeli authorities have both coordinated discourses of assimilation and exclusion as foundational components in the ongoing process of settler-state formation. We will consider these two case studies in turn, situating and historically analysing the racialisation of Indigenous people in the USA and that of Arab-Jews in Palestine/Israel.

As will be shown, while the racialisation of Indians in the USA evinces profound similarities to that of Indigenous Australians, similarities that reflect their also sharing the historical predicament of settler invasion, the racialisation (or non-racialisation) of Arab-Jews in Israel/Palestine bears distinct similarities to that of African Brazilians, who are also part of an unacknowledged majority. In this perhaps surprising correspondence, colonialism's classificatory workings emerge with particular clarity – as, I hope, do some of the directions we can take to rid our world of the historical iniquities of race, which is the hope on which this book concludes.

CHAPTER ONE

In Whole and In Part

The Racialisation of Indigenous People in Australia

Historically speaking, Australia followed the United States, a chronology that involved a degree of replication. While the differences between these two White-Anglo settler colonies are as marked as the continuities, the colonisation of Australia was too closely bound up with Britain's North American embarrassment to be considered separately. In terms of preaccumulation, settler policies in Australia were significantly informed by lessons learned in North America. An obvious example is the avoidance of chattel slavery. Of even greater significance for a discussion of race in Australia is the avoidance of Native sovereignty. As we shall see in this and other chapters, these twin absences, both reversing British colonial policy in North America, would have major consequences for the regime of race that settlers constructed in Australia.

As has often been noted, the dominant factor in the sequential relationship between Britain's establishment of settler colonies in North America and Australia (New Holland) was the industrial revolution. This is not only because English factories relied on colonial production for their raw materials, a consideration that did not significantly motivate the initial invasion of Australia. Of much greater significance for Australia was the Malthusian demographic problem (the ominously named 'redundant population') that industrialisation, especially the element of enclosure, was presenting to authorities in Britain. Prior to losing the war of independence, Britain had been using its North American colonies, especially the southern ones, to export the largely urban surplus population that enclosure and industrialisation had generated, whether as convicted felons, as indentured labour or as paupers. After 1783, however, as Coupland put it, 'independent America could no longer be used as a British dustbin'.[1]

---

1 R. Coupland, *The American Revolution and the British Empire* (London: Longmans, Green and Co., 1930), 253.

The victorious republicans' preferred source of exploitable labour being African rather than English, and vested with even fewer rights, the loss of the thirteen colonies had an immediate effect on the English landscape, as waterways crowded with prison hulks presented the most concrete domestic symptom of colonial defeat.[2]

Due no doubt to the scrupulous Eurocentrism that James Clifford has noted of him, Michel Foucault did not remark on the fullness with which the colonisation of Australia combined the narratives of his Madness and Civilization and Discipline and Punish.[3] Even the watery containment of the median condition – ship of fools, convict hulk – was common to both transitions, that from North America to Australia and that from leprous marginality to the Great Confinement. Had Foucault been more alert to colonialism, he might have noted that the historical progression on from the hulks, or from an overcrowded Newgate Prison, did not only lead to Jeremy Bentham's Panopticon. It also led to New South Wales and Van Diemen's Land.

This is not to try to score points from Foucault. It is rather to stress the intimacy, noted in the Introduction, between colonialism and modernity. As we shall see throughout this book, race provided an expedient resolution to the logical affront that colonialism presented to liberal-democratic ideology. As incubators and developers of modernity, Australian settlers would be in the vanguard of a number of democratic movements, including those for women's suffrage and trades-union rights.[4] At the same time, they would dispossess and maltreat Aborigines with all the ruthlessness of settlers elsewhere. Lorenzo Veracini has perceptively assigned these two characteristics of settler discourse – egalitarianism among settlers combined with exterminism towards Natives – to settlers' respective positioning in relation to metropolitan authority (the constraints of which they were united in resisting) and to Native territoriality (the claim to which they were united in suppressing).[5]

For Indigenous people, the concept of settler democracy can only be an oxymoron. Their attrition at the hands of that democracy reflects the

---

2   Alan Frost, *Convicts and Empire: A Naval Question, 1776–1811* (Melbourne: Oxford UP, 1980), 3–32.

3   Michel Foucault, *Madness and Civilization: A History of Insanity in the Age of Reason* (Richard Howard, trans., London: Tavistock, 1967); Foucault, *Discipline and Punish: The Birth of the Prison* (Alan Sheridan, trans., London: Allen Lane, 1977). For James Clifford, see 'On Orientalism', in Clifford, *The Predicament of Culture: Twentieth-Century Ethnography, Literature, and Art* (Cambridge, MA: Harvard UP, 1988), 255–76.

4   Brian McKinley, *A Documentary History of the Australian Labor Movement, 1850–1975* (Melbourne: Drummond, 1979); Marilyn Lake, *Getting Equal: The History of Australian Feminism* (Sydney: Allen & Unwin, 1999); Raymond Markey, 'Race and Organized Labor in Australia, 1850–1901', *Historian* 58, no. 2 (1996), 343–61.

5   Lorenzo Veracini, *Settler Colonialism: A Theoretical Introduction* (London: Palgrave Macmillan, 2010), 61.

core feature of settler colonialism, which is first and foremost a project of replacement. Settlers come to stay. In relation to Natives, as I have argued, settler colonialism is governed by a logic of elimination.[6] In destroying to replace, this logic encompasses more than the summary liquidation of Indigenous people. In common with genocide as Raphaël Lemkin characterised it,[7] settler colonialism has both negative and positive dimensions. Negatively, it strives for the dissolution of Native societies. Positively, the ongoing requirement to eliminate the Native alternative continues to shape the colonial society that settlers construct on their expropriated land base. In this positive sense, the logic of elimination marks a return whereby the Native repressed continues to structure settler-colonial society.

Thus elimination should be seen as an organising principal of settler-colonial society rather than a one-off (and superseded) occurrence. As Theodor Herzl, founding father of Zionism, observed in his allegorical manifesto/novel, 'If I wish to substitute a new building for an old one, I must demolish before I construct.'[8] In a kind of realisation that took place half a century later, the one-time deputy mayor of West Jerusalem, Meron Benvenisti, recalled, 'As a member of a pioneering youth movement, I myself "made the desert bloom" by uprooting the ancient olive trees of al-Bassa to clear the ground for a banana grove, as required by the "planned farming" principles of my kibbutz, Rosh Haniqra.'[9]

Invasion is a structure, not an event.[10] As we shall see in the chapters to come, the continuing operations of the logic of elimination can include officially encouraged miscegenation, the breaking-down of Native title into alienable individual freeholds, Native citizenship, child abduction, religious conversion, resocialisation in total institutions such as missions or boarding schools, and a whole range of cognate bio-cultural assimilations. All these strategies, including frontier homicide,

6   Patrick Wolfe, 'Nation and MiscegeNation: Discursive Continuity in the Post-Mabo Era', *Social Analysis* 34 (1994), 93–152; Wolfe, *Settler Colonialism and the Transformation of Anthropology: The Politics and Poetics of an Ethnographic Event* (London: Cassell, 1999).

7   '[O]ne, destruction of the national pattern of the oppressed group; the other, the imposition of the national pattern of the oppressor. This imposition, in turn, may be made upon the oppressed population which is allowed to remain, or upon the territory alone, after removal of the population and colonization of the area by the oppressor's own nationals.' Raphaël Lemkin, *Axis Rule in Occupied Europe: Laws of Occupation, Analysis of Government, Proposals for Redress* (Washington: Carnegie Endowment for International Peace, 1944), 79.

8   Theodor Herzl, *Old-New Land [Altneuland, 1902]* (Lotta Levensohn, trans., New York: Wiener/Markus, 1941), 38.

9   Meron Benvenisti, *Sacred Landscape: The Buried History of the Holy Land since 1948* (Berkeley: California UP, 2000), 2.

10   Wolfe, *Settler Colonialism and the Transformation of Anthropology*, 2; 'Nation and MiscegeNation', 96.

are modalities of settler colonialism. All of them come back to the issue of land.

Territoriality

Territoriality, the fusion of people and land, is settler colonialism's specific, irreducible element. Settlers' seizure of Natives' land is not simply a transfer of ownership. That can occur in a regular fashion within a system of ownership – by sale, inheritance, foreclosure and the like, rival claims being resolvable by appropriate arbitration. Rather than replacing one owner with another, settlers seek to replace an entire system of ownership with another. The settler/Native confrontation, in other words, is not between claims to ownership but between frameworks for allocating ownerships. It is between sovereignties, which are primordially external to one another. As Henry Reynolds observed, 'There has always been an international dimension to the relationship between Aborigines and the colonists.'[11] Given this externality, the settler legal system resolves issues of ownership within its jurisdictional limits. The question of its own externality is simply – and literally – beyond its power (*ultra vires*).

This is a straightforward matter that settler judiciaries typically express without qualms. To explain his denial of Indians' capacity to dispose of fee simple in their ancestral patrimony, for instance, Chief Justice John Marshall informed the US Supreme Court in the landmark case of *Johnson v. McIntosh* that 'this restriction may be opposed to natural right, and to the usages of civilized nations, yet, if it be indispensable to that system under which the country has been settled, and be adapted to the actual condition of the two people, it may, perhaps, be supported by reason, and certainly cannot be rejected by Courts of justice' – by which, of course, he meant settler courts of justice.[12] Marshall's position was faithfully echoed in the Australian case of *Coe v. Commonwealth*, which was devoted to the question, and taken for granted in statements such as the High Court of Australia's key decision in the Yorta Yorta case, which held that 'rights or interests in land created after sovereignty [by which the justices meant settler sovereignty] and which owed their origin and continued existence only to a normative system other than that of the new sovereign power, would not and will not be given effect by the legal order of the new sovereign'.[13]

---

11   Henry Reynolds, *Aboriginal Sovereignty: Reflections on Race, State and Nation* (Sydney: Allen & Unwin, 1996), 155.

12   *Johnson and Graham's Lessee v. William McIntosh* (21 *U.S.* 8 Wheat. 543) 1823 [*Johnson v. McIntosh*], 591–2.

13   *Coe v. Commonwealth*, HCA 42; (1993) 68 ALJR 110; (1993) 118 ALR 193 (17 August 1993); *Yorta Yorta v. Victoria*, HCA 58; 214 CLR 422; 194 ALR 538; 77 ALJR 356 (12 December 2002), 47.

The point is not to deplore these judgements. Given the circumstances, it is hard to see what else the judges could have said. The point is that having nothing to say about Native sovereignty has precisely that effect – nothing (notice that the Yorta Yorta judges' 'new sovereign' presupposed an old one). Marshall and the Australian judges (Gleeson, Gummow and Hayne) were not creating the basis on which the systems of ownership they adjudicated were founded. They were simply acknowledging that it was not up to them to question that basis. The law was not created by the law – in Carl Schmitt's terminology, it was created exceptionally.[14] Of itself, law does not conquer. It may express, legitimate, or even reinforce conquest, but these are elaborations on the datum of conquest, which is achieved by other means. To assume that Native sovereignty somehow evaporates in the aftermath of conquest is to go further than the judges, who remain silent on the matter.

Accordingly – and, it would seem, consistently with the judges' accounts – tracking what happens to the externality of Native sovereignty in the wake of the settler/Native confrontation requires us to look outside the settler legal system, a requirement that takes us directly to the priority of force. Peoples do not surrender their collective inheritances voluntarily. Thus there is no shortage of data relating to the force with which Natives were dispossessed. But possession is not ownership, with which it may or may not coexist, as in the case of tenancies. Even within the terms of the settler legal system, therefore – let alone in terms of the Native ones or in the space between the two – mere dispossession does not vitiate ownership, as is evidenced by the special requirements attending provisions such as adverse possession.

Thus the salient question to arise from the territorial dispossession of Native peoples is not that of whether or not it happened, since there can be no doubting that. Rather, it is the question of the subsequent career of Native ownership, which mere dispossession does not compromise.[15] The question, in other words, is one of strategy-analysis: How do settler societies deal with autonomous systems of ownership that are not susceptible to forcible seizure? This question acquires particular urgency in the context of a settler society's need to establish a rule of law with sufficient legitimacy to secure a viable level of consent to a recently promulgated set of social norms among an ever-aggregating and often diversely recruited immigrant populace.

For their own internal purposes, therefore, quite apart from international considerations, settler societies seek to neutralise the extraneous

---

14 Carl Schmitt, *Political Theology: Four Chapters on the Concept of Sovereignty* (George Schwab, trans., Chicago: Chicago UP, 1985).

15 'So if the Aborigines and Torres Strait Islanders did exercise sovereignty in Australia before the arrival of the British, what happened to it?' Reynolds, *Aboriginal Sovereignty*, 59 (asking the question within the terms of the settler legal system).

sovereignties that conquered Natives continue to instantiate. The most direct way to achieve this is through the physical liquidation of the bearers of those sovereignties. This solution becomes increasingly less viable as Natives are contained within the frontier, conflicting as it does with the emergent settler social order's requirement for the manifestation of due process. An alternative solution, exemplified in the US system of Indian treaties, is to secure a semblance of Native consent to a transfer of ownership – though this possibility was precluded in Australia, where Native ownership was not recognised. A third solution is physical removal and/or confinement, a merely temporary or provisional expedient if it takes place within the boundaries, existing or projected, of the settler nation-state.

A more permanent strategy is that of assimilation, whereby Natives' externality is dissolved through their incorporation into settler society. By this means, settler societies do not seek to resolve the problem of alternative systems of ownership. Rather, by doing away with alternative owners, they seek to obviate it. Assimilation, if it were to succeed, offers a more effective antidote to Native sovereignty than simple denial, which merely defers the problem, thus risking the emergence of circumstances less favourable to denial, as in the case of the impact of post-war decolonisation on Australian Aboriginal policy. These shifting racial modalities reflect settler colonialism's inability to replace Native society *tout court*. The quest to replace Native territoriality only maintains the refractory imprint of the Native counter-claim.

In their deployment, each of these strategies, which are not mutually exclusive, attests to the persistence of the problem of Natives' exteriority to settler sovereignty. This persistence accounts for the structural dimension of invasion, which has to suppress – or, at least, contain – the Native alternative across time. As observed, the structures are not inert. They are constituted through events, through practices that colonisers repeatedly strive to maintain, in various shifting adaptations to Natives' stubborn exteriority. As Elizabeth Strakosch and Alissa Macoun have observed, 'the flipside of invasion being a structure not an event is that [settler] sovereignty is a constant performance claiming to be an essence.'[16] Even in settler social discourse, albeit in the breach, Native sovereignty does not end with conquest any more than Native ownership ends with dispossession. Moreover, since Natives seek to exercise their countervailing sovereignties in whatever ways remain practicable, settler domestic discourse becomes refractorily politicised. As Philip Deloria observed of

---

16   Elizabeth Strakosch and Alissa Macoun, 'Land, Territory or Political Difference?', paper presented to the International Political Science Association Conference, 'The Politics of Indigeneity', Sydney, 2013. I am grateful to Liz Strakosch for pushing me to think harder about territoriality.

the post-frontier USA, 'while military conflict was no longer an option, the struggle between Native people and the United States had not concluded. Across Indian country, the recognition of military defeat had pushed Native people to develop strategies for continuing the struggle' (in which connection Deloria stresses the 'struggle waged on the cultural front').[17] This continuity – the ongoing refusal of a unilateral extinguishment – is also the import of the oft-repeated, deeply unsettling Australian Indigenous maxim, 'Always was, always will be, Aboriginal land'.

In seeking to suppress this autonomous counter-history, settler discourse is trapped into conceding institutional life to the very problem it seeks to eliminate. For something to be suppressed, it must first exist. By its very charter, an Aborigines Department or an Office of Indian Affairs attests to the persistence of the Native problem. Despite itself, it stands as an institutional trace of Native resistance, which it reluctantly acknowledges. During the era of the frontier, this is only to be expected. Territory, together with its Native population, remains to be conquered, so there remains an acknowledged external threat that requires institutional management. In the wake of the frontier, however, the continued need for institutional management becomes anomalous, attesting as it does to the persistence of an unreconciled externality that proclaims conquest not to be complete after all. So far as conquest remains incomplete, the settler state rests – or, more to the point, fails to rest – on incomplete foundations. For the settler state, therefore, the struggle to neutralise Indigenous externality is a struggle for its own integrity, an end to which assimilation offers the most effective means. This is where race comes in.

Domesticating Sovereignty

Once settlers deprive Natives of their bare usufruct, Natives' territoriality becomes inoperative as a source of subsistence. For the duration, therefore, their ownership, perforce detached from its object, becomes reduced to its political dimension. Whether or not settler legal systems formally acknowledge this continuing ownership, or regardless of the extent to which they acknowledge it, it is registered in other domains of settler social life, in particular cultural and administrative ones, which address Natives' unique relationship to the national polity in a variety of ways.

Administratively, for instance, the political nature of the Native problem is apparent in the disproportionate amount of energy that is devoted to a numerically insignificant group, a preoccupation that is unsuccessfully belied by the common conflation of Native affairs with administrative

---

17   Philip J. Deloria, *Indians in Unexpected Places* (Lawrence: Kansas UP, 2004), 104.

concerns such as crime, insanity and related forms of delinquency or neglect. For the external to be rendered internal, in other words, the *political* is rendered *technical*. A well-known, if premature, example of this device was the transfer of the US Office of Indian Affairs from the War Department to the newly created Department of the Interior, which took place in 1849, when the US Cavalry had barely set hoof on the Great Plains.[18] Comparably, though much more recently, in Australia in 2006, the ostensibly Indigenous-run Aboriginal and Torres Strait Islander Commission was replaced by a more openly government-run 'Office of Indigenous Policy Coordination' housed in the portmanteau Department of Families, Housing, Community Services and Indigenous Affairs. In rendering Indigenous issues a technical problem for specialists, typically embedded in the welfare bureaucracy at a substantial remove from the diplomatic service, the settler state seeks to depoliticise them.

In its ostensibly biological incarnation – which, as we shall see throughout this book, actually substitutes for history – race presents as a technical issue par excellence, the disciplinary preserve of natural science. As such, race is amenable to a range of scientific procedures, in particular measurement. In the case of practices such as skull-measurement and IQ testing, the politics become overwhelmed by the objective technicalities of numerical reasoning.[19] While Indigenous people in Australia and the United States have both been discredited on the basis of these computations, the pre-eminently racial technology that has been applied to them has been the measurement of blood quantum. As various scholars and activists have pointed out, blood quantum discourse serves to eliminate people from the Indigenous reckoning. While this consequence of blood quantum has been well critiqued[20] the operative terms of the idiom itself remain largely unexamined. Why, in particular, mathematics, and why its particular combination with blood? Posing the question thus highlights the simple fact that blood, being liquid, readily lends itself to quantification. It would be impossible to calibrate, say, culture or politics

---

18   Francis Paul Prucha, *The Great Father: The United States Government and the American Indians* (abridged ed., Lincoln: Nebraska UP, 1986), 111–12.

19   See Stephen Jay Gould, *The Mismeasure of Man* (Harmondsworth: Penguin, 1981); Richard J. Herrnstein and Charles Murray, *The Bell Curve: Intelligence and Class Structure in American Life* (New York: Free Press, 1994).

20   From a growing literature, see, for instance, Kimberly TallBear, 'DNA, Blood and Racializing the Tribe', *Wicazo Sá Review* 18/1 (2003), 81–107, developed and extended to DNA in TallBear, *Native American DNA: Tribal Belonging and the False Promise of Genetic Science* (Minneapolis: Minnesota UP, 2013). For a path-breaking analysis of blood quantum as 'statistical extermination', see M. Annette Jaimes, 'Federal Indian Identification Policy: A Usurpation of Indigenous Sovereignty in North America', in Jaimes (ed.), *The State of Native America: Genocide, Colonization, and Resistance* (Boston: South End Press, 1992), 123–38. For the discursively cognate Hawaiian case, see J. Kēhaulani Kauanui, *Hawaiian Blood: Colonialism and the Politics of Sovereignty and Indigeneity* (Durham: Duke UP, 2008).

with comparable precision. Blood, however, is well adapted to sustain the technical vocabulary that supplants the political language of external affairs in post-frontier settler discourse. In this regard, blood is like money, which also invokes liquidity to disguise the social relations that sustain it. As Marx and Engels influentially contended, political ideologies legitimate the hegemony of a particular social group, and they do so by assimilating that hegemony to nature, thus placing it beyond human intervention.[21] As a measurable liquid, blood straightforwardly constitutes an object of natural science, a quality that thereby naturalises the settler-colonial logic of elimination in one of its discreetly technocratic post-frontier modalities.

In providing for the social death of Nativeness – as an exteriority rather than as a mere tile in the multicultural mosaic – assimilation programmes acknowledge the historical tenacity of the autonomously constituted Native alternative. To this end, the racialisation of Indigenous people in both Australia and the United States has sought to minimise their resistance to the centripetal pull of settler-national state-formation. The racial characteristics attributed to Natives are maximally soluble, encouraging their disappearance into the settler mainstream. For all its obviousness, this strategy can be highly deceptive, even finding endorsement in some race-studies scholarship.

The fact that settler discourse constructs Indigenous people as racially fragile does not mean that Indigeneity itself is fragile, as if the elimination of Indigenous people is an insubstantial matter compared to the exclusion of groups whose alterities are deemed immutable. This problem can arise when the critique of essentialism is applied unrigorously. With essence mistaken for a quality (duration), those whose racialisation promotes permanent exclusion can figure as more substantially racialised than those whose racialisation promotes permanent disappearance.[22] Thus it is necessary to stress the centrality to post-frontier settler discourse of the claim that it is of the essence of Nativeness to be multidimensionally soluble. As the distinctive feature of Indigenous people's post-frontier racialisation, this solubility maintains and reproduces the historical elimination of the prior owners of the land.

---

21 For a concept that has proved so politically productive, ideology remained strikingly undefined in Marx and Engels's own writings, where it was exemplified in critical practice rather than formally spelled out. See, e.g., Marx and Engels, *German Ideology*, e.g. 64–5.

22 Apart from the contribution by Howard Winant, for instance, the house that race built would not seem to have a room for Indians: Wahneema Lubiano (ed.), *The House That Race Built* (New York: Vintage, 1997). Even George M. Fredrickson managed to write a book entitled *The Arrogance of Race* without allocating Indians more than three stray sentences. Fredrickson, *The Arrogance of Race: Historical Perspectives on Slavery, Racism, and Social Inequality* (Hanover: New England UP, 1988, sentences on pp. 16, 47 and 91). These examples are, of course, by no means isolated.

Settling Australia

How, then, did all this come to pass in Australia? It can hardly be said that, when the eleven ships of the First Fleet landed in January 1788, the scene was set for the replacement of the owners of a whole continent. While this outcome did indeed substantially eventuate, it had a historic-ity – it was brought about rather than foreordained. It took the discovery and development of a key export commodity, Australian merino wool, to provide the impetus for the frontier expansion and accompanying large-scale immigration that culminated in the settler takeover of the continent. This is not to suggest that measures to defray the cost of convict settle-ment were not considered. Prior to the merino revolution, for instance, along with the export staples of whaling and sealing, sheep provided a minor source of export revenue as meat.[23] Moreover, as Geoffrey Blainey recounted (albeit challenged by Alan Frost), plans for flax production, principally on Norfolk Island, were encouraged by the speculations of Captain Cook and the ambitions of Governor King (the scheme resulting in the production of two square yards of rough linen that were 'perhaps among the costliest textiles ever woven by man').[24] The straight Norfolk Island pines were also seen as a potential replacement for the towering New England white pine which, up to the loss of the North American colonies, had provided the British navy with its masts.[25]

Nonetheless, while none of this came to anything – and with the defeated Tory loyalists in North America preferring the prospect of Canada to the new Pacific outpost[26] – convict shipment still persisted. Moreover, mindful of the hazards of settler expansionism in the wake of the North American setback, the British imposed stricter bounds ('limits of location') for land claims in New South Wales. Such limits are vulner-able to the official blind eye. As James Boyce has revealingly shown, the settler takeover of Australia was not legislated. Rather, its primary dynamic arose permissively, in the absence of official regulation.[27] This highly pro-ductive absence should caution us against viewing settler colonialism as

23   E. Beever, 'The Origin of the Wool Industry in New South Wales', *Business Archives and History* 5, no. 2 (1965), 100–1.

24   Robert Hughes, *The Fatal Shore: A History of the Transportation of Convicts to Australia, 1787–1868* (London: Vintage, 1986), 101, citing Edward Lloyd; Geoffrey Blainey, *The Tyranny of Distance: How Distance Shaped Australia's History* (rev. ed., Sydney: Pan Macmillan, 2001), 37.

25   William Cronon, *Changes in the Land: Indians, Colonists, and the Ecology of New England* (New York: Hill and Wang, 1983), 109–11.

26   Coupland, *American Revolution and the British Empire*, 259–65.

27   'It was only after the abandonment of the long-established policy of concen-trated settlement that exclusive territorial claims beyond defined borders were made, perfect sovereignty over Aboriginal country was asserted, and the continental land rush began', James Boyce, *1835: The Founding of Melbourne & the Conquest of Australia* (Collingwood: Black Inc., 2011), xi.

a narrowly governmental project. Rather, as we shall see throughout this book, settler invasion typically combines a shifting balance of official and unofficial strategies, initially to seize Native territory and subsequently to consolidate its expropriation.

Rather than something separate from or running counter to the colonial state, the irregular activities of the frontier rabble constitute its principal means of expansion. These have occurred behind the screen of the frontier, in the wake of which, once the dust has settled, the exceptional acts that took place have been regularised and the boundaries of White settlement extended. Characteristically, officials express regret at the lawlessness of the dispossession while resigning themselves to its inevitability. In recent Australian jurisprudence, Justice Howard Olney invoked this inevitability as the 'tide of history', which provided the pretext for his notorious judgement in the Yorta Yorta case.[28]

The tide of history canonises the fait accompli, harnessing the diplomatic niceties of discovery to the maverick rapine of the squatters' posse within a cohesive project that implicates individual and nation-state, official and unofficial alike. In occupied Palestine today, Amana, the settler advance-guard of the fundamentalist Gush Emunim movement, hastens apace with the construction of its 'facts on the ground'. In this regard, the settlers are maintaining a tried and tested official strategy; indeed, Israel's 1949 campaign to seize the Negev before the impending armistice was codenamed uvda, Hebrew for 'fact'.[29] Settler colonialism, in short, is an inclusive, land-centred project that coordinates a comprehensive range of agencies, from the metropolitan centre to the frontier encampment, with a view to supplanting Indigenous ownership. Its operations are not dependent on the presence or absence of formal state institutions or functionaries.

In the 1820s, some years after soldier turned pastoralist John Macarthur's experiments with sheep-breeding had produced a particularly fine strain of wool that seemed superior even to that produced in Saxony, the rapid development of Yorkshire wool mills stimulated merino production in Britain's colonial limpet on the eastern edge of Australia and, further south, in the island colony of Van Diemen's Land (Tasmania).[30] In Van Diemen's Land, though there were few official

---

28 David Ritter, 'The Judgement of the World: The Yorta Yorta case and the "tide of history"', *Australian Historical Studies* 123 (April 2004), 106–21; Deborah Bird Rose, 'Reflections on the Use of Historical Evidence in the Yorta Yorta Case', in Mandy Paul and Geoffrey Gray (eds), *Through a Smoky Mirror: History and Native Title* (Canberra: Aboriginal Studies Press, n.d. [2002]), 35–48.

29 Ilan Pappe, *The Making of the Arab–Israeli Conflict, 1947–1951* (London: I.B. Tauris, 2001), 187.

30 Sylvia Morrissey, 'The Pastoral Economy, 1821–1850' in James Griffin (ed.), *Essays in Economic History of Australia* (Melbourne: Jacaranda, 1970), 58–61.

constraints on the seizure of grassland for pasturage and, as is well-known, Indigenous resistance was exhaustively suppressed, ecological conditions placed a limit on the amount of land available for wool-growing, a situation that encouraged Vandemonian settlers to cast their eyes northwards to the unconquered southern region of the New South Wales mainland, the Port Phillip District that would eventually become the colony (later state) of Victoria.[31] At the same time, further north, in the region around Sydney, the pressure for pastoral expansion was intensifying rapidly. Under conditions such as these, a territorial limit that had served to contain a disruptive convict outpost came to serve as an obstacle to the creation of wealth. As British Secretary of State Lord Glenelg observed, somewhat belatedly, in 1836,

> The whole surface of the country [New South Wales] exhibits a range of sheep walks which, though not naturally fertile, are yet, when occupied in large masses, of almost unrivalled value for the production of the finest description of wool ... The motives which are urging mankind to break through the [official] restraints are too strong to be encountered with effect by ordinary means. All that remains for the Government in such circumstances is to assume the guidance and direction of the enterprise which, though it cannot prevent or retard, it may yet conduct to happy results.[32]

Given the boom in wool exports, some ships could sail back and forth between Australia and England – at least, around the wool-gathering season of December to March – with less reliance on the Indian and Pacific ocean trading that many had engaged in once they had dropped off their human cargoes, together with supplies for those already there, earlier in the convict era. In maritime terms, a partial reversal set in. Whereas, in the early days, ships had left Britain with a cargo bound for Australia – which, as the flax disappointment illustrates, had little to send back – the merino revolution lessened the imbalance. As in the case of Brazil, which we shall consider below, a significant factor was human freight.[33] Given the merino revolution, the backloading could switch directions, or work both ways, with wave upon wave of settlers disembarking in Australia from ships that would return directly to Britain. The number of free settlers increased, aided by a bounty system that subsidised their passages, while convict transportation was stepped up, with emancipation generat-

---

31   Lloyd Robson, *A History of Tasmania*, vol. 1, *Van Diemen's Land from the Earliest Times up to 1850* (Melbourne: Oxford UP, 1983), 208; Boyce, *1835*, 19.

32   Glenelg quoted in Brian Fitzpatrick, *British Imperialism and Australia, 1783–1833: An Economic History of Australia* (Sydney: Sydney UP, 1939), 369.

33   'From the owner's viewpoint, passengers were just another way to fill a ship.' Frank Broeze, *Island Nation: A History of Australians and the Sea* (Sydney: Allen & Unwin, 1998), 83.

ing a constant demand for replacements – a departure from slavery that further expanded the settler population.[34]

To return for a moment to the question of Foucault and modernity, one of the Benthamite reforms that British Home Secretary Robert Peel introduced in concert with his reformed police force was the abolition of the death penalty for over a hundred offences. Instead of being hanged, the offenders were transported, a procedure that enhanced their utility.[35] In the event, in the decade of the 1830s, the White population of Australia rose by nearly 150 per cent (from 80,000 to 190,000).[36] Ultimately, the supply of convict labour no longer complemented what Brian Fitzpatrick termed 'the spontaneous colonial movement of expansion'. British policy shifted to a more flexible combination of capital and 'free' labour in the persons of

> tens of thousands of paupers, the necessary labour. Convict transportation to New South Wales was at length abandoned when, and only when, it had become clear that capital export and pauper emigration to Australia would be the most profitable form which English interest could take.[37]

Here, then, was settler colonialism's voracious dynamic, poised in a kind of pincer movement to the north and south of the Port Phillip District. In 1835, 'an illegal squatter camp was established on the banks of the Yarra River'. This was the beginning of Melbourne.[38] In the person of John Batman, the Vandemonians had arrived before the pastoral wave from further north, but that would not be long in converging on the lands and livelihoods of the Indigenous people of Victoria, collectively known today as Kooris. Batman, whose Tasmanian experience had hardened him in the ways of Native expropriation, opted for a softer approach on the mainland, conducting treaty negotiations on the Merri Creek, a tributary of the Yarra, proceedings that seem to have been attended by a young boy who would grow up to be called William Barak, whom we shall encounter presently.[39]

---

34 Wakefield's *Letter from Sydney* (written, appropriately enough, in Newgate gaol) was published in 1829.

35 Eric J. Evans, *Sir Robert Peel: Statesmanship, Power and Party* (2nd ed., London: Routledge, 1991), 17; T. A. Jenkins, *Sir Robert Peel* (London: Macmillan, 1999), 27–8.

36 Wray Vamplew, *Australians: Historical Statistics (Australians: A Historical Library*, vol. 10, Sydney: Fairfax, Syme and Weldon, 1987), 26.

37 Fitzpatrick, *British Imperialism and Australia*, 19. Fitzpatrick did not note the effects of the Irish famine for relieving the population pressure imposed on British society by mass poverty.

38 Boyce, *1835, xi*. The Henty brothers had crossed from Van Diemen's Land in 1834 and landed further west, to less substantial effect.

39 Bain Attwood with Helen Doyle, *Possession: Batman's Treaty and the Matter of History* (Carlton: Miegunyah, 2009).

Assuming the principle of pre-emption, a North American legacy that centralised land deals with Native peoples in the colonial government, Governor Bourke in Sydney rapidly repudiated Batman's Treaty, and colonists set about removing Native people from their rich Victorian grasslands with unparalleled speed and ruthlessness – in Richard Broome's estimation, 'as fast as any expansion in the history of European colonisation'.[40] So far as the interplay of official and unofficial strategies is concerned, it is apparent from Batman's overruled treaty that settlers could seize Aboriginal people's land without their consent but not with it. In Boyce's words:

> When Bourke belatedly heard that the squatters had committed their most brazen act of trespass yet – the colonisation of Port Phillip – the Governor viewed this as a strategic opportunity to break the impasse with London and let loose the benign spirit of private enterprise upon the vast wastelands of the continent.[41]

The all-engulfing ferocity of the Victorian land grab became even more destructive in 1851, when the discovery of gold caused large areas of the countryside to swarm with people whose only motivation for being there was greed. By the end of the 1850s, Indigenous people in Victoria had suffered a demographic collapse. According to the official figures of the colonial government's 'Board for the Protection of the Aborigines', 2,341 Aboriginal people remained alive in Victoria in 1861. Twenty-five years later, that figure had fallen to 806.[42] But the most intense attrition had occurred before 1861, especially in the decade following White colonisation in the mid-1830s. The lower end of estimates for the Aboriginal population as it stood in 1835 suggests a total of around 12,000 people (a figure already substantially reduced by smallpox epidemics).[43] Eight hundred and six being roughly 6 per cent of 12,000, it is misleading to talk of the Aboriginal population of Victoria as having been decimated, since the population level fell to well below 10 per cent. This is far and away the largest fact in Victoria's history, one that dwarfs the campaign for the eight-hour day, the career of Ned Kelly, the holding of the first

---

40   Richard Broome, *Aboriginal Victorians: A History Since 1800* (Crows Nest: Allen & Unwin, 2005), *xxiii*.

41   Boyce, *1835*, 32.

42   Annual reports for the Board for the Protection of Aborigines from 1861 to 1925 are available (open access) on line from the University of Melbourne at lib. unimelb.edu.au.

43   For discussion and further sources, see Broome, *Aboriginal Victorians*, 90–3, 146–7 (table), 194; Diane E. Barwick, 'Changes in the Aboriginal Population of Victoria, 1863–1966', in D. J. Mulvaney and J. Golson (eds), *Aboriginal Man and Environment in Australia* (Canberra: ANU Press, 1971), 288–315; M. F. Christie, *Aborigines in Colonial Victoria, 1835–86* (Sydney: Sydney UP, 1979), 206–7.

Australian federal parliaments or the staging of the Melbourne Olympics. The consequences of this foundational fact converged on a scattering of small portions of land that were set aside in the second half of the nineteenth century for the purpose of dealing with the problem of the Aboriginal 'remnant'.[44] Of these sites, Coranderrk Aboriginal Station was the one closest to Melbourne.

Coranderrk

Histories should, I believe, be written responsibly. I am writing this history on my verandah overlooking Healesville, in the Yarra Valley. The town is named after Richard Heales, a Congregationalist immigrant from London who made a name for himself in colonial Melbourne as a radical politician, temperance campaigner and founding president of the colonial legislature's 'Central Board to Watch Over the Interests of the Aborigines' (as it was initially called), before dying young in 1864. This year, our town is celebrating the sesquicentenary of its foundation – or, as it is somewhat nervously termed, 'settlement' – which took place a short while after Heales's death. Down below me to my right, where the buildings and paddocks give way to bushland, a patch of dark green marks the eastern end of the Coranderrk woods.

Terrible things were done at Coranderrk. When I go to the supermarket or the post office, I see descendants of people to whom these things were done. They generally keep themselves to themselves. They are in our town but not of it. They are of Wurundjeri country, which I am in but not of. The Wurundjeri (Woiworong) are part of a larger group of related peoples collectively called Kulin, whose country takes up the south-central region, including the greater Melbourne area, of the Australian state of Victoria. My house is built on Wurundjeri land, for which they have never received a cent. The least I can do is start this history at home, with what has happened here in Healesville, from which there can be no complete recovery. In any event, like so many Aboriginal histories, the Coranderrk story resonates widely. Australian settler colonialism has been nothing if not consistent. Similar things have been done to Indigenous peoples across the continent. The Coranderrk

---

44   It is hard to put a precise figure on the number of Aboriginal missions, stations and reserves. A figure of eight or ten is not unreasonable. Some (such as Acheron or Yelta) were short-lived and some (such as Ramahyuk and Lake Tyers) were merged, while some scholars (such as Broome, *Aboriginal Victorians*) do not seem to count Cummeragunja and Maloga as Victorian, presumably on account of their positioning in relation to the Murray River. In my view, while they were not Victorian Aboriginal missions for European administrative purposes, they were Victorian-Aboriginal missions for Koori community purposes. In excluding Cummeragunja, the priority accorded to the Eurocolonial category 'Victoria' over Indigenous community reckonings erases one of the vital hubs of Victorian Koori history and identity.

story tells of violence, theft, confinement, exploitation, banishment and betrayal. It also tells of resistance, steadfastness, adaptation, family and survival. In my view, it tells of the birth of the modern Aboriginal political movement.

Coranderrk's history was painstakingly reconstructed thirty or so years ago by the late Diane Barwick, her pioneering work being supplemented by Michael Christie and others. More recently, and in other media, it has been illuminated by two creative historical collaborations, that of Giordano Nanni and Andrea James, and that of Rachel Perkins and David Dale.[45] Summarising briefly from this body of work, Coranderrk was a rarity among Aboriginal reserves for being located at a site chosen by Aboriginal people themselves. It was their second attempt. They had previously selected a place called Acheron, over the Blacks' Spur (as it was then called) to the north-east, and had made a successful start to clearing and planting there – too successful as it turned out, as they were soon moved on and their selection allocated to local Whites who had come to covet the land once they saw what could be done with it. The Acheron 'second dispossession' is significant because it illustrates the fact that, by this stage (the early 1860s), the region had categorically entered the post-frontier era. Unallocated land was at a premium, with competition for it becoming intense. Indeed, the very establishment of the Aboriginal missions and reserves, essentially a confining provision, was symptomatic of this development.

After a period of uncertainty and another false start, the senior Wurundjeri elder (*ngurungaeta*), Simon Wonga, indicated to the Scottish lay preacher and Board for the Protection of Aborigines inspector John Green that they would like to set up a community at Coranderrk, where they were camping after the devastating loss of Acheron. In 1863, a year before the founding of Healesville, the community was established, initially without official gazetting, though this subsequently materialised. Wonga knew his man. The system of control that Green and his wife

---

45 The key work is Diane E. Barwick, *Rebellion at Coranderrk* (Laura E. Barwick and Richard E. Barwick, eds, Canberra: Aboriginal History Monograph 5, 1998 [1985]). See also Diane E. Barwick, 'Coranderrk and Cumeroogunga: Pioneers and Policy', in T. Scarlet Epstein and D. H. Penny (eds), *Opportunity and Response: Case Studies in Economic Development* (London: C. Hurst, 1972), 10–68; Christie, *Aborigines in Colonial Victoria*, 167–8, 182–99; Bain Attwood, *The Making of the Aborigines* (Sydney: Allen & Unwin, 1989), 90–103. Giordano Nanni and Andrea James, *Coranderrk: We Will Show the Country* (Canberra: Aboriginal Studies Press, 2013); Rachel Perkins and Darren Dale (prod. and dir.), *First Australians*, Episode 3: 'Freedom for Our Lifetime'. On demand at: sbs.com.au.

The following account of Victorian authorities' treatment of the Coranderrk community is principally indebted to these sources, together with conversations over the years with Aunty Joy Murphy Wandin. Giordano Nanni has been a patient and knowledgeable sounding-board for my reading of Coranderrk history.

Mary established at Coranderrk was astonishingly devolved by missionary standards of the time, the couple's policy being one of sharing governance with the community. In consequence, Aboriginal groups from other parts of Victoria were drawn to join the Coranderrk community, their leaders deferring to Wonga's authority as *ngurungaeta* of the country.

In John Green's capacity as Protection Board inspector, he was able to persuade a number of Aboriginal parents to entrust their children to his and his wife's care. He tended to recruit children who combined Aboriginal and European ancestry, so a significant proportion of the Coranderrk community, especially of its younger members, had relatively light complexions. In its early years, at least in relation to comparable institutions, Coranderrk succeeded, though it had to deal with constant harassment by White neighbours. Further, as the Greens' relatively humane management practices began to alarm the authoritarian governors of other missions, funding and oversight by the Board became sources of growing contention.

Aborigines were seen as an encumbrance rather than a clientele, and the Board failed to provide funding for basic capital works including housing, irrigation, storage, fencing and transport for produce. Coranderrk did not return an early profit and was held to be a liability to the colonial treasury, a perception that encouraged local Whites in their efforts to have the station sold off and fuelled arguments for residents' labour to be hired out, to defray the expenses of running the station. These pressures also reverberated within the community. In 1868, Wonga, together with his nephew, the now middle-aged William Barak (who would later succeed him as *ngurungaeta*) and fellow-resident Jemmy Barker, went to Melbourne to complain to the Board about Green's financial management. Green had been distributing the scarce funds available to him on a needs basis, which had disadvantaged some of the hardest workers on the station. All the while, surrounding White farmers were agitating for the station to be broken up and put on the market.

In the post-frontier era, then, Coranderrk confronted settler colonialism's twin priorities, the demand for cheap land and cheap labour to work it. Increasingly, these demands found racialised expression, voiced in the complaint that public money should not be wasted on supporting people who were not even proper Aborigines. The 'half-castes' should be made to work off the station. By the end of the decade, however, Green and the community were well reconciled and the pressure to single out people of mixed descent was resisted in major legislation that the colonial parliament introduced in 1869. In addition to providing for increased disciplinary control – a measure which, given the Greens' management policy, did not unduly affect Coranderrk – the 1869 legislation, as we shall see, regulated White pastoralists' use of Aboriginal labour and enabled Aboriginal people to be compulsorily confined on missions and reserves. Though these provisions were not enforced very rigorously, they had the effect of burdening the Coranderrk community with an increasing proportion of non-productive elderly and infirm members. Moreover, though resisted in the 1869 legislation, the racial dimension – most stridently voiced in parliament by the member for the constituency that included Coranderrk – had entered the public realm of politics.

The convergent pressures of financial uncertainty and the associated increase in Board interference eventually led to a major crisis. Hop growing was introduced at Coranderrk and proved to be an outstanding success, to the extent that the station returned a handsome profit that the Board could use to subsidise the other, church-run missions. Before long, the Board appointed White staff and labourers to produce the crop. White labourers would receive wages while Aboriginal ones would not. This was part of a programme of Board interference and criticism of the management style of John Green, who was eventually driven to resign his post at Coranderrk – a major tactical blunder that let down the Aborigines who had put their trust in his protection at the same time as it provided the Board with a pretext to be rid of its troublesome manager. Almost immediately, regretting his breach of trust, Green withdrew his resignation but the Board pressed its advantage and refused to reinstate him. This was the key moment in the Coranderrk rebellion, which, for all its impossible bravery and fortitude, would trigger measures whose consequences for Indigenous people in Victoria would fall squarely within the terms of the Genocide Convention that the General Assembly of the United Nations would approve, with Australian assent, sixty years later.[46]

In the wake of Green – who, despite bans, remained in the neighbourhood as a friend and advisor to the community – Coranderrk experienced a series of unwelcome replacements. Under Wonga and, after his death in 1875, his successor Barak, the Coranderrk Kooris mounted a sustained campaign of petition and protest, principally directed to the colonial parliament over the heads of the Protection Board. Initially seeking the reinstatement of John Green, the campaign subsequently widened to include a request for the abolition of the Board. Mary Green's educational efforts bore fruit in the felicity with which some of the younger members of the community, in particular Tom Dunolly and Robert Wandin, drafted letters and petitions to officials, parliamentarians and the radical Chief Secretary (leader of the colonial parliament) Graham Berry, who lent an ear to Barak in particular and provided significant support for the campaign while he remained in office.

The campaigners also secured the tireless support of a wealthy Scottish landowner, Anne Bon, who became a lifelong friend of Barak. Colonial

---

46   This assent was ratified in Australia's Genocide Convention Act, 1949.

newspapers, in particular the liberal *Age* and *Leader* newspapers of the Syme brothers David and George (the latter also being a member of the Board), printed the Coranderrk residents' letters and petitions and publicised their grievances, in particular their concern over the dismissal of John Green. Dramatically, Barak and others staged a series of walks into Melbourne to present their case to Berry and other officials, a journey of over forty miles each way (nowadays the round trip takes three hours to drive on tarmac highways). Growing public support was reflected in the appointment in 1881 of a parliamentary enquiry into 'the present condition and management of the Coranderrk Aboriginal Station', whose revealing proceedings included the testimonies of Coranderrk residents.[47] Though continuous with the armed resistance to colonial invasion that Wonga and Barak had experienced in their youth, this altogether lettered campaign, effectively orchestrated in the idiom of parliamentary agitation and without a spear in sight, constituted an utterly transformed mode of self-defence. The eventual colonial response was a catastrophe for Indigenous people in Victoria: an amendment to the 1869 legislation that was entitled the Aborigines Protection Act of 1886, universally referred to by Victorian Kooris to this day as the 'Half-Caste Act'.

In relation to the end of the frontier, and to the question of race in relation to land and sovereignty, it is instructive to compare the 1869 and 1886 Victorian acts, which encompass a key shift in the settler drive to eliminate Native territoriality.

The 1869 Act, legislated before sustained protests had arisen at Coranderrk and other missions, was essentially a matter of territorial consolidation. The land in its totality had been won from Aborigines, who were no longer in a position to contest its development. The 1869 Act provided for the regulation of the survivors in ways that would not obstruct settlers' orderly use of the land. Thus the government was empowered to prescribe 'the place where any aboriginal or any tribe of aborigines shall reside' (s. 2. i) and to prescribe the terms of work contracts between Aborigines and Europeans (s. 2. ii). In concert with routine provisions for the 'care custody and education' of Aboriginal children and measures to prevent adults from selling their government-issued blankets or moving outside the colony of Victoria (whereby they might evade the provisions of the act), the act provided for the spatial and financial control of Aborigines in a manner that would prevent them from impeding the workings of a predominantly pastoral economy.

Crucially, the arguments urged by the member for the electorate containing Coranderrk having been rejected, this control was undis-

---

47 These testimonies have been dramatised verbatim in Nanni and James, *Coranderrk: We Will Show the Country*.

criminating, the definition of Aboriginality being couched in terms of community affiliation rather than race. Section 8 of the 1869 Act defined 'an aboriginal' as: 'every aboriginal native of Australia and every aboriginal half-caste or child of a half-caste, such half-caste or child habitually associating and living with aboriginals'. All these people, wherever they were in the colony of Victoria, would be subject to control under the 1869 Act. Such an inclusive categorisation of Aboriginal people reflected the early ascendancy of a humanitarian faction on the Board, who advised the government on legislation relating to Aborigines. This group saw the missions as providing training that would enable Aborigines to survive the colonial onslaught as self-sufficient farming communities. On the basis of the humanitarian faction's desire for these communities to be viable, the number of labourers was maximised – a goal reflected in a style of racial classification not dissimilar to the one that we shall find associated with the reproduction of Black labour in the United States.[48] It was not to last long in colonial Victoria.

Seventeen years later, the main thing to change – for legislative purposes, that is – was the 1869 Act's definitional section 8, which the 1886 Act primarily held itself out as amending. In two consecutive sentences (section 2 and the first sentence of section 3), the 1886 Act introduced the racial distinction between 'half-castes' and Aborigines: 'Section eight of the [1869] Act is hereby repealed. The term "half-caste" whenever it occurs in this Act shall include as well half-castes as all other persons whatever of mixed Aboriginal blood.'

The amendment was crucial. Its awkward phrasing enabled the removal of all Indigenous people with any European ancestry from the provisions of the earlier 1869 Act, which had provided for Aboriginal people's admittance, including confinement, to missions and reserves. As such, it was the first occasion anywhere in the Australian colonies on which race constituted the operative criterion for legislation. It would by no means be the last. The most destructive consequence of the distinction drawn between those with and without European ancestry was spelled out in the new section 8 of the 1886 Act, which gave the government power to prescribe:

> the conditions on which the Board may license any half-castes to reside and be maintained on the place or places aforesaid where any aboriginal or tribe of aboriginals now or hereafter reside, and for limiting the period of such residence, and for regulating the removal or dismissal of any of such persons from any such place or places.[49]

---

48   I owe this insight to Giordano Nanni.
49   Aboriginal Protection Act 1886: *An Act to amend an Act intituled 'An Act to provide for the Protection and Management of the Aboriginal Natives of Victoria'* (PPV, 1886, no. 912).

With the temporary exception of children and the permanent exception of people aged thirty-five and over, whose days were on average numbered, this provision empowered the Board to break up Aboriginal families and communities on racial criteria that they themselves did not observe in their life together, permanently expelling kin from reserves and missions to which others were confined and condemning children and their families to the prospect of permanent separation when the children reached the age of thirteen. Within the space of two decades, the other mainland colonies and, after 1900, mainland states of Australia followed suit (Tasmania claiming that it had no surviving Aborigines).[50]

In the interval between the 1869 and 1886 Acts, the humanitarians had lost their dominance of the Board to a squatter clique who had no interest in Aborigines succeeding on land that could be taken over by White people. Rather than confining Aborigines to land committed to their cultivation in the manner of the 1869 Act, the 1886 Act provided for some Aborigines to spread out across the landscape, settler control of which was now taken for granted. The difference was that it no longer called the people concerned 'aborigines'. Rather, for settler purposes, a substantial proportion of the Aborigines controlled under the terms of the 1869 Act simply ceased to exist. Whatever threat to territorial order these people had posed in 1869 – a threat that had warranted their compulsory confinement – they no longer posed it.

Given the intervening disturbances at Coranderrk, along with other missions and reserves at a safer remove from Melbourne, this is surprising. It is all the more surprising in view of the fact that the insurgencies at Coranderrk and other missions were routinely blamed on 'half-castes', who were held to be more intelligent than Natives 'of the full blood'. On the face of it, then, the 1886 Act would seem to have provided for the letting loose on settler society of a group of notorious troublemakers. There is no need to pursue the absurdities. The 1886 Act was not aimed at individuals, whose behavioural characteristics it ignored. Nor was it aimed at territorial control, which it took for granted. It was aimed at Aboriginal collectivity. In the absence of land, we are back to the political dimension, Aboriginal territoriality, which finds expression in the technical language of race.

At a stroke, the 1886 Act sought to eliminate around half of Victoria's surviving Aboriginal population, a goal that was significantly achieved (by 1927, the Victorian Aboriginal population stood officially at 514, a drop of approximately 35 per cent from 1886[51]). The means to this

---

50 The list significantly includes the Aborigines Protection and Sale of Opium Act (Queensland, 1897), the Aborigines Protection Act (New South Wales, 1909) and the Aborigines Act (Western Australia, 1897).

51 Broome, *Aboriginal Victorians*, 209.

achievement were routinely forcible, with people being separated from their relatives by Victoria Police and Protection Board functionaries, in many cases to vanish thereafter into the settler mainstream. As observed, terrible things were done. Given these outcomes, it is hard to avoid questions of group psychology. Can it be that the bulk of the Legislative Assembly of Victoria – which, after all, represented the settler population as a whole – were psychopaths? The evidence does not permit such a simple interpretation. Rather, the rationales presented by proponents of the 1886 legislation evince a banality that Hannah Arendt would have recognised.[52] Giordano Nanni has pointed out to me that the rare debates on Aboriginal matters in the Legislative Assembly principally revolved around humdrum economic considerations, and were not conspicuously marked by the lurid cant of scientific racism.[53]

As we shall be reminded throughout this book, colonisers did not set out to create racial doctrine. They set out to create wealth. As Hansard reveals, the principal arguments for the 1886 Act boiled down to the related propositions that Aboriginal reserves were a drain on the public

---

52   Hannah Arendt, *Eichmann in Jerusalem: A Report on the Banality of Evil* (New York: Penguin, 1977 [1963]).

53   The following exchange from the parliamentary debate leading up to the 1886 Act is indicative of the framing of the issue (in this context, the term 'vote' refers to a sum of money that parliamentarians vote to allocate to a given end): 'On the vote of £6,084 to complete the vote (£10,584) for the aborigines, Mr BROWN observed that the vote showed an increase over the vote of last year. Surely, with the aboriginal race dying out, there should be reduction rather than increase.

Mr. BENT thought the Chief Secretary would do well to inform the committee what were their intentions for the Board for the Protection of the Aborigines with respect to half-castes. The last time this vote was under consideration it was promised that there should be more economy. It was stated that there was a large number of half-castes, and that the board would do something to procure their employment on work befitting their position. He would also like to hear some explanation for the item of £9,308 – a very large sum – for contingencies.

Mr. DEAKIN stated that the amount appropriated for salaries was comparatively very small. The bulk of the vote consisted of the £9,308 set down for contingencies, that was to say of money which was to go to the aborigines themselves in some form or other. The question of the expenditure upon the aborigines was an important one ... [notes that the expense was offset by the Coranderrk hops] ... The honourable member for Mandurang (Mr. Brown) very properly described the aborigines as a nearly extinct race, and, therefore the expense attending their maintenance ought to become less and less. There was at the present moment on the table a Bill [for the 1886 Act] under which it was proposed that the state [i.e., the colony] should get rid of the maintenance of the half-castes and quarter-castes of the aboriginal population; and the board hoped that that measure becoming law would soon enable them [the Board] to largely decrease their expenses.

(Mr. Zox – 'Are the half-castes and quarter-castes to merge into the general population?').

[Mr. Deakin] – 'That was the intention'. Victorian Parliamentary Debates (*Hansard*, session 1886, vol. 52, 1810). Alfred Deakin would later become prime minister of Australia.

purse, using up money that would be better spent on public works such as the railways, that this problem could be alleviated by removing the 'half-castes' so that they could contribute usefully to the Victorian economy, and that the reduced number of Aborigines remaining would need less land allocated to them, allowing portions of their reserves to be sold off (or even whole reserves if they could be amalgamated), the proceeds going to defray the public outlay on their maintenance.[54]

There is nothing deranged about these rationales, which are paradigm expressions of the settler-colonial logic of elimination. Indeed, there was a certain candour to the forthright acknowledgement of the attractive-ness of the mission land, reflecting the influence on Victorian Aboriginal policy of Protection Board members like the frontier-era squatter Edward Micklethwaite Curr, now in his sixties. Even Barak's friends and sup-porters Berry and Bon welcomed the passage of the 1886 Act, on the ground that it would stop public money being syphoned away from those for whom it was intended, 'full-blood' Aborigines.[55] Due process was vouchsafed. Accordingly, while many of these rationales were no doubt cynically expressed, and while it is clearly the case that part of the Protection Board's motivation for promoting the act was its resentment of the public success of the Coranderrk community's political campaign, the outcome for Victorian Aborigines cannot be reduced to a calculus of White people's intentions, which did not need to be consciously hostile. As Michael Christie observes, a feature of the Board's tactical shrewdness in getting the act passed was its accommodation of public support for the Coranderrk struggle: 'The public were less sympathetically disposed to the half-caste question – it lacked the dramatic appeal of a dispossessed but united people fighting to stay on a piece of land they considered theirs.'[56]

The Stolen Generations

The 1886 Victorian Act marks the legislative onset of the Australia-wide policy of Aboriginal child abduction, coordinated in 1937 but admin-istered individually by the separate states, the victims of which would come to be known as the Stolen Generations. Despite its ostensibly

---

54 Thus I diverge from the more narrowly doctrinal (in places, attitudinal) under-standing of race that characterises Bain Attwood's account of the 1886 Act, the origins of which, he asserts, 'did not rest exclusively in a *racial* ideology, if that is defined as a body of ideas associated with a racial structure, but lay initially in a general bourgeois ethos of individualism, economic self-help and moral improvement, and in an allied fear of pauperism.' Attwood, *Making of the Aborigines*, 98, emphasis in original.

55 Though Bon also asserted that it was 'unjust to the pure Aboriginals that the bounty of the State – a just recompense for deprived rights and privileges – should be lavished on the offspring of white immorality.' Quoted in Christie, *Aborigines in Colonial Victoria*, 201.

56 Christie, *Aborigines in Colonial Victoria*, 197.

selective nature – the preferential targeting of lighter-skinned children –
the policy was clearly aimed at the elimination of Aboriginal people as a
whole. As Joseph Carrodus, secretary of the federal Department of the
Interior, observed to the state delegates who assembled in Canberra in
1937 to devise a common Aboriginal policy, none of whom demurred:

> It would be desirable for us to deal first with the people of mixed blood.
> Ultimately, if history is repeated, the full bloods will become half-castes.[57]

On this basis, the delegates adopted as their national policy:

> That this Conference believes that the destiny of the natives of aboriginal
> origin, but not of the full blood, lies in their ultimate absorption by the
> people of the Commonwealth [Australia] and it therefore recommends that
> all efforts be directed to that end.[58]

The abductions were officially carried out until the 1960s. Aboriginal
children continue to be placed in care in disproportionate numbers.[59]
The details of this sustained historical trauma for Indigenous people in
Australia have been documented.[60] Our concern here is with what the
policy tells us about the work of race.

In this regard, it is apparent, first, that, despite the widespread talk
of Aboriginal people being congenitally inferior to Whites, the rationale for the policy of child abduction cannot have been genetic. Outside
homeopathy, at least, which did not determine Australian government
policy, it would make no sense to absorb defective material into one's
own gene pool. Nor, second, can the routinely cited allegations of the

---

57   'Aboriginal Welfare. – Initial Conference of Commonwealth and State Aboriginal
Authorities, held at Canberra, 21st to 23rd April, 1937' (Canberra: Government Printer,
1937), 21. Carrodus was responding to John Cleland, Chairman of the Advisory
Council of Aborigines for South Australia (whose qualification, significantly enough,
was as a professor of pathology), who had just expressed the same logic in cultural terms
('detribalization'): 'We would achieve exactly the same object in the ultimate if we dealt
first with natives of less than full blood.' With apparently unconscious irony, an Adelaide
kindergarten is currently named after Cleland.
58   'Aboriginal Welfare', 21.
59   'At June 2002, 22% (4,200) of children in out-of-home care were Aboriginal or
Torres Straight [sic] Islander children. This represented a much higher rate of children
in out-of-home care among Indigenous children than non-Indigenous children (20.1
per 1,000 compared with 3.2 per 1,000).' 'Children in out-of-home care,' in Australian
Bureau of Statistics, Australia Now (Canberra: Australian Bureau of Statistics, 2004),
s. 2, 'Australian social trends, 2003: family and community services: child protection'.
As this book was going to press, the Melbourne Age newspaper (13 June 2015, p. 3)
reported that 'a sharp increase in the rate of Indigenous children in Victoria being taken
from their families has prompted fears of a "lost generation" with broken cultural ties'.
60   Haebich, Broken Circles; National Inquiry into the Separation of Aboriginal and
Torres Strait Islander Children from Their Families, Bringing Them Home.

children's neglected state have been the rationale. Though the policy primarily targeted children with light skin, it was never claimed that their darker-skinned fellows were less neglected. Moreover, while children from other groups could also be taken away on the ground of parental neglect, as Peter Read discovered, 'being an Aboriginal' constituted the only ethnic category that could of itself constitute sufficient ground for taking a child.[61] This leaves a third option: colour. After she had been taken away, the late Lisa Bellear's White adoptive parents informed her repeatedly that she was really a Polynesian princess. Such stories are so common that the parents may have been officially instructed to explain the children's pigmentation to them on grounds other than Indigeneity, presumably to lower the likelihood of family reunion. In any event, spontaneous or otherwise, the deception was widespread. Clearly, the problem was not colour but history. The parents were seeking to exchange an Aboriginal provenance for another one, any other one. This is not to say that Polynesian, or, for that matter, other foreign ancestry of colour, was welcome in the era of the White Australia Policy. It is to say that Aboriginality was uniquely less welcome.

Though the Canberra conference standardised the policy of Aboriginal assimilation in 1937, for practical purposes it merely set the seal on a motley of cognate policies, varying in matters of detail, that had been incrementally adopted by the separate colonies and states three or four decades earlier, in the years surrounding federation and national independence, which had come into effect at the beginning of 1901.[62] For declarative purposes, federation signalled the ending of the frontier. The nation had matured and come to exercise its dominion, albeit somewhat patchily, over the continental landmass. Though individual Native groups would on occasion be hunted down up to the 1930s, federation marks the moment of nationhood, when the new Commonwealth came to determine its own constitution, including the matter of who should make it up, the fundamental questions of citizenship and entitlement to share in the national space. The vision being the making of a White nation, plans were drawn up to deport those of non-European ancestry.[63] Since

---

61 For Peter Read's pioneering contribution in this field, see Read, 'The Stolen Generations' (Sydney: Ministry of Aboriginal Affairs Occasional Paper no. 1, 1983); Read, '"A Rape of the Soul So Profound": Some Reflections on the Dispersal Policy in NSW', *Aboriginal History* 7 (1984), 1, 23–33; Coral Edwards and Peter Read (eds), *The Lost Children* (Sydney: Doubleday, 1989).

62 Aborigines Act (Western Australia, 1897); Aborigines Protection and Sale of Opium Act (Queensland, 1897); Aborigines Protection Act (New South Wales, 1909); Aborigines Act (South Australia, 1911); Aborigines Ordinance, 1918 (federal legislation re. Northern Territory).

63 Myra Willard, *History of the White Australia Policy to 1920* (Melbourne: Melbourne UP, 1923); Gwenda Tavan, *The Long, Slow Death of White Australia* (Melbourne: Scribe, 2005).

deportation was not an option in the case of Aboriginal people, to whom no extra-national homeland could plausibly be assigned, Aboriginal assimilation functioned as an internal correlate to the deportation of non-White foreigners. Though one included and the other excluded, the two strategies were coordinated at the level of the whole, together participating in the projected construction of a White Australia.

We shall encounter a similar complementarity of inclusive and exclusive strategies when we consider the distinctive racialisations of Indians and Black people in the USA, which, as we shall see, were contemporaneous with the Australian programme. Introduced in 1886, the Victorian legislation that marks the onset of the Australian programme of Aboriginal child abduction came a year before the General Allotment Act would signal the onset of the Dawes-era campaign in the United States against all things collectively Indian, a concerted post-frontier programme that coincided with the onset of the Jim Crow reign of racial terror that would be imposed on Black people in the US South from late in the 1880s. As in the case of Australia, the two US programmes were systematically conjoined, the inclusion of Indians converging with the exclusion of Black people in a range of ways that we shall consider below.

The coincidence was not merely chronological. In both Australia and the United States, concerted campaigns of Native assimilation commenced upon the ending of the frontier. In both countries, the cultural and biological aspects of assimilation fused inextricably, with blood quantum heuristically summarising a multidimensional engulfment. In the case of the Australian policy, as I have argued previously, the cultural and biological dimensions of assimilation recapitulated each other, sharing a narrative structure that eliminated interstitial elements from a governing polarity that was at once cultural, genetic and spatiotemporal.[64] On all these dimensions, White Australia was counterposed to an authentic Aboriginality that can be glossed as culturally traditional, genetically dark, spatially resident in the Outback (failing which, on reserves), and temporally discontinuous with the present.

The formula is familiar and hardly requires rehearsal. Its various dimensions complemented each other interchangeably. A remedy for the genetic defect of mixed bloodedness was the spatial device of removal, while the failure to be culturally traditional – epitomised in Tom Dunolly's too-clever-by-half letters to politicians – was held out as characteristic of 'half-castes'. Thus a campaign to eliminate people of mixed descent was realised spatially. In the wake of the 1886 Act, the Coranderrk community was systematically broken up, many of them transported to the Lake Tyers mission, which was eventually scheduled as the final repository of Victorian 'full bloods'. As Barwick recounted,

---

64 Wolfe, *Settler Colonialism and the Transformation of Anthropology*, 184–90.

The Board's 1921 annual report announced that only 42 residents remained at Coranderrk; the secretary's unpublished enumeration named another 47 'half castes' ineligible for aid or residence who were camped in the vicinity. Descendants [of the early Coranderrk families] ... were camped in huts and tents to be near their 'old people'. But the manager ... C. A. Robarts, punctiliously maintained the Board's rule that 'the outside half castes are restricted to one day a week to visit their relatives and friends'.[65]

But the Board was not acting alone. A wider cultural logic bore its members along:

In 1914 and 1915 Healesville residents petitioned the government to resume the reserve for a permanent military camp. Chief Secretary Murray refused, announcing that Coranderrk was the most suitable site for a central station housing all the surviving natives. The Healesville Shire Council then organised public protest meetings which complained that 'the congregation of a degenerate race a few miles from the township will ruin Healesville as a tourist resort'.[66]

Some of the names of the Shire councillors of 1915 adorn local businesses today, while the tourism industry has thrived. In the wake of the Council's campaign, the Coranderrk land was repeatedly excised, cut in two by the new Koo Wee Rup road, with the eastern half (which I look down on) becoming a cottage development for White people. By the end of World War II, everyone had been removed and all that was left to the Coranderrk Kooris was their cemetery. Though the ravaged community endured and has since staged a magnificent, albeit partial, recovery – managing among other things to buy back some of the Coranderrk land in 1998 – this has been achieved in spite of, not as a result of, our town's best efforts.

In sum, then, while the policy of child abduction was expressed in the language of race ('natives of aboriginal origin, but not of the full blood'), the Stolen Generations were the centrepiece of a comprehensive campaign that strove for the elimination of an entire group whose definition, as we have seen, is historical rather than biological. As prior owners of the land, Aboriginal people are unique. Their priority cannot be submerged in indiscriminate classifications based on colour, class or pathology. They are not Polynesians, royalty or otherwise, they are more than merely poor, and they may or may not be neglectful, but that is an individual matter. The attempt to assimilate them to such categories – biologically, culturally and spatially – has been part and parcel of the settler campaign to suppress their uniqueness, which irreducibly comes

---

65 Barwick, *Rebellion at Coranderrk*, 304.
66 Ibid., 306–7.

down to territoriality, to the political matter of their ongoing connectivity with the land that has been physically taken from them.

An anxious concession to this unredressed distinction sustains Aborigines' long-run prominence in Australian public discourse, which they dominate to an extent entirely disproportionate to their numerical status. The awareness to which this discrepancy attests is quintessentially historical. I have characterised this history as genocidal, denoting the gravest crime that can be perpetrated on the collective level. Since I have previously distinguished between the settler-colonial logic of elimination and genocide, arguing that the two typically converge but do not have to do so – one can exist without the other – it is necessary to be definitionally rigorous.[67]

Article II (d) of the UN Convention on Genocide includes among the acts that constitute genocide the imposition of 'measures intended to prevent births within the group'. Given that the Australian practice of abducting Aboriginal children, if 'successful', would bring about a situation in which second-generation offspring were born into a group different from the one from which the parent had originally been abducted, there is abundant evidence of genocide being practised in post-war Australia (i.e., after the adoption of the Genocide Convention) on the basis of Article II (d) alone. It is impossible to draw simple either/or lines between culture and biology in cases such as these. Though a child was physically abducted, the eventual outcome is as much a matter of a social classification as it is of a body count. It does not depend on the bare life of the child, which may be ongoing. The issue is the further births that the abductions prevented within the 'relinquishing' group.

This leaves the question of perpetrators' intentions. While this criterion obtains (regrettably, it might be thought) independently of victim groups' experiences, it is required under the opening clause of Article II of the Genocide Convention schedule, which defines genocide as 'acts committed with intent to destroy, in whole or in part, a national, ethnical [sic], racial or religious group, as such'. The 'as such' qualification is important. Genocide does not apply in situations where people are targeted for reasons that are not reducible to their group identity. The category 'natives of aboriginal origin, but not of the full blood' is, however, a group identity (racial and/or ethnical, whether or not 'national') – arguably a whole group, but certainly the Aboriginal group 'in part'.[68]

---

67 Patrick Wolfe, 'Settler Colonialism and the Elimination of the Native', *Journal of Genocide Research* 8 (2006), 387–409.

68 This is to leave aside the consideration that the category of the whole could itself be plural, referring to separate Aboriginal societies in their respective entireties: 'If this reasoning holds, then it is possible, by the UN definition, to regard as a genocide each willed act of extermination by settlers and/or the state of an entire Aboriginal group.

Thus the recommendation that 'all efforts' be directed to the 'end' of their 'ultimate absorption' by the people of the Commonwealth constitutes an explicit expression of genocidal intent at the highest official level, at least so far as the specified 'part' of the Aboriginal group was concerned.

Though this seems conclusive, one should, I think, pursue the matter further, since it is not the case that the 'half-caste' part of the whole Aboriginal group was viewed as stably distinct from it. Rather, as Carrodus made clear – and this is the significance of the other delegates accepting his statement without demur and moving straight from it to adopt the motion – the distinction between 'half-castes' and 'natives of the full blood' was seen as a descending one, whereby the 'full bloods' would merge steadily into the 'half-caste' category, thereby qualifying for absorption: 'It would be desirable for us to deal first with the people of mixed blood. Ultimately, if history is repeated, the full bloods will become half-castes.'[69]

The Victorian Protection Board would have approved. Fifty years earlier, in its first report to the Legislative Assembly on its implementation of the 1886 Act, the Board had observed with satisfaction that it represented 'the beginning of the end', which, within a few years, would leave 'only a few pure blacks' in official care.[70] The evidence resists 'bandying about'.[71] The genocidal practices authorised under the Australian policy of assimilation targeted Aboriginal people in whole and in part. Implications for redress present themselves.

The specificity of the Aboriginal category cannot be reduced to colour, any more than Aborigines' historical maltreatment can be trivialised as 'colour prejudice'. Beneath the indeterminate signifier of colour lies the historical continuity of dispossession, an irregularity that the inclusive regime of race has sought to neutralise. Thus it is consistent that another

---

In that case, Australia had many genocides, perhaps more than any other country.' A. Dirk Moses, 'An Antipodean Genocide? The Origins of the Genocidal Moment in the Colonization of Australia', *Journal of Genocide Research* 2 (2000), 93.

69   Carrodus in 'Aboriginal Welfare', 21.

70   'Parliament has passed a measure for merging the half-castes among the general population of the colony. For a long time the Board had been urging this policy on the attention of the country ... already the Board has made a fair beginning of a policy which is the beginning of the end, and which, in the course of a few years, will leave only a few pure blacks under the care of Government.' Alex Morrison (Board vice-chairman) in Board for the Protection of Aborigines, *23rd Report* (Melbourne: Government Printer, 1887), 3, 4.

71   I do not know how the term 'bandying about' came to feature in the script of genocide denial, but exponents would seem to regard it as indispensable. I have been accused of bandying about on a number of occasions, but not once by someone demonstrating awareness of the actual provisions of the Genocide Convention. I conclude that the bandying about of genocide denial is privileged in settler discourse, an exemption with very grave implications for Indigenous peoples' right to redress.

Black group, who were co-opted to very different ends by European colonisers, should come to be racialised in a correspondingly different manner. In the following chapter, we consider the racialisation of Black people in the United States.

CHAPTER TWO

The Two Minds of the South

Race and Democracy in the United States

When we shift from the racialisation of Black people in Australia to the racialisation of Black people in the United States, the difference is striking. In contrast to the regime in Australia, where Black women were obliged to become conduits to Whiteness, the United States presents the 'well-known anomaly of American racial convention' that Barbara Fields has characterised, which 'considers a white woman capable of giving birth to a black child but denies that a black woman can give birth to a white child'.[1] Given the regime of slavery, it is only consistent that Black women should have augmented White men's property by giving birth to additional slaves without regard to paternity, so the anomalousness presumably arose in the aftermath of slavery, when, in the absence of formal enactment, the subordination of African Americans came to rely more completely on colour. As we shall see, when the United States moved into the post-slavery era, a trace of slavery persisted in the fact that the paternity of Black women's children continued to have no effect on their status, which remained rigorously matrilineal.

Thus Black women are not only barred from having White children. Along with Black men, they are barred from having any children other than Black ones.[2] For our purposes, a significant consequence of this rule is that Black people cannot have Native children – a situation that is not so different from the Australian one after all. In its consequence for descent, the exclusive racialisation of Black people doubles as an eliminatory policy when it comes to the (non-)reproduction of Natives, a consequence that falls from view when racial politics in the United States

---

1 Barbara J. Fields, 'Ideology and Race in American History', in J. Morgan Kousser and James M. McPherson (eds), *Region, Race, and Reconstruction: Essays in Honor of C. Vann Woodward* (New York: Oxford UP, 1982), 149.

2 Strictly, therefore, Blackness operates ambilineally, including the preponderant matrilineality.

is viewed through the partial lens of a Black/White binary. Non-White is not necessarily Black.[3] At the level of the whole, therefore, we should adopt an integrated perspective that not only traces the historical racialisation of Black people in the United States but also coordinates that history with the concurrent racialisation of Indians.

In a letter of March 1757 to his brother Moses, Peter Fountaine, a Huguenot descendant of Westover, Virginia, complained of the 'many base wretches among us' who took up with Black women, 'by which means the country swarms with mulatto bastards' who, once three generations removed, would, 'by the indulgent laws of the country', be allowed to intermarry with Whites. He continued:

> Now, if, instead of this abominable practice which hath polluted the blood of so many among us, we had taken Indian wives in the first place, it would have been some compensation for their lands. They are a free people, and the offspring would not have been born in a state of slavery. We should become the rightful heirs to their lands and should not have smutted our blood.[4]

Fountaine was nothing if not succinct. This short passage bristles with themes that would animate North American racial discourse for the following century and beyond, in particular the hereditary nature of slavery and its linkage to Indian dispossession. At a stroke, Fountaine's connubial formula provided for Whites to acquire Indians' land and retain slaves to work it, a marriage of convenience if ever there was one. Few Australians would be pragmatic enough openly to advocate miscegenation as a solution to the ideological conundrum presented by the fact that settler institutions rested on the seizure of Aboriginal lands. Nonetheless, the principle that Indigenous people were assimilable into the European stock is common to the two national histories and contrasts sharply with the regime imposed on African Americans, whose difference was rendered absolute, ancestral and immutable.[5] In tracing the historical development of this peculiarly eternalised regime of race, which renders African heredity uniquely inexhaustible, we shall therefore keep in mind

---

3   An exclusive focus on Black mothers (Black woman/White man) is both a raced and a gendered binary, which excludes Black fathers and non-Black mothers (Black man/non-Black woman) from the parentage of Black children as well as some non-White fathers (non-Black, non-White man/Black woman).

4   Quoted in James Hugo Johnston, *Race Relations in Virginia and Miscegenation in the South, 1776–1860* (Amherst: Massachusetts UP, 1970), 170, who also quotes Colonel Byrd to almost identical effect.

5   'In appropriately altered circumstances Indians could become white men, a happy transformation indeed. It was precisely this transformation which Jefferson thought the Negro could never accomplish. By constantly referring to environment for one group and to nature for the other he effectively widened the gap which Americans had always placed between the two.' Jordan, *White over Black*, 478.

its antithetical complementarity with the concurrent racialisation of Native Americans.

Race and Slavery

The dating of race's emergence and of its harnessing to slavery remain controversial. Oceans of ink have been spilt on arguments over precisely when, once the first consignment of twenty Africans had been landed in Virginia in 1619, Africans became 'Negroes' (as opposed to 'heathens', 'savages', 'blackamores' and the like) and Negroes became slaves.[6] David Brion Davis quotes the English Puritan Paul Baines, who died in 1617, two years before the first landing, as stating that 'slavish' servants were 'perpetually put under the power of the master, as blackamores with us'.[7] So far as England's North American colonies are concerned, it is at least clear that, by the last quarter of the seventeenth century, the equation of Africanness and slavery was becoming well-established. As early as 1652, Rhode Island's antislavery legislation (which was to be ineffectual in practice) had presupposed that 'there is a common course practised amongst English men to buy negers, to that end they may have them for service or slaves forever'.[8]

It is not clear, though, whether 'forever' here (or, for that matter, Baines's 'perpetually') operated within an individual lifetime (durante vita) or conveyed a condition that was also transmitted to offspring in the manner that was to become characteristic of North America. It was not until the juridical opposition of slave versus free became mapped onto the hereditary opposition of Black versus White that being born a Black person meant being born a slave. By 1680, the English missionary Morgan Goodwyn could confidently express the developing North American presumption that the two words 'Negro' and 'Slave' had 'by custom grown Homogeneous and convertible', but he was a little ahead of his time.[9] In 1680, it was not yet the case that all slaves were necessarily Black, though the trend was increasingly in that direction, as fewer Indians and no Whites continued to be enslaved.[10] Ira Berlin has narrated

6   For an account of the protracted controversy over the priority of race or slavery, see Alden T. Vaughan, 'The Origins Debate: Slavery and Racism in Seventeenth-Century Virginia', *Virginia Magazine of History and Biography* 97 (1989), 311–54.

7   David Brion Davis, *The Problem of Slavery in Western Culture* (Ithaca: Cornell UP, 1966), 245.

8   Quoted in William M. Wiecek, 'The Statutory Law of Slavery and Race in the Thirteen Mainland Colonies of British America', *William and Mary Quarterly* 34 (1977), 260.

9   Quoted in James Walvin, *Questioning Slavery* (London: 1996), 79.

10   From a vast literature, see, e.g., Higginbotham, *In the Matter of Color*; Ira Berlin, 'From Creole to African: Atlantic Creoles and the Origins of African-American Society in Mainland North America', *William and Mary Quarterly*, 3ʳᵈ Series, 53 (1966),

how, around the turn of the eighteenth century, the 'relentless engine of plantation agriculture', driven by ruthless planters like Robert 'King' Carter, transformed the Chesapeake within the space of two generations, changing a society with slaves into a slave society, organised around the maintenance and reproduction of plantation slavery: 'a régime in which African descent was equated with slavery'.[11]

The consolidation of slave society in North America culminated a general realignment away from White indenture (even occasional slavery) and towards Black slavery that had been in train since around the middle of the seventeenth century. Prior to the 1650s, there had been a number of economic reasons for preferring White labour to Black. White labour was generally cheaper to import, the early-seventeenth-century slave trade from Africa and the Caribbean being dominated by Portuguese and Dutch traders whose high prices compared unfavourably with the cost of importing servants from England.[12] From the 1660s on, however, not only was the post–Civil War English Africa trade becoming increasingly well established, but English servants other than convicts were becoming harder to attract, in part because stories of the hardship of plantation life were in wide circulation in England.[13]

Slaves imported directly from Africa also became preferred over either Caribbean or Native ones. In the case of those who had already experienced slavery in the Caribbean – people who, in the unholy language of planter-speak, were 'seasoned' – the possession of pre-existent skills was offset by strategic familiarity with the system compounded by the potential for solidarity that flowed from the shared command of English. Alienated from their homelands, escaped Africans could not seek sanctuary through familiar Indigenous networks (maroon or *quilombo* settlements of escaped slaves did not develop in North America to the same extent as further south[14]). Having been in continental contact with Europeans for centuries, Africans shared resistance to many European diseases, as well as familiarity with European agricultural techniques. Moreover, the

---

288 (linking the trend to the rise of plantations); Davis, *Problem of Slavery in Western Culture*, 245.

11 Ira Berlin, *Many Thousands Gone: The First Two Centuries of Slavery in North America* (Cambridge, MA: Harvard UP, 1988), 109–26, quotation from Berlin, 'From Creole to African', 288.

12 Hilary Beckles, '"Black Men in White Skins": The Formation of a White Proletariat in West Indian Slave Society', *Journal of Imperial and Commonwealth History* 15 (1986), 8; T. H. Breen, 'A Changing Labor Force and Race Relations in Virginia, 1660–1710', in Breen (ed.), *Shaping Southern Society: The Colonial Experience* (New York: Oxford UP, 1976), 118.

13 Robin Blackburn, *The Making of New World Slavery: From the Baroque to the Modern, 1492–1800* (London: Verso, 1997), 319.

14 Berlin, *Many Thousands Gone*, 121. Berlin does not note the case of the Seminoles in Florida, presumably on account of their status as Indians.

awkward religious and ethical issues raised by the enslavement of Indians who had not been captured in war did not apply to Africans, who had already been in a state of slavery at the time of purchase – though these issues could as well be avoided by classificatory sleight of hand as by empirical ancestry. In eighteenth-century South Carolina, for instance, Indian slaves rapidly disappeared from census returns and plantation daybooks as plantation owners 'simply categorized their Indian slaves as Africans'.[15] For pragmatic reasons such as these, slavers in British North America steadily came to favour importing their labour directly from Africa. With slavery increasingly sharing boundaries with Blackness, laws relating to servitude were colour-coded accordingly.

From early in the eighteenth century, North American legislatures refashioned the English common-law concept of petty treason, which applied to offences committed against a person in a particular relationship of authority over the offender, to give it a general application to offences committed against Whites by Blacks.[16] This was part and parcel of the development of an across-the-board system of racial control whereby, in Frederick Cooper's words, 'planters as a class were equipped to take forceful measures to control slaves as a class, and they could count on the help of whites as a race to maintain order among blacks as a race'.[17]

This process of setting Blacks apart highlighted characteristics that were seen as manifestly distinguishing them from Whites, especially skin colour, facial shape and type of hair. Among first-generation slaves, these characteristics also included non-hereditary attributes such as language, religion and initiation marks. From the first creole generation on, however, such differences were radically levelled out, both among Blacks and, more dangerously, between Blacks and Whites, a situation that threatened White freedom and Black unfreedom alike. When boundaries could no longer be taken for granted, those who straddled them were targeted. Berlin has charted how, in the Chesapeake, the fortunes of 'free mulattos' – people who straddled both phenotypical and juridical boundaries – declined between 1660 and 1760 as the system of racial domination was consolidated: 'Since the Africans would shortly be creoles and since creoles shared so much with whites, distinctions among blacks threatened the racial division that underlay planter domination.'[18]

While the racialisation of people of African heritage as both Black and enslaved proceeded steadily, it was neither foreordained nor inevitable. As observed, colonisers – in this case, planters – did not set out to create

---

15   Blackburn, *The Making*, 123; Berlin, *Many Thousands Gone*, 145.

16   Wiecek, 'Statutory Law of Slavery and Race', 274.

17   Frederick Cooper, *Plantation Slavery on the East Coast of Africa* (New Haven: Yale UP, 1977), 259.

18   Ira Berlin, 'Time, Space, and the Evolution of Afro-American Society on British Mainland North America', *American Historical Review* 85 (1980), 73.

racial discrimination. They set out to create wealth.[19] In addition to its cir-
cumstantial trajectory, the developing equation of Blackness with slavery
needs to be understood in relation to its historicity: to the particular
conditions whereby this formula rather than any other – convict labour,
fixed-term slavery, a contract system – came to be selected as the optimal
arrangement for the achievement of overall social goals in British North
America. In a context that was simultaneously incubating a concern with
freedom, the development of a wholesale dependence on slavery, far from
being inevitable, requires explanation. Edmund Morgan provided such
an explanation.

The consolidation of African slavery took place in the very act of
refusing slavery, as submission to the despotic English yoke was often
depicted. Thus George Washington lamented that virtuous men should
be driven to choose war with the British crown on account of the 'sad
alternative' whereby 'the once happy and peaceful plains of America are
either to be drenched with Blood, or inhabited by Slaves'.[20] To a later
outsider's eye, the blind spot seems too glaring to be credited. After all,
as Morgan crisply noted, 'When Washington faced his sad alternative,
the happy and peaceful plains of Virginia had been inhabited by slaves
for more than a century, and 135 of them belonged to him.'[21] In providing a context for Washington's remark, however, Morgan went beyond a
critique of its manifest hypocrisy, which would have left it as an abstract
logical contradiction, to spell out its concrete historicity. The paradoxical
coexistence between the ideal of liberty and the practice of slavery had
arisen in North America, Morgan contended, as a result of the threat
that the presence of an unruly White working class, the so-called 'giddy
multitude' – precursors to those condemned to the hulks – had posed
to seventeenth-century Virginian society. In brief, as he put it, 'It could
be argued that Virginia had relieved one of England's social problems
by importing it.'[22]

The giddy multitude could find common cause with Black people,
Berlin's cosmopolitan 'charter generation', who, in the main, had arrived
from the Caribbean rather than directly from Africa.[23] Amid fears on
the part of the governing elite that the colony of Virginia was fast

19   '[T]he object was to produce cotton or sugar or rice or tobacco, not to produce
white supremacy.' Fields, 'Slavery, Race and Ideology', 111.

20   George Washington, *Writings* (J. Fitzpatrick, ed., Washington: 1931–44), vol.
3, 292.

21   Morgan, *American Slavery, American Freedom*, 4.

22   Morgan, *American Slavery, American Freedom*, 295. Cf. Edmund S. Morgan,
'Slavery and Freedom: The American Paradox', *Journal of American History* 59 (1972),
5–29.

23   Breen, 'A Changing Labor Force'. For the charter generation, see Berlin, 'From
Creole to African', 251–88; Berlin, *Many Thousands Gone*, 17–108.

becoming a 'sinke to drayne England of her filth and scum' – scum who, as Bacon's Revolt had made dramatically clear in the 1670s, could mobilise rebellious Africans – Virginia embarked on a twin programme that combined reductions in the importation of indentured English servants with a steep increase in the importation of enslaved Africans. Since these slaves did not have indentures that expired, they would not come to present the threat to order that White freedmen did. As Robin Blackburn has summarised the logic of this policy, the shift to a reliance on directly imported Africans 'reduced social antagonisms within the white colonial community by removing the axis of exploitation from inside it'.[24] Hence eighteenth-century Virginian planters were able to extol the ideal of a free White yeomanry and profess allegiance to the ancestral rights of Englishmen because the preponderance of Black slaves had pre-empted the development of a dangerous underclass of recently freed Whites.

Behind the theoretical contradiction that slavery presented to libertarian ideals, in other words, Morgan showed how, in material practice, the founding fathers' emancipatory ideology depended on slavery as a condition of its possibility. As he put it, slavery transformed 'the Virginia of Governor Berkeley to the Virginia of Jefferson ... [It was] slavery that made the Virginians dare to speak a political language that magnified the rights of freemen'.[25] Developing this profoundly subversive insight on Morgan's part, Davis observed that not only was it the case that Virginians could defend man's inalienable rights because the enslavement of Blacks had spared them the need to discipline a White proletariat but, reciprocally, condemnation of the same slavery would soon provide Englishmen with a means to demonstrate their own liberality in an era when, at home, 'they were beginning to find new uses for the self-same troublesome idle poor, who, after "proper admonition and tryals", could be molded into a compliant working class' (to which we might add – or transported).[26] Davis went on to spell out what had been implicit in Morgan's argument: Blacks, being deemed incapable of emancipating themselves, became a race apart in the late eighteenth century to an extent that warranted their exclusion from the universal humanity that bore the rights which the spokesmen of revolution were so loftily enunciating. Race, in short, became 'the central excuse for slavery'.[27]

---

24 Blackburn, *The Making*, 263.
25 Morgan, 'American Paradox', 29.
26 Davis, *Age of Revolution*, 264.
27 Ibid., 303–4. It should perhaps be noted that Morgan's own argument was becoming more explicitly couched in terms of race by 1975. 'Racism made it possible for white Virginians to develop a devotion to the equality that English republicans had declared to be the soul of liberty.' Morgan, *American Slavery, American Freedom*, 386.

Race and Citizenship

In situating the ideology of slavery in the material context to which it
dialectically contributed, Morgan and Davis were not discounting the
efficacy of ideology vis-à-vis practice. They were discounting the separation of the two. As oil to the wheel of slavery, the rights of man may
have been contradictory, but they worked. For the eighteenth-century
slaveholders who articulated them, mankind was not a category given
in nature. The qualifications that counted were not natural endow-
ments but attributes of citizenship. Citizenship, the ground of property,
was rational, volitional and achieved. On all these counts, Blacks failed
to qualify. As property themselves, Blacks were not rational subjects,
capable of contract, but a commodified object, labour, owned rather
than owning, externally directed, and lacking a will of its own. *Non cogito
ergo non sum* – in the vile pun penned by French race ideologue Comte
Joseph Arthur de Gobineau, 'black does not reflect'.[28] The voluntarist
aspect took on particular significance after the war of independence,
when liberty was viewed as a state that had been won, and at a cost to
which Blacks had not contributed.[29] Thus freeing Blacks would not only
conflict with slaveholders' property rights, which ranked alongside life
and liberty, but would also conflict with the principle that freedom was
an achievement of the will and the mind.

This qualification may not have applied to everyone, but in the case
of Blacks it did not apply to anyone. Soon after the 1803 Louisiana
Purchase, for instance, when French and Spanish settlers had requested
the rights of citizenship, Tom Paine responded that US citizens had
fought for their own rights, which did not make it 'incumbent upon
us to fight the battles of the world for the world's profit'.[30] But nor did
it make Frenchmen or Spaniards susceptible to enslavement. As aliens,
their disqualification was contingent rather than necessary and did
not make them ownable. As property, by contrast, slaves had no personhood, no basis for rights.[31] As early as 1669, the Virginia assembly
had declared that a master who killed his slave would not be guilty of
a felony, 'since it cannot be presumed that prepensed malice (which
alone makes murther Felony) should induce any man to destroy his
own estate'.[32]

---

28   Quoted in D. Marvin Jones, 'Darkness Made Visible: Law, Metaphor, and the
Racial Self', *Georgetown Law Journal* 82 (1993), 473.

29   The attribution to Crispus Attucks of the status of first casualty of the
Revolutionary War does not seem to have affected this rationale.

30   Thomas F. Gossett, *Race: The History of an Idea in America* (Dallas: Southern
Methodist UP, 1963), 230.

31   T. R. Cobb, *An Inquiry into the Law of Negro Slavery in the United States of
America* (Philadelphia, 1858), 238.

32   Quoted in Morgan, *American Slavery, American Freedom*, 312.

Since Blacks lacked the volitional ground for freedom, it was beyond the capacity of Whites to bestow it on them. Aliens such as French or Spanish settlers, by contrast, were potential citizens. They had the capacity to emancipate themselves under appropriate conditions. The lack of this capacity underlay the exclusion of Blacks from agency in the war of independence. The same lack enabled the double-speak whereby the Fathers of the Revolution could both deplore and persist in the practice of slavery. By the same token, slaves could no more enter into marriage than into any other form of contract, so they lacked family ties that could impede their being bought and sold at any stage (the condition that Orlando Patterson termed 'natal alienation').[33] Whatever slaves had, including their persons, was not theirs but their masters' to dispose of. As Judge Crenshaw of Alabama put it in 1838, 'Slaves have no legal rights in things, real or personal; but whatever they may acquire, belongs, in point of law, to their masters.'[34]

As property, slaves ranked with things (*Uncle Tom's Cabin* was originally subtitled *The Man Who Was Made a Thing*[35]) or, at any rate, with animals. But slavery only made sense on the basis that slaves were not animals. Otherwise, it would have been much less trouble to use animals. Obvious though this may seem, it reflects the core contradiction of slavery, which results from the attempt to treat humans as non-human. As Edgar Thompson had earlier observed, in his remarkable 1932 PhD dissertation:

> Regardless of his views concerning that abstract category 'the Negro', the planter became closely attached to individual Negroes, not because they were better than ordinary, but simply because he knew them ... The truth is that when planters began to look upon their slaves as human they themselves were no longer free; they could not disregard human claims and attachments.[36]

Time and time again, the convenience of denying slaves' personhood when it came to rights conflicted with the inconvenience of denying it when it came to responsibilities. Logically, the same denial of personhood that prevented slaves from owning property could also absolve them from responsibility for stealing it. It might even mean that Whites

---

33 Orlando Patterson, *Slavery and Social Death: A Comparative Study* (Boston: Harvard UP, 1985), *passim*. Where, as was sometimes the case, slaves were classified as real estate rather than as moveable chattels, this impeded an owner's right to sell them separately from the rest of the land. See, e.g., Davis, *Problem of Slavery in Western Culture*, 250–1.

34 Quoted in W. Goodell, *The American Slave Code* (New York, 1853), 88.

35 Werner Sollors, '"Never Was Born": The Mulatto, an American Tragedy?', *The Massachusetts Review* (Summer 1986), 297.

36 Edgar Tristram Thompson, *The Plantation* (PhD diss., Sociology Department, University of Chicago, 1932), 135.

could not be found guilty of conspiring with slaves or of aiding and abetting them in the commission of crimes. The logic that prevailed was not that of the logician, however, and slaves became subject to a double jeopardy.[37] As the court held in *Baker v. the State of Georgia*, in 1854, 'it is not true that slaves are only chattels ... and therefore, it is not true that it is not possible for them to be prisoners ... the Penal Code ... has them ... as persons capable of committing crimes; and as a ... consequence ... as capable of becoming prisoners.'[38] Slaves' conversion to Christianity raised similar issues. Responding to this problem as early as 1667, the Virginia assembly had resolved that 'Whereas some doubts have arisen ... baptism does not alter the condition of the person as to his bondage or freedom; masters freed from this doubt may more carefully propagate Christianity by permitting slaves to be admitted to that sacrament.'[39]

In disconnecting slavery from the cultural condition of heathenism, such provisions were turning points in the racialisation of slavery. In contrast to Blackness, heathenism was potentially correctable. The moment when slavery came to survive this correction marks the ascendancy of fixity over improvement. As distinct from the Catholic Portuguese, Protestants generally subscribed to an equality among believers that would have encouraged the manumission of converts – which is to say, it discouraged their conversion in the first place. Thus the tolerance of converts among the enslaved presupposed an alternative ground for their enslavement. With ancestry impervious to environment, slavery became racialised. In cases of doubt as to whether a person was a slave, the burden of proof was hereditary. 'The presumption of our law', as South Carolina justice William Harper would phrase this in 1856, 'is against a negro's freedom.'[40]

The case which enshrined Harper's remark, *Dred Scott v. Sandford*, has come to be seen as marking a kind of nadir, not so much for its endorsement of his presumption as for the blatant way in which it elevated de facto considerations over de jure ones. For not only did the presiding judge (John Marshall's successor, Justice Roger Taney) have to answer a question that had not been asked in order to deliver the part of his verdict that was to become infamous, but the rationale that he invoked

37 In Philip Schwarz's term, they were twice condemned. See Schwarz, *Twice Condemned: Slaves and the Criminal Laws of Virginia, 1705–1865* (Baton Rouge: Louisiana State UP, 1988).

38 Quoted in Arnold Sio, 'Interpretations of Slavery: The Slave Status in the Americas', *Comparative Studies in Society and History* 7 (1965), 301–2.

39 Quoted in Higginbotham, *In The Matter of Color*, 36–7. For other states, see Jordan, *White over Black*, 92–3, n. 115.

40 The wider context was Harper's famous *Monk v. Jenkins* opinion, Thomas C. Holt, *Black Over White: Negro Political Leadership in South Carolina during Reconstruction* (Urbana: Illinois UP, 1979), 43. For *Dred Scott*, see Don E. Fehrenbacher, *The Dred Scott Case: Its Significance in American Law and Politics* (New York: Oxford UP, 1978).

did not even pretend to constitutional sanction. It simply sanctified usage. Asked to decide whether a period spent in a free state extinguished a master's ownership of a slave, Taney gratuitously addressed the question of whether a free Black could bring an action in a US court – the very question that his predecessor had chosen to address thirty-five years earlier, only in relation to Indians, in the landmark case of *Cherokee v. Georgia*, which we shall consider below. Like Marshall before him, only in relation to Black people rather than Indians, Taney concluded that they could not bring such cases. For over a century, he declared, Blacks had been

> regarded as beings of an inferior order, and altogether unfit to associate with the white race, either in social or political relations; and so far inferior, that they had no rights which the white man was bound to respect; and that the negro might justly and lawfully be reduced to slavery for his [the white man's] benefit.[41]

For all its notoriety, however, it is not as if this passage was inaccurate as a description of customary usage in the South. Nor did Dred Scott provide for practical outcomes that were not already commonplace. What it did – along with re-enslaving Dred Scott – was dispense with the double-speak. Of course Blacks lacked rights. Indeed, Taney's bluntness serves to allay the notion that the framers of the Constitution might have been taken in by their own rhetoric. As Paul Finkelman has aptly pointed out,

> Throughout the Constitutional convention the framers used the terms 'blacks', 'negroes', and 'slaves' interchangeably. In fact, the framers used the racial designation more frequently than the term 'slave'. Similarly, white is used instead of 'free person'. In the end they chose not to use any of these terms, in hopes that the proslavery aspects of the Constitution would be hidden from voters in the North.[42]

'Race', as Finkelman continues, is present in the Constitution, 'even if the words "black", "Negro", and "white" are not.'[43] He might have added that the appeal of slavery may have been waning for voters in the North, but not the appeal of race.

---

41 *Scott v. Sandford* (*Dred Scott*), 60 *U.S.* 19 How. 393 393 (1856), 407.

42 Paul Finkelman, 'The Color of Law', *Northwestern University Law Review* 87 (1993), 958–9.

43 The term 'white' figured in the Articles of Confederation (Art. 9) but did not make it into the Constitution.

Naturalising Exclusion

As race increasingly coloured the space being vacated by a declining slavery, the juridical opposition of slave versus free gave way to the ostensibly natural one of Black versus White. The boundaries of the two did not necessarily coincide. When the primary concern had been the question of slave status, the blurring of boundaries had been dealt with by means of a range of juridical devices, in particular manumission (the formal release of individuals from their slavery) and the acknowledgement, against which Harper had presumed, of free Black status. Subsequently, just as the equation of Blackness and slavery had been established by degrees, so did the reverse process – whereby slavery was disconnected from Blackness – proceed incrementally. We have already noted a reference to 'free mulattos'. This was not necessarily redundant. In the eighteenth century, White blood had not been so inviolable that it could not be enslaved so long as it was mixed with Black. When the burden of Black subjugation finally passed from jurisprudence to biology, however, doctrinal authority for it passed from lawyers to scientists, who did not necessarily observe the same taxonomic boundaries.

The paradigm shift could be stressful. In an outraged response to the pamphlet that gave 'miscegenation' its name (Croly and Wakeman's anonymously published *Miscegenation* of 1863[44]), J. H. Van Evrie countered with a neologism of his own, 'subgenation': 'from sub, lower, and generatus and genus, a race born or created lower than another; i.e., the natural or normal relation of an inferior to a superior race'. For Van Evrie, the term 'miscegenation' had a proper application to relations between people of the same or equal races, but not to relations between Whites and Blacks, who represented different and unequal races. Such relations included slavery, which, as in the ancient world, obtained within a single race or between equal ones. Accordingly, 'The simple truth is – There is no slavery in this country; there are no slaves in the Southern States.'[45]

Such sentiments found scientific endorsement in the theory of polygenesis, which secured an appreciative audience in the South on account of its claim that the different races were separate stocks, descended, as it was often put, from different Adams. Even within the abstract domain of scientific speculation, however, the matter could hardly be left there. It was one thing for anthropological doyen Paul Broca, ensconced in Paris,

44   For Croly and Wakeman's famous Civil War hoax pamphlet of December 1863, *Miscegenation: The Theory of the Blending of the Races, Applied to the American White Man and Negro*, see Sidney Kaplan, 'The Miscegenation Issue in the Election of 1864', *Journal of Negro History* 34, iii (1949), 274–343.

45   J. H. Van Evrie, *Subgenation: The Theory of the Normal Relation of the Races – An Answer to 'Miscegenation'* (New York, 1864), 51–65.

to suppose that races were separate species and, accordingly, incapable of eugenesic crossings.[46] In the Atlantic theatre of applied encounter, such notions were abundantly confounded in the living flesh. Like engendered like. The fellow humanity of Black people could not be evaded so easily.

Whether slave or free, people of mixed ancestry compounded the contradiction between the slave as property and the slave as human being. There could be no more tangible symptom of this contradiction than the object of property who reconciled the humanity of the master with that of the slave within the compass of his or her own physical being. In some colonies and states, and at different times, a 'mulatto' category was officially acknowledged.[47] Significantly, this tended to occur when Whites were demographically outnumbered and, as in the highly labour-intensive rice economy of South Carolina, relied on a buffer population to stave off the threat of slave revolt.[48] For a brief period in eighteenth-century Georgia, free Blacks could even become White, though this extraordinary exception only obtained while Georgian Whites were in a frontier situation and needed assistance to suppress Native Americans and, to the south, the Spanish.[49]

Though the picture is, therefore, admittedly uneven, something remarkable begins to happen once slaves are emancipated. Along with the category 'free Black' (which ceases to have any meaning when all Blacks are free), the 'mulatto' category recedes as well.[50] This had begun to happen before the Civil War in the northern states, where all Blacks, whether classified mulatto or otherwise, were subjected to oppressive restrictions (Davis's 'substitute controls') that in many ways anticipated the Jim Crow system that was not to be established in the South until the late 1880s.[51]

---

46 Paul Broca, *On the Phenomena of Hybridity in the* Genus Homo (London, 1864).

47 After coming and going, the 'mulatto' category finally vanished for good from the US Census in 1920. Forbes, *Africans and Native Americans*, 203; Paul R. Spickard, 'The Illogic of American Racial Categories', in Maria P. P. Root (ed.), *Racially Mixed People in America* (London: Sage, 1992), 433, n. 27. See also Stephenson, *Race Distinctions in American Law*, 13.

48 Holt, *Black Over White*, 66; Peter H. Wood, *Black Majority: Negroes in Colonial South Carolina from 1670 through the Stono Rebellion* (New York: Norton, 1974), 131–66.

49 Though this became possible, it does not seem to have been realised in practice. See Winthrop Jordan, 'American Chiaroscuro: The Status and Definition of Mulattoes in the British Colonies', *William and Mary Quarterly* 19 (1962), 183–200; A. L. Higginbotham, Jr., and B. K. Kopytoff, 'Racial Purity and Interracial Sex in the Law of Colonial and Antebellum Virginia', *Georgetown Law Journal* 77 (1989), 1967–2029; Wiecek, 'Statutory Law', 261.

50 Goldberg, *Racial Subjects*, 35–42; Paul Spickard, *Mixed Blood: Intermarriage and Ethnic Identity in Twentieth-Century America* (Madison: Wisconsin UP, 1989), 433, n. 27; Stephenson, *Race Distinctions in American Law*, 13.

51 Davis, *Age of Revolution*, 305. See also George M. Fredrickson, *The Black Image*

This is very significant. What does it mean to free slaves and at the same time to homogenise the status of Blackness? Apart from anything else, it means that the boundary that had previously separated a Free Black from a slave disappears, which is to say that, in place of the slaves, a new and more inclusive oppressed category emerges, one which, being defined by race, does not admit the exceptions and contradictions that manumission had entailed for the peculiar institution of slavery.[52] In other words, emancipation cancelled out the exemption: you can be an ex-slave, but you can't be ex-Black.[53] This permanence had been prefigured in slavery's immunity to religious conversion, signifying the ascendancy of fixity over improvement. In the post-slavery era, the same ascendancy rendered race immune to emancipation. In dispensing with the 'free black' and 'mulatto' categories, emancipation marked out the unqualified Blackness that would become the object of persecution in the Jim Crow era.

Though born of slavery, therefore, race came into its own with slavery's abolition. So long as slavery persisted, race – for all its usefulness as a justification – was relatively redundant as a mode of domination. The point is, however, that the reverse also applies: given race, slavery becomes redundant as a mode of domination – along with its awkward burden of justification. Joanne Melish has documented how, as early as the late eighteenth century, perceptions of difference began to harden into 'notions of permanent and innate hierarchy – that is, "race"'. This trend was not simply a response to the problems that revolutionary rhetoric posed for the continuation of slavery. Rather, the intensified discourse of race 'began to emerge in the course of the first northern implementation of systematic emancipation'.[54]

In the absence of slavery, Blacks became superfluous. They had been imported for the purpose of unrestricted exploitation, and that purpose could no longer be fulfilled. There was no shortage of candidates for restricted exploitation in a nation of immigrants, which left emancipated Blacks in a situation comparable to that of Indians overtaken by the

---

in the White Mind: The Debate on Afro-American Character and Destiny, 1817–1914 (Hanover: Wesleyan UP, 1971), 4–5; Leon F. Litwack, *North of Slavery: The Negro in the Free States, 1790–1860* (Chicago: Chicago UP, 1961), but also see Stephen Riegel's questioning of Vann Woodward's watershed analysis in Woodward, *The Strange Career of Jim Crow* (New York: Oxford UP, 1955), cf. Riegel, 'The Persistent Career of Jim Crow: Lower Federal Courts and the "Separate but Equal" Doctrine, 1865–1896', *American Journal of Legal History* 28 (1984), 17–40.

52   As Dorothy Roberts expresses it, 'most Blacks were slaves, all were subordinate to whites.' Roberts, 'The Genetic Tie', *University of Chicago Law Review* 62 (1995), 228.

53   Thus 'passing' frustrates rather than furthers the regime. In Cheryl Harris's words, the practice involves 'not merely passing, but *trespassing*.' Harris, 'Whiteness as Property', *Harvard Law Review* 106 (1993), 1711.

54   Joanne Pope Melish, *Disowning Slavery: Gradual Emancipation and 'Race' in New England, 1780–1860* (Ithaca: Cornell UP, 1998).

frontier. Having yielded what had been theirs to yield – unfree labour and free land respectively – both became anomalies within. Why, then, did White society not seek to eliminate Black people in the same way as Indians, by assimilating them? Indeed, in a passage removed from subsequent editions of the Jeffersoniad, Thomas Jefferson himself has been cited as suggesting just this solution to the problem posed by emancipation: 'The course of events will likewise inevitably lead to a mixture of the whites and the blacks and as the former are about five times as numerous as the latter the blacks will ultimately be merged in the whites.'[55] But five to one is not nearly as comfortable a disproportion as fifty or a hundred to one.

Demographic imbalance is a product of history. In this case, it represents the difference between one group of people who had survived a centuries-long genocidal catastrophe with correspondingly depleted numbers, and another group whose reproduction had been fostered in common with that of other commodities. Moreover, these histories were ongoing. In large areas of the agricultural South, for instance, the ending of slavery did not mean that Blacks became anomalous overnight. On the contrary, they continued to furnish a rival and cheaper source of labour. Even when unemployed, their mere presence as a hyperexploitable alternative depressed White workers' wages. Thus a qualification is in order: in the aftermath of slavery, Blacks did not become physically anomalous as labour. They became juridically anomalous as equals.

On from Slavery

Since the exploitation of Blacks outlived emancipation, albeit in a more restricted form, we should not allow the abandonment of slavery to distract us from the continuities that obtain. As Frederick Cooper, Thomas Holt and Rebecca Scott (or one of them, at least) observed of histories that fail to link the slavery era to the present, 'Slave labour could be analysed in economic, social, and political terms, but free labour was often defined as simply the ending of coercion, not as a structure of labour control that needed to be analysed in its own way.'[56] With the ending of the false dawn of Reconstruction, race intensified as a structure of social control, its pervasive influence being expressed in a variety of ways, from mob barbarity to juridico-bureaucratic nicety. Miscegenation discourse encompassed the full range of race's dominion, from the 'black beast

---

55 Quoted in Joel A. Rogers, *Sex and Race: A History of White, Negro, and Indian Miscegenation in the Two Americas* (3 vols, New York: J. A. Rogers [private pub.], 1940–44), vol. 2, 186.

56 Thomas C. Holt, Rebecca Scott and Frederick Cooper (eds), *Beyond Slavery: Explorations of Race, Labor, and Citizenship in Postemancipation Societies* (Chapel Hill: North Carolina UP, 2000), 2–3.

rapist' that animated the rhetoric of lynching to the tortuous formula-
tions with which legislators and judges sought to locate the point where
Whiteness stopped and Blackness began. Jim Crow required a monolithic object. Even though some states retained legislation that technically
Whitened people with a blood quantum of no more than (usually) one-
sixteenth African descent, the trend – at least, after the landmark 1896
case of *Plessy v. Ferguson* – was steadily in the direction of what came to
be known as the 'one-drop rule', in which any evidence of any African
ancestry whatsoever, no matter how far back or remote and regardless of
phenotype, meant that one was classified Black.

There is, of course, considerable irony in the fact that the one-drop
rule makes Black blood so much stronger than White (or, for that matter,
any other) blood, even though, in White discourse, this strength consists
in an unlimited power to contaminate. The corollary to – or ideological
product of – the hyperpotency attributed to Black blood is White racial
purity. Even in Louisiana, where creole classification attains a complexity
that might seem to confound the rigid binarism of the one-drop rule,
one category – the White one – stands out as monolithically undivided,
leaving the rest as so many permutations of Black. Louisiana, after all,
was the location strategically (mis-)chosen for the put-up case of *Plessy v.
Ferguson*.[57]

The intensification of the one-drop rule took place in the continuing
vacuum created by the abolition of slavery and the demise of the Black
Codes, as post-Reconstruction state legislatures sought new mechanisms
to deliver an across-the-board system of racial control in place of the one
that had previously been delivered by slavery. Around the turn of the
twentieth century, Booker T. Washington noted that 'if a person is known
to have one per cent of African blood in his veins, he ceases to be a white
man. The ninety-nine per cent of Caucasian blood does not weigh by
the side of one per cent of African blood. The white blood counts for
nothing. The person is a Negro every time.'[58] Washington was not referring to an existing law, which popular usage would anyway have made
unnecessary. A further quarter-century would pass before Whiteness first

---

57 Raymond T. Diamond and Robert J. Cottrol, 'Codifying Caste: Louisiana's
Racial Classification Scheme and the Fourteenth Amendment', *Loyola Law Review*
29 (1983); Virginia Domínguez, *White By Definition: Social Classification in Creole
Louisiana* (New Brunswick: Rutgers UP, 1994).
58 Booker T. Washington, *The Future of the American Negro* (Boston, 1899), 158.
This claim has been exhaustively corroborated in F. James Davis, *Who Is Black?* Davis
overlooks some important counterexamples, so his account should be approached with
caution, hence my asserting no more than a steady trend. For qualifications, counterexamples and regional variations, see, e.g., Finkelman, 'Color of Law', 954–7; Ian F.
Haney Lopez, *White by Law: The Legal Construction of Race* (New York: New York UP,
1996), 118–19; Harris, 'Whiteness as Property', 1738–9; Mangum, *Legal Status of the
Negro*, 245–7; and, especially, Murray, *States' Laws on Race and Color, passim*.

came to be defined in law, under the Virginia anti-miscegenation legisla-tion of 1924.[59] Leon Higginbotham and Barbara Kopytoff summarised the trend to codification that this innovation capped off:

> In the early twentieth century, Virginians made the first change in their defi-nition of mulatto in 125 years. From the Act of 1785 to 1910, a mulatto, or 'colored' person was someone who had one-fourth or more Negro blood. In 1910, that category was expanded to include anyone with one-sixteenth or more Negro blood, and many people previously classified as white became legally colored. Then, in 1924, in a statute frankly entitled 'Preservation of Racial Integrity,' the legislators for the first time defined 'white' rather than 'mulatto' or 'colored.' The statute, which forbade a white person to marry any non-white, defined 'white' as someone who had 'no trace whatsoever of any blood other than Caucasian' or no more than one-sixteenth American Indian blood. In 1930, the Virginia legislature defined 'colored' in a similar, though slightly less restrictive way as any 'person in whom there is ascertain-able any negro blood'.[60]

From the point of view of our wider argument, a remarkable feature of the 1924 Act, which took the exclusion of Blacks to its formal extreme, is that even at this high-water mark in prescriptive racial hygiene, a provision is made for the incorporation of Indian blood: the so-called 'Pocahontas exception'.[61] True, there was a parochial motive for this clause, since it pleased some members of the planter elite in Virginia to claim descent from John Rolfe and Pocahontas, a provenance comfortably deeper than the four generations presumptively involved in a one-sixteenth ancestry. Yet such people were hardly likely to be removed across the tracks if the provision were not included (though it might have occasioned their quiet shelving of a shaky ancestral claim), so it remains remarkable that an exception should have been thinkable in a context of such extreme segregation. In fact, so extreme was this context that it actually makes no sense for it to have allowed an exception, let alone explicitly. It makes more sense not to view the proviso as an exception at all, but instead to consider the extent to which it conformed to the racial regime that Virginia was seeking to impose on Black people.

---

59 Higginbotham and Kopytoff, 'Racial Purity', 1977, n. 48; Peggy Pascoe, 'Miscegenation Law, Court Cases, and Ideologies of "Race" in Twentieth-Century America', *Journal of American History* 83 (1996), 59.

60 Higginbotham and Kopytoff, 'Racial Purity', 2020–1.

61 'It shall hereafter be unlawful for any white person in this State to marry any save a white person, or a person with no other admixture of blood than white and American Indian. For the purpose of this act, the term "white person" shall apply only to the person who has no trace whatsoever of any blood other than Caucasian; but persons who have one-sixteenth or less of the blood of the American Indian and have no other non-Caucasic blood shall be deemed to be white persons' (1924 Va. Acts, ch. 371, § 5). Go to: eugenicsarchive.org.

The wider Jim Crow context that the Virginia legislation articulated took recognisable shape on the ending of Reconstruction. Public lynchings of predominantly Black people began to multiply in the late 1880s. From this juncture, the racialisation of Black people, especially in the South, began to display characteristics that distinguished it from the congenital abasement that had characterised representations of the enslaved. Where slave corporeality had been governed by lack, in particular a lack of rational capacity, Blackness in the Jim Crow era came to be governed by threat. The mystical threat posed by the black beast rapist was as disproportionate as the potency ascribed to his blood. As in the cases of other shifts that we have noted, this discourse was not foreordained, so, with a view to historicity, we should consider the chaotic circumstances of the 1890s.

There are no grounds for discounting psychosocial factors in the sudden spread of Jim Crow persecution, in particular the coming of age of a generation of Whites who had grown up in the humiliating shadow of defeat (in common with the worst excesses of the Nazi Holocaust, the worst excesses of lynching set in around twenty-five years after the war had ended). For this group, not only could Blacks as a whole furnish a scapegoat for that defeat. In generational terms, Blacks of their own age were the first to have grown up without the restraining discipline of slavery, an irregularity that called for alternative methods of control.[62] Nor should we overlook the effect on employment of the global recession that deepened in the early 1890s, producing the 'Panic of '93'. Migration was also an issue – not so much the flood of foreign migrants who generally headed for industrial employment in the northern states, as Black workers seeking to escape the post-slavery peonage that prevailed for them (though they were also accused of strike-breaking) in the still primarily rural South.

The migrations were not only to the North. 'When blacks from the Deep South headed for Kansas in massive numbers, Southern whites first assassinated the leaders, then beat and lynched their followers.'[63] Once those who had evaded White attempts to prevent their escape arrived in Kansas, other Whites, with official encouragement in the form of 'sundowner' ordinances and related discriminations, took action to prevent them from staying.[64] Across the whole spectrum of social life,

---

62   William J. Cooper, Jr., and Thomas E. Terrill, *The American South: A History* (2nd ed., New York: McGraw-Hill, 1996), 526.

63   Jonathan M. Weiner, 'Class Structure and Economic Development in the American South, 1865–1955', *American Historical Review* 84 (1979), 983. See also Nell Painter, *Exodusters: Black Migration to Kansas after Reconstruction* (New York: Norton, 1976), 192–6.

64   Daniel M. Johnson and Rex R. Campbell, *Black Migration in America: A Social Demographic History* (Durham: Duke UP, 1981), 55.

industrialisation in the emergent New South was generating upheaval, with all the fear, suspicion and insecurity that it engendered.

Troublesome Blacks were not the only ones who did not know their place. Without understating the complexity of the situation, therefore – and certainly not suggesting a monocausal explanation – we might nonetheless factor in a profound historical shift, whose marginalisation in the historiography of Jim Crow would seem to reflect the segregation of African American and Native American studies. 1890, the year of General Nelson Miles's massacre at Wounded Knee, marks the end of the US frontier, a development that was also reported – though without mentioning the end of Indian military resistance – in the US Census for that year. Three years later, at the July 1893 meeting of the American Historical Association, held in Chicago, Frederick Jackson Turner read his paper 'The Significance of the Frontier in American History'.[65]

The ending of the contiguous frontier line did not put an end to US territorial expansion. Among overseas adventures, the 1890s also saw the invasions of the Philippines, Hawai'i, Puerto Rico and Cuba. With the partial exception of Hawai'i, however, these countries were not scheduled for incorporation into the US state and their inhabitants were not scheduled for citizenship.[66] So far as conquered peoples were concerned, the assimilability of colour stopped at the Indians. So too did the availability of cheap land through the treaty process, which, though legislatively discontinued in 1871, had persisted in the form of executive agreements.[67] In the absence – or, at least, radical curtailment – of further mainland territorial gains, the US economy had to abandon geography as a basis for its internal expansion and focus on the development of industrially and/ or financially generated growth, including the railroads and rapacious logging that devoured massive areas of the South, a dense involution that intensified the pressure on a job market already depleted by depression. The constraining effects of the ending of the frontier were as much social as geographical.

Thus the significance of the frontier for African American history is more than a matter of Black cowboys, important though their histories are. Even Edmund Morgan, for all the virtues of his analysis, largely

---

65 Turner's 'The Significance of the Frontier in American History' was read before the Chicago meeting of the American Historical Association in July 1893, subsequently being published in the *Proceedings of the State Historical Society of Wisconsin* in December 1893. See below, chapter 6, note 68.

66 See, e.g., Lanny Thompson, 'The Imperial Republic: A Comparison of the Insular Territories under US Dominion after 1898', *Pacific Historical Review* 71 (2002), 535–74; Christina Duffy Burnett and Burke Marshall (eds), *Foreign in a Domestic Sense: Puerto Rico, American Expansion, and the Constitution* (Durham: Duke UP, 2001).

67 Vine Deloria, Jr., and Raymond J. DeMallie, *Documents of American Indian Diplomacy: Treaties, Agreements, and Conventions, 1775–1979* (2 vols, Norman: Oklahoma UP, 1999), vol. 2, 249–560.

failed to factor in the contribution that Natives were obliged to make to the development of settler democracy. It has taken Aziz Rana, nearly four decades on, to explore how the 'essential connection between liberty and subordination' required the dispossession of Indigenous people just as foundationally as it did the enslavement of Africans.[68] Quite apart from the inherently expansive character of capitalist accumulation and the sleepless cupidity of speculators, both of which conduced to the ever-mobile frontier of Native dispossession – and, in turn, to the constant need for more immigrants to work the ever-expanding national estate – settler democracy required a constant supply of new territory with which to satisfy the proprietary aspirations of its burgeoning population, aspirations which, after all, had brought most of them to the country in the first place.

As it remorselessly ground on, the permanent but ever-moving frontier war brought together every dimension of settler selfhood: the material discourse of economic advancement, the national discourse of militarism, the ideological discourse of democratic concepts, and the psychological discourse of settler subject-formation participating inseparably in the process of Native dispossession. In Rana's dense encapsulation, 'If the republican goals of economic independence and freedom as self-rule necessitated territorial expansion, they also required enough people to work the land and to participate in projects of [Native] conquest.'[69]

In the aftermath of the frontier – both in Australia and, as will be shown in more detail below, in the USA – the racialisation of Indigenous people took the form of systematic programmes of Native assimilation centred about the technique of blood quantum. As we shall see, the introduction of this technique into US Indian-affairs discourse can be dated with some precision to 1892, the year of Sam Hose's death, the very time when the Jim Crow regime, centred on the intensifying one-drop rule, was consolidating its hold on the South. Even apart from their respective connections to the ending of the US frontier and their common phrasing in the idiom of blood, these phenomena were related in more than time. As indicated, in addition to rendering the exclusion of Black people complete and unqualified, the one-drop rule was integral to the statistical elimination of Indians, in that where Indians shared parentage with Black people it cut short the generations-long process of Indian dilution by Whiteness, providing for the immediate transmission of non-Indian status. Conversely, just as the assimilation of Whiteness into the Black 'bloodstock' did not conflict with the logic of elimination, so was the assimilation of Whites into the Indian

---

68 Rana, *Two Faces of American Freedom*, quote at p. 23.
69 Ibid., 116.

population ('squaw men', etc.) anathema to it.[70] The racialisation of Blacks and Indians was a coordinated programme of White supremacy. In admitting some Indian ancestry at the same time as it excluded all Black ancestry, the Pocahontas 'exception' was not exceptional at all. It only appears so when the two companion racialisations are viewed in isolation from one another.

White Nationalism

The dual utility of the one-drop rule in the United States enables us to appreciate settler racial discourse in a way that does not come out so clearly from the Australian case. From a methodological point of view, this example also illustrates a comparative approach's usefulness for mapping the linkages whereby the distinctive racialisations of different groups together subtend the maintenance of the colonial system as a whole.

To establish themselves, the Australian colonies did not import enslaved people (another legacy, as we have seen, of Britain's North American experience).[71] Australian convicts and indentured servants were an almost exclusively White group, who did not transmit their juridical condition to succeeding generations. Accordingly, as we have seen, Aboriginal assimilation provided for a departure from Aboriginality that was simultaneously an entry into Whiteness. The two were synonymous. Whiteness was the only destination. In the United States, however, there were other destinations, in particular the one afforded by the provision for Indigeneity to be overwhelmed by Blackness as well as by Whiteness.

Thus comparison with the one-drop rule enables us to clarify an ambiguity in settler discourse that is left unresolved in the Australian case. Native assimilation is not primarily a recruitment into Whiteness. If that were so, it would be hard to see the purpose, since supplementary White people can be acquired much more quickly through immigration. Rather, Native assimilation is primarily an elimination of Indigeneity. In the case of Indians being made Black under the provisions of the one-drop rule, two ethnocratic goals are achieved simultaneously: Indian elimination

---

70   In relation to Congress's destruction of the governments of the Five Civilized Tribes, Felix Cohen asserted that 'These governments ceased to exist as governments primarily because they had admitted to citizenship and the rights of occupancy in tribal lands, so many white men that the original Indian communities could no longer maintain a national existence apart from the white settlers.' Felix S. Cohen, 'How Long Will Indian Constitutions Last?', quoted in Cohen, *Handbook of Federal Indian Law* (Washington: US Govt Printing Office, 1945), 131.

71   'To establish themselves', because the situation of indentured Pacific Island labour in the late nineteenth century in some respects resembled slavery. Banivanua Mar, *Violence and Colonial Dialogue*.

and White racial hegemony. Those who promote racist exclusions within Indian tribes would do well to reflect on this consideration.[72]

The zeal with which Blackness was excluded in the Jim Crow era was one aspect of a wider polarisation in which Whiteness was being consolidated at a time when it was multiply threatened, not only by the persistent absence of the slavery that had once served to define it, but also by the continually renewed immigration of people who were neither Anglo-Saxon nor Protestant – including more than a million European Jews, mostly from Russia, whose racialisation will be considered in the next chapter. During the nineteenth century, in the United States as in much of Europe, race came to be bound up in nation-building, Whiteness becoming entangled with Manifest Destiny under the aegis of what George Fredrickson termed 'white nationalism'.[73] In the United States, a shared obsession with excluding Black people was part of the consolidation of a White proletariat from out of the fractious human mix engendered by the convergence of old and new migrations. Racial overlordship compensated for common deprivation. In Vann Woodward's list of White beneficiaries, the occupations – or lack of them – are revealing. As he observed, the Jim Crow laws 'put the authority of the state or city in the voice of the street-car conductor, the railway brakeman, the bus driver, the theater usher, and also into the voice of the hoodlum of the public parks and playgrounds'.[74] In keeping Blacks in their place, Whites endorsed their own.

Charged with the impossible burden of removing the fault-lines in White society, Black blood took on a mystic hyperpotency which, like sacredness for Durkheim, was omnipresent in a single drop, like the wine in a communion chalice or the tattered shred of a national flag. The mystical charging of Black blood represented mythologising of an order quite different from the profane calculus whereby planters had added Black women's offspring to their stock of slaves without reference to paternity. In its ritual dimension, this mythologising consecrated White solidarity in consensually scripted orgies of public barbarity. In its preoccupation with place, the language and imagery of Jim Crow are strikingly reminiscent of antisemitism, which was also becoming consolidated in the 1890s

---

72   For varying treatments of this disturbing phenomenon, see, e.g., Jodi A. Byrd, 'Been to the Nation, Lord, but I Couldn't Stay There', *Interventions: International Journal of Postcolonial Studies* 13, no. 1 (2011), 31–52; Kevin Noble Maillard, 'Redwashing History: Tribal Anachronisms in the *Seminole Nation* Cases', in Kristen A. Carpenter, Matthew L. M. Fletcher and Angela R. Riley (eds), *The Indian Civil Rights Act at Forty* (Los Angeles: American Indian Studies Center Press, 2012), 87–103; Circe Sturm, *Becoming Indian: The Struggle over Cherokee Identity in the Twenty-first Century* (Santa Fe: School for Advanced Research Press, 2010).

73   George M. Fredrickson, *White Supremacy: A Comparative Study in American and South African History* (New York: Oxford UP, 1981).

74   Vann Woodward, *Strange Career of Jim Crow*, 93.

and which, around the turn of the twentieth century, would inspire over a million European Jews to cross the Atlantic. Like Blackness in the United States, Jewishness in Europe would become vested with an ineradicable germ that could persist, to individuals' peril, down the generations. Moreover, in common with the Jim Crow regime, antisemitism emerged in the wake of emancipation.

In one sense, European antisemitism and the racialisation of African Americans were the mirror image of each other: while Jews stepped out from the segregation of the ghetto and thereby became anomalous, Blacks became anomalous and thereby found themselves segregated. In either case, however, as we shall see in the chapter to come, when the walls came down, physically or juridically, race took over.

CHAPTER THREE

Not About the Jews

Antisemitism in Central Europe

The modern emancipation of Jews in Europe coincided quite closely with that of enslaved people in the United States. After France had legislated emancipation in 1791, Napoleon extended it to Germany in 1808, at a time when Northern states were emancipating 'their' Negroes, the process continuing in Germany until the era of Reconstruction.[1] In broad terms, emancipation was straightforwardly symptomatic of the liberal ideology that accompanied the growth of industrial capitalism – to which, without controversy, we can add the rise of nationalism and the expansion of European colonialism – so that one might simply, and not unreasonably, put the coincidence of the two emancipations down to a liberal-capitalist zeitgeist taking hold of Western society.

Yet this does not address the marked differences between the historical experiences of Jewish people in Europe and of Black people in the United States. In contrast to enslaved people, Jews had not been exploited for their labour – quite the reverse: in their distancing from the labour market, Jews were more like Indians than African Americans. Moreover, in their ethnoreligious confinement, rigorously separated from the surrounding Christian society, Jewish ghettos in Europe were more like Indian reservations than the White-penetrated world of slavery. It was not until the Jim Crow era that physical segregation became central to the Black experience, by which time the walls of the Jewish ghetto had been at least nominally dismantled.

These differences notwithstanding, the post-emancipation experience of European Jews came to share important features with that of Black people in the United States. In both cases, after a period of seemingly genuine reprieve, inequity was not only restored but took on a generality

---

1 Christopher Clark, 'German Jews', in Rainer Liedtke and Stephan Wendehorst (eds), *The Emancipation of Catholics, Jews and Protestants: Minorities and the Nation State in Nineteenth-Century Europe* (Manchester: Manchester UP, 1999), 122–47.

of application that precluded the individual exceptions conceded in the pre-emancipation era. We have already noted how, in eliminating the 'free Black' and 'mulatto' categories, emancipation marked out the indiscriminate Blackness that would be the object of Jim Crow-era persecution. Comparably, in eliminating the court Jew and his privileged successors, along with the cleavage between Eastern and Western European Jews, emancipation marked out the monolithic Jewishness that would become antisemitism's object of persecution. In both cases, uniformity would come to be constructed genetically, as an ineradicable hereditary mystique common to every member of the persecuted community; a collective, though not always visible, mark of Cain. In both cases, in other words, emancipation inaugurated the racialisation of the community concerned.

To focus on the mystical dimension of the racialisation of Jewish and African American people – a dimension resistant to global explanations based on shifts in the realm of economic production – is to engage with the essential modernity of race. It is to move from Damien to Bentham.[2] As opposed to a heuristic grid whereby social groups were classified and assigned behavioural protocols to match, race presumed to determine the inner qualities of the individuals inhabiting its titular categories. As we shall see in the discussion of US Indian policy, at the same time as Black people in the United States were becoming vested with a special germ that ensured their perpetual exclusion, Indians were becoming vested with a congenital solvency that provided for their imminent merger, a strategy antithetical to the exclusion of both Jews in Europe and Black people in the USA. Moreover, in contrast to the situation of surviving Indigenous people in Australia and the United States, who came to share social space with Europeans by virtue of being invaded, the threat of encroachment that Jews and Blacks presented arose in the wake of their emancipation.

Thus it is very important to distinguish between emancipation and assimilation. Native Americans, in common with Indigenous people in Australia, have been targeted for assimilation rather than emancipation.[3] By contrast, though Jews and Black people were emancipated, stringent measures were adopted to prevent their assimilation. Either way – by assimilation or by emancipation – European society was seeking to rid itself of a population that, in its anomalous internality, had become problematic, whether as the Aboriginal problem, the Indian problem, the Negro problem or the Jewish problem. In turning to the Jewish problem (in more genteel usage, 'question'), and with the comparative example of the Negro problem in the United States in mind, we confront the tension

---

2 Foucault, *Discipline and Punish*, chapter 1.
3 The particularities of Indian citizenship, legislatively generalised in the United States in 1924, will be discussed below.

between emancipation and assimilation. In particular, we are led to ask what it is about emancipation that encourages the attribution to supposedly redeemed populations of distinctive qualities that mystically insulate them from the absorptive pull of liberal-capitalist social integration.

Moral Walls

Theodor Herzl, founder of political Zionism, succinctly depicted the intangible distancing that Jews experienced in emancipated Western Europe as a 'new ghetto'.[4] This formula captured the continuity between Jews' contemporary predicament and the mediaeval ghetto, at the same time as it pinpointed the crucial difference between the two. Though real enough, the new walls were moral ones, which did not mean that Jews were safe from physical harm. Rather, in contrast to the walls of the mediaeval ghetto (the concrete expression of the Church's official denunciation of Jews for their persistent rejection of the messianic redemption brought by Christ), late-nineteenth-century antisemitism was flourishing regardless of, rather than in conformity with, official policy.[5] A formal principle, the official policy of emancipation was failing to impede – or in its formality was actually abetting – the practical functioning of systemic Judaeophobia, as the claim that German culture was under threat from Judaisation (*Verjudung*) gained ground.[6]

In their abstraction, the moral walls were generic and individual, rounding the temples of every Jew. Contrary to the enlightened optimism of a Moses Mendelssohn or a Judah Leib Gordon, one entered the world outside the home not as an unmarked abstract individual but as a Jew. The abstract was not abstract but Gentile – there was no leaving

---

4 Theodor Herzl, *The New Ghetto: A Play in Four Acts* (H. Norden, trans., New York: Theodor Herzl Foundation, 1955). For discussion, see Gabriel Piterberg, *The Returns of Zionism: Myths, Politics and Scholarship in Israel* (London: Verso, 2008), 32–6.

5 In his electrifying speech to the first Zionist Congress, held in Basel in 1897, Max Nordau proclaimed a positive aspect: the securing of a Jewish inner community life free from Gentile interference, that transcended the walls of the mediaeval ghetto: 'invisible walls which were much thicker and higher than the stone walls that surrounded it physically'. Max Nordau, 'Speech to the first Zionist Congress' (Basel, 1897), in Arthur Hertzberg (ed.), *The Zionist Idea: A Historical Analysis and Reader* (Philadelphia: Jewish Publication Society, 1997), 236.

6 With the 'benefit' of hindsight, the catastrophe of Nazism has tended to accord a teleological inevitability to the career of antisemitism in Germany. At least in formal legislative terms, late-nineteenth-century German governments were by no means the most antisemitic in Europe. Indeed, despite its oppression of Catholics and banning of socialism, Germany did not legislate against Jews. Ritchie Robertson, *The Jewish Question' in German Literature, 1749–1939: Emancipation and Its Discontents* (Oxford: Oxford UP, 1999). For a discussion of 'Judaisation', which he traces back to Wagner, see Enzo Traverso, *The Jews & Germany: From the 'Judeo-German Symbiosis' to the Memory of Auschwitz* (Lincoln: Nebraska UP, 1995), 20–1.

one's Jewishness at home.[7] Rather than incorporating Jews as Jews, the freedoms that had been proclaimed by the Enlightenment universalised the Gentile norm, which – theism and secularism notwithstanding – remained implacably Christian. Ultimately, therefore, as the Russian Leon Pinsker had recognised in his celebrated pamphlet 'Auto-Emancipation', Jews were not the point. Rather, emancipation was a logical deduction from general principles that happened to catch Jews in its propositional net. Nothing personal was involved:

> The emancipation of the Jews naturally finds its justification in the fact that it will always be considered to have been a postulate of logic, of law, and of enlightened self-interest. It can never be regarded as a spontaneous expression of human feeling. Far from owing its origin to the spontaneous feeling of the peoples, it is never a matter of course; and it has never yet taken such deep root that discussion of it becomes unnecessary.[8]

In always requiring discussion, Jewish emancipation remained inorganic, alien to Gentile common sense, a gap that found informal expression in the new ghetto. Unlike the formality of emancipation, however, the new ghetto's moral walls were not inorganic to Gentile sentiment. Rather, in common with the Jim Crow regime in the United States, antisemitism did not need to be legislated.[9] In both cases, public sentiment exceeded the formal realm of official policy. To address antisemitism, therefore, it is not enough to view it as a popular reaction against official policy, which merely lifts it out of history, eternalising it as always already there and requiring no explanation. Politically, to posit antisemitism (or, for that matter, Negrophobia[10]) as a timeless proclivity of Western Christian culture is to render it unalterable, a toxic fallacy that Zionism and antisemitism together endorsed. The racialisation of Jewish people – on which Zionism and antisemitism also concurred – depended on this immutability, expressed as unconvertability, which (Darwin's

---

7 The reference is to Judah Leib Gordon's famous line, from his 'Awake, My People!' (1863), 'Be a man in the streets and a Jew at home' (literally, 'Be a man in your going out and a Jew in your tents'), which encapsulated Haskalah themes that had been commonplace since Mendelssohn a century earlier. For discussion and exegesis, see Michael Stanislawski, *For Whom Do I Toil? Judah Leib Gordon and the Crisis of Russian Jewry* (New York: Oxford UP, 1988), 49–51.

8 Leon Pinsker, *Auto-Emancipation: An appeal to his people by a Russian Jew* [1882], in Hertzberg, *Zionist Idea*, 187. As Nordau would later observe, 'the emancipation of the Jews was proclaimed in France, not out of fraternal feeling for the Jews but because logic demanded it.' Nordau, 'Speech to the first Zionist Congress', 236.

9 'German Jews and German Catholics alike suffered the effects of state discrimination after 1871, despite the absence of a legal sanction for such a policy.' Clark, 'German Jews', 144. In the US South, Jim Crow legislation was not framed in opposition to public opinion but in opposition to federal legislation.

10 This was the basic error guiding Winthrop Jordan's *White over Black*.

intervention notwithstanding) reflected the theme of fixity in Enlighten-ment thought. Neither emancipation nor antisemitism was timeless. Nor was either unprecedented. Both combined histories, related but distinct, that produced novel social forms in the nineteenth century. To oppose rather than appease antisemitism, therefore, we should first of all address its history.

Emancipation and Its Discontents

Antisemitism's propensity to seem external to history is not shared by emancipation. There is a lopsidedness to their pairing: while the histo-ricity of emancipation is taken for granted, antisemitism is consigned to primordiality, as evident in the frequency with which the term itself, a neologism coined in the 1870s to launch a political movement, has been displaced backwards onto earlier forms of Judaeophobia.[11] To rectify this imbalance, it is necessary for contingency, the essential difference between history and primordiality, to be restored to the account. This applies not only to the histories of emancipation and of antisemitism but also, since neither was merely a reflex of the other, to the material contingency of their conjuncture.

So far as the history of emancipation is concerned, it is generally accepted (and not only by Marxists) that the reform derived from the wider liberal ideology spawned by the market-place demand for freedom of trade. Emancipation, in keeping with its French-revolutionary cre-dentials, is obviously linked to the historical consolidation of bourgeois hegemony. Ideologically – whether or not the bourgeoisie supported emancipation in practice – the notion sought to popularise the interests of a class whose power and influence was derived from the ownership of movable capital in two directions. Upwards, as it were (or, perhaps, back-wards), emancipation was the logical conclusion to a social agenda which, in seeking to displace a fixed hereditary order founded on the immov-able ownership of land, had developed a distinctively universalist and meritocratic style of political rhetoric. Jews were, accordingly, incidental to this development, which also extended to Catholics – or, in Catholic countries, to Protestants – along with others.[12] Hence the trenchant

---

11 See, e.g., the assumption implicit in the title of Herbert A. Strauss (ed.), *Hostages of Modernization: Studies on Modern Antisemitism, 1870–1933/39. Germany, Great Britain, France* (Berlin: Walter de Gruyter, 1993). The term '*Antisemitismus*' was coined for political purposes in Germany in 1879 by the Judaeophobe Wilhelm Marr, though it (presumably as '*antisémitisme*') seems to have been used for polemical pur-poses by the Jewish scholar Moritz Steinschneider in France in 1860. See Alex Bein, *The Jewish Question: Biography of a World Problem* (Harry Zohn, trans., Rutherford: Herzl Press/Fairleigh Dickinson UP, 1990), 230; 593–622.

12 Liedtke and Wendehorst, *Emancipation of Catholics, Jews and Protestants.*

observation of Max Nordau, Herzl's number two at the World Zionist
Congress, that Jewish emancipation was merely an abstract entailment,
'solely the result of the geometrical mode of thought of French rational-
ism of the eighteenth century'.[13]

Overlooked in this perspective, however – and not, as I shall argue,
by Nordau alone – is the other direction in which liberal ideals sought to
popularise the interests of the bourgeoisie. Capitalism not only involves
capitalists. Looking downwards (or forwards) to the mass movements
that the formation of a relatively consolidated industrial proletariat
was generating, emancipation clothed the raw utilities of bourgeois
self-interest in the more appealing vestments of individual freedom. In
C. B. Macpherson's words, a 'newly moralized, liberal-democratic society
could claim, in a market society, to maximize individuals' chosen utilities,
and, as a free society, to maximize their powers.'[14] Again, therefore, Jews
were incidental. As Hannah Arendt declared in her magnificent unfinished essay on antisemitism (to which my own account is indebted, albeit
critically): 'The struggle to emancipate Jews was not about the Jews.'[15]

To state that emancipation was not about Jews is to state that it was
about something else – class ideology, a context-specific historical contingency. Thus the question arises of what *was* about Jews. The answer, of
course, is Judaeophobia – which emancipation, regardless of what it was
ultimately about, at least presupposed. Accepting the burden imposed by
this logic, and rejecting primordialism, Arendt insisted that, no less than
emancipation, antisemitism had antecedents that were the products of
particular circumstances, choices and activities. On this basis, she traced
the contingent historical trajectory of Judaeophobia so as to demonstrate
that antisemitism was neither spontaneous nor inevitable.

Her starting point was the stock image of Jewish life in mediaeval
and early-modern Europe as maximally enclosed and divorced from its
Gentile surrounds, with the great majority of Jews coming into contact
with other peoples 'only during catastrophes and expulsions'.[16] Otherwise
the ghetto's economic survival depended on the benevolence of moneylenders, the handful of wealthy intermediaries whose contact with the
outside world resulted from the religious ban on Christians practising
usury. As financiers and lenders to princely courts, some of these *shtadlan*
were able to use their political influence, though not always successfully,
to secure protection for their sequestered communities.[17]

---

13 Nordau, 'Speech to the first Zionist Congress', 236.

14 As Macpherson drily continued, 'Neither claim has stood up very well.' C. B.
Macpherson, *Democratic Theory: Essays in Retrieval* (Oxford: Clarendon Press, 1973), 6.

15 Hannah Arendt, 'Antisemitism', in Arendt, *The Jewish Writings* (various trans.,
Jerome Kohn and Ron H. Feldman, eds, New York: Schocken, 2007), 62.

16 Arendt, 'Antisemitism', 70.

17 Here and elsewhere, I adapt and/or supplement Arendt's account.

From this received depiction, Arendt departed from the hermetic binarism of ghetto and emancipation to trace the piecemeal developments
whereby increasing numbers of Jews had been able to access the dominant
echelons of Gentile society well before the Enlightenment. Anticipating
in their individual lives the general emancipation that was later to come,
notable Jews (not unlike some manumitted Blacks) had risen to opportunities presented by political developments in Gentile society from the
seventeenth century onwards. With the rise of the centralised absolutist
state (and accordingly, though Arendt does not discuss this, with the stir-
rings of enlightened despotism), the court Jew of the seventeenth and
early eighteenth centuries began to expand his operations, arranging the
substantial lines of credit that absolute rulers required for their habitual
war-making and establishing transnational networks to provide for the
supply of far-flung armies ('Jew Y could pay and deliver to armies fighting
far from home what Jew X had promised back in their homeland'[18]). In
Itzig and Ephraim, who provided the cannon balls from which Frederick
the Great hatched imperial Prussia, Arendt identified the prototypical
emancipated Jews, the first to leave the ghetto completely behind them,
an achievement that was their reward for 'highly dubious maneuvers that
brought in six million thalers annually during the last few years of the
Seven Years' War'.[19] While the Seven Years' War did not actually take
place as long before the Enlightenment as Arendt would have us think,
her wider point concerning the historicity of emancipation is impeccably
grounded. Strikingly, however, the bourgeoisie are conspicuous by their
low profile in her monarchical scenario. This is no accident.

Arendt is at pains to qualify 'the almost universally accepted thesis
that Jewish emancipation was directly dependent on the rise of the bourgeoisie', pointing out that formal emancipation did not come until 1868
in Britain ('the most bourgeois country in Europe') and until 1869 in
Prussia.[20] In this regard, her concern was not (or so I wish to argue) to
debunk the connection between emancipation and bourgeois ideology.

---

18   Arendt, 'Antisemitism', 78.
19   Ibid., 72.
20   In Switzerland, moreover, 'which has as good as always been ruled exclusively by the bourgeoisie, emancipation waged an especially hard struggle'; Arendt,
'Antisemitism', 82–3. It might, however, be noted that Moses Montefiore had become
the first Jew to hold public office in England (as Sheriff of the City of London) in
1838, while Prussia's first edict of emancipation had been passed in 1812. See, e.g.,
Liedtke and Wendehorst, *Emancipation of Catholics, Jews and Protestants*, 207–10;
Geoffrey Alderman, 'English Jews or Jews of the English Persuasion? Reflections on
the Emancipation of Anglo-Jewry', in Pierre Birnbaum and Ira Katznelson (eds), *Paths
of Emancipation: Jews, States and Citizenship* (Princeton: Princeton UP, 1995), 128–56;
U. R. Q. Henriques, 'The Jewish Emancipation Controversy in Nineteenth-Century
Britain', *Past & Present* 40 (1968), 126–46; Werner E. Mosse, 'From "*Schutzjuden*"
to "*deutsche Staatsbürger jüdischen Glaubens*": The Long and Bumpy Road of Jewish
Emancipation in Germany', in Birnbaum and Katznelson, *Paths of Emancipation*, 59–93.

Whether the bourgeoisie liked it or not, emancipation was championed in their vocabulary. Rather, her concern was with historicity. Emancipation did not spring out of nowhere once the bourgeoisie started talking about freedom. For our purposes, a key implication of this argument concerns the historicity of Judaeophobia rather than that of emancipation. Again, Itzig and Ephraim are pivotal. Despite being the first to step free of the ghetto, this singular pair did not thereby escape Judaeophobia. On the contrary, as Arendt makes clear, 'Frederick II might be able to pursue his Seven Years' War with the help of the tricks of Ephraim, the Jew he had put in charge of the mint, but the people did not hate Ephraim any less for it.'

This formulation (not least the word 'tricks') could seem to suggest a primordial Judaeophobia were it not for the fact that, in the following sentence, Arendt proceeds, crucially, to specify the operative context of Ephraim's unpopularity: 'Mercenary troops hired by one's own state were as feared as enemy armies.'[21] As a procurer of mercenaries, Ephraim would have been hated whether or not he was Jewish. The logic of this consideration has no dependence on blood libel.

In the wake of Ephraim's mercenaries, Arendt tracks the fortunes of Prussia's protected Jews through to the middle of the nineteenth century, finding that, though their proportion of the population grew considerably, Jews who enjoyed civic freedoms (or the dubious benefits of an official blind eye) remained a special class of 'exceptional' Jews – exceptional, that is, in relation to other Jews – who, despite their increasing numbers, continued to prove the rule depriving other Jews of civic and, in the main, economic rights. As a group, these exceptional Jews came to reside in and be identified with western Prussia, adding a spatial dimension to their collective privileging vis-à-vis the generality of their fellow Jews. After the Fourth Coalition's defeat by the French in 1807, however, Prussia was forced to surrender its eastern provinces, leaving the Jews in the west no longer exceptional – overnight, they had become practically the only Jews in Prussia. The protection that the exceptional Jews had enjoyed to this point having come from aristocratic rulers, it is not difficult for Arendt to point to bourgeois hostility towards them (even apart from the enmity that Napoleonic favour was earning them in Prussia's western residue). Thus she quotes bourgeois liberal Friedrich Buchholz's contention that getting rid of the aristocracy would first of all necessitate getting rid of the Jews: 'the aristocracy is so closely bound to the Jews that it cannot continue without them.'[22]

On this basis, by way of a complex historical survey that traces the steadily growing group of exceptional Jews' continued dependency on

21 Arendt, 'Antisemitism', 81–2.
22 Ibid., 92.

aristocratic protection, Arendt sets the scene for the Junker aristocracy's post-1807 abandonment of its special relationship with the group. The immediate cause of this was provided by the increasingly isolated and desperate Prussian monarchy, which Arendt somewhat arbitrarily separates from its aristocratic integument on grounds of state. In seeking to neutralise threats that it saw as coming simultaneously from both the nobility and the bourgeoisie, the 'independent' monarchy ('caught between Scylla and Charybdis') turned increasingly to Jewish financiers for support, causing the nobles to connect Jews to the state's burgeoning assaults on their traditional privileges, in particular the privatisation of landed property and the selling off of monarchical estates.[23]

Once again, in other words, it was not about Jews. Moreover, in the various counts of its indictment of the bourgeoisie – greed, novelty, cunning, inauthenticity, parasitism and the like – the aristocracy possessed a ready-made charge sheet to refocus against Jews, who emerged as an upstart pseudo-bourgeoisie, condemned by aristocracy and 'rabble' alike.

What, then, of the bourgeoisie itself? Would not all this make for a convenient alliance with a small but strategically significant group that had fallen out of favour with the bourgeoisie's own class enemies? At this point, Arendt's questioning of the link between Jewish emancipation and the rise of the bourgeoisie doubles as corroboration for the bourgeoisie's emergent antisemitism. Rather than coming to the defence of a group that was also under attack from the aristocracy, and with the same weapons, the bourgeoisie endorsed the aristocracy's hatred of the Jews – for the simple reason that it hated the same things in itself. The anxiety of the parvenu bespeaks a rootlessness that is cosmopolitan in its lack of fixity, a deterritorialised shiftiness that reflects capital's own movability. Culturally, in comparison to the ancestral legitimacy of the landed order that it had usurped, the bourgeoisie's market acumen was not competitive after all. Even politically, few bourgeois nationalists could have fared more plausibly than their Jewish counterparts when it came to claiming links to Charlemagne, let alone to Arminius or Vercingetorix. In invoking this anxiety (at least implicitly), Arendt completed the cross-class coalition confronting the Jews.

In so doing – and this is the reason for my extended adaptation of her account – she also completed the historical preconditions for their racialisation. As observed, antisemitism, in common with anti-Black racism in the USA, required a monolithic object of persecution. In homogenising the exceptional Jews of western Prussia, the defeat of 1807 prefigured that. Reciprocally, in consolidating the cross-class coalition formed against Jews – aristocracy, bourgeoisie and rabble – the internalised self-

---

23 Ibid., 102–3.

hatred of the parvenu completed the Gentile unity which, in opposition to the Jewish monolith, would come to constitute a racial polarity.

But something is glaringly missing from Arendt's account. 'Rabble' is hardly a rigorous category of class analysis.[24] Indeed, in its eternal disorder, the concept represents a primordialism of her own. The problem is not simply her elitism, which she makes no attempt to disguise. It is the lack of history inherent in the rabble's generic subalternity. Noting that Karl Wilhelm Friedrich Grattenauer's *Wider di Juden* [Against the Jews] was 'the first antisemitic tract for the rabble', Arendt hastens to clarify her time frame. Though Grattenauer's book was published in 1803, he was a few years too early: 'it was not yet time for an antisemitism of either the rabble or the bourgeoisie.'[25] That would have to wait on 1807 and the aristocracy, after which it would steadily become an antisemitism of all – or not actually all, since Arendt overlooks the arduous formation of a world-historical surge in the rabble's timeless flow, the industrial proletariat. The problem, then, is not with historicity. It is with Arendt's failure to live up to her own historicist agenda.

Bourgeois and Jew

It seems harsh to criticise an unfinished essay for its omissions. As an incompleteness, then, rather than necessarily a defect of the text, the German proletariat – which was congregating and mobilising throughout the nineteenth century, and which would duly furnish Bismarck with his war machine – is a crucial absence from Arendt's treatment, and not from hers alone. A pervasive elitism characterises accounts of the affinities linking liberalism, Jewish emancipation and antisemitism, an elitism consonant with founding Zionists' anger at the discrepancy between bourgeois rhetoric and their own cold-shouldering in bourgeois circles. This has had the effect of confining nineteenth-century antisemitism, along with the Zionist response to it, to the realm of ideas: antisemitism among the proletariat is not ignored so much as taken for granted, seen as operating at a level below that of ideas. Thus primordialism not only works chronologically, locating antisemitism in deep cultural time. It also works demographically, locating it in mass prejudice, where it figures as instinctual, deeply anchored in phylogenetic time.

For Nordau, mass consciousness incubated an unchanging Judaeophobia that required no substantiation. Impervious to philosophical niceties, this reservoir of prejudice ensured the failure of progressive

24　See also her 'The Alliance Between Mob and Capital', in Arendt, *Origins of Totalitarianism*, 147–57. Concerning the present book's analysis, the 'frontier rabble' is a figure of settler discourse (a disclaimer) rather than an empirical social category.

25　Arendt, 'Antisemitism', 93.

reform, warranting Zionist pessimism. Confronted with emancipation, he averred, 'popular sentiment indeed rebelled, but the philosophy of the [French] Revolution decreed that principles must be placed above sentiment'[26] – not for long, however, since everything else in his intoxicating speech to the first Zionist Congress was designed to demonstrate the inevitable prevalence of primordial sentiment. Antisemitism was eternal and unstoppable.

Yet there is no a priori reason why the Gentile working class should have echoed their class opponents' Judaeophobia. In overlooking the historical consolidation of the German proletariat, the elite perspective also trivialises the impact of the immigration from Eastern Europe of enormous numbers of rival workers. Over the final two decades of the nineteenth century, in the wake of the formation of the unified Reich, the steady growth in industrialisation that had occurred in Prussia for most of the nineteenth century accelerated dramatically.[27] The demographic consequences were extreme. As Klaus Bade has observed, Germany shifted from being a country of emigration to being a country of labour-importation.[28] Between 1873 and 1895, the population soared by over 25 per cent, from 41.6 million to 52 million.[29] But even this overall increase understates the astonishing number of immigrants, since emigration was not actually falling. Rather, the bare figures obscure the fact that the startling increase in total population took place at a time when the existing population was continuing to emigrate, in most cases to the USA, at a near steady rate.[30]

Compounding the growth in overall numbers, Germans were being replaced by immigrants, especially in the east, which was not only immigrants' first port of call but an area that German workers were abandoning for more highly paid employment in the heavy-industrial Ruhr Valley. Thus the increase in the non-German proportion of the population was even higher than the 25 per cent increase in the total figure. As in the case of the passing of the settler frontier, Germans found themselves having to share social space with outsiders, a national identity crisis that readily lent itself to xenophobia. In 1885, the *Posener Zeitung* warned its readers that 'it is precisely the eastern provinces that account for a hefty

---

26 Nordau, 'Speech to the first Zionist Congress', 236.
27 'The development of Central European anti-Semitism started with the transition to industrialization.' Hans Rosenberg, 'Anti-Semitism and the "Great Depression", 1873–1896', in Strauss, *Hostages of Modernization*, 19.
28 Klaus J. Bade, 'Labour, Migration, and the State: Germany from the Late 19th Century to the Onset of the Great Depression', in Bade (ed.), *Population, Labour and Migration in 19th- and 20th-Century Germany* (New York: Berg, 1987), 64.
29 Ulrich Herbert, *A History of Foreign Labor in Germany, 1880–1980: Seasonal Workers/Forced Laborers/Guest Workers* (William Templer, trans., Ann Arbor: Michigan UP, 1993), 9–10.
30 Ibid., 8–12.

contingent of German emigrants! Is this not sufficient proof that our own fellow Germans in the Reich are being driven from their homeland by foreigners?'[31]

In relation to the concurrent rise of antisemitism, the most significant feature of the avalanche of immigrants who arrived in Germany from the east is that the great majority of them were not Jewish. Moreover, of those who were Jewish, the majority did not stay in Germany but were merely passing through on their way to the United States, to which many departed on German liners, joining the flow of immigrants into the United States that we noted in the previous chapter. Others headed for France, England, Argentina and, in some cases, Palestine. Cited as disease prevention measures, strict transit migration controls (*Durchwandererkontrollen*) ensured that they kept moving.[32] Between the assassination of Tzar Alexander II and the outbreak of World War I, 'of the approximately two million Jews who passed through the Eastern borders ... roughly 78,000 remained in Germany, where they made up about 12% of the Jewish population'[33] – making the Jewish population roughly one and a half per cent of the German population as a whole, hardly a substantial minority.

Nonetheless, though German Slavophobia did not fail to target what Ulrich Herbert termed the 'bogey of Polonization', the campaign of vilification and expulsion mounted by German politicians and publicists against the Eastern Jews (who would come to be called *Ostjuden* during World War I) was considerably more intense, to the extent that restrictionist resistance to the continued immigration of Jews was initially voiced within the established German Jewish community itself (*reichsdeutsche Juden*), who rightly feared where the vilification might lead once it was afforded a tangible pretext.[34]

---

31 Quoted in Herbert, *Foreign Labor in Germany*, 12.

32 Klaus J. Bade, 'Germany: Migrations in Europe up to the End of the Weimar Republic', in Robin Cohen (ed.), *The Cambridge Survey of World Migration* (Cambridge: Cambridge UP, 1995), 133; Jack Wertheimer, *Unwelcome Strangers: East European Jews in Imperial Germany* (Oxford: Oxford UP, 1987), 14, 50–1.

33 Bade, 'Germany: Migrations in Europe', 133.

34 'Anti-Semitism did indeed follow the coming of the Eastern Jews to Germany, just as the German Jews had feared.' Michael Cohn, *Jewish Bridges: East to West* (Westport: Praeger, 1996), 37. The generally restrictionist attitude of German Jews subsequently changed in response to the recognition that 'the arguments of restrictionists relied heavily on the arsenal of anti-Semitic stereotypes employed in the battle against native Jews', Wertheimer, *Unwelcome Strangers*, 163. See also Jack Wertheimer, 'The Unwanted Element: East European Jews in Imperial Germany', in *Leo Baeck Institute Yearbook* 26 (New York: Leo Baeck Institute, 1981), 23–46; Geoff Eley, 'German Politics and Polish Nationality: The Dialectic of Nation-Forming in the East of Prussia', *East European Quarterly* 3 (September 1984), 335–59. 'Bogey of Polonization' in Herbert, *Foreign Labor in Germany*, 11. For the dating of the term '*Ostjuden*', see Wertheimer, *Unwelcome Strangers*, 6.

Rather than embodying the dimensions of the threat to German society in an era of chaotic transition, in other words, the Eastern Jews were ideologically recruited to the familiar role of scapegoat for it. In this regard, the extreme disproportion between Jews' actual demographic profile – the paucity of their real share of the population – and the scale of the social upheaval that was to be managed by way of their targeting is crucial. The smaller the social group whose demonisation serves to unite a given society, the larger the residual portion of society that is united by its shared hostility to that group. The energy with which antisemitism was mobilised was a response to the challenge to social cohesion that was being posed by an influx of non-Jews. In the wake of the national disaster of World War I, of course, antisemitism would provide the children and grandchildren of the immigration generation with even more demonic ways to assert their Germanness.

The full development of race was realised in antisemitism's collapsing together of the Eastern and the German Jews. The cultural differences between the two groups were substantial, the locals having assimilated almost seamlessly into German-bourgeois society over the course of the three generations that had elapsed since the Napoleonic era. Indeed, as the claim that German culture was under threat from Judaisation gained ground, it was their very similarity that was most threatening. In this context, as Steven Aschheim observes, 'It was the threat and perception of radical closeness that made "racial theory" extremely useful.'[35] By way of the doctrine of race, not only was this similarity denied. At the same time, the vehemence of that denial was combined with the xenophobia directed against the arrivals from the East, to produce an indiscriminate racial targeting that did not acknowledge any exceptional Jews.

The industrial proletariat did not turn antisemitic at their superiors' bidding. Those who did so had their own reasons for mistaking what was good for workers, and they were more likely to be finding them in the yellow press than in the pronouncements of a nationalist historian like Heinrich von Trietschke. Nonetheless, their rulers were not slow to exploit the correspondence between elite and popular antisemitisms. Moreover, the antisemitic Gentile front reciprocally unified its Jewish object. As the Ukrainian Marxist-Zionist Ber Borochov observed,

Anti-Semitism menaces both the poor helpless Jews and the all-powerful Rothschilds ... Were there no anti-Semitism, the misery and poverty of the Jewish emigrants [he was writing in Russia] would be of little concern to the Jewish upper bourgeoisie ... Everywhere the Jewish upper bourgeoisie

---

35   Steven E. Aschheim, *Brothers and Strangers: The East European Jews in Germany and German Jewish Consciousness, 1800–1923* (Madison: Wisconsin UP, 1982), 76.

is engaged in the search for a Jewish solution to the Jewish problem and a
means of being delivered of the Jewish masses.[36]

The cross-class accord that antisemitism facilitated had a counterpart
in settler racism. European society as a whole was in a dangerous and
sustained state of flux, as had been dramatically evidenced in the revolutionary fervour of 1848, the Paris Commune later in the century and the
ceaseless round of less publicised disturbances that betrayed the precari-
ousness of bourgeois rule. *Homo assimilans* was needed in the metropole
as well as in the colonies. In the German case, the most urgent requirement for social management was generated, in a context of rapid and
massive industrialisation, when the internal process of class formation
coincided with mass immigration. This situation further coincided
with the development of German colonialism in the years surrounding
Bismarck's Berlin Conference.[37]

A Frustrated Colonialism

The short and ignominious career of Bismarckian colonialism in Africa
is highly suggestive in regard to racial politics within Germany. From the
late 1870s onwards, colonialism was being championed as a universal
remedy for the gathering problems confronting the imperial Reich in
the wake of the recession that had commenced in 1873. The appeal of
the colonial propaganda urged by Friedrich Fabri ('father of the German
colonial movement') and others lay, as Bade has discerned, in its capacity
to combine

> all the national, economic, and social problems of the day and demolish ...
> any imaginable internal solutions, thus leaving just one way out – a supposed
> panacea for all national and political, all economic, demographic, and 'social'
> ills: colonial expansion.[38]

But, given the rapid waning of Bismarck's belated enthusiasm for Africa
('In October 1888, Bismarck curtly explained to Michahalles, German
Consul General in Zanzibar, that he had "had enough of colonies"'[39]),
this left only internal 'solutions'. In this context, the domestic language
of race, initially applied to self-affirmation in the romantic idiom of

---

36   Ber Borochov, 'Our Platform' (1906), selection in Herzberg, *Zionist Idea*, 361.
37   Stig Förster, Wolfgang J. Mommsen and Ronald Robinson (eds), *Bismarck,
Europe, and Africa: The Berlin Africa Conference 1884–1885 and the Onset of Partition*
(Oxford: Oxford UP/German Historical Institute London, 1988).
38   Klaus J. Bade, 'Imperial Germany and West Africa: Colonial Movement,
Business Interests, and Bismarck's "Colonial Policies"', Angela Davies, trans., in Förster
et al, *Bismarck, Europe, and Africa*, 122.
39   Ibid., 147.

European nationalism, became more explicitly other-directed, recruiting the supremacist xenophobia of colonial racism for internal use. Once again, it was not about the Jews.[40] Nonetheless, the hybrid image of Jews as both internal and external to European society made them ideal conduits between colonial and metropolitan ideologies, compounding local discredit with oriental menace.

There could hardly be a better example of this mediation than the infamous vilification of a rival that one of the most zeitgeist-attuned minds of his age, situated in England, expressed in private correspondence. In repeatedly referring to Ferdinand Lassalle as a 'Jewish nigger', Karl Marx was not merely ventilating a conjectural self-hatred of his own.[41] In voicing a transcontinental correspondence between the disparagement of Jews and Africans, Marx's nasty epithet anticipated the quasi-colonial racialisation of Jewish people that would presently take hold of his native Germany. Hence it is quite consistent that, in his overview of European racism, George Mosse should acquit one of racism's arch-prophets, writing in the mid-1850s, of the charge of antisemitism. It was only in late-nineteenth-century Germany, Mosse observes, that 'Gobineau's condemnation of the black and yellow races was turned against the Jew'. 'It was here', Mosse continues, 'that Gobineau got his undeserved reputation as an anti-Semite'.[42]

This is not to absolve Gobineau. It is rather to state that his manifesto for racism was not about Jews but about colonised peoples. Once coined, Gobineau's colonial typology, along with doctrinal racism in general, became discursively available for redirection into metropolitan practice.

---

40 'Anti-Semitism was the protest movement of all who were worried by the modernization of national and social life ... They called anyone they did not like a Jew, and denounced anything inconsistent with their views as Jewish.' Werner Jochmann, 'Structure and Functions of German Anti-Semitism 1878–1914', in Strauss, *Hostages of Modernization*, 60.

41 'It is now quite plain to me – as the shape of his head and the way his hair grows also testify – that he [Lassalle] is descended from the Negroes who accompanied Moses' flight from Egypt (unless his mother or paternal grandmother interbred with a nigger). Now, this blend of Jewishness and Germanness, on the one hand and basic negroid stock on the other, must inevitably give rise to a peculiar product. The fellow's importunity is also niggerlike.' Marx to Engels, 30 July 1862, in *Karl Marx–Frederick Engels Collected Works*, vol. 41, *Marx and Engels Correspondence, 1860–64* (London: Lawrence & Wishart, 1985), 390.

42 Mosse, *Toward the Final Solution*, 56. Mosse is attuned to the colonial dimension but, higher on the same page, asserts that 'The [German] acquisition of colonies in Africa in 1884 and the occupation of a base in China (1897) came too late to influence the development of racism in Germany', further asserting that Jews had long been the target of racism in Germany. As Bismarck's Berlin Congress demonstrated as early as 1878, however, Germany had not needed to possess extra-European colonies (Mosse does not consider Poland) to be already receptive to colonial discourse. Moreover, Mosse does not distinguish rigorously between racism and the generic Judaeophobia (Arendt's 'Jew-hatred') that German Jews had long been obliged to endure.

As Arendt observed in another scintillating essay (which, though completed, also disregarded the formation of the industrial proletariat), 'the fateful days of the "scramble for Africa"' constituted a turning point in the emergence of modern racism, a genealogy that she scrupulously acknowledged even in the darkest days of 1944.[43] In sealing the conjuncture between the external reverses of Bismarck's colonial project and the internal tumult of nationhood, industrialisation and mass immigration, antisemitism potently canalised the multiple stresses that were besetting the imperial Reich. Here again, therefore, and particularly starkly, the racialisation of the one group was critical to the consolidation of the social complex as a whole.

In view of the other commonalities that we have noted between the post-emancipation experiences of European Jews and of Black people in the USA, the affinity between their respective racialisations is not surprising. Both groups had featured centrally in elite polemics of the nineteenth century, which spawned a versatile range of collective aspersions, from Black people's abasement in scientific racism's cranial hierarchies to Jewish people's bourgeoisification by the Junker aristocracy. It was noted in the previous chapter that race was relatively redundant when Black people were already enslaved. To this we might add that race would also have been redundant when Jewish people were already walled in. In both cases, it was when European workers began to view emancipation as giving rise to a rival workforce – whether through the freeing of slaves or through the lifting of restrictions on immigration from the East – that proletarian discourse became receptive to elite racial doctrine. In either case, the historical preconditions for the full racialisation of the excluded community were achieved by this cross-class coalition, to which the threat of rivalry contributed. This development, rather than the demonopathy of some primordial rabble, completes the historicity of antisemitism and of Jim Crow alike.

To say that Jews were racialised in a manner reliant on colonial precedents is not to say that Jews were colonised. Without subscribing to a blue-water concept of colonialism (which overlooks the cumulative adjacencies of settler expansion), it is imperative to distinguish between metropole and colony. Otherwise, Native invasion falls from view, along with the crucial role played in colonialism by the metropolitan lower orders. Colonisers come from somewhere else, whether across oceans or

---

43   Arendt, 'Race-Thinking Before Racism', 37; 73 ('the "scramble for Africa" and the new era of imperialism ... exposed Western humanity to new and shocking experiences. Imperialism would have necessitated the invention of racism as the only possible "explanation" and excuse for its deeds, even if no race-thinking had ever existed in the civilized world'). Arendt asserted in another article that 'of the two main political devices of imperialist rule [the other being bureaucracy], race was discovered in South Africa.' Arendt, 'The Imperialist Character', in Arendt, *Origins of Totalitarianism*, 207.

across the frontier. The spatial element is irreducible. Thus to view Jews as colonised is to ratify the claim that their place is outside the metropole (a further claim shared by Zionism and antisemitism). Sympathetic though one may be to its intentions, therefore, the concept of internal colonialism is a pious oxymoron. If the concept is applied to Indigenous people, the element of internality undoes their sovereign externality, assimilating them to settler society by analytical fiat. Applied to the descendants of the enslaved, the colonial element distances White society from its responsibility for their incorporation, recapitulating segregation (James Baldwin discovered he was 'American' on encountering colonised Africans in Paris[44]).

Accordingly, to say that race is colonialism speaking is to say that colonialism came before race, which it created. To say otherwise – that race created colonialism – would be to subscribe to colonialism's own justification. In its origins, therefore, as a colonial invention, race was inherently spatial, predicated on externality. Inscribed within race, the spatial implication persists as a trace, distancing racialised communities within or, in the case of Indigenous people, undoing their externality. Jews had long been distanced within Europe, but in ways that presupposed inequality. Emancipation, the ghetto's misleading Joshua, compromised that inequality, which was restored by means of the thoroughly modern device of race, recalled from colonial service to effect a moral separation of Jewish people within Europe. In this light, we see that emancipation and assimilation are not merely distinct. They are strategic alternatives. Emancipation is a way not to assimilate: where assimilation denies the existence of difference, emancipation preserves liability for it.

Worker and Jew

This is not to countenance the functionalism whereby different forms of Judaeophobia become different ways of satisfying an eternal requirement for Jewish inequality, a formula that begs the question of where the inequality came from. Rather than taking inequality for granted, we should address the ways in which antisemitism inaugurated a specifically nineteenth-century mode of inequality.

Though Arendt recognised this question, her answer was uncharacteristically weak. As we have seen, a distinctive feature of antisemitism for

---

44 'To accept the reality of his being an American becomes a matter involving his integrity and his greatest hopes, for only by accepting this reality can he hope to make articulate to himself or to others the uniqueness of his experience, and to set free the spirit so long anonymous and caged.' James Baldwin, 'Encounter on the Seine: Black Meets Brown', in Baldwin, *Collected Essays* (New York: Library of America, 1998), 88. On the following page, Baldwin distinguishes between the 'Negro' and the 'African', 'who face each other ... over a gulf of three hundred years'.

Arendt was that it was not about Jews (so its history could be treated 'as a history of associations'). As such, antisemitism lacked the experiential foundation of earlier Judaeophobias, which had been based on 'concrete knowledge' of Jews: 'The history of the [earlier] hatred of Jews was about Jews, and not much more than that.'[45] But this concrete knowledge is hopelessly at odds with the depiction of a hidden people who are only encountered during catastrophes and expulsions. Despite this inconsistency, however, Arendt was, as always, onto something: Gentile knowledge of Jews *was* central to the crisis that antisemitism signalled, but the issue was not that Gentiles had known Jews in the past – they had not. Rather, I wish to argue, it was that they might start to know them in the present. This consideration takes us back to the nineteenth-century bourgeoisie and the emergent industrial capitalism that formed the basis of its existence.

The indictment that the self-hating bourgeoisie deflected onto Jews as a whole may or may not have applied to some Jews, but it certainly applied to the bourgeoisie's vital asset, only with its values reversed. When applied to capital, the negative qualities ascribed to Jews acquired positive complements: cunning, cupidity, parvenuism, pushiness and related vices figured as the market virtues of shrewdness, enterprise, innovation and drive. So long as it was not Jewish, greed was good. There was, however, an exception to this parallelism; one prominent stigma attached to Jews without being mirrored as a conversely valorised attribute of capital. The bourgeoisie, its grand touring notwithstanding, had no ideological counterpart to the wandering Jew.

In view of capital's constitutive mobility, the omission is significant. A liability incurred by capital's mobility is its besetting fear of labour matching its own global connectedness, forging international solidarities to frustrate the extraction of surplus value wherever that may take place. Given capital's reliance on the hyper-exploitation of labour in the colonies, this fear is most acute where the spectre of fellowship between metropolitan and colonial labour is concerned. As many have pointed out, nationalism provided the sovereign remedy for this threat, equipping global capital with an internal set of moral walls. European nationalism, as observed, had a Janus face, combining the unifying romance of self-assertion with the ethnocentric venom of colonial racism. As a displaced colonial surrogate within – out of place, dirty – the racialised Jew took on the xenophobic intensity of nationalism's outward thrust, furnishing a local proxy for the metropolitan proletariat to practise its recently acquired imperial subjecthood. With European nations gearing themselves up to fight the war of all wars over colonialism, it is only consistent that the wandering Jew, cave-shadow of capital's global mobility, should

----

45   Arendt, 'Antisemitism', 70.

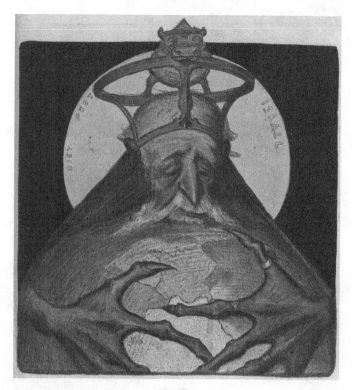

Fig. 2

morph into a worldwide conspiracy, threatening enough to reinforce the defensive cohesion of the nation-state (Fig. 2).[46] Representationally, as the twentieth century wore on, the globalising of the Jewish threat would be offset by an atomised imagery of capital, with international companies parochialising themselves, spore-like, as good national citizens in counterpoint to the denationalisation of the globalised Jew. By the time of the Nazi era, when the denationalisation of Jews would reach its demonic extreme, even Coca Cola could be teutonised (Fig. 3).[47]

---

46 Fig. 2, a caricature of Rothschild, was originally published in France by C. Léandre in 1898 but rapidly gained currency in Germany. This version appeared in Eduard Fuchs, *Die Juden in der Karikatur: Ein Beitrag zur Kulturgeschichte* (Munich: Albert Langen/Verlag, 1921), 209. The international character of antisemitic representations of the Jewish threat was much more general than the single case of the *Protocols of the Elders of Zion*, which, though initially composed at the behest of the Russian secret service around the turn of the twentieth century, did not acquire international currency until immediately after World War I. From a large literature see, e.g., Norman Cohn, *Warrant for Genocide: The Myth of the Jewish World Conspiracy and the 'Protocols of the Elders of Zion'* (London: Eyre & Spottiswood, 1967).

47 It is hard to tell whether Rudolf Streit-Scherz and Heinz Klüter were criticising or channelling this cultural code when they chose Figs 2 and 3 as facing pages in their facsimile selection from numbers of the *Berliner Illustrirte* spanning the period

Fig. 3

The industrial proletariat's relationship to colonialism constituted a historically unprecedented condition for the popularisation of antisemitism, a novel form of Judaeophobia. This material conjuncture was not necessary or foreordained. It was an elective affinity. The limitations of liberal ideology cannot account for it – working people had not been fooled by liberal ideology in the first place. Nor did popular antisemitism grow out of an alternation between known and unknown Jews. In their empirical humanity, Jews remained unknown throughout. Rather, the shift was from the Jew as outsider to the Jew as threat.

Here again, the Jewish experience had a counterpart in that of African Americans, who became eligible for lynching after they had joined the ranks of wage labour. Prior to their emancipation, Jewish workers had been excluded from productive industry, a constraint that had not affected Nordau and his colleagues in the Zionist elite.[48] As observed in

1891 to 1945, but the juxtaposition is revealing. *Facsimile Querschnitt durch die Berliner Illustrirte* (Munich: Sherz Verlag, 1965), selections from 26/1/1939 and 23/2/1939 (Fig. 3 on 23/2/1939).

48 'This is the Jewish spiritual misery, which is more painful than the physical because it affects men of higher station, who are prouder and more sensitive ... All the better Jews of western Europe groan under this misery and seek for salvation and

the introduction, however, while the perception of job-market rivalry can account for a ruthless degree of exclusion, it is not a sufficient condition for the elaborations that accompanied that exclusion. Though fin-de-siècle Germany had yet to develop a level of cruelty comparable to that on display in the US South, the obsessive focus on Jewishness was, as we have seen, radically disproportionate to Eastern Jews' actual impact on the labour market. Why, then, did so many of the Gentile working class so exceed the requirements for protecting their wages and conditions?

As an analytical method, the idea of thinking oneself into the psychology of antisemitism is not promising. Nonetheless, there is no mistaking the fact that Arendt, who had experienced the phenomenon at first hand, had compelling grounds for her repeated insistence that it was not about Jews. Arendt's conviction – to adapt the terminology of another profound Jewish thinker, who also took refuge from the phenomenon – suggests an ideological condensation, the channelling of a confused welter of latent resentments onto a single, clearly defined and locally available hate-object.[49] Refracted through the embodied, intensely cathected prism of race, antisemitism mobilised an emotional language intense enough to give vent to the diffuse discontents of a deeply disturbed class. Each and every Jew gathered all this unto him- or herself. It is in this concentrated-ness, I wish to suggest, that antisemitism partook of its mystic potency, inscribing its mark of Cain upon and within every Jew.

True, there were other factors. Nordau and Arendt were both right to point to bourgeois discourse's abiding fondness for abstraction, whereby Jewish people were condensed into 'the Jew', a generic monolith, lifted out of human commerce, that admitted no personal exceptions, whether by conversion or otherwise. For all its perspicacity, however, this insight

---

alleviation.' Nordau, 'Speech to the First Zionist Congress', 239. Thus Nordau 'was not beyond presenting Zionism as a kind of safety valve protecting the vital interests of German bourgeois Jewry', Aschheim, *Brothers and Strangers*, 88.

49 Being a feature of dream-work for Freud, condensation might seem to lack the radically uncensored virulent drive (*triebe*) animating antisemitism, which could alternatively (or also) be viewed as a species of paranoia. As Freud observed of the Schreber case, the paranoiac 'builds it [paranoia] up by the work of his delusions. The delusion-formation, which we take to be the pathological product, is in reality an attempt at recovery, a process of reconstruction ... the human subject has recaptured a relation, and often a very intense one, to the people and things of the world, even though the relation is a hostile one now.' Sigmund Freud, 'Psychoanalytic notes on an autobiographical account of a case of paranoia (*dementia paranoides*)', in *The Standard Edition of the Complete Psychological Works of Sigmund Freud* (James Strachey, ed., London: Hogarth, 1956–74), vol. 12, 70. Before his conversion to Zionism, the physician Nordau had made the relationship between antisemitism and hysteria explicit: 'German hysteria manifests itself in anti-Semitism, that most dangerous form of the persecution-mania, in which the person believing himself persecuted becomes a savage persecutor, capable of all crimes.' Max Simon Nordau, *Degeneration* (Memphis: General Books, 2010 [1892]), 166.

itself is somewhat abstract, in that it fails to capture the visceral hostility
that antisemitism licensed when it shifted from the exclusionary confines
of Nordau's elite to the humdrum level of the street. It misses the menace
attaching to an unseen power sensed as operating everywhere, orches-
trating the unhappiness of workaday life. As capital's Mr Hyde, it is no
wonder that the Jew behind the scenes, lurking everywhere and nowhere,
should soon enough become the worker-gone-wrong, the malign agent
of Bolshevism whose global tentacles shadowed those of capital itself.
This is not to impugn the distinguished contribution of some Jewish
people to the international workers' movement. The point is rather that,
in alienating workers from 'the Jew', antisemitism was alienating workers
from themselves. Either way, it was not about Jews.

In addition to its preoccupation with abstraction, the elite perspective overlooks the marginality of bourgeois-liberal discourse in Eastern
Europe. How was it that antisemitism – and, accordingly, the Zionist
response to it – could take hold in the western region of Tsarist Russia
and Poland? If antisemitism really was born of liberalism, it could only
have been stillborn in the residually feudal Pale of Settlement. An easy
response to this objection would be to invoke discursive contagion, a
kind of Leninism whereby movements grown elsewhere can subsequently
take root in soil otherwise historically unprepared for them. No doubt
there was an element of this (Pinsker was a scion of the Haskalah, or
Jewish Enlightenment, which had spread to Russia), but a more cogent
answer is that it is not actually the case that antisemitism took root in
the East after all, since Jewish difference there continued to be composed of religious materials. The pivotal 1881 pogroms (an established
Russian tradition deriving its name from the verb *pogromit*, to destroy)
were feudal irruptions encouraged, as is generally acknowledged, in the
hope of uniting the Gentile populace behind the crisis-prone Russian
ruling class in the wake of the portentous assassination of Tzar Alexander
II.[50] When Eastern-Jewish refugees migrated to Western Europe, one
of the languages available for them to discuss their established religious
oppression as Jews, along with the new form that they confronted on
arrival, was Zionism.[51] Being a response to antisemitism, Zionism, for all

---

50 See, e.g., John Doyle Klier, *Russians, Jews, and the Pogroms of 1881–1882*
(Cambridge: Cambridge UP, 2011), 17–39; Irwin M. Aronson, *Troubled Waters: The
Origins of the 1881 Anti-Jewish Pogroms in Russia* (Pittsburgh, PA: Pittsburgh UP, 1990);
Stephen M. Berk, *Year of Crisis, Year of Hope: Russian Jewry and the Pogroms of 1881–82*
(Westport, CT: Greenwood Press, 1985). For a comprehensive overview, see Jonathan
Frankel, *Prophecy and Politics: Socialism, Nationalism and the Russian Jews 1862–1917*
(Cambridge: Cambridge UP, 1981), 49–132.

51 Russian Jews had been emigrating in significant numbers since before the assas-
sination. See Jonathan Frankel, 'The Crisis of 1881–82 as a Turning Point in Modern
Jewish History', in David Berger (ed.), *The Legacy of Jewish Migration: 1881 and Its
Impact* (Brooklyn, NY: Brooklyn College Press, 1983, 9–22), 11.

its secularism, addressed the cumulative Judaeophobic history that anti-semitism encompassed, including the Russian feudal variant, the Spanish *limpieza de sangre* and the splenetic hostility of Luther.

Crucially, however, the reverse does not apply. In the absence of the diffusion eastwards of the Haskalah, Russian Judaism (as it remained, unemancipated and unsecularised) could not have come up with Zionism. On the basis of its historical experience, and confined to the conceptual vocabulary available to it in the depths of Tzarist feudalism, it could no more have framed a complaint about the shortcomings of liberal ideology than Spanish *marranos* or early-modern Germans had done before it. Though it may seem obvious, this point is very important. Historically, antisemitism was unique but not unprecedented. Larger than its precedents, it encompassed earlier Judaeophobias but, since it also incorporated elements they did not incorporate, they could not encompass it. This is its historicity, which primordialism suppresses. Antisemitism, in its modern fullness, cannot be read backwards onto earlier forms of Judaeophobia. By the same token, nor can it be ethnocentrically generalised outwards onto non-European forms of Judaeophobia, in particular to the everyday reciprocal disdain that characterised intercommunal relations among the millets of the Ottoman world.

Race and Nation

In contrast to the other regimes of race that this book considers, where the analysis of a colonial discourse does not involve speculation on the perspectives of the colonised people, the analysis of antisemitism has returned to Zionism at a number of points. It is worth considering why this should be. After all, it has not been necessary to discuss the Aboriginal Provisional Government in order to analyse Australian racism, or the NAACP to analyse Jim Crow.[52] But these movements have not participated in the colonial discourses that they have been predicated on resisting. Zionism, by contrast, was a conscious exercise in auto-racialisation. It embraced European colonial discourse, including race, nationalism and even, albeit strategically, antisemitism itself. In short, as Walter Laqueur has put it, Zionism was 'the product of Europe, not of the ghetto'.[53] As such, its discussion is part of our topic.

The key turning point for political Zionism was the idea of the nation – which, in nineteenth-century Europe, necessarily involved race. Nations were civilised, territorially bounded institutions inhabited by the

---

52 A partial exception, which hardly qualifies as a political movement, is that of the Indian tribes who exploit the one-drop rule to exclude members with Black ancestry.

53 Walter Laqueur, *A History of Zionism: From the French Revolution to the Establishment of the State of Israel* (New York: Schocken, 2003), 592.

European races that respectively made them up.[54] Herzl's breakthrough was his harnessing of the conviction that Jews should have a refuge outside Europe to the idea that Jews constituted a European nation like others.[55] In practical terms – since Herzl did not have unoccupied territory in mind – this meant that Europe should have a Jewish colony (as Nordau would put it, 'We intend to come to Palestine as the emissaries of culture and to expand the moral boundaries of Europe to the Euphrates').[56] This was consistent and unremarkable, the possession of colonies being an emblem of European nationhood in the 1890s.

In its political aspect, Herzl's nationalism provided that the means for the Jewish nation to acquire its territory should be governmental. Hence his recurrent overtures to heads of state. His Jewish outpost would be not just a place in which Jews might find refuge, a kind of escape-hatch from Europe, but, more positively, a national home, recognised by sovereign nations, in which the Jewish nation could exercise its own sovereignty in concert with and sanctioned by theirs – an emancipation which, though still imposed from above, would operate at the international level. As a territory outside Europe that would be provided by European governments (including, for this purpose, the Ottoman Empire), the Jewish national home was, by definition, a colonising vision. In its internationalism – its self-conscious candidature for membership of a European community of colonial nations defined by race – Herzl's Zionism was a qualitative departure from the ideological/spiritual nationalism of a Heinrich Graetz, a Moses Hess or even of Pinsker (whose emancipation had been first and foremost 'auto').[57]

All this hinged on Herzl's fateful embrace of the doctrine of race. This was not only on account of the nineteenth-century commonplace that race, nation and territory presupposed one another, whereby the existence of a race without a national home was anomalous. In addition, and more specifically, the only other denominator plausibly available to Herzl was religion, the obvious criterion for Jewishness, which was as

---

54 'The terms "people", "nation", and "race" tended at times to become identical during the second half of the nineteenth century, despite Herder's earlier efforts to keep them apart'. Mosse, *Toward the Final Solution*, 45.

55 Precedence for this idea has been claimed for Rabbi Yehudah Alkalai, 'the half forgotten Serbian rabbi and cabbalist of the old school, who was affected [in the 1840s] by the Balkan nationalist struggles which surrounded him' (Herzberg, *Zionist Idea*, 29). Whether or not this is the case, Alkalai's influence was hardly consequential.

56 Max Nordau, *Ketavim tsioniyim* (collected works, Jerusalem: Hasifriya Hatsionit, 1962), vol. 2, 113, quoted in Scott Atran, 'The Surrogate Colonization of Palestine, 1917–1939', *American Ethnologist* 16 (1989), 720.

57 The gap between Pinsker and political Zionism is obscured by Laqueur moving the date of Pinsker's death (which actually occurred in 1891) forwards to 1898, which would have had him overlap with the 1897 Basel Congress where political Zionism was launched. See Laqueur, *History of Zionism*, 74.

unwelcome to him as it was taken for granted by others.[58] Confronted with a Europe that, despite its modernity, had no remedy for abstract walls, Herzl did not give up on modernity; he gave up on Europe. To find a refuge in religion would have been to give up on modernity. Herzl wanted modernity's freedom – the freedom to be anonymous, not there for all to see – and that could only be achieved in a Europe that was not Europe, an old new land of colonialism's making. In excluding the most obvious criterion for Jewishness, religion, from the basis of his new movement, Herzl committed Zionism to a concept of race that reflected the volkisch colonial nationalism in the midst and likeness of which he had conceived his programme.

Thus it is consistent, rather than surprising, that Zionists should have echoed the racism, including the antisemitism, of colonial-nationalist discourse. Zionism's monolithic Jewish nation had the same boundaries as those of antisemitism. There is no need to rehearse the antisemitic sentiments, every bit as offensive as Marx's, to which prominent Zionists gave voice, and which have been amply documented elsewhere.[59] The point is not their incriminating verbiage but their conformity with the wider phenomenon of colonial thinking. In subscribing to the ideology of the colonial nation, Zionism reinscribed that ideology's racial premises, becoming an agent of the racialisation of Jewish people. As such, it is part of our topic.

Moreover, it is not as if antisemitism permitted no response other than Zionism. Even apart from the Orthodox condemnation as blasphemous of the idea that humans should pre-empt God's discretion in relation to the 'return' of Jews to Jerusalem,[60] contemporary secular-Jewish responses to antisemitism included non-Zionist, non-colonial perspectives such as those of the socialist Bund (Yiddish for 'alliance' – the avoidance of both Hebrew and Russian is significant) or of the

---

58 'With him [Herzl], the hope for a return to Palestine lost its religious and mystical character and became the basis for a modern, secular, political project; the creation of a Jewish national state. In this sense, he was the true originator of political Zionism.' Traverso, *Jews & Germany*, 90.

59 'We [Israelis] have been suffering from the disease of Jewish anti-Semitism ever since the *Haskalah* ... The poison that flows from Jewish nationalist sources is perhaps the most dangerous of them all ... Zionism actually based the [Jewish] national movement on a rationale of charges that it took over from the anti-Semites and attempted to find a core of justice in the hatred of the Jews.' Yehezkel Haufman, quoted in Michael Selzer, *The Aryanization of the Jewish State* (New York: Black Star, 1967), 36, where Selzer also provides incriminating quotations from the likes of Pinsker, Judah Leib Gordon and kibbutz-movement ideologue A. D. Gordon. For Herzl himself, see Albert S. Lindemann (who does not accuse), *The Jew Accused: Three Anti-Semitic Affairs (Dreyfus, Beilis, Frank), 1894–1915* (Cambridge: Cambridge UP, 1991), 85.

60 On the Orthodox (in his term, observant) rejection of Zionism, see Yakov M. Rabkin, *A Threat from Within: A Century of Jewish Opposition to Zionism* (London: Zed Books, 2006).

'conscious pariah' Bernard Lazare, whose humane Jewish universalism would later be picked up by Arendt and after her, in a companion spirit, by Gabriel Piterberg.[61] By 1906, the Bund – founded in Vilna in 1897, the year of the first Zionist Congress – had achieved a Russian membership of over 40,000.[62] Zionism, like antisemitism, was neither primordial nor inevitable. It had a history. There were alternatives.

The trace of Judaeophobia that Zionism and antisemitism together brought to the racialisation of Jewish people was the desirability of their exclusion from Europe. As a distinctly nineteenth-century discourse, however, Zionism framed this exclusion in a new way. In preference to the traditional alternatives of either confining Jews to bounded spaces within or expelling them to boundless space without, Zionism provided for a bounded space without. The basis on which Zionism asserted its charter to this colonial space was also new, the doctrine of race. Race set Jews apart at the same time as it delineated their nationhood, a concept that presupposed a territorial complement. In aspiring to export its racial monolith, Zionism did not seek to undo antisemitism. It did not aspire to a race-free or a multiracial society. Rather it retained the racial topography that it shared with antisemitism and sought to project it, structurally intact, to another country. Accordingly, when we move, in later chapters, to the colonisation of Palestine, we shall follow Zionism's staging of an unacknowledged return: its projection of metropolitan racial discourse back out onto the colonial world.

As we shall see, the regime of race that Zionism sought to impose in Palestine retained and redirected the Judaeophobic trace – the project of exclusion – that Zionism shared with antisemitism in Europe. Yet continuity is not identity. Having arrived in Palestine, Zionism confronted different historical conditions, including the challenge presented to its monolithic racial topography by Arab-Jews. These conditions prompted new discursive strategies as Zionism shifted from being a derivative response to racial dominance within Europe to itself exercising racial

---

61 'For groups such as the Bund ... or for liberal religious [Jewish] groups, a denial of migration as a means for solving key problems of Jewish life was a central element of their self-definition.' Shaul Stampfer, 'The Geographic Background of East European Jewish Migration to the United States before World War I', in Ira A. Glazier and Luigi De Rosa (eds), *Migration across Time and Nations: Population Mobility in Historical Contexts* (New York: Holmes and Meier, 1986), 221. For the Bund, see Henry J. Tobias, *The Jewish Bund in Russia from Its Origins to 1905* (Stanford: Stanford UP, 1972). For Lazare, see Arendt, 'The Jew as Pariah: A hidden tradition', in Arendt, *Jewish Writings*, 283–97; Arendt, 'Herzl and Lazare', in ibid., 338–42; Piterberg, *Returns of Zionism*, 1–50. For a number of less explicitly Judaeocentric alternatives (including those of Eduard Bernstein and Rosa Luxemburg), see Adam M. Weisberger, *The Jewish Ethic and the Spirit of Socialism* (New York: Peter Lang, 1997).

62 Steven Cassedy, *To the Other Shore: The Russian Jewish Intellectuals Who Came to America* (Princeton: Princeton UP, 1997), 54.

dominance outside Europe. Accordingly, the regime of race that Zionism has sought to construct in Palestine/Israel is related to but distinct from antisemitism, and will be discussed separately. An understanding of the emergence of antisemitism within Europe does not depend upon it.

Having noted a number of ways in which antisemitism in Europe corresponded to the Jim Crow regime in the USA, we might add that the Black experience in the USA also gave rise to separatist initiatives whereby Black thinkers envisaged the removal of their people to external locations. Examples include the nineteenth-century Colonization Movement (insofar as it was supported by Black people) and Marcus Garvey's much more significant twentieth-century Universal Negro Improvement Association.[63]

Garvey's movement did not seek emigration in order to replace Black people already living in a target destination, but to unite with them under the overarching principle of Africa. Nonetheless, in a manner at least partly reminiscent of Zionism, Garvey's movement more or less accepted White supremacism's binary racial topography.[64] The same cannot be said for the relationship between Garvey's racial classifications and those operating in Brazil, where Blackness is conspicuous – or inconspicuous – on account of its submersion beneath a baroque profusion of colour classifications that could hardly be less binary. In shifting to Brazil, therefore, we shift from a situation in which the racialisation of a group of White people in Europe shares ground with the racialisation of Black people in the USA, to a situation in which the racialisation of Black people in another part of America is altogether different from the racialisation of Black people in the USA. Again, therefore, colour is not the issue.

---

63 For the Colonization Movement, see, e.g., Emma J. Lapsanskey-Werner and Margaret Hope Bacon (eds), *Back to Africa: Benjamin Coates and the Colonization Movement in America, 1848–1880* (Pennsylvania: Pennsylvania UP, 2005). For Garvey, see, e.g., Marcus Garvey, *The Philosophy and Opinions of Marcus Garvey, or Africa for the Africans* (Amy Jacques-Garvey, ed., Dover: Majority Press, 1986); Ibrahim K. Sundiata, *Brothers and Strangers: Black Zion, Black Slavery, 1914–1940* (Durham: Duke UP, 2003).

64 As is notorious, Garvey was less inclined than White supremacists to include lighter-complexioned Black people in the African American category, a perspective that may have reflected his West Indian background: 'I had promised not to waste much more of the space of the *Negro World* on the cross-breed Dutch-French-Negro editor of the *Crisis* [W.E.B. Du Bois], the official organ of the National Association of the Advancement of "Certain" People', Garvey in *Negro World* on 10 May 1924, quoted in Tony Martin, *Race First: The Ideological and Organizational Struggles of Marcus Garvey and the Universal Negro Improvement Association* (Westport: Greenwood Press, 1976), 273.

CHAPTER FOUR

Whoever Says Brazil Says Angola

Africans, Natives and Colour in Brazil

Compare the hard and fast polarity of the one-drop rule, or Australia's one-way racial attrition, with the extravagance of Brazilian[1] colour classifications (Fig. 4).

---

branco, preto, moreno claro, moreno escuro, mulato, moreno, mulato claro, mulato escuro, negro, caboclo, escuro, cabo verde, claro, araçuaba, roxo, amarelo, sarará escuro, côr de canela, preto claro, roxo claro, côr de cinza, vermelho, caboclo escuro, pardo, branco sarará, mambebe, branco caboclado, moreno escuro, mulato sarará, gazula, côr de cinza clara, creolo, louro, moreno claro, caboclado, mulato bem claro, branco mulato, roxo de cabelo bom, preto escuro, pelé

Fig. 4

If ever there was a worthy challenge to class analysis, this system surely offers it. Truly baroque in its excess, it would seem to explode any limit to ethnic differentiation. While it should be acknowledged that many of these terms are neither widely distributed nor regularly used, this list is by no any means comprehensive (Marvin Harris's most extensive compilation included nearly 500 terms). The point is not the particular details of the system, however, but its extraordinary plurality, remarkable even by the standards of Louisiana, Mexico or Jamaica.[2] Through

---

1 Brazil has never been homogeneous. Many scholars have overlooked the substantial differences between the different types of slavery obtaining in different regions (Bahia, Minas Gerais, etc.), different industries (sugar, mining, coffee, domestic slavery, etc.), and between town and country. The following analysis has specific reference to the sugar industry in Bahia, which was Gilberto Freyre's focus and the cradle of the Atlantic slave trade. Thus 'Brazil' always includes that local industry, and sometimes, but not always, includes others.

2 Diamond and Cottrol, 'Codfying Caste'; Domínguez, *White by Definition*; J. Jorge Klor de Alva, 'The Postcolonization of the (Latin) American Experience: A

all this plurality, it is noticeable that the relatively few terms referring to Natives (derivatives of Caboclo, Indian/White) reduce Indigeneity to the quality of colour along a spectrum of Black and White.[3] In this regard, the Brazilian system compares with the one-drop rule, which likewise contributes to Native elimination while excluding African Americans. C. R. Boxer's comment on the contrast between the assimilability of Indian ancestry and the exclusion of African descent in eighteenth-century Brazil could well have sounded familiar in the twentieth-century USA: 'Colonial legislation discriminated against persons with an infusion of Negro blood much more than it did against Mamelucos, Caboclos, and other examples of cross-breeding between Whites and Amerindians.'[4] In the Brazilian case, however, rather than racialising the descendants of the enslaved in a binary fashion, the colour chart operates to suppress any suggestion of a binarism of Black and White. Rather than a polarity, the Brazilian scheme is a carnival of interstices.

The way that this system so spectacularly abjures binarism has sustained a misleading historiography of slavery and race relations in Brazil. The inspiration for this stemmed principally from Gilberto Freyre, historian to the Brazilian establishment, whose *Casa-Grande and Senzala*, originally published in Portuguese in 1933 (appearing in English translation as *The Masters and the Slaves* in 1946), fostered the myth that the Portuguese had been relatively benign slavers. Freyre's claims inspired a number of American historians – in particular Frank Tannenbaum, Stanley Elkins and, to a lesser extent, Winthrop Jordan – to assert that Brazilian slavery had been milder than the North American variant because, whereas Iberians in the New World were familiar with slavery, which had been codified and regulated in a passably humane manner

Reconsideration of "Colonialism", "Postcolonialism", and "Mestizaje"', in Gyan Prakash (ed.), *After Colonialism: Imperial Histories and Postcolonial Displacements* (Princeton: Princeton UP, 1995), 241–75.

3   There is no authoritative schedule. This is Harris and Kotak's list, which I cite here because it was elicited with some system. Marvin Harris and Conrad Kotak, 'The Structural Significance of Brazilian Categories', *Sociologica* 25 (1963), 203 n. Harris subsequently listed the twelve terms most commonly employed in his survey, 'each of which occurred more than one hundred times', none of which referred to Indigeneity: *moreno, branco, mulato, preto, negro, alvo, moreno-claro, cabo verde, claro, sarará, escurinho, escuro.* Marvin Harris, 'Referential Ambiguity in the Calculus of Brazilian Racial Identity', in Norman E. Whitten, Jr. and John F. Szwed (eds), *Afro-American Anthropology: Contemporary Perspectives* (New York: The Free Press, 1970), 77. 'More than 300 terms are employed in Brazil to distinguish the immense variety of racial types, in a manner enabling individuals' social status to be determined on the basis of their features, their education and manners, income, occupation, personality, which contrasts starkly [*nitidamente*] with countries where Blacks and Mestizos are indiscriminately labelled "Negros".' Thales de Azevedo, *Democracia Racial: Ideologia e realidade* (Petrópolis: Editora Vozes, 1975), 28–9.

4   C. R. Boxer, *Race Relations in the Portuguese Colonial Empire, 1415–1825* (Oxford: Clarendon Press, 1963), 116.

derived from Roman Law and filtered through the Catholic church, slavery had not been institutionalised in England for centuries and so there existed no rules to regulate the practice and restrain its excesses.[5]

The relatively high incidence of manumission was central to this culturalist apology for Brazilian slavers. Brazil's complex system of ethnic classification testified to the system's alleged mildness, since it indicated that, rather than a rigorously polarised society that ruthlessly distinguished between master and slave, the Portuguese had presided over an integrated polity in which manumission had been commonplace and people could move up and down the hierarchy with relative ease.[6] So far as the Portuguese are concerned – and without holding any brief for Anglo-American slavers – little could be further from the truth.

Slaves and Natives

Though slaves ceased to be imported into the United States around the end of the eighteenth century, this did not greatly affect the system of slavery there, since slaves could and did reproduce themselves, to the extent that slave numbers grew in the nineteenth-century South. In Brazil, on the other hand, there was no pretence of endogenous increase. Rather, slaves were constantly replaced with fresh imports from Africa.[7]

---

5 Gilberto Freyre, *The Masters and the Slaves: A Study in the Development of Brazilian Civilization* (Samuel Putnam, trans., Berkeley: California UP, 1986); Frank Tannenbaum, *Slave and Citizen: The Negro in the Americas* (New York: Knopf, 1946); Stanley M. Elkins, *Slavery: A Problem in American Institutional and Intellectual Life* (Chicago: Chicago UP, 1959); Winthrop Jordan, 'Unthinking Decision: Enslavement of Negroes in America to 1700', in Breen, *Shaping Southern Society*. Toynbee's claim that 'race feeling' in the contemporary West had no precedent in mediaeval Europe, which included colonising Spain and Portugal but not colonising England, bears marked similarities to the Freyre/Tannenbaum thesis but does not appear to have influenced its formulation. Arnold Toynbee, *A Study of History* (Oxford: Oxford UP, 1934), vol. 1, 223–5. See also de Azevedo, *Democracia Racial*, 28–30.

6 'Portuguese colonization produced a fluid structure, making possible the transmutation from class to class, from race to race, and producing a new biological type, and new values in human beauty ... In Brazil and Spanish America the law, the church, and custom put few impediments in the way of vertical mobility of race and class, and in some measure favored it. In the British, French, and United States slave systems the law attempted to fix the pattern and stratify the social classes and the racial groups.' Tannenbaum, *Slave and Citizen*, 119–20, 127.

7 'Throughout the entire four-century history of the Atlantic slave trade the United States [including British North America] imported only 400,000 slaves. Yet, by 1860 there were over 4,000,000 slaves in the United States. Brazil, on the other hand, imported close to 3,600,000 slaves over this same period, yet there were only 1,500,000 slaves in Brazil in 1872.' Thomas W. Merrick and Douglas H. Graham, *Population and Economic Development in Brazil: 1800 to the Present* (Baltimore: Johns Hopkins UP, 1979), 56. The classic account of Atlantic slave trade demography, whose findings have been modified by subsequent research, is Philip D. Curtin, *The Atlantic Slave Trade: A Census* (Madison: Wisconsin UP, 1969). See also Blackburn, *The Making*,

The importation continued until the early 1850s, when the British finally terminated it by means of a naval blockade, whereupon Brazilian slavery began to break down.[8] While estimates continue to vary as to the precise numbers involved in the negative demographic regime whereby high death and low fertility rates coincided with constant resupplies from Africa, few would now quarrel with Stuart Schwartz's characterisation of the adult mortality and general fertility rates among slaves in eighteenth-century Brazil as 'staggering ... far worse than recorded in other slave regimes'.[9]

The negative demographic regime also applied to Brazilian Natives, whose numbers declined dramatically in the wake of the Portuguese invasion.[10] We should not take this decline for granted, as a kind of collateral damage resulting from the plantation economy. Native people in Brazil were targeted for elimination as systematically as their counterparts in Australia. In contrast to Aborigines' unrivalled centrality to the historiography of race in Australia, however, Natives have been marginalised in histories of race relations in Brazil, which have overwhelmingly concentrated on the enslavement of Africans in Brazil and its aftermath. It is as if the two nightmares are separate stories, with Natives apparently subjected to a relatively short period of slavery and abuse before a

---

460; Davis, *Problem of Slavery in Western Culture*, 232–3; Celso Furtado, *The Economic Growth of Brazil: A Survey from Colonial to Modern Times* (R. W. de Aguiar and E. C. Drysdale, trans., Berkeley: California UP, 1971), 127–8; de Azevedo, *Democracia Racial*, 14–16. In this connection, it might be noted that the free Black population in Brazil was able to reproduce itself: George Reid Andrews, *Slavery and Race Relations in Brazil* (Albuquerque: University of New Mexico Latin American Institute, 1997), 7.

8   Though Brazilian slaves were not to be emancipated until 1888, the combination of the curtailment of the trade from Africa, which had ceased altogether by 1853, and the effects of the law of 1871, whereby the condition of slavery was no longer transmitted to offspring, meant, in the words of Richard Graham, that 'no new slaves would be available either from Africa or from procreation [i.e., from either importation or local birth].' Graham, 'Action and Ideas in the Abolitionist Movement', 63.

9   The term 'negative demographic regime' comes from Stuart B. Schwartz (*Slaves, Peasants, and Rebels: Reconsidering Brazilian Slavery* [Urbana: Illinois UP, 1992], 11). The quotation comes from Schwartz, *Sugar Plantations in the Formation of Brazilian Society: Bahia, 1550–1835* (Cambridge: Cambridge UP, 1985), 373.

10   On Gomes's estimate, Brazil's Indian population, having fallen from around 5 million in 1500 to around 120,000 in 1955, stood at around 250,000 in 2000: Mercio P. Gomes, *The Indians and Brazil* (John W. Moon, trans., Gainesville: Florida UP, 2000), 249, Appendix B. 'Since the 1950s ... a dramatic resurgence in Brazil's indigenous population, by some estimates an increase of 300 per cent, can be attributed in large measure to people once classified as pardos now identifying themselves as natives, claiming or reclaiming a native past.' Stuart B. Schwartz and Hal Langfur, 'Tapanhuas, Negros da Terra, and Curibacas: Common Cause and Confrontation between Blacks and Natives in Colonial Brazil', in Matthew Restall (ed.), *Beyond Black and Red: African-Native Relations in Colonial Latin America* (Albuquerque: New Mexico UP, 2005), 106. See also Jonathan W. Warren, *Racial Revolutions: Antiracism and Native Resurgence in Brazil* (Durham: Duke UP, 2001), especially chapter 1.

combination of disease, legislation and missionary sequestration effectively takes them out of the picture, apart from occasional reappearances as slave-catchers (a legacy that has underlain tensions between Indigenous people and African Brazilians).

To this extent, race historiography on Brazil has participated in its own object, recapitulating in narrative form the elimination of Indigenous Brazilians. This representational complicity persists in the present-day marginalisation of the elimination of Amazon communities, whose contemporary dispossession appears no less disconnected from mainstream historiography on race in Brazil than their rainforest homelands appear disconnected from the rest of the world. Nonetheless, in comparison to Native Brazilians outside the Amazon region, who lack the rainforest communities' first-world environmentalist cachet, Amazon Natives have succeeded in attracting an impressive degree of international support.[11]

The catastrophic attrition of Natives in Brazil raises the fundamental question of why the Portuguese took Africans there at all. Unlike the Australian case, where the aim of the programme of Aboriginal elimination was, and is, their replacement by a White majority; and unlike the case of the United States, where (with the short-lived exceptions we noted in Georgia and South Carolina), slaves constituted a numerical minority, Indigenous Brazilians were demographically overwhelmed by a majority who were not themselves the conquerors: the millions of enslaved Africans who, by the late sixteenth century, had all but supplanted enslaved Native labour in the Brazilian colonial economy. Thus the racial regime in Brazil presents a distinctive configuration. In addition to the elimination of Indigenous people, it was structured to accommodate a Portuguese minority's coercion of the African majority who were being imported to replace them. As we are seeing throughout this book, subjugated populations are racialised in distinct but complementary ways that together sustain the overall dominance of European colonisers.

Schwartz – who, to his credit, has documented the central role played by Natives in the establishment of the Portuguese plantation economy – tracks the replacement of Natives by Africans in seventeenth-century Bahia.[12] In contrast to the English in North America, as Schwartz

---

11 One example is Survival International ('the movement for tribal peoples'), which has an unfortunate tendency to romanticisation. See survivalinternational.org.

12 'The transition of the labor force from Indians to Africans took place slowly over a period of about half a century [the second half of the sixteenth]', Stuart B. Schwartz, 'A Commonwealth within Itself: The Early Brazilian Sugar Industry, 1550–1670', in Schwartz (ed.), *Tropical Babylons: Sugar and the Making of the Atlantic World, 1450–1680* (Chapel Hill: North Carolina UP, 2004), 188–9. See also Schwartz, 'Indian Labor and New World Plantations: European Demand and Indian Responses in Northeastern Brazil', *American Historical Review* 8 (1978), 43–79; Schwartz, *Sugar Plantations*, 35–72.

demonstrates, the Portuguese succeeded in staffing Brazilian plantations with Native labour. As in other settler colonies, the effects of European diseases made reliance on Native labour problematic for plantation owners, to which, in the case of Brazil, we should add the difficulty presented by the alternative to plantation life that was offered by Jesuit missions. Yet Portuguese plantations in Brazil had managed to remain reasonably profitable before embarking on the wholesale replacement of Natives with African imports.

In this regard, it is significant that they were not the only Iberians to enslave South American Natives. At the same time, enslaved Natives were furnishing the Spanish with the precious metals that their American project was fixatedly devoted to securing. In the absence of precious minerals in Brazil (prior to their industry-scale exploitation in the eighteenth century), Portugal established a production economy with a view, at least in part, to defending its possessions there from the ambitions of European rivals.[13] The same consideration also operated in favour of importing Africans, an activity that underwrote Portugal's maintenance of a maritime presence in the region. Moreover, so far as missionaries were concerned, Africa was a lost cause – lost, that is, to Islam, as well as being unpenetrated by Europeans – so missionary objections to the enslavement of beings created by God in His image tended not to extend to those He had chosen to create in Africa. As Harris argued, Africans could conveniently be enslaved in place of the Natives whose confinement enabled Jesuits to proselytise them.[14] Iberian Muslims had ceased to be an option after the *Reconquista*, completed a few months before Columbus set off on his first voyage, while Ottoman suzerainty had closed off the supply of Balkan peoples whose very name designated the condition of slavery.

All these considerations played a part, and it would be misleading in the extreme to seek to reduce the situation to a single cause. As a factor that was critical rather than exclusive, therefore, we can focus on the asymmetry of the sugar trade. Like wool from Australia, sugar only accounts for Portuguese voyages out from the colony. The African slave trade operated inwards, the indispensable fulfilment of profitable voyaging. What else could you keep on taking to Brazil?

The life and death statistics of Brazilian slavery are not only staggering on humanitarian grounds. American slavery as a whole is egregious on those grounds, so comparisons are idle. Rather, Brazilian slavery's internal failure to reproduce itself makes no sense at all in terms of the economic logic of slavers in the United States. Whereas the lives of North

---

13 Furtado, *Economic Growth of Brazil*, 3–5.
14 Marvin Harris, *Patterns of Race in the Americas* (New York: Norton, 1964), 16–17.

American slaves represented a valuable commodity to their masters and were thus carefully – albeit not kindly – preserved, Africans who were enslaved onto Brazilian plantations could expect radically truncated lives unless they were manumitted.[15] In some respects – again going by the logic of slavers in the United States – it was as if Brazilian slavers deliberately harmed their own interests in treating their human property so negligently. This not only applies to the apparently casual squandering of slave lives. So far as the reproduction of those lives was concerned – reproduction being the core concern of any economic system – Brazilian slavery consistently produced a demographic imbalance in favour of adult males, to the relative exclusion of both reproducers – women – and the reproduced – children. Yet Brazilian slavery had been established for a century before the British first brought enslaved Africans to North America, and it outlived United States slavery by a quarter of a century; so it cannot have been altogether illogical. We should therefore distinguish between the reproduction of enslaved people and the reproduction of a system of slavery.

To appreciate the logic of a given system of slavery, we should look further than its capacity to reproduce itself, a purpose for which a convergence of biology and politics will suffice. We also need to chart the ways in which a system of slavery needs to reproduce the enabling conditions whereby it can go on reproducing itself in future generations, conditions that are not necessarily local or internal to it.[16] In the United States, these conditions were locally determined, so, as observed, slavery could survive the ending of the slave trade. Slavery's demise in the United States resulted from the failure of its political warrant, a process to which biology was incidental. In Brazil, by contrast, it was the politics that were incidental, while the role of biology was not (or was much less) local. New slaves were disproportionately produced in Africa, making Brazilian

---

15 Contemporary accounts put eighteenth-century Brazilian slave life expectancy at between seven and fifteen years: C. R. Boxer, *The Golden Age of Brazil, 1695–1750: Growing Pains of a Colonial Society* (Berkeley: California UP, 1969), 174; Robert Edgar Conrad, *World of Sorrow: The African Slave Trade to Brazil* (Baton Rouge: Louisiana State UP, 1986), 17. Such estimates have been qualified by Emilia Viotti da Costa, *The Brazilian Empire: Myths and Histories* (Chicago: Chicago UP, 1985), 134–5, and challenged, though for the era succeeding the termination of the slave trade in 1851, by Robert Slenes, *The Demography and Economics of Brazilian Slavery, 1850–1888* (PhD diss., Stanford University, 1976), 370.

16 A point eventually arrived at, in the context of sustained debate, by Claude Meillassoux, *Maidens, Meal, and Money: Capitalism and the Domestic Community* (Cambridge: Cambridge UP, 1981). For some of the lead-up, see also Emmanuel Terray, 'Classes and Class Consciousness in the Abron Kingdom of Gyaman', in Maurice Bloch (ed.), *Marxist Analyses and Social Anthropology* (London: Malaby, 1975), 85–135; George Dupré and Pierre Philippe Rey, 'Reflections on the Pertinence of a Theory of the History of Exchange', in Harold Wolpe (ed.), *The Articulation of Modes of Production* (London: Routledge & Kegan Paul, 1980), 128–60.

slavery vulnerable to the ending of the slave trade. Once that finally came about, in 1850, slavery began to break down (and planters began to treat their slaves more considerately[17]).

Furthermore, the politics involved in slavery's demise were much less spectacular in Brazil, which did not experience a civil war, than they had been in the United States. In order to understand how Brazilian slavers sought to reproduce the conditions whereby their system could go on reproducing itself in the future, therefore, we should not assume the Anglophone distinction between the practice of slavery and the slave trade. Brazilian slavery was instead an integrated coordination of the two. Once we recognise the Brazilian system as an ongoing transatlantic process – as the saying went, 'whoever says sugar says Brazil and whoever says Brazil says Angola'[18] – we begin to understand its operative logic, which was different from that of slavery in the United States. In the process, we also begin to understand how it was that Brazilian slavery escaped so lightly in political terms, with abolition taking place relatively bloodlessly.

Slavery and Empire

In its Portuguese-imperial origins, there were various reasons for Brazilian slavery's comparatively high expenditure of human resources. In the first place, the voyage from West Africa to Bahia was considerably – almost 50 per cent – shorter than the one to North America, making it much cheaper to ship Africans to Brazil[19] (Fig. 5). Since the Portuguese controlled both ends of the Brazil slave trade, there were fewer middlemen and levies to be factored into the price paid by purchasers. The Portuguese did, however, impose per capita levies on both Angolan exports and Brazilian imports, which encouraged maximising cargoes so as to reduce the shipping portion of the 'item' price.[20] The price of

---

17 '[L]iving conditions seem to have improved after the abolition of the slave trade in 1850, when the price of slaves increased and slaveowners became more concerned with keeping their slaves in good health. In the twenty years from 1855 to 1875, slave prices almost trebled.' Viotti da Costa, *Brazilian Empire*, 144.

18 This 'famous phrase of Padre António Vieira ... was actually a common expression'. Schwartz, *Sugar Plantations*, 339.

19 Blackburn, *The Making*, 170. The journey from Angola to Bahia took up to forty days: José Honório Rodrigues, 'The Influence of Africa on Brazil and of Brazil on Africa', *Journal of African History* 3 (1962), 55. Journeys to the Caribbean or North America took two months: Herbert Klein, 'The Atlantic Slave Trade to 1650', in Schwartz, *Tropical Babylons*, 228 (where the Bahia journey is estimated at one month).

20 Luiz Felipe de Alencastro, 'The apprenticeship of colonization', in Barbara L. Solow (ed.), *Slavery and the Rise of the Atlantic System* (Cambridge: Cambridge UP/ Harvard Du Bois Institute, 1991), 167–8; Joseph C. Miller, 'Some Aspects of the Commercial Organization of Slaving at Luanda, Angola, 1760–1830', in Henry A. Gemery and Jan S. Hogendorn (eds), *The Uncommon Market: Essays in the Economic*

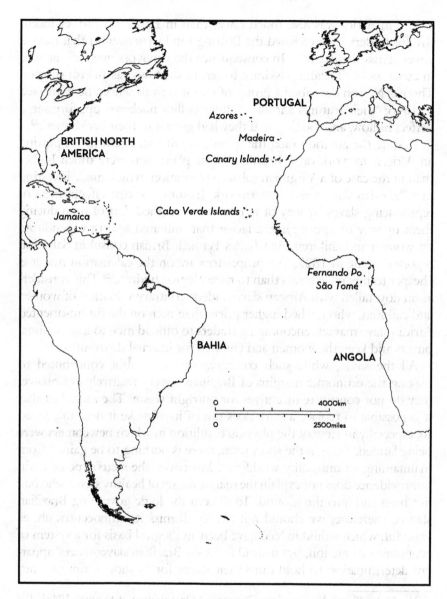

Fig. 5

History of the Atlantic Slave Trade (New York: Academic Press, 1979), 105; Hugh
Thomas, *The Slave Trade: A History of the Atlantic Slave Trade, 1440–1870* (London:
Picador, 1997), 541. Eric Williams cites what would seem to be a limiting case of the
itemisation of human beings: 'One meeting of the two sovereigns of Spain and Portugal
was held in 1701 to discuss the arithmetical problem posed by a contract for ten thou-
sand "tons" of Negroes granted the Portuguese.' Williams, *Capitalism & Slavery*, 39.

a slave in Africa was also much lower than in Brazil,[21] a further incentive for traders to overcrowd the floating tombs (*tumbeiros*) that carried slaves across the Atlantic. In consequence the survivors generally arrived in extremes of ill health – 'skinny, tottering shadows', as British surgeon Thomas Nelson described a group of recent arrivals whom he witnessed in 1846; 'their features shrunk ... their bellies puckered up, forming a perfect hollow, and looking as if they had grown to their backbones'.[22]

Despite the attrition rate, the immediate financial returns on putting an African to work on a Brazilian sugar plantation were much higher than in the case of a Virginian tobacco plantation, which made investing in a Brazilian slave a shorter-term risk. In sum, the cost-effectiveness of reproducing slaves by way of purchase outweighed that of reproducing them by way of upbringing, a factor that militated against expenditure on women and children. As Charles Pennell, British consul in Salvador, reported home in 1827, 'the proprietors act on the calculation that it is cheaper to buy male slaves than to raise Negro children.'[23] This consideration dovetailed with African slave traders' contrary valuation of women and children, who fetched higher prices than men on the future-oriented African slave market, encouraging traders to offload men to international buyers and keep the women and children for internal distribution.[24]

All the same, while such considerations no doubt contributed to making the economic margins of Brazilian slavery relatively permissive, they do not constitute incentives for outright waste. The mere fact that it is possible to replace a slave does not of itself make it desirable to do so, especially in view of the physical condition in which newcomers were being landed. Even in the short term, there is nothing to be gained from maintaining an unhealthy workforce. Moreover, the stereotype of Latin improvidence does not explain the manumitting of healthy slaves who had not been run into the ground. To discern the logic governing Brazilian slavery, therefore, we should not simply dismiss it, ethnocentrically, as wasteful, which would indeed have been an illogical basis for a system of economic production, but instead focus on Brazilian slaveowners' apparent determination to hold onto their slaves for as short a time as they

---

21   Miller, 'Some Aspects of the Commercial Organization of Slaving', 104–5. For the economics of the Portuguese Atlantic slave trade generally, see Joseph C. Miller, *Way of Death: Merchant Capitalism and the Angolan Slave Trade, 1730–1830* (Madison: Wisconsin UP, 1988).

22   In addition to *túmulos flutuantes* (floating tombs), slave ships were known as *tumbeiros* (tomb- or pall-bearers), a term that 'also referred to those in Africa who hunted or bought slaves and who marched them to the coast.' Conrad, *World of Sorrow*, 4, n. Nelson quoted on p. 16.

23   Quoted in Schwartz, *Sugar Plantations*, 365.

24   Kátia M. de Queirós Mattoso, 'Slave, Free, and Freed Family Structures in Nineteenth-Century Salvador, Bahia', *Luso-Brazilian Review* 25 (1988), 83 (quoting João José Reis).

could.[25] Externally, this concern takes us out beyond the hemispheric interchange between Brazil and Africa to the global context of Portugal's maritime empire as a whole, while, internally, the same concern takes us to the remarkable depoliticisation of slavery in Brazilian society. As we shall see, for all its deceptive simplicity, the logic of a fast turnover in slaves simultaneously contributed both to the maintenance of an international mercantile system and to the safeguarding of planter hegemony in Brazilian national culture. Thus its longevity is not surprising.

The mercantile and the maritime characteristics of Portugal's global empire were two sides of the one coin of metropolitan demography. In contrast to England, Portugal did not enclose pasturage. A rural population was not driven off the land and into burgeoning industrial cities to negotiate the alternatives of proletarian wage-labour or lumpenproletarian unemployment. Crucially, therefore, Portugal did not develop the giddy-multitude style of population surplus that Britain would export to settler colonies in North America and Australia.[26] If anything, the reverse was the case, with Portuguese officials worrying that the deployment overseas of imperial functionaries could leave the kingdom vulnerable at home. As the Jesuit António Vieira exclaimed: 'Where are our men? Upon every alarm in Alentejo it is necessary to take students from the university, tradesmen from their shops, labourers from the plough!'[27]

Thus Portugal's imperial project came to be staffed by a minimal contingent of Portuguese people, a requirement conducive to a colonialism of the surfaces that placed a premium on confining mercantile activity to coastal exchanges.[28] Portuguese imperialists operated at the edges, preferring to delegate production of the commodities in which they traded – the spice-harvesting, the silk- and cotton-growing, the slave-hunting, the timber-felling – to local management.[29] In the main, the value that Portuguese traders added to their commodities was achieved by shipping them from coast to coast. In this regard, being both reproductive and territorially settled, Brazil's plantation economy constituted something

---

25 The idea that Brazilian slavery failed through waste, neglect and improvidence is a commonplace of the Anglophone literature, which generally takes for granted North-American criteria for 'success'. See, e.g., Conrad, *World of Sorrow*, 7–15 ('Why the Slave Population in Brazil Could Not Renew Itself').

26 Furtado, *Economic Growth of Brazil*, 21.

27 Harris, *Patterns of Race in the Americas*, 82.

28 A. H. de Oliveira Marques, *History of Portugal*, vol. 2, *From Empire to Corporate State* (New York: Columbia UP, 1972), 80–1; A. J. R. Russell-Wood, 'The Ebb and Flow of Commodities', in Russell-Wood, *A World on the Move: The Portuguese in Africa, Asia, and America, 1415–1808* (New York: St Martin's, 1992), 123–47.

29 'As early as the beginning of the sixteenth century, royal revenue deriving from overseas commerce (African gold, slaves and spices; Asian spices brought by the Cape route; and Atlantic island sugar, dyes and cotton) comprised no less than two-thirds of the [Portuguese] Crown's total income.' Blackburn, *The Making*, 114.

of an exception within the Portuguese maritime empire. Nonetheless, it was not exceptional in its minimisation of Portuguese personnel. In a further, decisive and related regard, however, Portugal's Brazil operation was altogether exceptional. Sugar is not indigenous to Brazil. The Portuguese had to take it there. This basic consideration is crucial to understanding Brazilian slavery.

We should not assume that the Portuguese had any particular commitment to sugar as a substance. On the other hand, there is no question that they had a commitment to Africans as a commodity. Apart from real ivory, slaves – 'black ivory' – were just about all that West African merchants had to exchange for trade items that Portuguese navigators were extremely keen to sell to them.[30] As a result, underpopulated Portugal acquired a chronic surplus of slaves whom its domestic economy could not support. This surplus would become a potent preaccumulation. To provide an outlet for excess slaves acquired in the course of opening up African markets, Portugal supplied slaves to Spain for its New World colonies and established the sugar plantations on the Atlantic islands of São Tomé and Fernando Po from which the Brazilian industry would be developed.[31] These islands (along with Madeira and Cabo Verde) had yet to reach their absorptive capacity by the time Columbus returned with news of territory even further to the west, but the possibility was opened up. By 1532, it seems, African slaves were already in Brazil.[32] By the end of the sixteenth century, enslaved Africans had replaced Natives as the engine driving Brazilian sugar.[33]

Thus it is misleading to assume, as many have, that the Portuguese wished to grow sugar in the New World and this prompted a requirement for slaves, Indigenous or otherwise, to grow it. As Fernando Novais argued over forty years ago, with the expansion of the Atlantic-island sugar industry reaching its limits, the Portuguese required another destination to which they could export slaves, and sugar provided the requisite outlet for the labour of those slaves.[34] Slaves need something to

---

30   'Angola exported practically nothing besides Bantu slaves and elephants' tusks – "black" and "white" ivory in other words.' Boxer, *The Golden Age of Brazil*, 25.

31   Franklin W. Knight, 'Slavery and lagging capitalism in the Spanish and Portuguese American empires, 1492–1713', in Solow, *Slavery and the Rise of the Atlantic System*, 69; Blackburn, *The Making*, 117.

32   A. J. R. Russell-Wood, 'Iberian Expansion and the Issue of Black Slavery: Changing Portuguese Attitudes, 1440–1770', *American Historical Review* 83 (1978), 33.

33   Stuart B. Schwartz, 'Indian Labor and New World Plantations: European Demand and Indian Responses in Northeastern Brazil', *American Historical Review* 8 (1978), 43–79; Schwartz, *Sugar Plantations*, 35–72.

34   Fernando Novais, *Estrutura e Dinâmica do Antigo Sistema Colonial (Séculos XVI–XVIII)* (São Paulo: Centro brasileiro de análise e planejamento [CEBRAP], 1974), 23–32, where Novais developed analyses by Eric Williams and by Caio Prado, Jr.

work on. The sugar sustained the slavery, not the other way around.[35] It did not have to be sugar, but it did have to be slaves.

We need to be rigorous in following through the implications of the commodification of human beings. Instead of talking, in the manner conventional to comparative slavery studies, of slaves in the sugar industry as distinct from, say, slaves in the rice industry or slaves in the cotton industry, we might do better – at least, where the Portuguese are concerned – to talk of sugar, rice or cotton in the slave industry.[36] To do so involves looking further than the immediate site at which slave labour is exploited and out to the structure and pricing of the wider economy in which this particular exploitation participated. From this perspective, we can ask potentially revealing questions – how, for instance, did the price discrepancy between a purchase in Angola and a sale in Bahia come to be so marked? We can also dispense with counterfactual speculations of the type favoured by Robert Conrad among others, as to what would have happened 'if African slaves reaching Brazil had lived a normal span of years' – a non-occurrence that makes it obvious for Conrad that 'the need for rapid replacement would have been less compelling, and the volume of traffic would therefore have been smaller.'[37]

With the full implications of human commodification at the centre of our thinking, we can begin to account for the high turnover of slaves in Brazil in terms of the system's own logic. We can also contextualise the bias in favour of importing Africans rather than enslaving Natives, a growing preference that was not only a response to disease. Here too, the elimination of Natives harmonised with the exploitation of imported labour. Native superfluity was a consequence of the commitment to African slavery. To track down the systemic motivation for such phenomena, we should put aside ethnocentric assumptions born of the rationality associated with slavery in the United States, and think in

---

35 While endorsing (and learning from) Luiz Felipe de Alencastro's system-wide analysis of the dispensability that the surplus of slaves occasioned, I question the priorities in his section heading, 'The slave trade as an instrument of colonial policy'. Without simply reversing that priority, I think that Alencastro's section understates the extent to which Portuguese colonial policy was dictated by the *sui generis* requirements of the slave trade. Alencastro, 'Apprenticeship of Colonization', 169–73. For an outright reversal ('the key to understanding African colonial slavery is the slave trade, and not the other way round'), see Lúcio Kowarick, *The Subjugation of Labour: The Constitution of Capitalism in Brazil* (Kevin Mundi, trans., Amsterdam: CEDLA, 1987), 12. The priority is, of course, systemic rather than chronological. Though slaves had worked the sugar industry in the Madeira of Columbus's childhood, he took trial sugar seedlings to Brazil in 1493 but not slaves to work them. Carl O. Sauer, *The Early Spanish Main* (Berkeley: California UP, 1966), 210–11.

36 Sugar-trade vessels from non-Portuguese ports (the Baltic, the Netherlands, Venice, subsequently England and France) were, of course, a different matter and, to that extent, qualify the argument.

37 Conrad, *World of Sorrow*, 15.

terms of the Portuguese-imperial context in which Brazilian slavery was
conducted.

In addition to Portugal's reluctance to export manpower, its domestic
economy was basically agricultural, producing little for export.[38] In relation to both these disadvantages, Portugal stood to gain from dealing in
commodities that others had produced. Thus there was strong motivation for a circulation economy in which a complex range of commodities,
including slaves, indirectly complemented one another at the level of the
whole. Political independence did not replace the ownership of this mercantile system, which imperial Brazil inherited. Nor were individual links
in the global chain independent of each other. Silk leaving Macao or
cotton leaving Goa could put African bodies on *tumbeiros*, the proceeds
of a voyage between the Pacific and Indian oceans eventually affecting
how many slaves a trader might purchase on the Atlantic coast of Africa.
Of even greater significance for the Atlantic link, overall economic
returns were a function of the entire chain. If an individual voyage failed
to return a profit, the remedy was not to repeat it but to keep sailing, and
hope to make up the deficit further down the line. Moreover, the pirated
and war-prone Atlantic was a hazardous seaway for merchant traffic, a
factor that added a heavy insurance burden.[39] On each individual voyage,
therefore, the imperative was to ship as much merchandise as possible.
African slave traders must have been pinching themselves.

As indicated, however, the logic of a fast turnover in slaves was not
only geared externally, to the needs of a maritime empire. Internally, the
same logic also sustained the political dominance of the ruling planter
class. It is the combination of these two crucial advantages that explains
the systemic value of Brazil's negative demographic regime. The link
between the two is the practice of manumission, which provided an alternative to death as a way out of slavery.

So far as the economics of slave-trade supply and demand were concerned, it made little difference which alternative applied so long as the
market for fresh slaves remained buoyant. Internally, however, it made a
big difference since, unlike dead slaves, disgruntled slaves who had been
around long enough to become savvy in the ways of planter society posed
a pressing threat from within.[40] The constant replacement of experienced

---

38   Knight, 'Slavery and Lagging Capitalism', 68.
39   Schwartz, 'A Commonwealth within Itself', 175. Herbert Klein asserts that the
leg out from America to Europe 'was the least important part of the slaving voyage',
which he depicts as bilateral and limited to slavery (with specialist ships). Klein's study
is not confined to Brazil. Moreover, he does not pursue the implications of his statement
that 'It usually took three full years to complete a voyage with a merchant needing to
sell the constantly arriving colonial goods (by which most of the slaves were paid for)
to local importers.' Klein, 'Atlantic Slave Trade to 1650', 222.
40   Cardoso asserted that planters' failure to allocate time for the peasant breach

slaves with fresh imports from Africa militated against the development of a culture of resistance among them. The prevention of slave solidarity could be achieved not only by death, which made for unproductive workers before it took place, but also by manumission, which offered planters a way to prevent the contagion of creole discontent from spreading to new arrivals. It also militated against the development of kinship networks among enslaved people.

In place of a sterile alternation between apologists who stress the manumissions while discounting the mortality rates, and critics who reciprocally discount the manumissions in favour of the deaths, we should therefore see the two features of the Brazilian system as together pre-empting the threat that slave solidarity would pose to the reproduction of a social system based on slavery.

Unity and Division

In discouraging slaves from developing the consciousness of a social group capable of acting for itself, the combination of manumission and the high slave death rate safeguarded the domestic political interests of the planter class at the same time as it served the empire-wide requirement for a constant flow of trade. The issue, then, was slave solidarity, as well it needed to be in the radically imbalanced demographic context that Portuguese colonial policy had engendered. As we have seen, that policy tailored the management of a mercantile system to the needs of a relatively underpopulated metropolis. The management of a settled, labour-intensive plantation industry was by no means tailored to the same needs. In such a precarious context of minority rule, planter unity and slave disunity were both critical.

Thus the reason why the Portuguese should have gone to such roundabout lengths to prevent the development of solidarity among its African slaves and ex-slaves is only too obvious. The Africans massively outnumbered the Portuguese, and would have had little trouble in overthrowing them if ever (or, perhaps, if only) they had set their collective mind to it.[41] That they have not done so – at least, have not mobilised a broad enough collectivity to do so successfully – is a matter of record. Accordingly, throughout Brazilian history, Blacks have consistently occupied the

---

(slaves' independent economic activity) 'risked the outbreak of some kind of rebellion.' Ciro Flamarion S. Cardoso, 'The Peasant Breach in the Slave System: New Developments in Brazil', *Luso-Brazilian Review* 25 (1988), 61.

41 As Dauril Alden observed of the disproportionate official response to the 1798 Bahia Tailors' Revolt, in relation to which no revolutionary plan was ever uncovered, Salvador was a city 'where two out of three persons were black or brown and in a captaincy where whites were outnumbered five to one.' Alden, 'Late Colonial Brazil, 1750–1808', in Bethell, *Cambridge History*, vol. 3, 656.

lowest, most impoverished and exploited positions in society. To this day, though it is a Brazilian cliché that money whitens, since there are some well-off Blacks and a larger number of poor Whites, the great majority of Blacks are poor and the great majority of the elite are White.[42] Moreover, and crucially, even this subversive observation overlooks a wider solidarity capable of incorporating Indigenous people as well as Blacks.

In 'post'colonial Brazil's nineteenth-century imperial era, the significance of the divisions that plantation society strove to impose on slaves, ex-slaves, their successors and descendants lies in the simple fact of division itself. The longer Africans survived in Brazil, the more the European minority sought to divide them up into separate juridical and ethnic categories. Thus some planters' purchasing policy was geared to Africa-born slaves, selected for the regional, linguistic, cultural and religious differences among them. Others were more ambivalent about slave creolisation. On the one hand, sharing the language and culture of slavery was seen as facilitating collective militancy, while, on the other hand, the same qualifications could be seen as conducive to planter control. As Schwartz has shown, this ambivalence manifested itself as a division between two schools of slaveholders, 'those who thought that permitting slaves to maintain their African cultures was a positive way of stimulating differences among them and thus an effective social control, and those who thought that such cultural persistence stimulated rebellion'.[43]

Thus it would seem that the concern was not so much either African birth or creolisation per se as the threat posed by homogeneity – a fear dramatically realised in the great slave revolts in Bahia, which were mobilised around a shared culture of Islam.[44] Dividing around such questions, Brazilian planters were not, however, divided to an extent comparable to the divisions they imposed on those of African descent. In times of crisis, planters of all persuasions knew only too well where their collective interest lay, and seamlessly closed ranks. Correspondingly, a great deal of effort and ingenuity went into imposing divisions on the enslaved and the formerly enslaved.[45]

---

42 See, e.g., Andrews, *Blacks and Whites*, 126–7; Peggy A. Lovell, 'Race, Gender and Development in Brazil', *Latin American Research Review* 29 (1994), 19–22, Thomas E. Skidmore, *Black into White: Race and Nationality in Brazilian Thought* (Durham: Duke UP, 1993 [1974]), 376. As Nelson do Valle Silva drily concluded, 'Summarizing our findings, we can say that we now know the cost of not being white in the Brazilian "racial democracy": about 566 cruzeiros a month in 1976.' Silva, 'Updating the Cost of Not Being White in Brazil', in Pierre-Michel Fontaine (ed.), *Race, Class, and Power in Brazil* (Los Angeles: UCLA Center for Afro-American Studies, 1985), 55.

43 Schwartz, *Sugar Plantations*, 342; 468–86.

44 João José Reis, *Slave Rebellion in Brazil: The Muslim Uprising of 1835 in Bahia* (Arthur Brakel, trans., Baltimore: Johns Hopkins UP, 1993).

45 'The slaves' potential for rebellion was contained not only by repression, but also by the rivalries and enmities that divided the slave community ... Maids, cooks, seam-

Juridically, African Brazilians were divided into slave versus free, with freed slaves in turn being divided into those born free versus those who had been manumitted (*libertos*) and, after about 1830, those who had been released from slave ships intercepted by the British (emancipados). After the passing of the 'free womb' law of 1871, children born to slave mothers but destined for freedom became known as *ingênuos*. In addition to these juridical boundaries, a range of informal social distinctions obtained: African versus creole; Black versus mulato and Caboclo, together with a regionally varied range of phenotypical oppositions.[46] Prior to the abolition of slavery, however, the distinction that dominated all others was the fundamental opposition between slavery and freedom, which formed the juridical matrix from which divisions such as those between *libertos*, *emancipados* and *ingênuos* were elaborated.

For our purposes, however, there is a significant difference between the latter two categories, which only emerged in the nineteenth century, and the category comprising *libertos* and their descendants. Neither emancipados nor *ingênuos* had been manumitted. Their juridical freedom had come about through other means. As the nineteenth century wore on, and other American slave regimes either tumbled or showed signs of doing so, Brazil evinced an increasing preparedness to contemplate alternatives to slavery, though these did not constitute alternatives to exploitation. Rather, Brazilian planters were seeking new means to the same end. An obvious strategy – one half-realised by the intercepted *emancipados* – was to continue importing fresh labour from overseas, but dropping the requirement for it to be enslaved. Such a strategy would continue to hamper the formation of solidarities between the newcomers and the existing slave population. Moreover, in an international trading context dominated by the growth of industrial capitalism, the possibility of free labour offered planters a more flexible set of options than the arthritic traditions of slavery permitted.

As Marx was incisively aware, one of the principal freedoms of 'free' labour was the freedom from burdening employers with subsistence demands between periods of productive activity.[47] Slaves, by contrast,

---

stresses, coachmen, pages, washerwomen, and nursemaids received special treatment and had greater opportunities to gain their freedom through manumission than did fieldhands.' Viotti da Costa, *Brazilian Empire*, 141. 'City police, slave hunters, regular army troops, a good part of the civilian contingent in the National Guard ... consisted of free people of color born in Brazil ... the planter class could always count on Afro-Bahians during crises created by foreigners, be they African or Portuguese.' Reis, *Slave Rebellion in Brazil*, 143.

46 See, for instance, Appendix B ('Brazilian Racial Terminology') in George Reid Andrews, *Blacks and Whites in São Paulo, Brazil, 1888–1988* (Madison: Wisconsin UP, 1991), 249–58; Harris and Kotak, 'Structural Significance of Brazilian Categories'.

47 'The owner of the labour-power should sell it only for a definite period, for if he were to sell it rump and stump, once for all, he would be selling himself, converting

had to be maintained during the off-season and during periods of illness as well as during the life-cycle disabilities of childhood and old age. In regard to seasonal fluctuations, slavery was awkwardly inelastic, especially since all the plantations in a given area tended to experience peak labour demand at the same time, which ruled out sharing slaves around to balance each other's needs. This problem could be alleviated by the presence of a free-labour alternative who could be hired during times of increased demand. Free labour also had the advantage of being employable on the high-risk tasks for which masters were reluctant to endanger the lives or limbs of slaves, who constituted a major capital investment.[48]

To these ends, the existence of free or cheaply available land could also work to slaveholders' advantage. The fall-back option of personal plots enabled free labourers to stay in one place to be available for work on local plantations as occasion arose. Complementarily, the cultivation of personal plots could allow slaves to survive independently of the slaveholder's support during low-workload periods in the plantation cycle, so their provision was not necessarily an outcome of planter benevolence or a concession won by slaves.

The allocation of personal plots, often associated with Ciro Cardoso's concept of the 'peasant breach' (*brecha camponesa*), which Cardoso himself attributed to Tadeusz Lepkowski, was central to the set of 'opportunities for independent action and social advancement' that Schwartz identified as characteristic of Brazilian slavery.[49] Slaves could and did save income generated from their private plots to purchase manumissions for themselves and, more significantly, for their descendants. Here too, however, we should not assume benevolence on the part of slaveholders. The ultimate concession won by slaves – the quilombos, or independent, self-governing maroon communities – occurred in spite of, rather than

---

himself from a free man into a slave, from an owner of a commodity [labour-power] into a commodity ... For the conversion of his money into capital, therefore, the owner of money must meet in the market with the free labourer, free in the double sense, that as a free man he can dispose of his labour-power as his own commodity, and that on the other hand he has no other commodity for sale, is short of everything necessary for the realisation of his labour-power'. Or again: 'Free labourers, in the double sense that neither they themselves form part and parcel of the means of production, as in the case of slaves, bondsmen, &c ... They are, therefore, free from, unencumbered by, any means of production of their own. With this polarisation of the market for commodities, the fundamental conditions of capitalist production are given', Marx, *Capital*, vol. 1, 165–6, 668.

48   Stanley J. Stein, *Vassouras: A Brazilian Coffee County, 1850–1900. The Roles of Planter and Slave in a Plantation Society* (revised ed., Princeton: Princeton UP, 1985), 58; Robert Brent Toplin, *The Abolition of Slavery in Brazil* (New York: Atheneum, 1972), 5.

49   Tadeusz Lepkowski, *Haiti* (Havana: Casa de las Americas, 1968), vol. 1, 59–60, cited in Cardoso, 'Peasant Breach', 49. Quotation from Stuart B. Schwartz, 'Resistance and Accommodation in Eighteenth-Century Brazil: The Slaves' View of Slavery', *Hispanic American Historical Review* 57 (1977), 69–81.

as a result of, slaveholders' best efforts.[50] In contrast, the sale of manumissions enabled planters to recoup the purchase price of slaves after extracting years' worth of value from their labour, the proceeds going to the purchase of less worn-out replacements. As a bonus, slaveholders could relieve themselves of liability for the upkeep of old slaves and the unproductive children of freed slaves, a consideration that casts light on the fact that, despite the demographic preponderance of male slaves, slaveholders disproportionately manumitted females, who – in contrast to their men – would automatically transmit their status to children.[51] All this accrued as a return on the allocation of private plots to slaves. Furthermore, the mere possibility of manumission, for all its pitfalls, provided planters with an inducement that they could use to encourage docility among their unfree workforce – a tactic cheaper and more effective than pure coercion.

In addition to affording this degree of strategic flexibility to slaveholders, available extra land also enabled them to expand their plantations outwards without needing to modify either the relations or the technologies of production, or to increase the intensity of the productive process. Moreover, the clearing and preparation of additional land could provide a profitable outlet for labour during off-peak periods on the established plantation.[52] On all these counts, the availability of extra land could enable plantation owners, particularly in frontier areas, to mitigate the burden of maintaining a full complement of manpower during off-season periods of reduced workforce involvement.

The problem for planters was, of course, that the same considerations could often work the other way, to their disadvantage. In particular, as H. J. Nieboer recognised over a century ago, when land is easily available unenslaved labourers can also acquire it, freeing themselves from having to sell their labour when planters need extra hands. At the least – assuming a modicum of worker mobilisation – it raises the price they can charge for their labour and allows them to be more assertive about working conditions.[53] Paradoxically, therefore, plantation owners in outlying frontier areas can become supportive of an intrusive level of state power in order to render the coercion of unenslaved workers economically viable. On counts such as these, the issues of manumission and the importation of free immigrants, both of which produced a free labouring

---

50   Conrad, *World of Sorrow*, 20; Reis, *Slave Rebellion in Brazil*, 40–62; Stuart B. Schwartz, 'The *Mocambo*: Slave Resistance in Colonial Bahia', *Journal of Social History* 3 (1970), 313–33.

51   George Reid Andrews, 'Race and the State in Colonial Brazil', *Latin American Research Review* 19 (1984), 209.

52   Stein, *Vassouras*, 57–8; 214–16.

53   The situation that Nieboer termed 'close resources'. H. J. Nieboer, *Slavery as an Industrial System* (The Hague: Martinus Nijhoff, 1900), 420–2.

class, regularly and controversially converged in Brazil, especially as the prospect of the abolition of slavery became more and more unavoidable.

From early in the nineteenth century, planters who supported the importation of immigrant labour as a precaution against the abolition of slavery had agitated for legislation that would prevent newly arrived immigrants from purchasing land.[54] These planters generally came from frontier areas, land being too expensive elsewhere for the problem to arise. Planters in traditional areas, where spare land was not available, supported the distribution of land in frontier areas to European immigrants on the ground that the communities they would establish (*nucleos coloniais*) would expand the area of Brazilian 'civilisation'. As Emilia Viotti da Costa pointedly concluded, 'Both systems – using immigrants as plantation workers and promoting *nucleos coloniais* – were tried in the coffee areas during the first half of the [nineteenth] century and failed.'[55] These considerations would continue to obtain. As a member of a prominent traditional slaveholding family from the São Paulo coffee-growing region would put it later in the century, with abolition imminent: 'immigrants with money are of no use to us.'[56]

Immigrants' usefulness – so long as they were free of money – was as a replacement workforce. Planters like Martinho Prado, who uttered the foregoing remark, did not view life after slavery as the emancipation of human beings but as the abolition of one form of coercion in favour of another. Abolition would not do away with African Brazilians. It would do away with their lack of rights. In seeking immigrants, therefore, Prado was not seeking more workers. He was seeking an alternative source of rightlessness. Moreover, he was unlikely to find it so long as slavery persisted, since foreign workers tended not to emigrate to places where they would have to compete with slaves in the race to the bottom. Rather than fighting a civil war over the issue, therefore, a number of Brazilian planters actually welcomed the prospect of abolition as enabling them to secure workers who, rather than free, would be even more governable than either slaves, whose unruliness was a prime factor in the shift towards abolition, or freed Brazilian men and women, of whom there was no shortage.[57] Flooding the market with foreign labour would depress

---

54   Viotti da Costa, *Brazilian Empire*, 94.
55   Ibid.
56   Martinho Prado, speech delivered on 27 January 1888, quoted in Kowarick, *Subjugation of Labour*, 69, citing Michael Hall's 1969 PhD thesis.
57   Various scholars have noted that slave and ex-slave dissidence was cited as a pretext for the immigration programme. See, e.g., Florestan Fernandes, 'The Weight of the Past', in John Hope Franklin (ed.), *Color and Race* (Boston: Houghton Mifflin, 1968), 282–301; Robert M. Levine, '"Turning on the Lights": Brazilian Slavery Reconsidered One Hundred Years after Abolition', *Latin American Research Review* 24 (1989), 207.

the wages that workers could demand, especially as the amount of available land was decreasing.[58] Moreover, in contrast to freed Brazilians, some foreigners, especially Italians, could be relied on to allow women and children to work alongside men during periods of peak demand, a cultural factor that expanded the seasonal adaptability of individual hires.[59]

By this stage in the nineteenth century, abolitionists could invoke European racial doctrine to argue that White labour was inherently better than Black.[60] In common with their republican counterparts further north, however, Brazilian planters' priority was not to make racial prejudice but to make money – though of course the outcome was the same. Prado's preference for biddable immigrants over people who had won their freedom – whether in the past or in the immediate future – doubled as a preference for people of European descent over people of African descent. As upkeep gave way to wages, therefore, so did slavery give way to race, with no let-up in the logic of exploitation. When the juridical distinction between free and unfree people of African descent was finally removed, their collectivity became opposed to that of people from Europe.

As in the case of the United States, therefore, abolition completed the racialisation of Africanness in Brazil. In the wake of abolition, Brazil's response to a labour surplus was to import extra labour from overseas.[61] As we shall see below, this would also be Israel's response to the labour surplus that arose in the wake of independence. In both cases, the labour problem was not that it was lacking but that it was local.

Since African Brazilian deprivation survived the emancipation decree of 1888, it is important not to exaggerate the significance of that decree. Nonetheless, in dispensing with the condition of slavery, abolition removed the juridical distinctions that had served to divide African Brazilians. This left the unofficial distinctions, which were predominantly couched in terms of colour. In the twentieth century, these informal distinctions blossomed into the full excess of the Brazilian baroque.[62] Prior to abolition, the juridical permutations of slavery and freedom had produced a degree of diversity among the enslaved and the formerly enslaved that had sustained the dominance of the planter class, the only group

---

58 Stein, *Vassouras*, 45–7.
59 George Reid Andrews, 'Black and White Workers: São Paulo, Brazil, 1888–1928', in Rebecca J. Scott et al., *The Abolition of Slavery and the Aftermath of Emancipation in Brazil* (Durham: Duke UP, 1988), 111.
60 Toplin, *Abolition of Slavery in Brazil*, 147, 263.
61 Thomas E. Skidmore, 'Racial Ideas and Social Policy in Brazil, 1870–1940', in Richard Graham (ed), *The Idea of Race in Latin America, 1870–1940* (Austin: Texas UP, 1990), 7–36; Andrews, *Black and Whites in São Paulo*; 135–6, 177–8; Kowarick, *Subjugation of Labour*, 68–9; Ademir Gebara, *O mercado de trabalho livre no Brasil, 1871–1888* (São Paulo: Brasiliense, 1986).
62 Andrews, *Blacks and Whites in São Paulo*, 249.

whose divisions could be relied on to dissolve when collective interests were threatened. The baroque system of nomenclature grew out of and compounded this diversity, on whose reproduction across time planter hegemony depended.

The term 'baroque' does not here refer to an era, since the nomenclature's most elaborate development took place in the nineteenth century. It refers to the system's Gordian extravagance. The relatively straightforward permutations of slavery and freedom began to complexify in the nineteenth century, during the period when planters, with varying degrees of reluctance, were coming to terms with the impending demise of slavery. Hence the reason for preferring the term 'abolition' to 'emancipation' is that, in a manner reminiscent of the experience of European Jews, emancipation was not about the slaves. Rather, Brazilian authorities acted as if, along with slavery, they had also dispensed with the slaves. Ex-slaves in Brazil were more marginalised than Blacks in the US South, whose labour continued to be exploited under changed forms of control. Black Brazilians, in contrast, found themselves systematically bypassed – although, as an impoverished potential alternative, they could serve by their mere presence to discipline the newcomers. Indeed, when immigrants showed signs of having imported disruptive European ideologies such as socialism or syndicalism, they could find themselves passed over in favour of African Brazilians.[63]

Race and Emancipation

The correspondences between this phenomenon and the post-emancipation racialisation of Black people in the United States are pronounced. In particular, both abolitions signalled an intensification of miscegenation discourse. Yet the outcomes of this intensification in the two societies were the inverse of each other. Whereas, in the United States, the one-drop rule policed the most thoroughgoing of racial polarities, the Brazilian baroque suppressed an empirical polarity in which African extraction overwhelmingly correlated with deprivation. Where one promoted solidarity among a White majority, the other promoted fragmentation among a non-White majority. Quite straightforwardly, then, the contrast between the Brazilian and US regimes of difference reflects the different demographies that the two regimes have sought to construct and maintain. A rule that made Blacks of people who were anything other than a hundred per cent White would have had terminal consequences for minority rule in Brazil, where any pretext for incorporating people into the White category, including non-biological ones,

---

63 Andrews, 'Black and White Workers', 103–7; 115–18; Andrews, *Blacks and Whites in São Paulo*, 55, 58, 151.

was acceptable. As we saw, something comparable could also happen in Georgia and South Carolina under appropriate demographic conditions.

Clearly, then, the issue is not colour at all. It is the use to which colour is put. What, then, is that use? Rather than describing an inherently precarious situation in which a few people exercise privilege over most people with their consent, the Brazilian baroque *mis*describes that situation – which is to say, it safeguards it. In their lack of clarity, the myriad colour classifications perform a socially reproductive function continuous with that which, in the slave era, was performed by the combination of manumission, high mortality and juridical heterogeneity. These factors cooperated to prevent a hyperexploited majority from realising its community. Since slavery was abolished in Brazil, the heterogeneity – a burden now borne by the colour classification system – is the only one of these three complementary strategies to survive into the present (though Black life expectancy remains commensurate with impoverishment). In the wake of abolition, a depoliticised set of colour classifications acquired increased salience as the other factors became obsolete. Subsequently, in combination with the programme of White immigration, the elaboration of colour classifications helped prolong the oppression of African Brazilians into the post-slavery era.

Rather than elucidating this situation, historians such as Tannenbaum and Elkins were recapitulating Brazilian racial ideology. On the other hand, though Carl Degler's famous 'mulatto escape hatch'[64] was not well received by Brazilian critics at the time, we should recognise the value of the insight, which Marcus Garvey ignored, that categories intervening between Black and White can function to discourage non-Whites from electing to be the majority. We should, however, amend Degler's thesis, since the reprieve that counts is not opened up for individual mulatos but for the dominant group as a whole. The Brazilian baroque is a ruling-class escape hatch.

Here again, then, we encounter a regime of race that does not essentialise. If anything, the opposite is the case. Though inequality in Brazil is orchestrated by means of a calculus of White and Black, the Brazilian categories are not racial in a sense that corresponds to the racialisation of African Americans or European Jews. Full siblings in Brazil can be assigned different classifications, which vary with the judgements of individuals and can change across time.[65] This is the reason for referring to

---

64   Carl Degler, *Neither Black Nor White: Slavery and Race Relations in Brazil and the United States* (New York: Macmillan, 1971), 224–5. In response to Degler, Eduardo de Oliveira e Oliveira suggested the term *alcapao* for an escape hatch, *alcapao* signifying both an emergency exit and an animal trap: 'emergency exit from the system itself, but a prison for the mulato, incapable of acquiring a sense of self [*uma consciência própria*]', Oliveira, 'O mulato, um obstáculo epistemológico', 70.

65   Over half a century ago, Oracy Nogueira distinguished cogently between

the Brazilian system as one of colour rather than race. In Brazil, race operates in denial. It is denied by colour, a sous rature mode of racialisation that suppresses the very essentialism that is seen as defining race in other contexts.

Despite this major difference, however, the regimes of difference obtaining in Brazil and the United States both reproduce colonial relationships, whether by maintaining social divisions that would otherwise be incoherent or by effacing social divisions that would otherwise be coherent. When we view the Brazilian regime of race as a whole, the surface dazzle of its myriad categories emerges as a latter-day instantiation of Brazil's long-run history of planter domination. In their very lack of apparent system, the endless gradations of Black/White admixture sustain a twin project that combines the subjugation of African Brazilians with the elimination of Native Brazilians.

Indians and the Nation

Thus we come to the Natives, who have been conspicuous for their low profile in our discussion of Brazil. But their marginalisation is the point. It is a productive absence, which reinforces the logic of the system as a whole. In Roland Barthes's terms, Natives constitute an absent centre, invisibly ordering the random proliferation of ethnic categories.[66] A classificatory system governed by mixtures of Black and White is not natural or foreordained. It is a contingent product of history.

In the beginning, the governing opposition was between Natives and invaders.[67] Natives could not have been excluded from a Portuguese/African dichotomy when Africans had yet to be introduced. The question of the exclusion of Natives is, therefore, an empirical one. I confess that

---

constructions of race based on 'mark' and on 'origin', respectively associated with Brazilian and US racial discourse. A race of mark is based on external appearance (hence full siblings can be differently classified) whilst a race of origin is based, selectively, on heredity, which may or may not harmonise with external appearance, and which necessarily classifies full siblings together. Nogueira, 'Preconceito racial de marca e preconceito racial de origem', *Anals do XXXI Congresso Internacional de Americanistas* (São Paulo, 1955); Nogueira, 'Skin Color and Social Class', in *Plantation Systems of the New World* (Washington: Pan American Union Social Science Monographs no. 7, 1959), 164–78.

66 For the concept of the absent centre, see Roland Barthes, *Camera Lucida: Reflections on Photography* (Richard Howard, trans., New York: Farrar, Straus and Giroux, Inc., 1981), 5–6, 87; Jacques Derrida, 'Signature, Event, Context', in *Glyph 1* (Samuel Weber and Jeffrey Mehlman, trans., Baltimore: Johns Hopkins UP, 1977), 180.

67 Although it should be noted that this could change rapidly. In the records of the chapel for the Engenho Sergipe and surrounding area, the term 'negro' was used to refer to both African and Indian slaves early in the seventeenth century: Schwartz, *Sugar Plantations*, 516, n. 31.

I do not have an answer to just when or how this exclusion came about, or to how, some time in the sixteenth century, the master/slave opposition became coded Portuguese/African rather than Portuguese/Native. I suspect that the Jesuits played a part through their redeeming of Indians from slavery and for conversion – a redemption that placed Natives on the Portuguese side of the eschatological chasm separating those possessed of redeemable souls from Africans – and they certainly had a hand in ending Indians' legal enslavement; but the cultural question is wider than this.

Without diminishing the importance of a question I cannot answer, however, we can at least gauge the continuing implications of the absence – or, perhaps, the non-triangulation – of a Native pole in Brazil's chromatic taxonomy. Dispossession is no more expressible in the language of colour than is enslavement. Lacking chromatic designation, the systemic community between enslavement and dispossession does not provide ground for solidarity, while those as yet undispossessed in the Amazon region are not a colour (brown?) but something categorically external to a chromatically ordered typology: Indians.

Despite itself, therefore, the ideology of whitening ultimately depends on a binarism of Black and White, with White as its final – which is to say, its cumulative – destination. This binarism is that which the colour spectrum lies in between, comprising so many intervening degrees of unfinished Whiteness. The existence of a third pole to which Blackness could be drawn would undo the majority's stake in the Whiteness they are supposedly destined to share. A cumulative demography of dispossession, resistant to the assimilatory pull of *branqueamento*, is the precise possibility that Brazilian racial ideology is structured to preclude. Moreover, in contrast to the whitening power of money, the threat of nativism among African Brazilians has no ideological antidote. Even Frente Negra Brasileira has risked inadvertently recapitulating the marginalisation of Natives.[68] In a silent way, then, the exclusion of Indians is central to the work of the Brazilian baroque. The totality of this exclusion, whereby Indigeneity is uniquely discontinuous with the otherwise comprehensive continuity of Brazil's ethnic schedule, burst into public view in 1952 with the controversial 'Diacuí case' (*o caso Diacuí*).

Ayres Câmara Cunha, a state forest worker, was in danger of losing his job when his sexual relationship with a young Indigenous woman from the forest, Diacuí Canualo Aiute, came to light. Affirming the

---

68   See, for instance, Quilombhoje (org.), *Frente Negra Brasileira – Depoimentos* (São Paulo: Ministério da Cultura, 1998); de Azevedo, *Democracia Racial*, 30 (also noting *União do Negro Brasileiro*); John Burdick, 'Brazil's Black Consciousness Movement', *Report on the Americas* 25, no. 4 (1992), 23–7; Lélia Gonzalez, 'The Unified Black Movement: A New Stage in Black Political Mobilization', in Fontaine (ed.), *Race, Class, and Power in Brazil*, 120–34.

couple's true love, Cunha sought to marry Aiute, his professed intention, as Tracy Devine Guzmán recounts, being to 'live forever in the forest among his indigenous friends and help them morally and materially'.[69] The chief impediment was the fact that, as an Indian, Aiute was a ward of the state, so that the marriage would have to be approved by Brazil's Indian Protection Service (which, as if to mark the crossed frontier that the couple's liaison epitomised, had been shifted, US Indian Office-style, from the War Ministry to the Ministry of Agriculture). When the official response indicated that his application was doomed, Cunha went to the press. 'Within days, newspapers throughout the country transformed the affair into a Romeo and Juliet production intriguing enough to rival modern-day Brazilian soap operas'.[70]

In the event, Cunha and Aiute succeeded. The point, however, is the dramatic extent to which the controversy surrounding their union belied the official culture of whitening, which was meant to encourage rather than proscribe miscegenation. Would not the proposed marriage have set Aiute on the path to whiteness? In her case, that prospect frustrated rather than furthered national policy, which set 'isolated Indians' apart from the integrated plurality of the national mainstream. As noted, for all its multifarious variety, the Brazilian baroque does not include an 'indígena' category. Again, therefore, the racialisation of Indigenous people need not entail solubility. In the Brazilian case, in contrast to the racial regime in the United States, national ideology excludes isolated Indians, who remain across a conceptual (albeit ever-receding) frontier, at the same time as it strives to dissolve Blackness into the mainstream.

Scholarly concern with Brazilian slavery has tended to obscure the role of territorial dispossession in the making of Brazilian settler society, as if the two were separate topics. As in the case of the United States, however, dispossession was preconditional to Brazilian slavery, the imported Africans being set to work on expropriated Indian land. In contrast to slavery, however, which only persists at a reduced and informal level, the territorial dispossession has never been interrupted. To continue its expansion, the Brazilian state requires more land, and Amazon communities have land – as Alcida Rita Ramos has put it, Amazonia remains 'no man's land, everybody's business'.[71] In dispersing Indigeneity among its miscellany of colour classifications, the Brazilian baroque masks this continuity. Amazon communities are not Caboclos – at least, not yet. Rather than embodying the latest phase in the dispossessive continuity

---

69   Tracy Devine Guzmán, *Native and National in Brazil: Indigeneity after Independence* (Chapel Hill: North Carolina UP, 2013), 134.

70   Ibid., 134–5.

71   Alcida Rita Ramos, *Indigenism: Ethnic Politics in Brazil* (Madison: Wisconsin UP, 1998), 222.

of Brazilian state-formation, they figure as denizens of some extra-civic space running parallel to modern Brazil. The Jesuits would approve. Amazon communities exist outside history.[72] When they eventually join modern Brazil, as they steadily do, they acquire colours to complement their immersion in its undiscriminating ocean of poverty. Paradoxically, therefore, coming into colour makes once-were-Amazons invisible. As they shift from cultural curio to social problem – from anthropology to sociology – a further casualty is history: the same history as slavery. Accordingly, scholars of slavery need to address Amazon communities. By the same token, so does Survival International need to address the favelas.

In the case of Brazil, then, the (non-)racialisation of people of African descent reproduces the politics of minority domination in an era when juridical discriminations have ceased to be viable. This discursive continuity occurs in tandem with the continuity of Indian dispossession, which the Brazilian baroque masks in a different way, by omission rather than by obfuscation. As in the case of the United States, these two modes of racialisation interweave with each other historically. In the second half of this book, we shall consider two histories of racialisation in rather more detail, allocating two chapters each to case studies of the racialisation of Native Americans in the USA and of Arab-Jews in Palestine/Israel. In either case, the historical relationship that the particular regime of race maintains into the present will be outlined in the first of the two chapters, whereupon the second chapter will address the shifting ways in which the basic characteristics of that relationship have been reproduced by race.

As will emerge, in their different contexts, each of these national regimes of race combine discursive strategies that we have already seen in operation, in particular the strategies of inclusion (Indigenous people in Australia), exclusion (African Americans, European Jews), marginalisation (Native Brazilians) and deracination (African Brazilians). While this discursive repertoire is strikingly simple, its practical combinations can be very complex. Beneath all the complexity, however, lie fundamentally simple relationships of inequality: conquest, dispossession, exploitation, removal, replacement, assimilation and elimination.

---

72 This externality perpetuates the colonial pattern noted by Hemming: 'Those tribes which had managed to retreat deeper into the interior before the advancing Portuguese, to avoid destruction or absorption into Portuguese Brazil, were no more than a vague threat on a distant frontier.' John Hemming, 'Indians and the Frontier', in Leslie Bethell (ed.), *Colonial Brazil* (Cambridge: Cambridge UP, 1987), 189.

CHAPTER FIVE

The Red Race on Our Borders

Dispossessing Indians, Making the United States

The process whereby Indians shifted from being external to Euroamerican society to being incorporated within it was piecemeal and drawn-out. In anglophone North America, it spanned three centuries, the seventeenth, eighteenth and nineteenth, extending from the era of the Powhatan Confederacy to that of Wounded Knee. On the demise of the frontier, as we shall see in the following chapter, the racialisation of Indians became an integrated national discourse that we can trace through federal Indian policy and that relied on blood quantum criteria. For all its domesticity, however, this internalised identity politics retained the inherently international concept of the treaty, a legacy that continues to testify to Indians' extended historical transition from externality to interiority in relation to Euroamerican society. To situate the racialisation of Indians, therefore, this chapter will trace the process through which Indians' progressive containment within the federal body politic was registered and enacted in US Indian policy – which is to say, it will trace the politico-juridical dimensions of invasion. On this basis, the following chapter will explore the racialisation of Indians in the post-frontier era.

The doctrine of discovery, initially formulated in response to the conquest of the Americas, encompassed the apologetic repertoire whereby European sovereignty was first asserted over the lands and inhabitants of the New World. In that it suggests singularity, the term 'doctrine' of discovery is misleading, since it glosses a range of positions within the disputatious arena that would come to be known as the law of nations or, later, international law. Nonetheless, certain themes are constant, in particular the unequivocal distinction between dominion, which inhered in European sovereigns alone, and the lesser right of occupancy or possession that the doctrine assigned to Natives. The right of occupancy entitled Natives to use a territory that Europeans had discovered, even though ultimate title, or dominion, vested in the European sovereign.[1]

The distinction between dominion and possession presupposed a long-held asymmetry whereby Native entitlements were held to be axiomatically inferior to those enjoyed by Europeans (or Christians). On the cusp of modernity, Francisco de Vitoria had reformulated this ancient discrepancy a few years after Columbus had precipitated a religious crisis in the shape of humans whose relationship to Adam was at best unclear. Though the inhabitants of the Indies lacked access to the gospel, it was necessary for them to be normatively intelligible to Europeans. In particular, for Vitoria to integrate them into his scheme, they had to be subject to the *jus gentium* (law of peoples or nations). His solution (perhaps the only one in the circumstances) was a universal rationality whereby all people created by God could discern the order in His creation. A consequence of this universal competence was a shared responsibility to adhere to the *jus gentium*, a responsibility that the allegedly incestuous, human-sacrificing and bestial cannibals of the New World were conspicuously failing to discharge.

On the one hand, therefore, the inhabitants of the Indies were possessed of reason, and thus equivalent to everyone else – which is to say, equivalent to the Spanish – while, on the other hand, their sociocultural demeanour was at variance with the *jus gentium* (which was also, of course, equivalent to the Spanish). Though possessed of an unquestionable right of occupancy, therefore, they also required Spanish intervention, an occurrence that was rendered likely by the fact that Vitoria held the Spanish entitled to travel, trade and proselytise in the Indians' country.[2]

The British in North America retained the Spanish claim to a basic asymmetry between Natives' right of occupancy and the property rights that could accrue to Europeans. Since Christian monarchs had ultimate title to land, individuals' ownership of it had to be traceable to an original transfer from the crown (or, after the Revolutionary War, from the US government). Given a legitimate transfer from the sovereign, landownership came to participate in the quality of sovereignty, conferring rights that the state was committed to defending. These rights, which were

---

1 See especially Robert A. Williams, Jr., *The American Indian in Western Legal Thought: The Discourses of Conquest* (New York: Oxford UP, 1990) as well as the classic but still reliable Mark F. Lindley, *The Acquisition and Government of Backward Territory in International Law* (London: Longman, Green & Co., 1926).

2 Vitoria in Ernest Nys (ed.), *De Indis et De Iure Belli Relectiones, being parts of Relectiones Theologicae XII by Franciscus de Victoria* (John P. Bate, trans., New York: Oceania/Wildy & Sons, 1964 [1917], S. 3, proposition 4), 157. See also Antonio Truyol Serra (ed.), *The Principles of Political and International Law in the Work of Francisco de Vitoria* (Madrid: Ediciones Cultura Hispánica, 1946); Williams, *American Indian in Western Legal Thought*, 96–118.

available to Europeans or their creole successors, were categorically superior to Natives' rights over the land that they occupied. The key word is 'occupy': under certain conditions, Natives' immemorial occupancy entitled them to a right of soil or usufruct, understood as hunting and gathering rather than as agriculture. This right was inalienable. Under the principle of pre-emption – an idea memorably expressed by the plaintiffs' counsel in *Cherokee v. Georgia* as 'a principle settled among themselves [European powers] for their own convenience, in adjusting their mutual acts of rapine on the western world'[3] – a discoverer secured the exclusive right, on behalf of his sovereign and vis-à-vis other Europeans who came after him, to acquire land from the Natives. This right gave the discovering power (or, in the US case, its successors) a monopoly over land transactions with the Natives, who were prevented from disposing of their land to any other European power. Thus the Royal Proclamation of 1763 assigned the key components of Indian relations (land, trade, diplomacy) to the central government in London.[4]

On the face of it, this would seem to pose little threat to people who did not wish to surrender their land to anyone. Indeed, this semblance of Native voluntarism has provided scope for judicial magnanimity in regard to Indian sovereignty. In practice, however, the corollary did not apply. Pre-emption sanctioned European priority but not Indigenous freedom of choice. As Harvey Rosenthal observed of the concept's extension into the US constitutional environment, 'the American right to buy always superseded the Indian right not to sell.'[5] Underlying this disparity was the simple but crucial assumption that the terms 'European' and 'native' were of a different order. The same logic did not apply to both. As L. C. Green and Olive Dickason put it, in terms reminiscent of Taney's notorious language in the Dred Scott case, 'international law did not recognise the aboriginal inhabitants of … newly discovered territories as having any legal rights that were good as against those who "discovered" and settled in their territories'.[6]

In a colonial context, pre-emption enlists Native title to the service of the sovereign as against his or her diasporan subjects. The Native right of occupancy is good against everyone except the sovereign. In practice,

---

3 Quoted in Harvey D. Rosenthal, 'Indian Claims and the American Conscience: A Brief History of the Indian Claims Commission', in Imre Sutton et al., *Irredeemable America: The Indians' Estate and Land Claims* (Albuquerque: New Mexico UP, 1985), 36.

4 'Proclamation of 1763', reproduced in Robert N. Clinton, 'The Proclamation of 1763: Colonial Prelude to Two Centuries of Federal-State Conflict Over the Management of Indian Affairs', *Boston University Law Review* 69 (1989), 382–5.

5 Rosenthal, 'Indian Claims and the American Conscience', 36.

6 L. C. Green and Olive P. Dickason, *The Law of Nations and the New World* (Alberta: Alberta UP, 1989), 125–6.

this apparent concession to Native rights was a pragmatic acknowledgment of the lethal interlude that would intervene between the conceit of discovery, when navigators proclaimed European territorial dominion over already-owned regions to trees or deserted beaches, and the practical realisation of that conceit in the final securing of European settlement, formally consummated in the extinguishment of Native title. Pending the extinguishment of Native title, however, no one else could pre-empt the sovereign's prior entitlement. Thus pre-emption had a dual consequence. As between the crown and Natives, it spanned the interlude between the theoretical conquest inherent in discovery and the reality of effective conquest, manifest in extinguishment, while, as between the crown and its diasporan subjects, the same principle recruited Natives to fill the spaces left by the empirical patchiness of colonial settlement.

These implications were not, however, commensurate. Ultimately, the rights that pre-emption sanctimoniously assigned to Indians were meaningless. They existed pending extinguishment. In the wake of extinguishment, however, sovereign transfers of title in fee produced homogeneity between settler subjects and the crown. This homogeneity, an outcome of conquest, existed vis-à-vis the Natives, uniting Europeans in a refusal to share ownership with them. Though yet to be couched in the language of race, the demography of sovereignty anticipated its categorical boundaries.

Understood as an assertion of Indigenous entitlement, the distinction between dominion and occupancy dissolves into incoherence. Understood processually, however, as a stage in the formation of the settler-colonial state (specifically, the stage linking the assertion and the realisation of territorial acquisition[7]), the distinction is consistent. Pre-emption provided that Indians could transfer their right of occupancy to the sovereign and to no one else. They could not transfer dominion, because it was not theirs to transfer; that inhered in the crown, and had done so from the moment of discovery. Dominion without settlement constitutes the theoretical (or inchoate) stage of territorial sovereignty.[8] In US Chief Justice John Marshall's words, it remained to be 'consummated by possession'.[9] Upon this consummation, the completion of conquest, the sovereign gathered together the totality of rights attaching to the territory concerned. From this consolidated set of rights, the sovereign transferred to settlers an entitlement, fee simple, that was greater than the sum of the rights that the Natives had surrendered. Collectively,

---

7 Philip Deloria's 'ambiguous period in which the US colonial administration exerted only partial control' extended into the late nineteenth century. Deloria, *Indians in Unexpected Places*, 21, referring to US/Lakota relations.

8 Williams, *American Indian in Western Legal Thought*, 269.

9 *Johnson v. McIntosh*, 573.

in other words, the process yielded more than land for settlers. It also yielded sovereign subjecthood: settlers became the kind of people who could own rather than merely occupy.

What, then, was the supplement that the sovereign added to Natives' right of occupancy to produce the expanded confection that was passed on to the settler? This supplement, which reflected and consolidated settlers' axiomatic superiority to Natives, inhered in the element of dominion, asserted by the sovereign at the moment of discovery, which had not been the Natives' to transfer. Again, therefore, sovereignty's limits anticipated those of race: only Indian occupancy was detachable from title. Fee simple in the United States, as in other settler colonies, remains traceable to a sovereign grant on the part of the colonising power. Property starts where Indianness stops.

Once the theoretical expropriation asserted at discovery had been realised in practice, the distinction between occupancy and dominion lost its primary function, persisting as a contradiction with which Natives might embarrass the moral pretensions of the settler state. The right of occupancy has produced utterances in statutes, treaties and court decisions that would enable sympathetic judges to find in favour of Indian claimants. In the context of the whole, however, these concessions seem a small price to pay. A key feature of discovery is that it was instantaneous. From the moment of assertion, it covered the whole of a discovered territory, shielding it from the ambitions of other European powers. The military metaphor is advised, since the scheme was ultimately grounded in violence. The assertion of sovereignty vis-à-vis other European powers did not require that the territory in question had been settled and regulated by the discovering power. Rather, it was an assertion that the discoverer was capable of warding off other Europeans.[10] Should another European power prevail in a war for the territory, then sovereignty would pass to that power.

All this took place in the realm of dominion, so the Natives were not involved. Their right of occupancy obtained in a lower realm, where the process of acquisition was anything but instantaneous. Nation by nation, tribe by tribe, band by band, the ceaseless movement of the frontier was inherently uneven. In combination, the instantaneous assertion of sovereignty and the piecemeal extinguishment of Native occupancy produced the international and the domestic faces of the emergent settler nation-state. As Jill Norgren has observed, succession to the British crown's assertion of discovery enabled the United States to claim dominion over all Indian lands in one fell swoop. Indian affairs and foreign policy coincided as the crown's original pre-emption vis-à-vis other European powers

---

10 L. C. Green, 'Claims to Territory in Colonial America', in Green and Dickason, *Law of Nations*, 125.

was applied to the new republic's hemispheric neighbours: 'Discovery thus supported the assertion of American hegemony over the continent, a diplomatic stance reiterated during Marshall's time in the 1823 Monroe Doctrine.'[11] President Monroe announced his bedrock foreign-policy doctrine in the same year as Marshall's *Johnson v. McIntosh* decision formally incorporated the monarchical distinction between occupancy and dominion into republican jurisprudence.

Domesticating Discovery

Thus we move from the general discourse of discovery to its selective incorporation into US Indian policy. As will emerge, the relationship between Indian tribes and the federal government was founded, as it remains founded, on the Marshall court's twin concepts of wardship and domestic dependent nationhood. Moreover, these concepts themselves instantiate the two core principles that organised the doctrine of discovery. As stated, these two principles are: first, the hierarchical distinction between the dominion that the doctrine assigned to European sovereigns and the occupancy that characterised the Native realm; and, second, the fact that discovery governed relations between Europeans rather than between Europeans and Natives. In combination, as adapted to domestic jurisdiction by the Marshall court, these two principles would seal US Indian policy's transition from foreign policy to settler-colonial governance. We shall trace this transition from the era when Indian Affairs constituted foreign policy.

In addition to constituting the territories that the French had surrendered at the end of the French and Indian (Six-Year) War, the Proclamation of 1763 had, for the first time, established a boundary (effectively, the crest of the Appalachians) between the Native realm and the English mainland colonies. As such, the Royal Proclamation constitutes the first official specification of a bounded zone, beyond the limits of colonial settlement, that was designated Indian country.[12] Across this boundary, Indian law obtained (subject, theoretically, to the pre-emptive right).[13] On the British, eastern side of the boundary, though Indians retained possessory rights that were good so far as third parties were concerned,

---

11   Jill Norgren, *The Cherokee Cases: The Confrontation of Law and Politics* (New York: McGraw-Hill, 1996), 90.

12   At the colony level (New York), Daniel M. Friedenberg has traced the division back to the 1758 treaty of Easton, Friedenberg, *Life, Liberty, and the Pursuit of Land: The Plunder of Early America* (Buffalo, NY: Prometheus, 1992), 105.

13   With the possible exception, one might surmise, of those non-landed charter colonies that did not claim continental crown grants extending to the Pacific. I have not been able to find a resolution concerning this possibility, which Robert J. Miller raised in conversation with me.

the crown claimed radical or ultimate title, and Indian land could only be transferred to colonial ownership through the mediation of the crown.[14]

In the wake of the war of independence, the victorious republicans were hardly disposed to defer to a proclamation that had been issued by the reviled George III. Nonetheless, the Constitution and early Indian legislation marked a retreat from the aggressively state-oriented interlude of the Articles of Confederation period, back to a British-style centralisation of Indian affairs in the federal government.[15] This shift reflected the fact that, in the late eighteenth century, Indians still presented a military threat sufficient to preclude the downgrading of relations with them. Indeed, Peter Silver has convincingly documented his contention that what he calls the 'anti-Indian sublime', an 'enraptured discourse of fear' that colonists refined, played a formative role in the emergence of 'a new group, more and more often invoked in the middle colonies after mid-[eighteenth]century: "the white people"'.[16] It is crucial to remember that Indian affairs represented the fledgling republic's foundational foreign policy. Indeed, the Indian threat was of such magnitude that, despite the profound misgivings of a number of the framers of the Constitution, it led to the creation of a standing army, with all the freshly remembered potential for tyranny that this entailed.[17]

In the preconstitutional 1780s, Alexander Hamilton had already warned of the dangers of Indian alliances with the British and the Spanish:

> The savage tribes on our Western frontier ought to be regarded as our natural enemies, their [British and Spanish] natural allies, because they have most to fear from us, and most to hope from them.[18]

Hamilton was reacting to what he saw as the dangerous excesses of the years immediately following independence, when many of the successful revolutionaries had been in no mood to appease tribes who, in

---

14   Robert J. Miller, *Native America, Discovered and Conquered: Thomas Jefferson, Lewis and Clark, and Manifest Destiny* (Lincoln, NE: Nebraska UP, 2008), 31–2.

15   *Articles of Confederation*, Art. 9, cl. 4 (US 1781); Stuart Banner, *How the Indians Lost Their Land: Law and Power on the Frontier* (Cambridge, MA: Harvard UP, 2005), 131; Walter H. Mohr, *Federal Indian Relations 1774–1788* (Philadelphia, PA: Philadelphia UP, 1933), 173–199.

16   Peter Silver, *Our Savage Neighbors: How Indian War Transformed Early America* (New York: Norton, 2008), xix–xx.

17   Alexander Hamilton ('Publius') in *The Federalist* [*Papers*], no. 24, 1787 (reprint, Jacob E. Cooke, ed., Middletown: Wesleyan UP, 1961), 152–7.

18   Ibid., 160. Marshall would recognise the continuing currency of this concern in his *Worcester v. Georgia* judgement: 'early journals of Congress exhibit the most anxious desire to conciliate the Indian nations …The most strenuous exertions were made to procure those supplies on which Indian friendships were supposed to depend, and everything which might excite [Indian] hostility was avoided.' *Worcester v. Georgia*, (31 US. 6 Pet. 515, 1832), 515, 549.

many cases, had sided with the British. In 1786, Congress, fearing that Virginia's threatened invasion of Indian country could unite the southern tribes in a hostile alliance, urged Virginia to 'abstain from committing Hostilities against, making Reprisals upon, or entering into War with all or any Tribes or Nation of Indians with which the United States are in Peace or any other'.[19] Other state legislatures – Georgia, North Carolina and New York in particular – sought to run their own Indian affairs, a situation that threatened to get out of hand when, in Robert Clinton's words, 'Georgia's unilateral efforts at cessions and treaty-making with rump delegations of the Creek Nation spawned an Indian war on the eve of the Constitutional Convention.'[20] The response of a committee of the Continental Congress would echo down the annals of federal Indian policy:

> An avaricious disposition in some of our people to acquire large tracts of land and often by unfair means, appears to be the principal source of difficulties with the Indians ... The committee conceives that it has been long the opinion of the country, supported by Justice and humanity, that the Indians have just claims to all lands occupied by and not fairly purchased from them ... and no particular state can have an exclusive interest in the management of Affairs with any of the tribes.[21]

The solution that the framers of the Constitution adopted, almost without debate,[22] consisted in a reassertion of the sovereign's pre-emptive monopoly over land transactions with Indians. The so-called 'treaty clause' of the Constitution gave the president 'power, by and with the advice of the Senate, to make treaties, provided two-thirds of the Senators present concur'.[23] An equally consequential five words were the 'and with the Indian tribes' that the Constitutional Convention added onto the end of the commerce clause of the Constitution, the earlier draft of which had merely given Congress the power to regulate commerce 'with foreign nations, and among the several States'.[24] On the basis of the Indian reference in the commerce clause, as Charles Wilkinson has pointed out, the first five weeks of the First Congress saw the enactment of no less

---

19 *Journals of the Continental Congress*, vol. 31 (14 September 1786), 657.

20 Clinton, 'Proclamation', 371; U.S. Constitutional Convention, *Journal of the Federal Convention* (E. H. Scott, ed., Washington: Govt Printing Office, 1893 [1787]), 47.

21 *Journals of the Continental Congress*, vol. 33 (3 August 1787), 457, 459.

22 Robert J. Miller, 'American Indian Influence on the United States Constitution and Its Framers', *American Indian Law Review* 18 (1993), 153; Francis P. Prucha, *American Indian Policy in the Formative Years: The Indian Trade and Intercourse Acts, 1790–1834* (Cambridge, MA: Harvard UP, 1962), 41.

23 Art. 2, s. 2, para. 2.

24 Art. 1, s. 8, para. 3.

than four major statutes devoted to Indian affairs.[25] In his third annual address, delivered in 1791, President Washington expressed the hope that 'all need of coercion in future may cease and that an intimate intercourse may succeed, calculated to advance the happiness of the Indians and', as he continued significantly, 'to attach them firmly to the United States'.[26] Washington was only too aware that, in the British and the Spanish, the Indians had alternative options for attachment (options that would not become available to Indigenous people in Australia, whose sovereignty would remain correspondingly unacknowledged). Moreover, as Supreme Court Justice and Constitution-signer James Wilson observed, 'there were neither men nor supplies for the defence of the frontier'.[27]

In the event, Congress – whose initial act had been to set up the Department of War with special responsibility for hostilities with Indians – passed a series of trade and intercourse acts intended to regulate relations between Indians and Whites. Four of these acts were passed in Congress's first decade (in 1790, 1793, 1796 and 1799[28]). Together, they were intended to ensure that Indian affairs became a federal preserve (shared between the president and the Senate), principally through federal control of land acquisitions, as under the doctrine of preemption, but also through federal controls on Indian trade and Indian-related criminal proceedings. This outcome perpetuated the doctrine of discovery. As noted above, the concept of pre-emption both regulated relations between European sovereigns and subordinated local colonial governance to the metropolitan centre. Both these outcomes continued straightforwardly from the federalising of Indian affairs, which, on the one hand, proscribed diplomacy between Indian nations and European ones and, on the other, subordinated the states to the federal government.

Though the trade and intercourse acts provided for federal primacy in Indian affairs, they did not clarify the status of the tribes or nations with whom the federal government could enter into its exclusive arrangements. Constitutionally, this remained an open question since, in response to Congressional concern over the republic's Indian alliances in relation to the British and the Spanish, the Constitution had ratified previous treaties agreed between Indian nations and the British.[29] Having

---

25 Charles Wilkinson, *American Indians, Time, and the Law* (New Haven: Yale UP, 1985), 13.

26 Quoted in Phillip B. Kurland and Ralph Lerner (eds), *The Founder's Constitution* (Chicago: Chicago UP, 1987), vol. 2, 531 (Article 1, Section 8, Clause 3 [Indians], Document 6).

27 Quoted in Page Smith, *James Wilson: Founding Father, 1742–1798* (Chapel Hill: North Carolina UP for the Institute of Early American History and Culture, 1956), 70–1.

28 1 *Stat.* 137, 1 *Stat.* 329, 1 *Stat.* 469, 1 *Stat.* 743.

29 Art. 6, para. 2.

acknowledged a sovereignty that had been in place in the British period, the Constitution could not simultaneously negate that sovereignty or reduce it to its own specifications. Rather, the acknowledgement itself entailed the recognition that Indian sovereignty was prior to and independent of the US Constitution.[30] Accordingly, the Constitution was silent on the matter.

Initially, the new republic maintained the British policy of treating the Indian nations as practical counterparts. As the military balance tilted the United States' way, however, control over White people's dealings with Indians, an internal matter, inexorably expanded into control over Indians themselves. In this enhanced strategic environment, various attempts were made to get around what was increasingly viewed as a constitutional anomaly. It was asserted that tribes who had sided with the British had been conquered in a just war, thereby forfeiting their sovereignty.[31] But this by no means accounted for all the Indian nations with land in the territory claimed by the United States. An ostensibly more benign (and, as it turned out, more consequential) alternative was enunciated in 1795 at the treaty of Greenville, whose paternalistic language anticipated the fiduciary rhetoric of wards and guardianship that would later come to characterise the Marshall judgements.[32]

This language not only invested Indian dispossession with humanitarian appeal. It also signalled the shift from British treaty-making with Indians – a way of coming to terms with a military rival – to the US treaty system, which was premised on a strong power's dominance over weaker ones. But the USA and the British crown had fundamentally different strategic agendas. In particular, the British had been relatively anti-expansionist, since they feared (rightly, as it turned out) that expansion would render the colonists unmanageable.[33] On this basis, it was prudent not to attempt to destroy the power of Indigenous neighbours who, in addition to providing assistance against the French, Dutch and Spanish, might also contribute useful support should the crown's own colonial subjects prove troublesome. In the wake of independence, however, there was a marked shift to expansionism, not least because sales of public land,

---

30   This situation entails continuing disadvantages for Indian peoples whom the British conquered without making treaties. 'The United States came into existence long after English colonialism largely dispossessed New England Indians, and tribes there lack a treaty relationship *with the United States*': Jean M. O'Brien, *Firsting and Lasting: Writing Indians Out of Existence in New England* (Minneapolis: Minnesota UP, 2010), 203.

31   *Journals of the Continental Congress*, vol. 25 (15 October 1783), 683; vol. 27 (28 May 1784), 456.

32   Anthony F. C. Wallace, *The Long, Bitter Trail: Andrew Jackson and the Indians* (Eric Foner, ed., New York: Hill & Wang, 1993), 27.

33   See also Tim A. Garrison, *The Legal Ideology of Removal: The Southern Judiciary and the Sovereignty of Native American Nations* (Athens: Georgia UP, 2002), 47.

which was most cheaply available from Indians, provided a means for the federal government to pay off its substantial war debts.[34] Moreover, so far as Indians were concerned – whichever side they may have taken in the war of independence – the shift from the British to the USA involved a shift from colonial subjecthood to non-citizenship. A corollary to the increased responsiveness to citizens that democratic republicanism introduced was a reduced level of responsiveness to non-citizens, a factor that favoured those who coveted the vast expanses of productive land that remained in Indian hands.

As the nineteenth century moved on, Indians rapidly lost their strategic assets. In 1803, any threat that the French might have posed was removed by the Louisiana Purchase. A decade later, in concluding the War of 1812, the Treaty of Ghent finally ended the British threat. The Spanish being marginal in Florida, this left Indians alone to face one of the most aggressive mass movements in history, logistically buttressed by the burgeoning canal network and steamboats, which first appeared in 1807.[35] Andrew Jackson's vanquishing of the British at New Orleans anticipated the comprehensive defeat, in the North-West in the following year, of Tecumseh's British-allied pan-Indian uprising. The year after that, in 1814, Jackson routed the Creek Redsticks at Horseshoe Bend, extending US military hegemony from the Mississippi to the Atlantic and from Canada to Mexico. Given the efficiency of the recently invented cotton gin, combined with cotton's rapid exhaustion of the soil (which generated a constant need for new plantations), this victory sealed the fate of the south-eastern tribes.

Nearly half a century after the signing of the Constitution, in this very different strategic context, the Marshall court finally confronted the wild card of Indian sovereignty, domesticating it to the republican constitutional environment. Though synthetic, in that it combined elements from the established discourse of discovery, the court's version of Indian sovereignty was an invention contrived to accommodate the novel circumstance of settler-colonial nationhood. As such, the concept inaugurated 'post'colonial jurisprudence, adapting a horizontal vocabulary to a vertical mode of domination. Given the parlous strategic circumstances to which Indians had been reduced (in Thomas Jefferson's words, 'we have only to shut our hand to crush them'[36]), the question remains of why the United States maintained the notion of Indian sovereignty and persisted with the treaty-making that followed from it. How should we

---

34　Wallace, *Long, Bitter Trail*, 31.

35　George R. Taylor, *The Transportation Revolution, 1815–1860* (New York: Holt, Rinehart and Winston, 1951), especially 22, 57–64.

36　Letter to Governor William Henry Harrison, 27 February 1803, in *Jefferson Papers*, first series, vol. 9, no. 208, also in Francis P. Prucha (ed.), *Documents of United States Indian Policy* (Lincoln: Nebraska UP, 1975), 22.

read the scrupulosity with which, no matter how thoroughly a people had been conquered, the United States insisted on acknowledging their sovereignty prior to removing, confining or otherwise dispossessing them?

The Innocence of Conquest

This question takes us back to the earliest days of the new republic, when Congressional trepidation over Indians' military capacity was mixed with a sensitivity that was to be of much longer duration. Policy directives evinced anxiety over the discrepancy between the rhetoric of human entitlement, to which US officials were characteristically addicted, and the actual treatment that Indians were receiving. On 18 July 1788, for instance, Secretary at War Henry Knox reported to the Continental Congress that it appeared:

> that the white inhabitants on the frontiers of North Carolina in the vicinity of Chota on the Tenessee [sic] river, have frequently committed the most unprovoked and direct outrages against the Cherokee Indians. That this unworthy conduct is an open violation of the treaty of peace made by the United States with the said Indians at Hopewell on the Keowee the 30th of November 1785. That the said enormities have arisen at length to such a height as to amount to an actual although informal war of the said white inhabitants against the said Cherokees ... the principles of good Faith sound policy and every respect which a nation, owes to its own reputation and dignity require if the union possess sufficient power that it be exerted to enforce a due observance of the said treaty ... in order to vindicate the sovereignty of the Union from reproach, your secretary is of the opinion, that, the sentiments, and decision, of Congress should be fully expressed to the said white inhabitants, who have so flagitiously stained the American name.[37]

Given that the date was 1788, the strategic implications of Knox's concern can be appreciated. Within a few years, however, as noted, a major change had begun to set in. Nonetheless, over the momentous decades that followed, there was continuity in one respect. No matter how inexorably the United States consolidated its military domination of neighbouring tribes, the rhetoric of Indian sovereignty remained in place. Prior to the Marshall judgements, however, there was no authoritative statement as to quite what that sovereignty might mean.

It could be said that, even in the wake of the Marshall judgements, there existed no single or coherent statement of Indian sovereignty. This is because a number of commentators have asserted a rupture between Marshall's *Johnson v. McIntosh* judgement of 1823, which is widely seen

---

37 *Journals of the Continental Congress*, vol. 34 (18 July 1788), 342–3.

to have been repressive, and his *Worcester v. Georgia* judgement of 1832, which some scholars have seen as designed to undo the harsh consequences of *Johnson v. McIntosh*.[38] On this basis, the *Cherokee v. Georgia* ruling of 1831, in which the foundational Indian-policy principles of wardship and domestic dependent nationhood were enunciated, appears as somewhat awkwardly bridging the two.

Yet those who contend that Marshall's two Cherokee judgements of the 1830s represent a benign attempt on the chief justice's part to improve the situation engendered by his earlier decision have to account for the fact that the Cherokee judgements did not overturn his earlier ruling. On the contrary, Johnson remains good law and continues to be cited in Supreme Court rulings. My concern is with the outcomes of US Indian-affairs discourse, rather than with which Marshall was the real or the better Marshall. In this regard, the three judgements can be seen to cohere harmoniously once they are understood as acts of state-formation governed by the two core principles of discovery that we have noted. All three judgements expressed Euroamerican superiority over Indians in terms of dominion as opposed to occupancy; they also arbitrated between Europeans rather than between Europeans and Natives. In combination, these two principles produced a juridically voided Indian subjecthood that I term *corpus nullius*.[39] Thus we turn to the rulings themselves.

Marshall's *Johnson v. McIntosh* ruling straightforwardly exemplifies the principles that we have noted:

> Indian inhabitants are to be considered merely as occupants, to be protected, indeed, while in peace, in the possession of their lands, but to be deemed incapable of transferring the absolute title to others.[40]

Delivered eight years before *Cherokee v. Georgia*, Johnson anticipated the later judgement's concept of wardship, only in a context where the implications of subordination were unsoftened by the rhetoric of paternalism. In Johnson, Indians were not 'citizens in the ordinary sense of that term',

> since they are destitute of the most essential rights which belong to that character. They are of that class who are said by jurists not to be citizens, but perpetual inhabitants with diminutive rights. The statutes of Virginia, and of

---

38　For examples and critique, see Patrick Wolfe, 'Against the Intentional Fallacy: Legocentrism and Continuity in the Rhetoric of Indian Dispossession', *American Indian Culture and Research Journal* 36 (2012), 3–45.

39　Patrick Wolfe, '*Corpus Nullius*: The Exception of Indians and Other Aliens in US Constitutional Discourse', *Postcolonial Studies* 10 (2007), 127–51.

40　*Johnson v. McIntosh*, 591–2.

all the other colonies, and of the United States, treat them as an inferior race
of people, without the privileges of citizens, and under the perpetual protection and pupilage of the government.[41]

Such assertions have been held to conflict with the apparently international status that the later Worcester judgement can be read as assigning
to Indian sovereignty:[42]

> The Constitution, by declaring treaties already made, as well as those to be
> made, to be the supreme law of the land, has adopted and sanctioned the
> previous treaties with the Indian nations, and consequently admits their
> rank among those powers who are capable of making treaties. The words
> 'treaty' and 'nation' are words of our own language, selected in our diplo-
> matic and legislative proceedings, by ourselves, having each a definite and
> well understood meaning. We have applied them to Indians, as we have
> applied them to the other nations of the earth. They are applied to all in the
> same sense.[43]

A year before Worcester, in *Cherokee v. Georgia*, Marshall had coined the
'domestic dependent nation' formula, continuing from it to acknowledge
that Indians had 'an unquestionable, and, heretofore, unquestioned right
to the lands they occupy, and that right shall be extinguished [i.e., shall
only be extinguished] by a voluntary cession to our government'.[44] At
first sight, this statement might seem to affirm Indian sovereignty in a
manner inconsistent with *Johnson v. McIntosh*. We should, however, be
alert to the telltale word 'occupy', repeated from the Johnson decision,
which, as we have seen, was conventionally used to reduce Native rights
to a level below those that attached to Europeans. And sure enough, this
stout assertion of Native entitlement was followed, without any percep-
tible sense of awkwardness, by the assertion that Indians were 'in a state
of pupilage; their relation to the United States resembl[ing] that of a
ward to his guardian'.[45] This reduction reflects the practical outcome of
the case. For, despite Marshall's endorsement of Indian sovereignty, the
status of domestic dependent nationhood was so disabling that, in one
sense, it is misleading to talk of *Cherokee v. Georgia* as a case at all. Before
the proceedings could properly start, the court had to decide whether
or not the Cherokees could even bring a case before the US Supreme
Court. Strictly, therefore, Marshall's comments on the wider relationship

---

41   Ibid., 569.
42   Milner S. Ball, 'Constitution, Court, Indian Tribes', *American Bar Foundation Research Journal* 1 (1987), 31–3.
43   *Samuel A. Worcester, Plaintiff in Error, v. The State of Georgia* (31 US. 6 Pet. 515) 1832 [*Worcester v. Georgia*], 559.
44   *The Cherokee Nation versus the State of Georgia* (30 US 5 Pet. 1 1831), 17.
45   Ibid., 17.

between the US government and the Cherokee were mere dicta. Yet they could hardly have been more consequential:

> it may well be doubted whether those tribes which reside within the acknowledged boundaries of the United States, can, with strict accuracy, be denominated foreign nations. They may, more correctly, perhaps, be denominated domestic dependent nations. They occupy a territory to which we assert a title independent of their will, which must take effect in point of possession when their right of possession ceases. Meanwhile they are in a state of pupilage. Their relation to the United States resembles that of a ward to his guardian.[46]

On this basis, the substance of the Cherokees' plea never got to trial. Being a domestic dependent nation, as opposed to a foreign one, they were barred from applying to the Supreme Court to have the treaties that they had signed upheld. As Marshall's brother judge, Justice Baldwin, put it, almost too-perfectly exemplifying the concept of *corpus nullius*, 'there is no plaintiff in this case'.[47]

In resolving the constitutional conundrum over Indian sovereignty, the domestic dependent nation formula provided a foundation stone for US Indian law. This formula would echo repeatedly through subsequent litigation. The notion of wardship was inherently ambivalent. On the one hand, wards, like children, were entitled to care and protection. Thus Marshall went on from his analogy between Indians' relationship to the United States and the ward–guardian relationship to observe that 'they look to our government for protection; rely upon its kindness and its power; appeal to it for relief to their wants; and address the president as their great father ...'[48] On the other hand, however, the condition of childhood was demeaning and inferior – adult African males, after all, were routinely called 'boy'. The infantilisation of Indians that the notion of wardship entailed was more deleterious than the defeat-in-war formula, because it compromised the acknowledgement of a prior capacity. As wards or minors, Indians were not competent to be vested with the full rights that were exercised by Europeans (adults, personified in the 'great father'). In other words, though Indians' prior sovereignty could not be undone, it could be diminished.

This disabling outcome had been expressed less delicately in the *Johnson v. McIntosh* judgement, which declared Indians' diminished status to have already been in place at the moment of discovery. Diminution was not a new development, the result of military defeat, but a pre-existent feature of Indians' inherent characteristics, a corollary to their undevel-

---

46 Ibid., 21.
47 Ibid., 30.
48 Ibid., 21.

oped state in relation to Europeans ('the actual condition of the two peoples'). By means of this proto-evolutionist formula, Marshall could retain the constitutional acknowledgement of Indian sovereignty while simultaneously reducing it to the mere possessory or usufructory rights from which European-style dominion was categorically distinguished. Hence 'Indian inhabitants are to be considered merely as occupants, to be protected, indeed, while in peace, in the possession of their lands, but to be deemed incapable of transferring the absolute title to others.' They were incapable of transferring absolute title to others because, as wards or minors, they were incapable of holding it in the first place. In this formula, the asymmetry between Native rights and European ones was not quantitative, a consequence of the relative size or strength of the two parties, but qualitative, a consequence of the developmental disparity in their human capacities. As Frank Shockey has pointedly observed, though Europe contained both large and small nations, none of them 'seriously contended that the citizens of another European nation held their lands under a different, and less secure, title than its own subjects'.[49]

Why, then, having arrived at this formula for negating Indian sovereignty, did the Marshall of *Cherokee v. Georgia* subsequently seem to surrender the advantage? In that judgement, the requisite diminution was expressed as resulting from the European takeover rather than from qualities that were intrinsic to Indians themselves. As we have seen, however, the rhetorical variance between Johnson and the two 1830s judgements did not subtend a corresponding difference of practical outcome. Marshall was aware that, though separated by nearly a decade in his professional life, his judgements would stand coevally in black letters to be compared and cross-referenced by generations of lawyers. He did not hold out his judgement in either the Cherokee or the Worcester case as modifying *Johnson v. McIntosh*. Thus we should identify the grounds on which the three decisions cohere.

I contend that the requisite grounds are to be found in two closely related constitutional dimensions of a novel form of polity that was still at a formative stage of self-construction. These dimensions are the diachronic one of the republic's accession to rights that had previously attached to the English crown, and the synchronic principle of federalism. From early in his career as a state politician in Virginia, and unwaveringly from his appointment as federal chief justice in 1801, Marshall had championed the twin ideals of nationalism and federalism.[50] Put briefly,

---

49 Frank Shockey, '"Invidious" American Indian Tribal Sovereignty: *Morton v. Mancari* contra *Adarand Constructors, Inc. v. Peña*, *Rice v. Cayetano*, and other recent cases', *American Indian Law Review* 25 (2001), 279.
50 David S. Robarge, *A Chief Justice's Progress: John Marshall, from Revolutionary*

the former ideal was at issue in *Johnson v. McIntosh* and the latter in the two Georgia cases.[51]

To take Marshall's nationalism first: in *Johnson v. McIntosh*, he found that the US government had legitimately succeeded to the title acquired by the British crown under the doctrine of discovery (as he put it, 'The British government, which was then our government, and whose rights have passed to the United States, asserted a title to all the lands occupied by Indians, within the chartered limits of the British colonies'[52]). The issue here was not, in other words, the rights of Indians, but the successive rights in relation to Indians of the British crown and the US government. Now, so far as the later two Cherokee judgements are concerned, the same principle applies – the rights of Indians were incidental. This time, however, the primary concern was not the successive rights in relation to each other of the US government and the English crown, but the coexistent rights in relation to each other of the US government and the states of the Union. In this connection, and altogether consistently, the federalist-nationalist Marshall came down in favour of the federal government.

Cherokee v. Georgia and *Worcester v. Georgia* both involved pleas in which the Supreme Court was asked to intervene to restrain the state of Georgia from violating treaties that the federal government had entered into. As we have seen, when the interests at stake had been Cherokee ones, Marshall had sidestepped the issue by finding that domestic dependent nations could not bring cases before the Supreme Court. The following year, taking hints in Marshall's own judgement and, especially, in the dissenting judgement of Justice Thompson, who had found in their favour, the Cherokees were back at the Supreme Court. This time, however, they did not appear on their own account but, in a put-up case, through the person of a White US citizen from Vermont, Samuel Worcester.

Worcester was one of two missionaries whom the Georgia court had sentenced to four years' hard labour for being on Cherokee land without the approval of the state government, an action that infringed a statute that Georgia had recently passed as part of a programme of negating the Cherokee sovereignty that treaties with the federal government had

---

Virginia to the Supreme Court (Westport: Greenwood Press, 2000), 97–8, 298–301; Francis N. Stites, *John Marshall: Defender of the Constitution* (Oscar Handlyn, ed., Boston: Little, Brown & Co., 1981), 38–76.

51 Thus I endorse Joyotpaul Chaudhuri's assertion, which he did not develop, that 'The *McIntosh* decision is consistent with Marshall's nationalism and his imperial conceptions of the unitary state. The *Worcester* decision conforms to his Federalist and antistate politics.' Chaudhuri, 'American Indian Policy: An Overview', in Vine Deloria, Jr. (ed.), *American Indian Policy in the Twentieth Century* (Norman: Oklahoma UP, 1985), 25.

52 *Johnson v. McIntosh*, 588.

recognised. The missionaries had appealed to the Supreme Court, who then issued a writ of error to the Superior Court of Georgia. Governor Wilson Lumpkin reacted to this writ with a defiant message to the Georgia legislature, who responded, in what Charles Warren termed 'rebellious resolutions,' by directing the governor that 'any attempt to reverse the decision of the Superior Court ... by the Supreme Court of the United States, will be held by this State as an unconstitutional and arbitrary interference in the administration of her criminal laws and will be treated as such.'[53]

It was in this abrasive context that the Supreme Court came to consider the missionaries' appeals. Though the question was the same as in the previous year's case – could a state suborn the federal government's agreements with Indian nations? – this time the plaintiffs were not domestic dependent nations, but US citizens, citizens and foreign nations having undisputed access to the Supreme Court. Thus the federal/state issue became unavoidable. Since this issue obtained between Europeans, however, resolving it in favour of the federal government would not affect the diminution of Indian sovereignty. Worcester's 'strong' version of Indian sovereignty did not change this.

On this basis, it is entirely consistent that, in contrast to Marshall's Johnson decision, the Cherokee judgements should express Indians' diminished status as resulting from the European takeover rather than as inhering in Indians themselves. For, in the context of Marshall's *federalist* agenda, to maintain his earlier denial of Indians' precontact incapacity to exercise full national sovereignty would have been to lose the ground that he needed to rule that the relevant jurisdiction lay with the federal government rather than with the state of Georgia. As a state of the Union, Georgia was precluded from engaging in international relations. That was the prerogative of the federal government alone. For relations with the Cherokee to be international, the Cherokee had first to be a sovereign nation, capable of independent self-regulation. As such, they would constitute a sovereign entity to which the pre-emptive federal monopoly would apply. Thus Marshall's pro-Indian pronouncements in Worcester were a rhetorical device to the federalist end of promoting the primacy of the US government. In Johnson, by contrast, his primary concern had been the nationalist one of the republic's succession from the British crown. In the pre-eminent context of state-formation, there is no inconsistency, let alone rupture, between the three judgements.

In this light, it is not surprising that such sovereignty as Indians have been accorded has so often turned out to be hollow when put to the test.

---

53   Charles Warren, *The Supreme Court in United States History*, vol. 2: *1821–1855* (Boston: Little, Brown & Co., 1922), 213–14.

The final two Marshall judgements coincided with the beginning of the systematic campaign of Indian removal that was formally inaugurated, during the presidency of Andrew Jackson, by the Indian Removal Act of 1830. Over the following decade or so, the majority of Indians from the South and East (including the North-East) were relocated west of the Mississippi by force, fraud or, more often, both – a process through which, apart from loss of life, Indians lost millions of acres of land. In the wake of the Marshall decisions, the United States expanded southwards and westwards, either by engaging in treaties with Indians held representative of wider tribal groupings or through warfare with and purchase from Mexico, whereby the USA acquired rights originally negotiated with Indigenous groups by the Spanish. Thus treaties with Indians constitute the principal means whereby the United States acquired its national territory.

Treaties require and presuppose national sovereignty on the part of signatories. In terms of state-formation, therefore, it was Indian nations' sovereignty that enabled their respective territories to be converted into so many parts of the United States. It follows that dispossession was consummated by Indian sovereignty – had Marshall not acknowledged that sovereignty, then the basis on which the United States went on to acquire the majority of its present territory would be invalidated. This degree of ongoing compatibility between Indian dispossession and Indian sovereignty as formulated in the Marshall decisions obliges us to view that formulation of sovereignty as a conduit – rather than an impediment – to dispossession.

This conclusion illuminates how the flood of removals and re-removals that followed in the wake of the Marshall judgements embodied the spirit of those judgements. Consider the key phrase 'domestic dependent nation' itself. Indian nations were not 'domestic' in the conventional sense of having a proper (even familial) place within the republican social order. On the contrary, their domestic status excluded them from a juridical domain that even foreign nations could enter. Rather than Indians themselves, it was their inconvenient sovereignty that was being domesticated. In the event, the judgements were a prelude to Indians' removal beyond the spatial bounds of the social order. 'Dependent' is similarly double-edged, since, as Marshall himself made clear, dependency, like wardship, connotes both a condition that warrants protection and a state of subordination. In the event, the former provided rhetorical cover for the latter.

Thus the terms 'domestic' and 'dependent' combined the twin principles of discovery that we have noted, with 'domestic' signifying that Indians were not parties to arrangements that obtained between European sovereigns, while 'dependent' summarised the inferiority that accompanied their status as mere occupants. Moreover, for all its flattering of White-appointed treaty signatories, the term 'nation' was necessary for them to sign away their peoples' homelands. In short, rather than conflicting with the Marshall version of sovereignty, Indian dispossession was of its essence.

Wardship and Removal

In this connection, it is crucial to note the simple but generally overlooked fact that Marshall spoke in the plural. It was not just the Cherokee nation, beleaguered by encroaching Whites, that was domesticated and dependent, but, as we have seen, 'tribes which reside within the acknowledged boundaries of the United States'. Given the elasticity of a frontier that was remorselessly moving west as Marshall spoke, this meant that all Indian societies were already domestic dependent nations, albeit many of them in waiting. Indians west of the Mississippi, Plains nations with whom the federal government was still agreeing treaties whose wording was reminiscent of British-era compacts between equals – all Indian societies, whether or not they had had formative contact with the White republic, were generically scheduled to become domesticated and dependent. The phrase was not so much a description as a manifesto.

This inclusiveness of scope underscores a further feature of Indian treaties: their tactical versatility. In the 1830s, with the prairie teeming with buffalo, the westward expansion of the United States was inhibited by a daunting military obstacle. This problem existed to a much lesser extent to the east of the Mississippi (though Seminole Florida remained defiant). It hardly existed at all in the North-East. In this uneven setting, the utility of Indian sovereignty lay in its semantic flexibility. It could encompass the whole range of settler-colonial articulations at once, from the unpacified cross-frontier realm of international relations, where grandiloquent concessions to Indian nationhood were in order, to the internal extreme of assimilation, where the domestic and dependent aspects overwhelmed the national ones. For juridical purposes, therefore, Marshall's formula filled the space of Manifest Destiny, the genocidal interlude between dominion and conquest. As observed, dominion without settlement constitutes the theoretical or inchoate stage in the formation of the settler-colonial state. At the cost of a minimal residue (literally, 'residual sovereignty'[54]), Marshall's formula brought legitimacy to the nation-founding violence of expropriation.

---

54 Residual (or inherent) sovereignty refers to the residuum left over from treaties through which Indian tribes surrendered or modified specified aspects of their primordial sovereignty: 'What is not expressly limited remains within the domain of tribal sovereignty', Cohen, *Handbook of Indian Law*, 122.

The anxiety over the legitimacy of conquest that the Marshall judgements sought to resolve, an anxiety that undid the declared boundary between national and international affairs, had been evident from the beginning. In the early republic, an era resounding with altitudinous declarations, the right of occupancy had provided grounds for the fledgling US government to proclaim an appropriately fulsome Indian policy. The cornerstone of this policy was to be the treaties whereby Indian nations relinquished occupancy to the United States:

> The utmost good faith shall always be observed towards the Indians, their lands and property shall never be taken from them without their consent; and in their property, rights and liberty, they shall never be invaded or disturbed, unless in just and lawful wars authorized by Congress; but laws founded in justice and humanity shall from time to time be made, for preventing wrongs being done to them, and for preserving peace and friendship with them.[55]

This celebrated passage comes from the Northwest Ordinance of 1787.[56] Significantly, the Indian nations in the region to the north-west of the new republic were effectively unpacified and in close contact with the British. Dorothy Jones has suggested that historians have been deceived by the US government's desire for a uniform Indian policy into believing that it actually had one. In practice, Jones argues, for all the rhetoric of uniformity, early US governments maintained three distinct policy approaches to their Indian neighbours: one each for the South, the North-West and the North-East.[57] The variety that Jones identifies underscores the importance of distinguishing between official policy on Indians and the local calculations that governed actual interchanges with them. In the 1820s, for instance, when the passion for removing Indians from the South was reaching its climax, the Senate was ratifying treaties with powerful Plains nations to the north-west in terms reminiscent of British-era compacts between autonomous foreign powers.[58] Fifteen years earlier, in the North-East, Iroquois sachems had asked President Madison to remove them to Ohio. They were told that, while they were welcome to leave New York, they could not remove to Ohio because 'the Government was even then contemplating a consolidation of settlements this side of Michigan as a safeguard should another war break out with Great Britain'.[59]

---

55 *Northwest Ordinance* (1787), *Journals of the Continental Congress*, vol. 42, 340–1.

56 Ratified by Congress in August 1789 (1 Stat. 50).

57 Dorothy V. Jones, *License for Empire: Colonialism by Treaty in Early America* (Chicago: Chicago UP, 1982), 169.

58 See, e.g., the 1825 treaties with the Sioune, Hunkpapa and Oglala bands of the Sioux and with the Cheyenne, Charles J. Kappler, (ed.), *Indian Treaties 1778–1883* (*Indian Affairs: Laws and Treaties*, vol. 2, Washington: Govt Printing Office), 230–6.

59 Annie H. Abel, 'The History of Events Resulting in Indian Consolidation West

Such tactical considerations take us behind the uniformly sententious rhetoric in which treaties were framed to the strategic constants that the various approaches sustained. The primary and overriding constant being territorial acquisition, treaties provided for Indians to make territorial concessions. These included rights of access as well as cessions of parts of tribal territory (from an Indian perspective, confinement to other parts), and, increasingly from the Indian Removal Act until the end of the Civil War, provided for Indian societies to be uprooted and removed to remoter locations.

A salient feature of the policy of Indian removal was that, along with greed for land, the programme inscribed a hardening pessimism, a sense of fixity whereby not only were Indians and Whites unable to live together: they would remain so.[60] Such pessimism was not, however, a matter of race. Indeed, it had been a recurrent feature of Euroamerican discourse on Indians since well before the advent of race (a comparable perspective had hardened Puritan attitudes in the wake of the Pequot War, for instance[61]). Indians' refractory condition allowed two possibilities: either they could cease to be Indians – i.e., assimilate or die – or they could remove. These alternatives existed in each other's shadow. Thomas Jefferson and Andrew Jackson were principally responsible for bringing them together. In 1817, when removal and assimilation were explicitly linked in treaty bargaining, General Jackson recalled a talk that President Jefferson had given to the Cherokees eight years previously. As an inducement to the tribe to exchange its land for land in Arkansas, Jefferson had offered those who did not want to go west the option of staying behind, only on 640-acre individual allotments rather than on tribal land.[62] Returning to this idea in 1817, Jackson posed the alternatives of remaining tribal and removing or remaining on traditional land in an untraditional way, as holders of individual allotments subject to state law. In Michael Rogin's words, these alternatives 'shared an underlying identity'.[63] Either way, as Indians, Indians would lose their land.

The Royal Proclamation, as observed, had represented the first occasion on which territory was designated Indian country. The existence of

of the Mississippi River', *American Historical Association Annual Report for 1906* (vol. 2, Washington: Govt Printing Office, 1908), 307.

60   An example that influenced the passage of the Indian Removal Act was a pamphlet published anonymously by Lewis Cass, subsequently war secretary in the Jackson administration: 'Removal of the Indians', *North American Review* 30 (1830), 62–121, especially 72–3.

61   Charles M. Segal and David C. Stineback, *Puritans, Indians, and Manifest Destiny* (New York: Putnam & Sons, 1977), 221; Stineback, 'White Nationalism and Native Cultures', *American Indian Culture and Research Journal* 2, no. 2 (1978), 10.

62   Abel, 'History of Events', 254–5.

63   Michael P. Rogin, *Fathers and Children: Andrew Jackson and the Subjugation of the American Indian* (New York: Knopf, 1975), 179.

such a zone was prerequisite, both conceptually and physically, to the policy of Indian removal. In a 1789 report to Congress, for instance, Henry Knox recommended that the best way to avoid conflict was to set aside territory for Indians.[64] Some of the colonies had taken such measures. As Annie Abel pointed out, though, Jefferson was different. Colonies may have reserved ad hoc spaces for individual groups, but only Jefferson 'contemplated the organization of what would have become an Indian Territory, perhaps an Indian state, to which all tribes might be removed'.[65] Jefferson not only came up with the idea. Through the Louisiana Purchase, he gave it spatial feasibility. The 'greatest real estate deal in history' was motivated by the possibility of Indian removal: Section 15 of the Louisiana Territorial Act of 1804 provided that

> The President of the United States is hereby authorised to stipulate with any Indian tribes owning land on the east side of the Mississippi, and residing thereon, for an exchange of lands, the property of the United States, on the west side of the Mississippi, in case the said tribes shall remove and settle thereon.[66]

Along with territory west of the Mississippi came the promise of the federal government being able to sign Indian treaties without making territorial concessions that would antagonise the states. In addition to preserving the Union, therefore, the Purchase forged a union between treaties and removal. The outcome could not have been more fateful for Indians and Blacks alike. The development of the plantation economy in Georgia, Tennessee, Arkansas, Louisiana, Mississippi, Alabama and Florida was conditional upon Indian removal. The Purchase provided the territory west of the Mississippi that the US government exchanged for the homelands that removing tribes were obliged to surrender by way of treaties. Cultivated by Black labour, these expropriated Indian lands produced cotton.

Removal and Assimilation

The proposition that removal and assimilation were two sides of the same coin is at odds with the conventional view of them as antithetical. According to Nancy Carter, for instance, the US government had

---

64 Knox to George Washington, 7 July 1789, in *American State Papers, Indian Affairs* (vol. 1, *A Century of Lawmaking for a New Nation: US Congressional Documents and Debates, 1774–1875*, Washington: Library of Congress), 53.

65 Abel, 'History of Events', 244.

66 'An act erecting Louisiana into two territories, and providing for the temporary government thereof', *United States Statutes at Large* (8th Congress, Session I, Chapter 38, 26 March 1804, 283–9), in Library of Congress, *A Century of Lawmaking for a New Nation*.

an 'early posture of nonassimilation', which dealt with Indian tribes 'as entities to be dealt with by treaty', rather than with Indian individuals 'as citizens to be brought under the laws of the nation'.[67] It would indeed be hard to find a more thoroughgoing form of segregation than one in which, instead of being restricted to particular residential neighbourhoods and public facilities, people were actually hidden over the horizon, beyond any form of contact. But to assume that such a strategy is incompatible with assimilation is to misapply the model of Black racialisation, on which basis Indian removal could seem to represent a fulfilment of the separatist dream underlying the Colonization Movement and Jim Crow.[68]

This is not only misleading. It is one of the points at which race can most clearly be seen to constitute a trace of history. In the Indigenous case, in stark contrast to the racialisation of the formerly enslaved, removal and assimilation commonly furthered the settler-colonial logic of elimination – albeit, in the case of removal, a provisional or temporary form of elimination. Nonetheless, while it may only have postponed the 'Indian problem', so long as removal remained spatially viable it was considerably faster than assimilation. Admittedly, as will be seen in the next chapter, assimilatory measures came to predominate after treaty-making was abolished in 1871. By that time, however, there was little vacant land left beyond the penumbra of White settlement, so, of the two complementary strategies, only assimilation remained viable. When this happened, Indians could no longer be moved on to free up their land for White appropriation. They could, however, be moved *in* to free up their land for White appropriation, embarking on the path to citizenship through becoming the individual proprietors of alienable allotments.

In view of the positive valorisation attaching to citizenship, it is not surprising that this complementarity should be mistaken for tension. Indeed, the ironies of Indian citizenship instance a more general historical pattern, whereby Indians' elimination was routinely hampered by the success with which they had been able to mimic the ways of White people. Premised on Indian recalcitrance, removal was vulnerable to their civility. Thus it is no accident that, regardless of the profound sociocultural differences distinguishing them, the programme's primary

---

67 Nancy Carol Carter, 'Race and Power Politics as Aspects of Federal Guardianship over American Indians: Land-Related Cases, 1887–1924', *American Indian Law Review* 4 (1976), 198. See also Young, *Redskins, Ruffleshirts, and Rednecks*, 5.

68 'Time and time again blacks have told me how lucky they were not to have been placed on reservations after the Civil War. I don't think they were lucky at all. I think it was absolute disaster that blacks were not given reservations': Vine Deloria, Jr., *Custer Died for Your Sins: An Indian Manifesto* (Norman: Oklahoma UP, 1969), 194. For incisive discussion of this point, see Kevin Bruyneel, *The Third Space of Sovereignty: The Postcolonial Politics of U.S.-Indigenous Relations* (Minnesota: Minneapolis UP, 2007), 148–53.

targets (the Choctaw, Chickasaw, Cherokee, Creek and Seminole peoples) should find themselves collectively designated 'The Five Civilized Tribes' in Euromerican parlance.

There was a distinctively Edenic cast to the predicament of civility. Indians who tasted the fruit of civilisation lost their innocence, gaining cunning rather than knowledge. This perverse approximation to Whiteness lent itself to the idiom of heredity. In 1816, for instance, Jackson complained of the 'designing half-breeds and renegade white men' who had encouraged Chickasaw reluctance to cede land.[69] When Indians invoked the vocabulary of American freedom, their impertinence could be put down to European ancestry. No one was more subject to this reproach than John Ross, the Cherokee leader who, as hostile Whites never tired of pointing out, was of largely Scottish biological extraction.[70] Prominent figures such as Creek leader Alexander McGillivray, Chickasaw leader Levi Colbert and Choctaw leader Greenwood LeFlore were also discredited on account of their White ancestry. Opposition to removal was routinely attributed to the machinations of self-serving half-breeds, who allegedly connived to frustrate the intentions of full-blood traditionalists who saw removal as an opportunity to protect their people from the disruptive influence of Whites.[71]

Whether or not such a division obtained in Indian society (there were tribespeople with European ancestry on either side of the Indian controversy over removal[72]), the issue certainly reflected a schism within European society. Removal threatened to make proselytisation more difficult for missionaries, who generally opposed it. In 1826, for instance, LeFlore, David Folsom and Samuel Garland, all Choctaws descended from White fathers and opposed to removal, replaced the old 'full-blood' leadership at a time when the United States was seeking a treaty of cession

---

69 Theda Perdue, *'Mixed Blood' Indians: Racial Construction in the Early South* (Athens: Georgia UP, 2003), 70, 95–6. Concerning Georgia and the Cherokees in particular, Georgia Governor Wilson Lumpkin repeatedly charged that resistance to removal was encouraged by a combination of mixed-bloods and northern troublemakers: 'Those [Cherokees] who have emigrated [to Arkansas] are delighted with their new homes, and most of their brethren who remain in the States would gladly improve their present condition by joining them; but their lordly chiefs, of the white blood, with their Northern allies, "will not let the people go".' Lumpkin, *The Removal of the Cherokee Indians from Georgia* (New York: Dodd, Mead & Co., 1907), 61.

70 In terms of the argument of this book, it is surely significant that, having a one-eighth proportion of biologically defined Cherokee ancestry, John Ross was Indian to the same degree as Homer Plessy was Black.

71 Richard White, *The Roots of Dependency: Subsistence, Environment, and Social Change among the Choctaws, Pawnees, and Navajo* (Lincoln: Nebraska UP, 1983), 125–6, 138–9; Young, *Redskins, Ruffleshirts and Rednecks*, 22–3, 27; Thomas N. Ingersoll, *To Intermix With Our White Brothers: Indian Mixed Bloods in the United States from Earliest Times to the Indian Removals* (Albuquerque: New Mexico UP, 2005), 225–33.

72 Perdue, 'Race and Culture', 711.

from the Choctaws. Soon afterwards, missionaries encouraged Choctaw Christian preachers to launch a 'Great Revival', a campaign with which the new leadership was identified.

Some of the strongest opposition came from John Pitchlynn, who, like the three new chiefs, was a White trader's son. Pitchlynn, who allied himself to the disaffected 'full-blood' chief Moshulatubbee, parodied Folsom's gospel as 'Join the church and keep your country'.[73] To retain their leadership, the old chiefs offered to remove. The local Indian agent approved, reporting to the government, in terms that could hardly express the affinity between assimilation and removal more succinctly, that 'the greater part of the full Bloods would follow, and the half-breeds could be made full citizens'.[74] As if to bear him out, LeFlore – who, in the meantime, had become principal Choctaw chief – eventually converted to the cause of removal and signed the requisite treaty, only to stay behind himself, accept citizenship and go on to a distinguished career in Mississippi politics.[75]

The primary technique of assimilation was allotment, whereby, as the proprietors of individual parcels of land, Indians would become agriculturalists.[76] Ideologically, allotment furnished an answer to critics who complained that removal was oppressive. More immediately, it also provided a way for White traders to recover debts incurred by individual Indians, who could not offer tribal land in settlement. Nonetheless, LeFlore's choice (in which he was joined by thousands of fellow-Choctaws[77]) was not how nomads were meant to behave.

The difficulty cut to the core of the nascent racialisation inherent in the removal programme. The prospect of improvable Indians undermined the principal justification for removal, which was that Indians' incurable savagery made it impossible for Whites to coexist with them. In keeping with the Lockean narrative informing the wider discourse of discovery, a stubborn incapacity for agriculture was central to this savagery. At least so far as Indians in the South were concerned, there was a contradiction in all this, as the oxymoron 'civilized tribes' attested. These Indians had been agriculturalists for millennia. They had taught White people to grow corn and tobacco. In return, White people had taught them the wandering ways of the sylvan romance, which they had been obliged to learn rather quickly as a consequence of having their homes and crops burned by land-hungry invaders.

---

73 Young, *Redskins, Ruffleshirts, and Rednecks*, 28.
74 Ibid.
75 Florence R. Ray, *Greenwood LeFlore: Last Chief of the Choctaws East of the Mississippi River* (Memphis: Davis Printing Co., 1930), 29; Ronald N. Satz, *American Indian Policy in the Jacksonian Era* (Lincoln: Nebraska UP, 1975), 86.
76 Perdue, *'Mixed Blood'*, 68.
77 Satz, *American Indian Policy*, 83.

Gerald Sider has illustrated the depth and tenacity of this potent ideological inversion. Recalling his distress at witnessing young Lumbee men lining up to volunteer as scouts in Vietnam, a group who suffered one of the highest mortality rates in field combat, Sider reflected on the irony of these descendants of expelled agriculturalists identifying with the wandering forest life that settler ideology had exchanged for their farms: 'What these Indian children often said, before they went off to their doom, was a pack of self-assertive, self-destructive, imposed and claimed lies: We Indians have special abilities to move silently through the forest; we Indians have special skills as scouts and as hunters – we Indians will show them'.[78]

Nomadism naturalised removal. The image of the roaming Indian, forever passing though, endlessly surveying the horizon, attenuated Indians' acknowledged ties to land, assuaging the violence that removal did to common-sense understandings of property. People who were routinely on the move would not be unduly inconvenienced. Noting that settlers had uprooted themselves to remove from Europe, Jackson rhetorically asked if it was to be supposed that 'the wandering savage has a stronger attachment to his home than the settled, civilized Christian?'[79] In this connection, no problem arose when Indians behaved like Whites. Nor did they merely vacate their own homelands. In resettling across the Mississippi, removing tribes acted as proxy invaders in relation to the peoples who already lived there, and who were beginning to feel the game-depletion that settler encroachment occasioned.[80]

To acquire territory that it could exchange for the land that removing tribes were relinquishing in the South (which was rapidly becoming the South-East), the US government solicited treaties with the Osage and other Plains societies in the West. Being only too aware of the provocative impact of alien incursions, the Chickasaws had a clause included in the first section of their 1834 removal treaty obliging the US to protect them from the traditional owners of their new home across the Mississippi.[81] Crueller still was the irony whereby those Cherokees who had heeded Jefferson's talk and removed to Arkansas found their new country threatened, twenty-five years on, by an influx of Eastern Cherokees who had originally chosen to stay but, by 1834, were facing forced removal. An additional quarter-century's worth of civilising – including the invention of a Cherokee script, the publishing of a newspaper (the progressively named Cherokee Phoenix) and the drawing-up of a

78 Gerald M. Sider, *Lumbee Indian Histories: Race, Ethnicity, and Indian Identity in the Southern United States* (Cambridge: Cambridge UP, 2004), 208.

79 Quoted in Rogin, *Fathers and Children*, 216.

80 Beaumont, *Marie*, 162; Grant Foreman, *Advancing the Frontier, 1830–1860* (Norman: Oklahoma UP, 1933), 107–16, 147–8.

81 Kappler, *Indian Treaties*, 309.

constitution – had failed to render these genteel refugees any more accept-able to their White neighbours. The Cherokees' cultural achievements stood out as such singular provocations to the officials and legislators of the state of Georgia for one simple reason, attested over and over again in public statements and correspondence: the Cherokees' farms, planta-tions, slaves, and written constitution all signified permanence.[82]

The key contradiction of civility was that it lifted Indians out of pre-history and inserted them into the future. Elimination was inherently chronological – whether dead, removed or assimilated, Indians would pass into memory. Euroamerican time, as Benjamin Lee Whorf put it, flows out of a future, through a present and into a past.[83] Correspondingly, as their nomadic condition attested, Indians – or, at least, good Indians – were impervious to linear temporality. Nomadism was not only condu-cive to removal. Nomads were bound into the realm of disappearance at a deeper level, subsisting on dwindling indigenous resources whose reproduction was finite. Agriculture is inherently reproductive, generat-ing capital that projects into a future where it repeats itself. Farming, like the Cherokee Constitution, staked a claim on the here that transcended the now. As individuals, Indians would not disrupt the forward flow of Euroamerican history, the time of the nation – not merely because they could be relied on to sell their private plots, but more profoundly because, as individuals, they would cease being Indian. Detribalised, they would merge into the future, the challenge that they presented to the rule of private property evaporating as surely as removing tribes evaporated into the West.

Heredity could be invoked to disguise this transformation, substitut-ing phenotype for social type. In the end, however, no matter how often John Ross's Scottish ancestry might be cited as a bar to his Cherokee credentials, it proved no bar to his losing his wife, Quatie, on the Trail of Tears.[84] Like his light skin, Ross's optimistic Constitution encroached on a future that had no place for collective ownership. Across the Mississippi,

82   The capacity to achieve permanence was typically put down to European ances-try, as in Andrew Jackson's exasperated disparagement of the 'designing half-breeds and renegade white men' who had encouraged Chickasaw reluctance to cede land. Perdue, 'Mixed Blood', 70, 95–6.

83   'Or in which, to reverse the picture, the observer is being carried in the stream of duration continuously away from a past and into a future': Benjamin Lee Whorf, Language, Thought, and Reality: Selected Writings of Benjamin Lee Whorf (John B. Carroll, ed., New York: M.I.T. Press/Wiley & Sons, 1956), 57.

84   Mrs Ross, known in life as Quatie, was named Elizabeth on her tombstone at Little Rock, Arkansas, where she died, having given her blanket to a freezing child, as the steamboat Victoria docked on or about 1 February 1839. Angie Debo, A History of the Indians of the United States (London: Pimlico, 1995), 125; Grant Foreman, Indian Removal: The Emigration of the Five Civilized Tribes of Indians (2nd ed., Norman: Oklahoma UP, 1953), 310.

outside national time, he could remain principal chief, implementing the Cherokee Constitution. If Ross had stayed behind, his light skin might have proved an asset, like Greenwood LeFlore's. He could have joined in the future. But he would have ceased being Indian.

The Individual and the Tribe

On the face of it, the reproach of hybridity that was levelled against Ross might seem to anticipate the Dawes-era blood quantum discourse that will be the subject of the next chapter. But this would be to mistake surface detail for historical motivation. There is a fundamental difference between ancestral slurs intended to discredit Ross's personal intransigence and the genetic calculus that would seek to destroy tribal organisation through impartially assimilating Indians as Indians, a blanket category impervious to personal demeanour or affiliation.

The adoption of this strategy into national policy would mark the closure of the frontier, a development that culminated the long-run process whereby Indians' relationship with settler society shifted from one of externality to one of interiority. Once the territory bounded by Mexico, Canada, the Atlantic and the Pacific had been stably colonised, the only space left available for expansion was within, a condition that rendered the frontier coterminal with reservation boundaries. Prior to this development, however, space had provided an alternative to race, banishment across the frontier (or, later, confinement to reservations) providing favoured techniques of elimination. Consider, for example, Article 3 of the treaty that the Poncas were induced to sign before being removed (for the first time) in 1858:

> The Ponca being desirous of making provision for their half-breed relatives, it is agreed that those who prefer and elect to reside among them shall be permitted to do so, and be entitled to and enjoy all the rights and privileges of members of the tribe, but to those who have chosen and left the tribe to reside among the whites and follow the pursuits of civilized life, viz: [eight individuals, with separate residences specified] ... there shall be issued scrip for one hundred and sixty acres of land each.[85]

---

85 Kappler, *Indian Treaties*, 774. Treaty precedents extend at least as far back as article 8 of the 1817 treaty with the Wyandot, Seneca, Delaware, Shawnee, Potawatomie, Ottawa and Chippewa peoples, which provided ('At the special request of the said Indians') for allotment in the case of 'persons hereinafter mentioned, all of whom are connected with said Indians, by blood or adoption', who included, e.g., 'the children of the late William M'Collock ... who are quarter-blood Wyandot Indians, one section ... To Anthony Shane, a half-blood Ottawa Indian, one section of land': Kappler, *Indian Treaties*, 147–8.

Here, in the antebellum era, for Poncas who choose to stay behind (named members of the 'mixed-blood' elite through whose good offices the treaty had been arranged), core elements of the fin-de-siècle Dawes programme are already in place: individuals assimilate into White society by means of allotments, while the tribe ceases to obstruct White access to its homeland.

One aspect of the Ponca treaty does, however, stand out in contradistinction to the later Dawes regime. Though mixed-bloodedness is an operator (in that it denotes those eligible for assimilation), it lacks implications for tribal membership. Here we begin to see the relationship, which the following chapter will explore, between blood quantum discourse – which is to say, race discourse in its specifically Indian application – and the internalisation of Indian societies. The Poncas whose mixed-bloodedness was without consequence were those who remained external by virtue of consenting to remove. They were those who chose John Ross's way rather than that of Greenwood LeFlore. Externally, the US government's Indian problem was a tribal one. Assimilating individual members would not make tribal territory, which was collectively held, available (indeed, it could have the reverse effect, since treaty negotiators regularly relied on 'mixed-blood' elites to secure tribal acceptance of treaties). Moreover, for treaty purposes, it was in the US's interest for tribes to be composite. Breaking them down into smaller units would only necessitate additional treaties. Prior to internalisation, in other words, the US government relied on the very tribal governments that it would subsequently seek to dismantle.

At this stage, White ancestry could be cited to impugn uncooperative leaders such as McGillivray or Ross, while the presence of White or Black elements in a tribe's makeup could be seen to aggravate the military threat that it posed, as in the case of the Seminoles.[86] But such assertions were part of the polemics of removal, aimed at the leaders' refusal to sign treaties rather than at their putative genetic characteristics. Over the frontier, neither civility nor mixed-bloodedness posed a problem – even Jackson had not minded a Cherokee Constitution operating in Oklahoma.[87]

Once a tribe was internalised, however, its government constituted an obstacle that frustrated the US government's access to individual Indians with privately owned property. The impediment to assimilating tribes into the body politic was not simply that they were collective groupings, since the United States encompassed other collectivities – in particular, of course, the states themselves but also, from late-century

---

86 Kenneth W. Porter, *The Negro on the American Frontier* (New York: Arno, 1971).
87 Wilkinson, *American Indians, Time, and the Law*, 17.

on, corporations.[88] Rather, tribes were inassimilable because they were independently constituted entities whose organising principles were discordant with those that governed the structurally regular institutions of US society, uniformly constituted around the centrality of private property. Thus the obstacle to the Indian Territory's admission to statehood was not its demographics but its commitment to collective ownership.[89] Indians were the original communist menace.

Thus we move from the formalities of discovery to the depoliticised workings of settler governmentality. In the following chapter, we shift from Indians' protracted journey from autonomy to containment, to a post-frontier history in which international relations became reduced to identity politics. In formal institutional terms, we have noted that this extended process found condensed expression in 1849, when the Office of Indian Affairs was shifted from the War Department to the Department of the Interior.[90] No doubt the symbolism of this shift was highly significant. Nonetheless, this chapter has tried to show that, in formalising the concepts of diminution, wardship and domestic dependent nationhood, the Marshall court had already encapsulated and given juridical substance to the long-run process of Indian incorporation, a process that was fatally intensifying as the chief justice spoke. In the chapter to come, we will stay with the Marshall judgements – for so have the Supreme Court and the Bureau of Indian Affairs – in order to investigate the implications of US Indian policy's loss of its international dimension, when the 'nation' component of Marshall's fertile phrase became submerged beneath the 'domestic' and 'dependent' aspects.

---

88 The concept of corporate personhood was first enunciated in 1886 in the Supreme Court case of *Santa Clara County v. Southern Pacific Railroad* (118 U.S. 394, 1886).

89 Vine Deloria, Jr., and Clifford M. Lytle, *The Nations Within: The Past and the Future of American Indian Sovereignty* (Austin: Texas UP, 1984), 24–5.

90 Miller, 'American Indian Influence', 157; Prucha, *Great Father*, 112.

CHAPTER SIX

The Red Race in Our Bosom

Racialising Indians in the United States

On the passing of the frontier, US Indian policy sought to incorporate Indians into settler society not as so many separate tribes but generically, individually and as a whole – which is to say, as a race. When Indian societies finally became contained within the territorial bounds of settler society, blood quantum discourse yielded a monolithic Indianness that transcended distinctions between good and bad or civilised and uncivilised, yielding an inherently unstable racial condition whose salient tendency was disappearance.

As observed, in the twentieth century, mixed-bloodedness became the post-frontier version of the Vanishing Indian, an outcome which, as we saw in the previous chapter, the nineteenth century had principally achieved through removal. In tracing the career of blood quanta as a settler-colonial strategy, therefore, our analysis departs from the traditional territory of race studies and into the legal and bureaucratic discourses that blood quanta gathered together. In combination, however, they harmoniously subtended the project of eliminating settler society's enduring 'Indian problem'. To establish this continuity, we shall return to the removal era and follow eliminationist logic through to the 1930s – the era when, it will be argued, even tribes themselves were finally incorporated into settler society.

With Andrew Jackson as president, Congress passed federal removal legislation in 1830.[1] By the end of the 1830s, the Creek, Choctaw, Chickasaw and Cherokee peoples had been removed west of the Mississippi while, in Florida, ceded by the Spanish, the majority Seminoles' days were numbered. Less well-known but comparably brutal removals had also taken place in the North.[2] In 1845, Texas joined the

---

1   U.S. Statutes at Large, 4 (28 May 1830), 411–12.

2   See, e.g., the 1838 treaty with the New York Indians. Kappler, *Indian Treaties*, vol. 2, 502–16.

Union. Over the following two years, under pressure of war, Mexico yielded territory from Texas to the Pacific. Two decades later, the Civil War enormously intensified the militarisation of the United States.[3] In the postbellum era, augmented by industrial development, railroad penetration, telegraphic communication, buffalo culls and a population endlessly replenished by immigration, this enhanced military capacity enabled the lightning-war conquest of the warrior/hunting nations of the Great Plains, who were rapidly relegated to reservations, out of the path of the settler nation's westward expansion.[4] Once confined to reservations, Indians became, in Colonel Dodge's words, prisoners of war.[5] Through all these developments, the rhetoric of sovereignty continued to characterise treaty-making – though the treaties that the Sioux signed in the 1860s provided for a very different future from the ones that they had signed thirty years earlier.[6]

By the end of the nineteenth century, the United States had completed the defeat and territorial containment of Indian societies within its continental boundaries. For military purposes – though not, as Philip Deloria has crucially insisted, for cultural and other ones – the Indians had been conquered.[7] Strikingly, however, treaties rigorously avoided the language of conquest.[8] In preference to claiming title by right of conquest (whereby surrender would have sanctioned annexation), treaties persisted with the formula of cession by agreement. In particular, they dispensed with the claim that Indians had been conquered in 'just wars' – which is to say, in wars where they had been the aggressors,

---

3 Robert M. Utley, *The Indian Frontier of the American West, 1846–1890* (Albuquerque: New Mexico UP, 1984), 93–7. Postbellum militarisation applied not only to the official military. Following Samuel Colt's patenting of the first revolver in 1836, the culture of the gun spread very rapidly among US households, especially on the frontier. Michael A. Bellesiles, 'The Origins of Gun Culture in the United States, 1760–1865', *Journal of American History* 83 (1966), 455.

4 See, e.g., Utley, *Indian Frontier*; Richard White, *'It's Your Misfortune and None of My Own': A New History of the American West* (Norman: Oklahoma UP, 1991), 94–109.

5 Colonel Richard Irving Dodge, *Our Wild Indians: Thirty-Three Years' Personal Experience Among the Red Men of the Great West* (New York: Archer, 1882), 644.

6 Compare, for instance, the treaty that the Santee band of the Sioux signed on 15 July 1830 (Kappler, *Indian Treaties*, 305–10) with the one that they signed on 29 April 1868 (ibid., 998–1007).

7 Deloria, *Indians in Unexpected Places*, 104, 229.

8 An exception has been claimed for 'the case of the Sioux Indians in Minnesota, after the outbreak of 1862': Cyrus Thomas, 'Introduction' to Charles C. Royce (comp.), *Indian Land Cessions in the United States* (Bureau of American Ethnology 18th Annual Report, for 1896–97, 2 parts, Washington: Govt Printing Office, 1899), part 2, 640. No such treaty appears in either Kappler or Deloria and DeMallie, the only 1862 treaty involving either Minnesota or the Sioux being one between the state (!) of Minnesota and 'certain bands of Chippewa [Ojibway]'. Vine Deloria, Jr., and Raymond J. DeMallie, *Documents of American Indian Diplomacy: Treaties, Agreements, and Conventions, 1775–1979* (2 vols, Norman: Oklahoma UP, 1999), vol. 2, 1084.

a theme that had occupied the Marshall court.[9] Given the pragmatics of the frontier, this condition was hardly insuperable. Time and time again, on the Plains, the US cavalry was sent into Indian country to protect encroaching Whites from attack by its Indian owners. Moreover, as Raymond DeMallie remarked, treaty-makers were not above signing a treaty 'so that when it was broken there would be legal justification for sending in the army'.[10] For all practical purposes, therefore, conquest took place. Why else should ostensibly sovereign nations decide to surrender their ancestral homelands?

More often than not, the agency that reduced Indian peoples to this abjection was not some state instrumentality but irregular, land-hungry invaders (Ned Blackhawk's 'imperial precursors') who had no intention of allowing the formalities of federal law to impede their access to the riches available in, under, and on Indian soil.[11] If the government notionally held itself aloof from such disreputable proceedings, however, it was never far away. Consider the complicity between bayonet-wielding troops and the 'lawless rabble' in the following account of events immediately preceding the Eastern Cherokees' catastrophic 'Trail of Tears', one of many comparable 1830s removals whereby Indians from the South-East were displaced west of the Mississippi to make way for the development of the slave-plantation economy in the Deep South. The removals illustrate the pragmatics of discovery particularly clearly. As noted in the previous chapter, dominion without conquest constitutes the theoretical (or 'inchoate') stage of territorial sovereignty. In Marshall's words, it remained to be 'consummated by possession'.[12] This delicately phrased 'consummation' is precisely what the rabble were achieving at Cherokee New Echota in 1838:

> Families at dinner were startled by the sudden gleam of bayonets in the doorway and rose up to be driven with blows and oaths along the weary miles of trail that led to the stockade [where they were held prior to the removal itself]. Men were seized in their fields or going along the road, women were taken from their wheels and children from their play. In many cases, on turning for one last look as they crossed the ridge, they saw their homes in flames, fired by the lawless rabble that followed on the heels of the soldiers to loot and pillage. So keen were these outlaws on the scent that in some instances they were driving off the cattle and other stock of the

---

9 *Johnson v. McIntosh*, 587, 588; *Worcester v. Georgia*, 545.

10 Raymond J. DeMallie, 'American Indian Treaty Making: Motives and Meanings', *American Indian Journal* 3, no. 1 (1977), 9.

11 Ned Blackhawk, *Violence over the Land: Indians and Empires in the Early American West* (Cambridge, MA: Harvard UP, 2006, 169). On this basis, I register my disagreement with Blackhawk's assertion, further up the same page, that the seasonal trappers to whom he was referring were 'not settlers'.

12 *Johnson v. McIntosh*, 573

Indians almost before the soldiers had fairly started their owners in the other direction. Systematic hunts were made by the same men for Indian graves, to rob them of the silver pendants and other valuables deposited with the dead. A Georgia volunteer, afterward a colonel in the Confederate service, said: 'I fought through the civil war and have seen men shot to pieces and slaughtered by thousands, but the Cherokee removal was the cruelest work I ever knew'.[13]

On the basis of this passage alone, the structural complexity of settler colonialism could sustain libraries of elaboration. A global dimension to the frenzy for Native land is reflected in the fact that, as economic immigrants, the rabble were often drawn from the ranks of Europe's landless. The cattle and other stock were not only being driven off Cherokee land; they were being driven into private ownership. Once evacuated, the Red man's land would be mixed with Black labour to produce cotton, the white gold of the Deep South. To this end, African American slavery and the highest echelons of the formal state apparatus converged across three continents with the disorderly pillaging of a nomadic horde who may or may not have been 'lawless' but who were categorically settlers. Moreover, in their indiscriminate lust for any value that could be extracted from the Cherokees' homeland, the grave-robbers are unlikely to have stopped at the pendants. The burgeoning science of craniology, which provided a distinctively post-eighteenth-century validation for settlers' claim to a racial superiority that entitled them to other people's lands, made Cherokee skulls too marketable a commodity to be overlooked.[14] In its endless multidimensionality, there was nothing singular about this one sorry removal, which all of modernity attended.

Invasion and the Long Run

The iconic status of the Cherokee Trail of Tears is apt to give the misleading impression that it was an isolated or exceptional event. As observed, the Cherokees were by no means the only people to be removed, to which we should add that other removals had taken place before the 1830s and would continue after them.[15] In regard to the long-run character

---

13 James M. Mooney, *Historical Sketch of the Cherokee* (Washington, DC: Smithsonian Institute, 1975 [1900]), 124. On this basis, to return to Blackhawk's 'settler' category (n. 11 above), it seems to me that Cherokees, along with certain Indians elsewhere in North America, would question Blackhawk's assertion that 'Utah's Indian wars were unique in that the settlers themselves became the initial agents of violence, followed by the U.S. Army', Blackhawk, *Violence over the Land*, 230.

14 Gould, *Mismeasure of Man*.

15 The nineteenth-century campaign seems to have originated with Jefferson in the wake of the Louisiana Purchase. Knox or his successor, Timothy Pickering, may

of Indians' incorporation into settler society. The Trail of Tears, far from being isolated in time, was one episode in the protracted historical process whereby the Cherokees became contained within settler society.

We should resist the idea that, in being driven onto the Trail of Tears, the Cherokees were being driven into history, as if they had been waiting in some pristine Indigenous space over the frontier until the tide of White settlement eventually caught up with them. By 1838, Cherokee society had been experiencing a continuous series of transformations that had been occurring in and through their contact with Europeans for over a century and a half. Their southern Appalachian homeland had placed them between the English on the Atlantic coast, the French in the Ohio and Mississippi valleys, and the Spanish in Florida. As a result, they had long been central to these rival powers' ceaseless competition for Indian allies. Different tribes were armed and supplied by European powers who fomented hostilities between them, a situation that had placed Cherokee society on something like a permanent war footing, bringing about a centralising of the cellular village structure that had generally obtained until quite late in the seventeenth century.[16]

Until enslavement became an almost exclusively African condition towards the end of the seventeenth century, the Cherokees had been involved in the Indian and Black slave trade with Europeans, a lucrative undertaking that exacerbated the belligerent situation by encouraging slave raids on surrounding Native peoples.[17] The Europeans traded their manufactured goods for war prisoners, so this commodification stimulated the Indians to further conflict. As chattel slavery became increasingly Africanised, Cherokees' trade with Europeans came to centre on deerskins, an important commodity in Europe (where, with cattle depleted by continental epidemics, deerskins provided goods ranging from military uniforms to book-bindings). As a result, Charleston, the principal export centre for Appalachian deerskin, soon rivalled Albany, capital of the northern fur trade, in the volume and value of its animal exports to Europe. Whether for hunting, slaving or warring, men's constant absences had a

---

have suggested the idea to him. There were relatively minor colonial precedents. Abel, 'History of Events', vol. 2, 244. For Indian removal in California in the 1860s, see Robert F. Heizer (ed.), *The Destruction of California Indians* (Lincoln: Bison Books/ Nebraska UP, 1993), 154–61.

16 Robert J. Conley, *The Cherokee Nation: A History* (Albuquerque: New Mexico UP, 2005), 25–9; Gary C. Goodwin, *Cherokees in Transition: A Study of Changing Culture and Environment Prior to 1775* (Chicago: University of Chicago Dept. of Geography Research Paper no. 181, 1977), 112–24; Steven Oatis, *A Colonial Complex: South Carolina's Frontiers in the Era of the Yamasee War, 1680–1730* (Lincoln: Nebraska UP, 2004), 244–75.

17 Theda Perdue, *Slavery and the Evolution of Cherokee Society, 1540–1866* (Knoxville: Tennessee UP, 1979), 19–40; R. Halliburton, Jr., *Red over Black: Black Slavery among the Cherokee Indians* (Westport: Greenwood Press, 1977), 3–19.

significant impact on gender and family roles.[18] Economic historian Wilma Dunaway has aptly sketched the transnational density of the situation:

> The Cherokees marketed slaves and deerskins to Charleston for re-export to the West Indies and to the northern colonies ... In return, Charleston received sugar and tobacco from the West Indies and rum from the northern colonies. The rum traded to Charleston merchants, a large part of which ended up in Cherokee villages, had its origins in West Indian molasses, for which the northern colonies swapped lumber and provisions. In exchange for the deerskins exported to England, Charleston received manufactured goods – including woolens, clothing, guns, and iron tools that were bartered to the Indians for slaves and deerskins. In return for the luxury goods it manufactured from Cherokee deerskins, England received raw materials, luxury goods, and meat provisions from all over the globe.[19]

The outcome of this involvement in global capitalism was predictable enough. Cherokee society rapidly became deindustrialised and dependent. Dependency concedes power – especially, where Europeans were concerned, the power to threaten to cut off trade. As Daniel Richter tersely observed of the Iroquois North-East as early as the mid-seventeenth century: 'Ironically, to continue to live as "Indians", Native people needed to trade with Europeans.'[20] In 1751, over eighty years before the Trail of Tears, Cherokee chief Skiagonota was already acknowledging the loss of self-sufficiency: 'The clothes we wear we cannot make for ourselves. They are made for us. We use their ammunition, with which we kill deer. We cannot make our guns. Every necessity of life we have from the White people.'[21]

For all its concentrated horror, therefore, the Trail of Tears was not an isolated event. As the Middle Passage cannot be separated out from the continuum of African American slavery, so the Trail of Tears brought together key components of an eliminatory process that was not only long-established, but would continue long after most of the Cherokee had crossed the Mississippi into the federal realm of Indian Territory. By the end of the century, in the Indian country that was poised to become Oklahoma, the removed Western Cherokees would become one of the

---

18 For diametrically opposing accounts of how Cherokee women's traditional relationship to agriculture was affected by dependency, see Perdue, *Slavery and the Evolution of Cherokee Society*, 53, *cf.* Wilma A. Dunaway, *The First American Frontier: Transition to Capitalism in Southern Appalachia, 1700–1860* (Chapel Hill: North Carolina UP, 1996), 37.

19 Dunaway, *First American Frontier*, 34.

20 Daniel K. Richter, *Facing East from Indian Country: A Native History of Early America* (Cambridge, MA: Harvard UP, 2001), 51.

21 Quoted in Dunaway, *First American Frontier*, 39.

central targets of the allotment campaign.[22] Thus the idea of the frontier catching up with them is multiply misleading. There was no dividing-line in space but a complex and uneven historical process. Moreover, this process never passed over them, so there is no dividing-line in time either: not an event but a structure. Accordingly, rather than viewing the Trail of Tears, for all its stark containedness, as a monolithic occurrence, we should see it as a cumulative event that condensed key features of an extended historical transformation. The Cherokees are but one example of a very general long-run phenomenon.[23]

Territoriality

The constant that imposes ultimate order on the otherwise shifting and episodic long-run histories of Indian dependency that have been narrated by scholars such as Blackhawk and Richard White is the insatiable dynamic whereby settler colonialism always needs more land.[24] In keeping with Lockean fundamentals, the primary motive is often agriculture, though by no means always. The whole range of primary sectors can sustain the project. In addition to agriculture, therefore, we should think in terms of forestry, fishing, pastoralism, and mining (the last straw for the Cherokees was the discovery of gold on their land). With the exception of agriculture, however (and, for some peoples, pastoralism), none of these provides a sufficient basis for social life. You cannot eat lumber or gold; fishing for the world market requires canneries. Sooner or later, miners move on, while forests and eventually even fish become exhausted or need to be farmed.

Agriculture not only supports the other sectors. It is inherently sedentary and, therefore, permanent. In contrast to extractive industries, which rely on what just happens to be there, agriculture is geared to vouchsafing its own reproduction, generating capital that projects into a future where it repeats itself (hence the farmer's dread of being reduced to consuming seed-stock). Moreover, to recall Locke again, it supports a larger population than non-sedentary modes of production. In settler-colonial terms, this means that an agricultural population can be expanded by continuing immigration at the expense of Native lands and livelihoods. As observed, in contrast to the fixed Native stock, there are always more

---

22 Kent Carter, *The Dawes Commission and the Allotment of the Five Civilized Tribes, 1893–1914* (Orem: Ancestry, 1999); D. S. Otis, *The Dawes Act and the Allotment of Indian Lands* (Francis Paul Prucha, ed., Norman: Oklahoma UP, 1973 [1934]).

23 For an example much further West, see Blackhawk's account of the complex and ever-shifting historical incorporation of Ute, Paiute and Shoshone societies in the Great Basin. Blackhawk, *Violence over the Land*.

24 Blackhawk, *Violence over the Land*; White, *Roots of Dependency*; White, *'It's Your Misfortune'*; White, *Middle Ground*.

settlers where the first ones came from. The inequities, contradictions, and pogroms of metropolitan society ensure a recurrent supply of fresh immigrants – especially, as noted, from among the landless. In this way, individual motivations dovetail with the global market's imperative for expansion.

Territorial expansion can override the most cherished of ideological objectives. When large expanses beckoned, even Jefferson and Jackson's hallowed yeoman farmer could be hustled out of the way by absentee speculators.[25] Displaced by speculators, many smallholders found them-selves steered into manufacturing industry to provide a market for the agricultural surplus. Jackson's manufacturing-oriented 'tariff of abomina-tions' maintained this industry.[26] Mary Young documented how, in the wake of Indian removal, Jacksonian policies favoured speculators over settlers. Driven to recoup the cost of removal, the government 'made a consistent practice of offering more land for sale each year than could possibly be purchased [by settlers ... This] threw large areas into the market before many settlers had realized enough from their crops to pur-chase their claims.'[27] The frontier was led from behind.

Through its ceaseless expansion, agriculture (including, for this purpose, commercial pastoralism) progressively eats into Indigenous ter-ritory, a primitive accumulation that turns native flora and fauna into a dwindling resource and curtails the reproduction of Indigenous modes of production. In the event, Indigenous people are either rendered depend-ent on the introduced economy or reduced to the stock-raids that provide the classic pretext for settler death squads. Neither alternative signifi-cantly obstructs the expansion of the settler economy. When it comes to the threat of permanence, however, as observed in relation to the Cherokee Constitution, Natives pose an irreducible obstacle to settler expansion. As Justice William Johnson put it in his concurring judge-ment in Cherokee v. Georgia: 'The hunter state bore within itself the

---

25   Donald B. Cole, *The Presidency of Andrew Jackson* (Lawrence: Kansas UP), 118; Richard Slotkin, *The Fatal Environment: The Myth of the Frontier in the Age of Industrialization, 1800–1900* (Norman: Oklahoma UP, 1985), 110–12, 127.

26   Since tariffs were seen to encourage retaliatory measures on the part of foreign countries that constituted the primary export market for the plantation economy, they were seen to favour the industrial North at the expense of the South, a division that reinforced the differences over slavery. See, e.g., Louis P. Masur, *1831: Year of Eclipse* (New York: Hill & Wang, 2001), 153–6. In this connection, Indian removal provided an issue that was capable of reconciling northerners such as Jackson's silvertail vice president Martin Van Buren and the southern slaveholding interest. Indeed, for Richard B. Latner, Indian removal furnished a basis for unifying the fledgling Democratic Party: Latner, *The Presidency of Andrew Jackson: White House Politics 1829–1837* (Athens: Georgia UP, 1979), 97–8.

27   Young, *Redskins, Ruffleshirts, and Rednecks*, 182. See also Daniel Feller, *The Public Lands in Jacksonian Politics* (Madison: Wisconsin UP, 1984), 80; Peter Temin, *The Jacksonian Economy* (New York: Norton, 1969), 96.

promise of vacating the territory, because when game ceased, the hunter would go elsewhere to seek it. But a more fixed state of society would amount to a permanent destruction of the hope, and, of consequence, of the beneficial character of the pre-emptive right.'[28] The first thing that the rabble did, let us remember, was burn the Cherokees' houses.

After the Civil War, when the primary focus of Indian dispossession switched to the Plains, removal morphed into the cognate policy of reservation.[29] As Robert Trennert observed, the early reservation policy, which sought to protect White travellers, was necessitated by the fact that the more mobile people of the Plains (who 'moved easily from one location to another, had no permanent villages or agricultural fields for whites to destroy, and were usually able to choose between battle or retreat as the situation demanded'[30]) needed to be handled differently. Through this shift, however, the strategic essentials remained the same. To exchange the buffalo road for the cow road, Plains Indians had to be 'settled on fixed reservations, since only then could their tribal land be assigned to individuals'.[31]

This continuity notwithstanding, there is a major difference between a pre–Civil War Indian policy dominated by removal and a post-war one dominated by the concept of the reservation, a solution first officially adopted in the late 1860s under President Ulysses S. Grant's so-called 'peace policy'.[32] The difference is that, by leaving Indians on a parcel of their own land, however limited, a reservation concedes permanence. The word itself denotes a continuing portion of Indians' primordial title, a portion that was 'reserved', or not surrendered, in treaties. By contrast, removal consummated the de facto extinguishment of Indians' right of occupancy that flowed with the tide of White incursion. 'Titles given in the West proved less substantial than those in the East,' Abel concluded her classic essay, 'for they had no foundation in antiquity.'[33] Excisions, repeat removals and the enforced sharing of territory granted more than once by different treaties were the practical face of removal's temporariness, which kept time with the westward march of the nation. There was anyway a limit to the West, which was also closing in from the Pacific, imposing a final constraint on removal.

---

28 *Cherokee v. Georgia*, 23.
29 Lewis Cass had used the term 'reservation' in the course of advocating the removal policy: 'Removal of the Indians', 66, 68.
30 Robert A. Trennert, Jr., *Alternative to Extinction: Federal Indian Policy and the Beginnings of the Reservation System, 1846–51* (Philadelphia: Temple UP, 1975), 14.
31 Rennard Strickland, 'Genocide-at-Law: An Historic and Contemporary View of the Native American Experience', *Kansas Law Review* 34 (1986), 725.
32 Prucha, *Great Father*, 152–64; David Sim, 'The Peace Policy of Ulysses S. Grant', *American Nineteenth Century History* 9 (2008), 241–68; White, *'It's Your Misfortune'*, 103–4.
33 Abel, *History of Events*, 412.

For settler purposes, however, it made little difference whether Indians had been removed to other tribes' homelands or confined to a portion of their own. They were on reservations, and there was nowhere else to put them. By the final quarter of the nineteenth century, practically all the territory within the contiguous United States that remained outside some form of US ownership (including public domain) was the territory held by or reserved to Indians under treaties. Thus treaties could no longer serve the purpose of converting Indian homelands into so many parts of the United States. Rather, they had come to constitute islands of incompleteness in the settler project. As such, they were historically as well as strategically temporary. A Turneresque outgrowth of expansion, the treaty was endemic to the nineteenth century. Thus it was timely that Congress should resolve, on 3 March 1871, that: 'No Indian nation or tribe within the territory of the United States shall be acknowledged or recognized as an independent nation, tribe, or power with whom the United States may contract by treaty.'[34] The era of treaty-making with Indian tribes was formally over.

After the Frontier

Despite the seemingly momentous nature of this development, some scholars have questioned its significance. The circumstances were hardly grandiose, treaty-making coming to an end as the result of an individual member's rider to a House appropriations bill. Moreover, until 1919 at least, variously named conventions and agreements continued to be made with Indian tribes. So far as the tribes themselves were concerned, it would be hard to identify any major difference of outcome between these instruments and treaties.[35] Nor was it as if treaties had brought unqualified blessings to Indians. Indeed, Ely Parker, the Seneca lawyer who came to be appointed Commissioner for Indian Affairs, argued that treaties were not worth preserving ('great injury has been done by the government in deluding [Indians] into the belief of their being independent sovereignties, while they were at the same time recognized only as its dependents and wards'[36]).

---

34   16 *Stat.*, 566, c. 120, s. 1.

35   Vine Deloria, Jr., and David E. Wilkins, *Tribes, Treaties, and Constitutional Tribulations* (Austin: Texas UP, 1999), 60–1; Vine Deloria, Jr., & Clifford Lytle, *American Indians, American Justice* (Austin: Texas UP, 1983), 37; Wilkinson, *American Indians, Time, and the Law*, 8. So far as the US was concerned, a major difference between these agreements and treaties was that, whereas under Article II, Section 2 of the Constitution, treaties involved both the executive and legislative branches (presidential representatives and a two-thirds Senate majority), the agreements merely required simple majorities in Congress and the Senate. See Deloria and DeMallie, *Documents of American Indian Diplomacy*, vol. 1, 249.

36   *Report of the Board of Indian Commissioners* (Washington: Govt Printing Office, 1869), 10.

Moreover, hostility to treaties could unite friends and foes of the Indian, the former being troubled by treaties' openness to abuse while the latter objected to any form of concession to Indians, or even to anything that impeded their extermination.[37] It can also be said that the end of treaty-making was not so much an Indian policy initiative as the by-product of a states' rights issue. The House of Representatives was growing tired of appropriating funds to an end that was determined by the Senate.

For such reasons, we need not be too concerned with the precise circumstances or details of the amendment.[38] Nor should we expect to find the years 1870 and 1872 distinguished by a hiatus in the conduct of Indian affairs. In the historical long run, however, as a marker of the final internalisation of Indian societies, the importance of the end of treaty-making can hardly be overstated. In separating Indian affairs from treaty discourse, the 1871 act completed *Cherokee v. Georgia*'s exclusion of Indian nations from the protection of international law. The outcome was a thoroughgoing domestication whereby, through being rendered internal, the Indian problem became administrative rather than political. Treaties had presupposed a measure of exteriority, one that the removals had provisionally maintained. Moreover, for all their shortcomings, treaties had at least required a semblance of bipartisanship – though possibly drunk, bribed and/or intimidated, there still had to be Indian signatories, and the government still had to go out West and talk to them. After 1871 – in theory at least, and increasingly in practice – congressmen merely had to talk to each other to change the ways in which Indians were controlled. Robert Oliver characterised this shift as a move from 'governing by bilateral agreement to governing by unilateral legislation'.[39]

Though governed, however, Indians were not citizens. For all the shortcomings of treaties, they were the only source of rights that Indians had. In the absence of treaties, they became unrelievedly subject to the power of Congress. Russel Barsh and James Youngblood Henderson have spelled out the totality of this subjection:

> Treaties, like contracts, are unenforceable except against those agreeing specifically and expressly to be bound by them. Legislation, however, is presumed to be legitimate when enacted, and enforceable against all persons

---

37 John R. Wunder, *'Retained by the People': A History of American Indians and the Bill of Rights* (New York: Oxford UP, 1994), 29.

38 Kevin Bruyneel has argued cogently that the 1871 amendment was a conscious and acknowledged departure. While I am not so sure about this, the important point, on which Bruyneel and I agree, is that the 1871 amendment marks a fundamental turning point in US Indian policy. See Bruyneel, *Third Space of Sovereignty*, 65–95, especially p. 66.

39 Robert W. Oliver, 'The Legal Status of American Indian Tribes', *Oregon Law Review* 38, no. 3, (1959), 200.

within the power of the legislature. Consent is neither specific nor express, but general and implied in the right to vote. Tribal Indians in 1871 could not vote. Thus what appeared to be a transfer of responsibility between branches of the federal government, was in actuality an assertion or arrogation of the power to govern tribes without their consent.[40]

This unqualified subjection is the essential feature of the doctrine of Congressional plenary power. In a double jeopardy reminiscent of *Cherokee v. Georgia* – whereby the Cherokee were neither citizens nor a foreign nation – Indians without treaties fell between two stools after 1871. Lacking a social contract, they became subject to the whim of Congress. Thus we see more clearly why the prescient Marshall should have rejected the notion of conquest. Conquered populations have rights under international law. By contrast, the regime that emerged after 1871 – the juridical forerunner, only on a much larger scale, to Guantánamo Bay[41] – represented a constitutional no-man's-land without limit or constraint.

Applying to Indians unprotected by treaties, this post-frontier condition was initially selective. As the nineteenth century drew to a close, however, Congress and the Supreme Court combined in an attempt to generalise it to all Indians. The cornerstone of this concerted campaign was the policy of allotment. Ostensibly, allotment provided for a cultural transformation whereby the experience of private property ownership would propel Indians from the collective inertia of tribal membership into the progressive individualism of the American dream. In the outcome, however, allotment's principal consequence was to detach Indians from their land, enabling the US government to extinguish tribal title to it – which is to say, Indian sovereignty over it. This occurred because individual allotments, usually of 160 acres, were smaller than a pro rata division of tribal territory would have yielded. Before allottees could begin to sell their plots, therefore, the government had already appropriated the surplus. Moreover, as Cole Harris has observed, capitalism benefited doubly from allotment, 'acquiring access to land freed by small reserves and to cheap labour detached from land'.[42]

Allotment also marked a refusal of collective organisation. 'A protected Indian title to land', enthused the Indian Rights Association in 1885, two years before the passage of the allotment legislation which it had championed, 'is the entering-wedge by which tribal organization is to

---

40 Russel L. Barsh and James Y. Henderson, *The Road: Indian Tribes and Political Liberty* (Berkeley: California UP, 1980), 69.

41 Sarah H. Cleveland, 'Powers Inherent in Sovereignty: Indians, Aliens, Territories, and the Nineteenth-Century Origins of Plenary Power over Foreign Affairs', *Texas Law Review* 81 (2002), 1–284.

42 Cole Harris, 'How Did Colonialism Dispossess? Comments from an Edge of Empire', *Annals of the Association of American Geographers* 94 (2004), 172.

be rent asunder.'[43] Theodore Roosevelt agreed, extolling the General Allotment Act in his message to Congress of December 1901 as 'a mighty pulverizing engine to break up the tribal mass'.[44] Given such basic correspondences, it is not surprising that nascent forms of both removal and allotment should have existed from the early days of White settlement. The General Allotment Act did not invent allotment; it sought to make it general.

Though it certainly brought increased system, the divisive technique that the act enshrined was by no means an invention of the 1880s.[45] Previous treaties had not, however, sought to generalise allotment to all Indians.[46] Indeed, in the 1830s, federal officials had assumed that allotment would encourage voluntary removal rather than assimilation: allottees would sell their plots in order to join tribal fellows who had moved west. 'President Jackson and his advisers were caught off guard, therefore,' commented Ronald Satz, 'when thousands of Choctaws decided to take advantage of the allotment provisions and become homesteaders and American citizens in Mississippi.'[47]

There was nothing special about Choctaws to make them particularly congenial to White society. Few of them were like Chief LeFlore, who had a White father, light skin, wealth, education and influential connections in Euroamerican society.[48] Moreover, a majority of the Choctaws were removed, like Ross and the Cherokees. The reason the remainder were acceptable had nothing to do with their being Choctaw. On the contrary, it had to do with their not (or, at least, no longer) being Choctaw. They had become 'homesteaders and American citizens'. In a word, they had become individuals. Choctaws who stayed became the proprietors, each to his own, of separately allotted fragments of what had

---

43 ' Quoted in Francis Paul Prucha, *Americanizing the American Indians: Writings by the 'Friends of the Indian', 1880–1900* (Cambridge, MA: Harvard UP, 1973), 172–84.

44 Theodore Roosevelt, first State of the Union Address, 3 December, 1901.

45 Paul W. Gates, 'Indian Allotments Preceding the Dawes Act', in John G. Clark (ed.), *The Frontier Challenge: Responses to the Trans-Mississippi West* (Lawrence: Kansas UP, 1971), 141; Young, *Redskins, Ruffleshirts, and Rednecks, passim*. J. P. Kinney found a legislative order of the General Court of Massachusetts which declared as early as 1633 that 'if any of the Indians shall be brought to civility, and shall come among the English to inhabit, in any of their plantations, and shall there live civily [sic] and orderly ... such Indians shall have allotments amongst the English, according to the custom of the English in like case.' Kinney, *A Continent Lost – A Civilization Won: Indian Land Tenure in America* (Baltimore: Johns Hopkins UP, 1937), 6.

46 Hence it is consistent that Senator Dawes should have advocated the discontinuation of treaty-making on the ground that this would conduce to general allotment. See Wilcomb E. Washburn, *The Assault on Indian Tribalism: The General Allotment Law (Dawes Act) of 1887* (Philadelphia: J. B. Lippincott, 1975), 25.

47 Satz, *American Indian Policy*, 83.

48 Mrs Lee J. Langley, 'Malmaison: Palace in a Wilderness, Home of General LeFlore, Mississippi's Remarkable Indian Statesman', *Chronicles of Oklahoma* 5, no. 4 (1927), 371–80.

previously been the tribal estate, theirs to sell to White people if they chose to. Without the tribe, though, for all practical purposes they were no longer Indians.

Here, in essence, is assimilation's Faustian bargain – have our settler world, but lose your Indigenous soul. Beyond any doubt, this is a kind of death. Assimilationists recognised this very clearly. On the face of it, one might not expect to find much in common between Captain Richard Pratt, founder of the Carlisle boarding school for Indian youth and leading light of the philanthropic 'Friends of the Indian' group, and General Phil Sheridan, scourge of the Plains and author of the deathless maxim, 'The only good Indian is a dead Indian'.[49] As Pratt was keenly aware, however, the irreconcilable Native difference that settler polities seek to eliminate can be detached from the individual, whose bare life can be reassigned within the set of settler social categories, yielding a social death of Nativeness. Thus the training in individualism that Pratt provided at his school was designed to cause the tribe to disappear while its members stayed behind – a metaphysical variant on the Choctaw scenario. This would offer a solution to reformers' disquiet over the national discredit attaching to the Vanishing Indian. In a paper for the 1892 Charities and Correction Conference held in Denver, Pratt explic- itly endorsed Sheridan's maxim, 'but only in this: that all the Indian there is in the race should be dead. Kill the Indian in him and save the man.'[50] In killing the Indian within – thereby interrupting individuals' succession from the tribes who had originally signed treaties – assimilation would also provide a means of treaty-abrogation.

Refraining from making new treaties was a partial measure, apply- ing only to those who had not already entered into them. Generalising its effects would require the abrogation of treaties that had already been signed. This objective, which would remove the legal protection, however insubstantial, that treaties formally provided, was central to the post-1871 policy framework that John Wunder has termed 'the New Colonialism': a reservation-based discursive formation that 'attacked every aspect of Native American life – religion, speech, political free- doms, economic liberty, and cultural diversity'.[51] The link that Wunder notes between the break-up of the treaty system and the imposition of a bureaucratic regime of institutional conditioning is crucial. The

---

49   It should be acknowledged that Pratt himself had previously served out West as a cavalry officer. The point is the consistency linking his various dealings with Indians.

50   Richard H. Pratt, 'The Advantages of Mingling Indians with Whites' [1892], selection in Prucha, *Americanizing the American Indians*, 261. Ward Churchill, *Kill the Indian, Save the Man: The Genocidal Impact of American Indian Residential Schools* (San Francisco: City Lights, 2004) illustrates the genocidal consequences of Friends of the Indian–style total institutions.

51   Wunder, *'Retained by the People'*, 39, 17.

depoliticisation of Indian affairs required that they be detached from the realm of international relations. Once detached, the internalised Indian problem took on the characteristics of a Foucauldian discourse, becoming a technical issue which, like crime or insanity, was to be shaped and managed by a bureaucratically credentialled coterie of specialists whose disciplinary mission was the reconstitution of Indian subjecthood.[52]

In the three or four decades after treaty-making was discontinued, the discourse of conquest turned inwards, seeking to penetrate through the tribal surface to the individual Indian below, whose individuality corresponded to a particular fragment of the tribal estate. The outcome was a two-way loss whereby culture and biology supplemented each other. Mixed-bloodedness operated as a synonym for – or, at least, conduit to – a wider cultural and political assimilation whose achievement would amount to the dissolution of Indianness, a process that Annette Jaimes has termed 'statistical extermination'.[53] As Senator Higgins put it in Congress: 'It seems to me one of the ways of getting rid of the Indian question is just this of intermarriage, and the gradual fading out of the Indian blood; the whole quality and character of the aborigine disappears, they lose all of the traditions of the race'.[54]

Culturally, through what Lewis Meriam sarcastically dubbed 'the magic in individual ownership of property', Indians would be co-opted out of the tribe, which would be depleted accordingly, and into White society.[55] The Greenwood LeFlore model would be generalised. With every man his own chief, there would be no more Indians. Colonel Pratt estimated that allotted Indians could be assimilated in a mere three to five years so long as they were evenly spread (which would 'only make nine Indians to a county throughout the United States'). Justice William Strong concurred: 'I would, if I had my way in the matter, plant no allotment of an Indian family within ten miles of another.'[56] But the final boundary of the Indian domain was Indianness itself, persisting within every individual who remained Indian. In the end, blood quanta crossed even this boundary, allotting the Indianness beneath the skin.

---

52 By 1910, Francis E. Leupp, former Commissioner of Indian Affairs, would feel able to state that the Indian problem had 'now reached a stage where its solution is almost wholly a matter of administration', Leupp, *The Indian and His Problem* (New York: Charles Scribner's Sons, 1910), *vii*.

53 Jaimes, 'Federal Indian Identification Policy', 137.

54 Congressional Record quoted in Spruhan, 'Legal History of Blood Quantum', 32.

55 Lewis Meriam et al., *The Problem of Indian Administration. Summary of Findings and Recommendations* [Meriam Report] (Washington, DC: [Brookings] Institute for Government Research, 1928), 7. 'If we can watch our body of dependent Indians shrink even by one member at a time, we may congratulate ourselves that the complete solution is only a question of patience', Leupp, *Indian and His Problem*, 49.

56 Quoted in Otis, *Dawes Act*, 67.

As a strategy of elimination, assimilation promises to be more effective than either homicide or a spatial device. Unlike homicide, it does not jeopardise settler social order, since the policy is invariably presented, in philanthropic terms, as offering Natives the same opportunities as are available to Whites. Correspondingly, unlike the spatial techniques of removal and/or confinement, assimilation is seen as permanent and not susceptible to the settler land-hunger that sooner or later arrives at the boundaries of the Native enclave. Above all, though, assimilation is total. In neutralising a seat of consciousness, it eliminates a competing sovereignty. Confined Natives, relatives and descendants of conquered Natives, remember their dispossession. That memory inscribes the foundational violence of settler democracy. Assimilated Natives, by contrast, do not even exist. There are only White people, settlers, bereft of memory.

Or so might the Native Administrator's wish be fulfilled. Natives can see things – and, more to the point, act on things – in other ways.[57] Given the power imbalance involved, however, resistance entails the most hazardous degree of risk-assessment, as in the case of those who boycotted the Dawes rolls and thereby disinherited their descendants.[58]

Plenitude and Power

For all its fame, or notoriety, the Dawes (or General Allotment) Act of 1887 was just one component in an avalanche of legislative and judicial initiatives that succeeded the final containment of Indian peoples. In combination, these concerted initiatives, which adapted the frontier logic of the Marshall judgements to twentieth-century conditions, converged on the specifically Indian-focused racial discourse of blood quanta. The Dawes Act is best understood in the context of the Seven Major Crimes (or Offenses) Act of two years earlier, which, in subordinating tribal law to US jurisdiction on reservations, struck at the heart of tribal authority.[59] Two years previously, in the Crow Dog case, the Supreme Court had reversed the conviction of Crow Dog, a Sioux who had allegedly murdered the White-aligned chief Spotted Tail, on the ground that tribal law should apply to cases of major crime.[60]

---

57 It is crucial not to grant Congressional intentions the status of faits accomplis. Indians resisted these measures at every turn, with locally varying degrees of success. Vine Deloria repeatedly complained that scholarship on Indian law (to which we might add Indian policy) has confused prescription and description, as if 'tribes meekly bowed to the dictates of federal actions simply because these actions were clothed in the trappings of law.' Deloria, 'Laws Founded in Justice and Humanity: Reflections on the Content and Character of Federal Indian Law', *Arizona Law Review* 31 (1989), 205.

58 Carter, 'Snakes & Scribes'.

59 Act of 3 March 1885, 23 *Stat.*, 362.

60 *Ex Parte Crow Dog*, 109 U.S. 556 (1883).

Sydney Harring has convincingly argued, on the basis of a careful archival reading, that the case had been orchestrated by the Bureau of Indian Affairs with a view to turning public opinion against the maintenance of tribal law on reservations. The hue and cry that followed the Crow Dog judgement prompted Congress to pass the Seven Major Crimes Act, which, in removing major offences from tribal jurisdiction (the Five Civilized Tribes were excepted), critically undermined tribal authority on reservations, encouraging a growth in disorder that warranted the granting of further powers to the BIA. In 1898, the Assimilative Crimes Act made more minor offences subject to state law on reservations, despite their federal standing.[61] The previous week, the relatively privileged status that had been accorded to the Five Civilized Tribes as a consequence of treaty undertakings had been definitively overturned by the Curtis Act, which dismantled their tribal legal systems and left them with the non-choice of agreeing to allotment provisions with the federal government or having the Dawes Commission allot their land for them.[62] The crucial factor in this development was not the legislation itself so much as the intervening judicial development that had enabled it.

Smarting from the public opprobrium to which the Crow Dog judgement had exposed it, the Supreme Court had proved to be a fast learner. In 1886, the year following the Major Crimes Act, the Court had been called on to decide whether it was constitutional for Congress to legislate for acts that took place between Indians within the boundaries of an Indian reservation. The judgement in this case (*Kagama*) maintained the distinctively sanctimonious idiom that we have seen to characterise Indian affairs, holding out the power that flowed from wardship as consonant with the federal government's duty to protect Indians from the states ('They [Indians] owe no allegiance to the States, and receive from them no protection. Because of the local ill-feeling, the people of the States where they are found are often their deadliest enemies'[63]).

Yet the judgement's conclusion could hardly have diverged more markedly from the court's position three years earlier in Crow Dog. In what Lawrence Baca has reasonably termed 'perhaps the single most powerful expression of the authority of the federal government over Indian tribes', the Kagama court relied on Marshall's concept of wardship to hold that, by ending treaty-making, the 1871 amendment had provided that Indians should be governed by acts of Congress. At this much-quoted moment, when the Supreme Court deferred to Congressional authority

---

61 Act of 7 July 1898, S. 2, 30 *Stat.*, 717. The court in *McBratney v. United States* (104 U.S. 621 [1881]) had paved the way for this development by upholding state jurisdiction over crimes involving non-Indians on reservations.

62 Act of 28 June 1898, 30 *Stat.*, 495.

63 *Kagama*, 118 U.S. 375 (1886), 383–4.

over Indian affairs, not only was the passing of the frontier acknowledged but the federal government became general and the tribes became
a race:

> The power of the General Government over these remnants of a race once
> powerful, now weak and diminished in numbers, is necessary to their protec-
> tion, as well as to the safety of those among whom they dwell. It must exist
> in that government, because it never has existed anywhere else, *because the
> theater of its existence is within the geographical limits of the United States* [my
> emphasis], because it has never been denied, and because it alone can enforce
> its laws on all the tribes.[64]

The year after *Kagama*, the Dawes Act was passed. A few years later,
at the dawn of the twentieth century, the totalitarian edifice of plenary
power was completed when the Supreme Court in *Lone Wolf v. Hitchcock*
determined that 'the power exists to abrogate the provisions of an
Indian treaty'.[65] This ruling 'essentially freed Congress from any linger-
ing concern that it had to get Indian consent before it could dispose of
Indian lands'.[66] In the same judgement, the Court unilaterally surrendered its power to review Congressional activity in the special realm of
Indian affairs, declaring that Indian affairs were a political question and,
as such, the preserve of the legislature. In completing the depoliticisation
of Indian affairs through the ironic device of the political question, the
Lone Wolf v. Hitchcock court took *Cherokee v. Georgia*'s removal of judicial
protection to its logical conclusion. In the time that had elapsed since
the *Kagama* judgement, Congress had not failed to take advantage of
the licence it had received from the court. The Dawes Act, which gave
the federal government power to negotiate with individual Indians, is
probably less significant than the 1891 amendment to it, which, fatefully, gave the Bureau of Indian Affairs power of attorney – including
powers of lease or sale – over the land of Indians deemed incompetent
to deal with their own affairs (as Vine Deloria commented, 'presumably
the Secretary would learn the lessons of private property on behalf of
the Indians'[67]).

The depoliticisation of Indian affairs centred on the BIA's blood
quantum reckonings, which reflected the exigencies of tribal enrollment and titular succession from the allotment rolls that were instituted
at the dawn of the twentieth century. As we have seen, terms such as

---

64   *Kagama*, 118 U.S. 375 (1886), 384.
65   187 U.S. 553 (1903), 566.
66   Spruhan, 'Legal History of Blood Quantum', 40.
67   Vine Deloria, Jr., '"Congress in Its Wisdom": The course of Indian legislation',
in Sandra L. Cadwalader and Vine Deloria, Jr. (eds), *The Aggressions of Civilization:
Federal Indian Policy since the 1880s* (Philadelphia: 1984, Temple UP, 1984), 116.

'full-blood', 'mixed-blood', and 'half-breed' had been common enough for most of the nineteenth century, but it was not until Dawes commissioners confronted the problem of determining which Indians should be entitled to individual allotments of reservation land, and of what extent, that these casual designations came to acquire mathematical refinement. This development can be dated, with some precision, from the year before Turner published his seminal essay on the frontier.[68] Writing in 1892, Indian Affairs Commissioner T. J. Morgan distinguished the rigorous quantifications necessitated by the administrative requirements of tribal allotment from the looser usage of earlier eras.[69] In 1856, Morgan declared, it had been enough for Attorney-General Caleb Cushing simply to recommend that: 'half-breeds (and in his opinion he seems to use the expressions half-breeds and mixed-bloods interchangeably) should be treated by the executive as Indians in all respects so long as they retain their tribal relations.'[70]

So unfamiliar was his refinement, however, that Morgan proceeded immediately to ignore it, going on to refer to Ross, whose detractors never tired of pointing to his seven White great-grandparents, as 'a Cherokee chief, who was a half-breed'.[71] Ultimately, however, Morgan's innovation would be adopted and practically elaborated, with disastrous consequences for the thousands of Indians who found themselves excluded (or, with political misjudgement, excluded themselves) from the Dawes rolls, consequences that persist into the present.

On the ground, mixed-bloodedness does not seem to have significantly affected individual Indians' entitlement to being placed on the

---

68 Turner's 'The Significance of the Frontier in American History' was read before the Chicago meeting of the American Historical Association in July 1893, subsequently being published in the *Proceedings of the State Historical Society of Wisconsin* in December 1893. For the full text, go to: xroads.virginia.edu. An earlier version of its central thesis, entitled 'Problems in American History', had been published in the Wisconsin student publication *The Ægis* in November 1892, a bare three months after Commissioner Morgan's report. Two years previously, in 1890, less than two years after the passing of the Dawes Severalty Act of 1887, the US Bureau of the Census had reported the disappearance of a contiguous frontier line. Robert Porter, Henry Gannett and William Hunt, 'Progress of the Nation', in *Report on Population of the United States at the Eleventh Census: 1890, Part 1* (Washington: Bureau of the Census, 1895, xviii–xxiv).

69 'In close connection with the subject of Government control over the Indians and methods of administration, an interesting question has recently arisen, namely, What is an Indian? One would have supposed that this question would have been considered a hundred years ago and been adjudicated long before this. Singularly enough, however, it has remained in abeyance, and the Government has gone on legislating and administering law without carefully discriminating as to those over whom it had a right to exercise such control. The question has arisen latterly in connection with the allotment of lands.' T. J. Morgan, *Sixty-First Annual Report of the Commissioner for Indian Affairs* (Washington: Govt Printing Office, 1892), 31.

70 Ibid., 34.

71 Ibid.

Dawes rolls and allotted. But land loss was the result not of allotments being allocated, but of their being sold or leased. Thus it was crucial that restrictions which prevented 'full-bloods' from selling or leasing their allotments (to prevent them from being duped) were relaxed in the case of the allegedly more savvy 'mixed-bloods', whose losses were disproportionately higher.[72] In the authoritative report that found its way into the Indian Reorganization Act of 1934, D. S. Otis stressed that leasing was 'a spur to the taking of allotments':

> But it seems hardly to have been a spur to the Indian becoming a farmer. Perhaps some Indian lessors learned the doctrine of hard work from their white tenants. But evidence seems to show that what they learned mostly was to reap where they did not sow.[73]

Thus could incompetent Indians sit out the twenty-five years before they could sell their allotments. Moreover, as Otis acidly noted, it soon became clear that 'either the Indians were growing more incompetent or more incompetent Indians were being discovered, for leasing increased by leaps and bounds'.[74]

In the aftermath of the frontier, which had relied on treaties for its expansion, plenary power removed the remaining obstacles that Indian sovereignty presented to the twin process of dismantling tribal government and breaking tribal territory down into alienable private lots. Indeed, so unfettered was the apparatus of plenary power that, in 1913, the *Sandoval* court felt obliged to insulate the rest of the population from the possibility that Congress could deprive any group of its rights by the simple expedient of 'arbitrarily calling them an Indian tribe'.[75]

In the years between the discontinuing of treaty-making in 1871 and *Lone Wolf v. Hitchcock* in 1903, Congress (with varying degrees of success) sought to discontinue treaty-making, subvert tribal law on reservations and generalise allotment. In territorial terms, the outcome of this collusion of the powers was that, within the same three decades, Indians lost half their land (from over 155 million acres in 1881 to under 80 million in 1900[76]), a faster rate of dispossession than had

---

72 As Kent Carter noted in his thorough account of the allotment of the Five Civilized Tribes, 'An allottee's right to manage his property was now [in 1906] based on degree of blood.' Carter, *Dawes Commission and the Five Civilized Tribes*, 176. See also Cohen, *Handbook of Federal Indian Law*, 169; Angie Debo, *And Still the Waters Run* (Princeton: Princeton UP, 1940), 36–52; Land Division of the Indian Office statistics are quoted in Otis, *Dawes Act*, 86–7.

73 Otis, *Dawes Act*, 125.

74 Ibid., 120.

75 *U.S. v. Sandoval* (231 U.S., 1913, 28), 46.

76 *Statistical Abstract of the United States* (US Bureau of the Census, Department of Commerce, 1955), 180.

previously been provided by the US Cavalry. As the Hoover Commission would belatedly conclude, 'the rationalization behind this policy [allotment] is so obviously false that it could not have prevailed for so long a time if not supported by the avid demands of others for Indian land.'[77] Immiseration kept pace with the land loss. At the turn of the twentieth century, Indian population numbers hit the lowest level they would ever plumb.[78] Needless to say, the coincidence between the demographic statistics and the landownership ones was no coincidence. Thus reduced, Indians were increasingly seen as becoming eligible for the generalised citizenship that would cap their assimilation.[79]

A large step in this direction took place in 1919, when Indians who had contributed to the war effort were rewarded with citizenship. Indian citizenship was finally generalised in 1924 – though not in a form that was equal to that of other citizens since, uniquely, Indian citizenship permitted the continuation of wardship. In individual cases, citizenship had already been made available to Indians who allotted and distanced themselves from tribal organisation (though the case of John Elk – an assimilated town-dweller who was nonetheless barred from voting – had illustrated the limitations of this concession[80]). For Indian people, therefore, citizenship and racialisation converged. Both tended towards assimilation.

Here again, and particularly starkly, we see the fundamental disparity between Indian people's racialisation and that of Black people, which, as we saw in chapter three, also reached a high point in 1924 in the Virginia anti-miscegenation statute that conceded the Pocahontas exception. Rather than converging with their citizenship, Black people's racialisation negated it. The hysterical policing of the one-drop rule that characterised the Jim Crow era was above all directed towards undoing the equality that Black people's formal citizenship entailed. The difference could not be clearer. Black people did not need to be equal to be exploited. Their inclusion did not add millions of acres to the national estate.

---

77 Charles J. Rhoads, John R. Nichols, Gilbert Darlington, George A. Graham, 'Report of the Commission of Indian Affairs to the Commission on Organization of the Executive Branch of the Government' (unpublished manuscript, October 1948, 15–16, quoted in S. Lyman Tyler, *Indian Affairs: A Work Paper on Termination with an Attempt to Show Its Antecedents* [Provo: Institute of American Indian Studies, Brigham Young University, 1964], 6).

78 Thornton, *Holocaust and Survival*, 133.

79 For discussions of Indian leaders' varying reactions to this development, see Bruyneel, *Third Space of Sovereignty*, 102–20.

80 *Elk v. Wilkins*, 112 U.S. 94 (1884).

Colonising the Tribe

The allotment policy was formally discontinued by the New Deal reforms associated with John Collier's dynamic stint as commissioner of Indian Affairs, which enshrined the principle of tribal self-government. To its undeniable credit, the 1934 Indian Reorganization (Wheeler-Howard) Act put an end to the catastrophic process of tribal allotment and returned surplus tribal lands that had not yet been sold off. It also curtailed the sale of tribal assets to outsiders. In addition, the act and related legislation improved Indians' freedom of religion and speech, established a more equitable criminal-justice system on reservations and provided funds for land acquisition and economic development, among other improvements.[81]

All this came at a price, however. Collier's vision for tribal organisation reflected his own Pueblo romance, a 'Red Atlantis' that he had discovered during a sojourn in New Mexico in the early 1920s. In Robert Berkhofer's words, the Pueblos became Collier's 'personal countercultural utopia'.[82] Nonetheless, tribes that reorganised under the act found themselves adopting a distinctly Western style of governance by way of the Bureau of Indian Affairs' model constitution.[83] Though the act ostensibly abandoned the campaign to assimilate individual Indians, its prescription for reinforcing tribal government was to anglicise it. Constitutions typically introduced tribal elections, specified blood quantum–based membership criteria and included the phrase 'subject to the approval of the Secretary of the Interior', whereby tribes surrendered final say over expenditure or land use. An indication of the practical substance of the act's version of tribal independence is the fact that the reforms were to be administered by the BIA, the single organisation with most to lose from Indian self-government.

Where tribal authorities evinced unwillingness to exchange their own political processes for Western-style electoral contestation, Collier sought to replace them with imposed political structures of Interior Department design. Indian resistance was widespread. The objections did not come only from traditionalist diehards. Christianised Indians reacted against the threat of being returned to ways of life that they had repudiated; allotted individuals resisted the idea of surrendering their holdings to the

81 John Collier, 'Indian Religious Freedom and Indian Culture' (Interior Department Circular no. 2970, January 1934). See also Jay B. Nash (ed.), *New Day for the Indians: A Survey of the Workings of the Indian Reorganization Act of 1934* (New York: Academy Press, 1938), 26.

82 Robert F. Berkhofer, Jr., *The White Man's Indian: Images of the American Indian from Columbus to the Present* (New York: Vintage, 1979), 178.

83 See, e.g., Graham D. Taylor, *The New Deal and American Indian Tribalism: The Administration of the Indian Reorganization Act, 1934–45* (Lincoln, NE: Nebraska UP, 1980), 37; 96.

collectivity; Oklahoma tribes 'believed they would have to return their oil wells to tribal governments that existed only as paper organizations',[84] while the Navajos, the largest tribe of all, politely heard Collier out and wanted nothing to do with his system.[85] For the Department of the Interior, however, one model fitted all. Ten years after the act had been passed, Assistant Solicitor Charlotte Westwood reported to the Senate Committee on Indian Affairs that the degree of standardisation of tribal constitutions was so 'incredibly high' that the conclusion was warranted that 'these constitutions are nothing more than new Indian Office [BIA] regulations'.[86]

In an important sense, however, the model constitutions were much more than new BIA regulations. Rather, they fundamentally shifted the level of regulation itself. Whereas, in the allotment era, tribal government had been routinely demonised, there was no suggestion that it was anything other than an alien entity. The allotment programme was premised on an unmediated opposition between tribal organisation and US society. In seeking to dismantle that opposition, the Indian Reorganization Act sought to raise the scope of assimilation from the level of the individual to that of the tribe itself. Where Dawes-style assimilation had reconstituted individual Indians as property-owners, and thus sought to eliminate them as Indians, the Indian Reorganization Act reconstituted tribes into structural conformity with White institutions – which is to say, it sought to eliminate them as Indian institutions.

The Indian Reorganization Act was championed with a tribal-rights enthusiasm that was reminiscent of Marshall's pro-Indian rhetoric. Moreover, the semblance of tribal consent that had been so important for treaty-making remained central to the process of securing tribal acceptance of the new constitutions, though this did not stop the BIA from defining and circumscribing tribes' powers for them. Bureau interference extended right down to a tribe's capacity to define its own membership, a function that was usurped by the model constitution's blood quantum requirement. In response to this requirement, Frank Ducheneaux, leader of the Cheyenne River Sioux, complained that the legislation not only kept Indians under the control of Congress and the secretary of the interior, but 'limited their sovereign rights, which had never been done before formally'.[87]

---

84 Lawrence M. Hauptman, 'The Indian Reorganization Act', in Cadwalader and Deloria, *Aggressions of Civilization* (131–48), 137.

85 Lawrence C. Kelly, 'The Indian Reorganization Act: The Dream and the Reality', *Historical Review* (44, 1975, 291–312), 296–7, 303–4; Wunder, *'Retained by the People'*, 67–8.

86 Barsh and Henderson, *The Road*, 121–2, quoting Senate Report no. 1031, 78th Congress, 2nd Session (1944), 5.

87 Quoted in Wunder, *'Retained by the People'*, 114.

It is important to widen the narrow focus that would confine the Indian Reorganization Act to US national history. Such a focus, which fails to recognise Indians as colonised peoples, merely endorses the post-frontier depoliticisation whereby Indian affairs were relegated from the realm of international relations to that of municipal administration, a phenomenon that we should be analysing rather than reproducing. The context in which the act was introduced was not merely that of the New Deal United States. Globally, it was an era in which White authorities were introducing systems of indirect or delegated governance with a view to assuaging colonial-nationalist sentiment in the colonies. Collier derived inspiration for his model of tribal government, which he even termed 'indirect administration', from Lord Lugard's plan for the indirect rule of British colonies.[88] Rather than fostering national independence, Lugard's intention had been to postpone it indefinitely. Thus it is not surprising that the Indians whom Collier recruited to the scheme should have found themselves in an impossible situation. As Laurence Hauptman has noted, '"Bureau Indians" had been viewed as traitors by many Indians since the days of Carlos Montezuma.'[89]

Blood Quantum

The reconfiguration of tribal governments into structural harmony with Euroamerican institutions was tellingly reflected in a concomitant elaboration of blood quantum criteria, in which the depoliticisation of Indian sovereignty through the bureaucratic technology of race emerges with particular clarity. In April 1934, a few weeks before the passing of the Indian Reorganization Act, President Franklin D. Roosevelt signed Executive Order 6676, which, for the first time, formally specified a quarter-degree requirement (in this case, for employment preference with the BIA).[90] Soon afterwards, section 19 of the Indian Reorganization Act would provide that:

> The term 'Indian' as used in this Act shall include all persons of Indian descent who are members of any recognized Indian tribe now under Federal jurisdiction, and all persons who are descendants of such members who were, on June 1, 1934, residing within the present boundaries of any reservation, and shall further include all other persons of one-half or more Indian blood.[91]

88 John Collier, *America's Colonial Record* (London: Victor Gollancz, 1947); Scudder Mekeel, 'An Appraisal of the Indian Reorganization Act', *American Anthropologist* 46 (1944), 209.

89 Hauptman, 'Indian Reorganization Act', 142.

90 Anita Vogt, 'Eligibility for Indian Employment Preference', *Indian Law Reporter* 1, no. 6, June 1974), 33.

91 *Indian Reorganization* (Wheeler-Howard) *Act*, s. 19.

A major shift has taken place here. Under the Dawes regime, hybridity had furnished a means to fragment the tribe. As of 1 June 1934, however, reservation Indians were no longer segregated into differently entitled categories. On the contrary, mixed-bloodedness seems to lack implications for tribal membership (though, as we have also seen, the model constitutions would seek to remedy this). Rather than tribal organisation, blood quantum discourse was now aimed primarily at people living *off* the reservations, the 'all other persons' who were not 'of one-half or more Indian blood'. This takes us back behind Dawes to the removal era, when, as the Ponca example illustrated, those whose mixed-bloodedness had been without consequence were those who had removed over the frontier.[92] As we have seen, it had been the Poncas' 'half-breed relatives', forsaking the tribe and living among White people, who had been eligible for allotments. In contrast to the assimilable individual, tribal organisation had been incompatible with the structurally regular institutions of US society, which meant that it had to be removed and, when that option was no longer available, dismantled. In the wake of the frontier, when the inassimilable tribe had finally been encompassed within White society, mixed-bloodedness came to operate within the confines of the tribe, which it served to break up.

Under the Indian Reorganization Act, by contrast – at least, as Congress passed it, before the BIA took over its implementation – mixed-bloodedness ceased to operate within the tribe, which was seen as confined to the space of the reservation.[93] But this is entirely consistent since, at the same time, tribal organisation ceased to be structurally incompatible with the institutions of US society. In other words, as the frontier receded from living memory, the act consolidated the invasion, achieving on paper the same end as removal had previously achieved on the ground. It rid US society of the inassimilable features of the tribe.

The Indian Reorganization Act's incorporation of the reconstituted tribe had profound implications for the complex interplay between civic and geographical space, Kevin Bruyneel's 'third space of sovereignty', that shaped the racialisation of Indian people.[94] As we have seen, when the destruction of tribal organisation was the primary target of US Indian policy, geographical withdrawal from the tribe was the key step

---

92 Thus it is significant that a form of blood quantum calculus that at least partially anticipated the genetic arithmetic of the Dawes era had already emerged earlier in the nineteenth century in Connecticut, at the expense of the Narragansett – New England being well and truly in a post-frontier condition by this stage. For a telling example, see O'Brien, *Firsting and Lasting*, 128.

93 The BIA has repeatedly applied blood quantum requirements more zealously than other agencies and sometimes in excess of legislation. Vogt, 'Indian Employment Preferences', 37. See also Hagan, 'Problem of Indian Identity', 319.

94 Bruyneel, *Third Space of Sovereignty*.

in an individual's assimilation into White society. Once the reformed tribe had been domesticated, however, the anomaly of an Indianness that persisted beyond tribal boundaries intensified accordingly. At this point, race ceased to operate on the reservation. There being no further need to eliminate an Indianness that had a licensed place, blood quantum discourse came to focus exclusively on Indianness as it endured off the reservation. All these years on, the abruptness of the reversal still has the capacity to astonish. Consider the following interchange from the House Committee on Indian Affairs' hearing into the Indian Reorganization Bill:

> SENATOR THOMAS: Well, if someone could show that they were a descendant of Pocahontas, although they might be only five-hundredth Indian blood, they would come under the terms of this act.

> COMMISSIONER COLLIER: If they are actually residing within the present boundaries of an Indian reservation at the present time.[95]

Off the reservation, however, one needed to boast half a degree to qualify. Failing this, blood quanta would continue to declassify Indians as they had earlier done within the tribe. When five-hundredth-degree descendants of Pocohantas – or, for that matter, quarter-degree people who had qualified for preferential BIA employment under Roosevelt's Executive Order – passed over the reservation boundary, therefore, they changed colour. Indians with African ancestry turned from Red to Black. So long as they did not possess a single drop of Black blood, other Indians could turn White. Either way, they ceased being Indian. There could hardly be a clearer example of race intensifying in White social space. Such anomalies reflect the persistence of settler-colonial thinking in the New Deal reforms, which located Indianness in a confined realm that was not merely geographical (the physical space of the reservation). By the same token, the Indian Reorganization Act's incorporation of the tribe into structural conformity with its civic environment culminated the racialisation of Indian people.

There could be no more unstable racial identity than one that transforms itself, trickster-like, at the reservation gate. Nor could the contrast with the fixity of Blackness be more complete. As we have seen, instability – susceptibility to being changed into something else – is a distinctive attribute of Indianness in US settler-colonial discourse. In comparison to this extreme, the nineteenth-century savagery that was either located or removable over the frontier was hardly unstable at all: as noted, Indians'

---

95 *Hearings on S. 2755 and S. 3645. Before the Senate Committee on Indian Affairs*, 73rd Congress, 2nd Session (1934), 264.

incapacity for agriculture figured as irredeemable in removalist propaganda. As we also saw, on the basis of Dawes-era logic, throughout the relentless attack against it, the tribe still incubated an alterity that was contrapuntal to White society. With the Indian Reorganization Act, however, the Indian problem became finally contained. This was the ultimate end of the frontier.

The bizarre formula that made chameleons of Indians as they moved on and off reservations is the obverse of a rule that assigned African Americans to Blackness without reference to phenotype. The ramifications of these historically produced differences are fundamental. As a number of scholars have noted, for instance, the Fifteenth Amendment could theoretically jeopardise Indians' distinctive rights, which could be interpreted as racially based.[96] Correspondingly, as noted at the outset, the African American civil-rights era campaign to be included on equal terms with White society represented an agenda that, on their own account, Indigenous people in the United States (as in Australia) have had to devote much of their political energies to resisting. Assimilation is typically championed as affording Natives the same freedoms as White people. As Senator Arthur Watkins of Utah, tireless advocate of the disastrous post-World War II policy of terminating Indian tribes, extolled the policy: 'Following in the footsteps of the Emancipation Proclamation of ninety-four years ago, I see the following words emblazoned in letters of fire above the heads of the Indians – THESE PEOPLE SHALL BE FREE!'[97]

Thus there is no paradox in the fact that, whereas forty acres and a mule were alleged to be enough to satisfy Black aspirations in the post-bellum era, the 160-acre sections that were allotted to individual Indians under the Dawes legislation were the centrepiece of a campaign to destroy tribal organisation.[98] The disparity reflects the antithetical complementarity that the colonial rule of private property has imposed on the two populations. From an Indigenous point of view, whether the arrival of particular intruders is voluntary or coerced does not affect these

96   The Fifteenth Amendment to the US Constitution prohibits the federal and state governments from denying a citizen the right to vote based on that citizen's 'race, color, or previous condition of servitude' (the latter meaning slavery).

For a cautionary discussion of the federal implications of the Hawaiian state case of *Rice v. Cayetano* (in concert with *Adarand* and the Alaskan *Bakke* case), see Shockey, '"Invidious" American Indian Tribal Sovereignty', especially 311.

97   Arthur V. Watkins, 'Termination of Federal Supervision: The Removal of Restrictions over Indian Property and Person', *Annals of the American Academy of Political and Social Science* (no. 311, 1955), 55.

98   Otis's *Dawes Act*, which originated as a report that found its way into the House hearings preceding the *Indian Reorganization Act*, remains a reliable source. For the Five Civilized Tribes in particular, see Carter's excellent *Dawes Commission and the Five Civilized Tribes*.

intruders' standing as rivals for their space and vital resources.[99] The logic of elimination is not reducible to voluntarism. As we have seen, enslaved Africans participated in Indian dispossession. Conversely, many Indians not only owned but bought and sold Black slaves. Indeed, Stand Watie, one of the leaders of the Cherokee treaty faction at the time of the Trail of Tears, was a slaveholder who went on to become the last Confederate general to surrender in the Civil War. In a Manichean moral universe, the empirical anomaly of good guys behaving like bad guys is hard to accommodate, confounding the liberal shibboleth of subaltern agency. For the liberal conscience, Black invaders and Indian slaveowners can represent altogether too much agency. The discomfort arises from the assumption that the enslaved and the banished – James Madison's 'the black race within our bosom and the red on our borders'[100] – should naturally be companions in more than misfortune. The surprise occasioned by tensions between Blacks and Indians reflects a static multiculturalism that views difference anachronistically, as a set of appearances endlessly reborn in the present.

It cannot be stated too strongly that discourses on Indians and on Blacks should be situated in relation to each other. As we have seen, the one-drop rule, apparently so specifically targeted at African descent, not only sanitises the White population but simultaneously eliminates Indians through its assimilation of Red-Black people to the Black category. As observed, those who promote racist exclusions within Indian tribes might reflect on the contribution their policy makes to the furtherance of White supremacy. As in the case of White supremacism in Australia, which produced the Stolen Generations of Aboriginal children, the one-drop rule provides for Native parents to produce non-Native children.

For all their formal differences, US policy on Indians and Australian policy on Aborigines evince fundamental commonalities with regard to a basic set of settler-colonial strategies of elimination. These commonalities persist beneath major constitutional distinctions such as the presence or absence of treaties or the opposition between monarchical and republican forms of government. The territorial expedients of clearance, removal, and confinement are directly analogous. Moreover, in each case, policies of biocultural assimilation, instantiated in various forms of genetic arithmetic, intensify on the closure of the frontier, which forestalls spatial stopgaps such as removal. In the post-frontier era, settler

99 For critiques of Asian immigrants' pretensions to Native ('local') status in Hawai'i, for instance, see most of the articles in Candace Fujikane and Jonathan Y. Okamura (eds), *Asian Settler Colonialism* (Honolulu: Hawai'i UP, 2008).

100 James Madison, *The Writings of James Madison* (9 vols, New York: G. P. Putnam's Sons, 1900–1910), vol. 3, 515.

authorities characteristically seek to depoliticise Indigenous external-ity by reducing international relations to a set of technical problems for internal administration.

This does not, however, mean that Native assimilation is an invari-able feature of settler colonialism. On the contrary, as we saw, removal represented an alternative to assimilation. Rather than an invariable strat-egy, assimilation is one among a range of eliminatory techniques that become favoured under different historical circumstances, the ending of the frontier being particularly conducive to its deployment. In the case of Zionism, which is the subject of the following two chapters, the Palestine/Israel frontier remains incomplete and the most strenuous measures have been adopted to avoid assimilating the Native popula-tion. Thus the problem is not assimilation per se, but its furthering of the settler project. Elimination, rather than its strategic repertoire, is the core feature. On this basis, we turn now to the Zionist colonisation of Palestine.

CHAPTER SEVEN

Purchase by Other Means

Dispossessing the Natives in Palestine

In the annals of settler colonialism, Zionism presents an unparalleled example of deliberate, explicit planning. No campaign of territorial dispossession was ever waged more thoughtfully. Methodologically, this characteristic makes Zionism a particularly revealing archive for research into the logic of settler colonialism. As we shall see in this and the following chapter, the programme consciously systematised by Zionist planners combined elements that had converged more haphazardly in other dispossessions, organised and prioritised with an express method that facilitates reconstruction.

While this characteristic is convenient for analytical purposes, it also entails a hazard. As observed, the settler logic of elimination is not reducible to voluntarism. It may involve deliberate premeditation on the part of individual agents – indeed, in the Zionist case, it involves the most careful forethought – but it does not depend on it. Palestinian entitlement does not depend on whether or not it can be shown that, somewhere in nineteenth-century Europe, a Jewish theorist or theorists imagined expelling the Natives from the land of Zion (or, if they did imagine this, whether or not they did so publicly).[1] The issue, once again, is the outcome, which obtains at the level of usufruct. Even if it could be shown that a people had been dispossessed absent-mindedly, or through some mistaken exercise of good intent, this would alter neither the fact of that people's dispossession nor the fact that the settlers who replaced them thereby became colonisers. By the same token – again, with reference to collective outcomes rather than individual representations – there is no necessary tension between being a refugee and being a settler.

---

1 'We shall try to spirit the penniless population across the border by procuring employment for it in the transit countries, while denying it any employment in our own country.' *The Complete Diaries of Theodor Herzl* (Raphael Patai, ed., Harry Zohn, trans., New York: Herzl Press/Yoseloff, 1960), vol. 1, 88.

Obvious though it may seem, this point has important implications for the legitimation of Israeli settler colonialism and, accordingly, for Western blindness concerning the ongoing catastrophe of Palestine. This is because evidence that Zionists planned the expulsion of the Natives in advance of Palestinians' 'miraculous' 1948 mass flight is seen as injurious to the crucial image of Israelis as victims. So long as Israelis are cast as victims, their opponents figure contrapuntally as the persecutors of Jews, a formula whereby Palestinians have even been cast as succeeding to the mantle of Nazism.[2] Thus it is understandable that a number of scholars should have devoted considerable energy to demonstrating that the 'transfer' of Palestine's Arab population was actively envisaged and systematically planned from the very beginnings of Zionism.[3]

Revealing though such findings are, however, intentionality itself is not the issue. Individual Jewish settlers may have arrived in Palestine with commendable motivations that did not include malevolence towards the Natives. Indeed, a number of them were surprised to find that Palestine was inhabited at all, let alone by the established agricultural community that they found there,[4] a surprise that testified to the success of Zionism's ideological claim that a land without a people was waiting for a people without a land.[5] Moreover, for every incriminating statement that early Zionists made (usually in private), it is easy enough to find a number of soothing assurances, coined for public consumption, in which the same Zionists asserted their intention to live in harmony with Palestine's Arab population. Dupes or not, however, the arrivals, refugees and otherwise, were nonetheless settlers, since the Natives whom some of them may

---

2   Seemingly oblivious to the Holocaust-trivialisation that this analogy entails, Zionist publicists have embraced it. For comment and sources, see Joseph A. Massad, *The Persistence of the Palestinian Question: Essays on Zionism and the Palestinians* (New York: Routledge, 2006), 132–4.

3   The most comprehensive account is Nur Masalha, *Expulsion of the Palestinians: The Concept of 'Transfer' in Zionist Political Thought, 1882–1948* (Washington: Institute for Palestine Studies, 1992). See also, e.g., Benny Morris, 'Yosef Weitz and the Transfer Committees, 1948–1949', *Middle Eastern Studies* 22 (1986), 522–61; David Hirst, *The Gun and the Olive Branch: The Roots of Violence in the Middle East* (London: Futura, 1978), 129–30; Israel Shahak, 'A History of the Concept of "Transfer" in Zionism', *Journal of Palestine Studies* 18, no. 3 (1989), 22–37; Marion Woolfson, *Prophets in Babylon: Jews in the Arab World* (London: Faber & Faber, 1980), 121–6.

4   Neville J. Mandel, *The Arabs and Zionism before World War I* (Berkeley: California UP, 1976), 31.

5   Israel Zangwill seems to have introduced the phrase into Zionist parlance, though he himself credited Lord Shaftesbury: Zangwill, *The Voice of Jerusalem* (London: Heinemann, 1920), 104. The phrase had, however, been used earlier, principally by nineteenth-century Christian-romantic proto-Zionists. See Adam M. Garfinkle, 'On the Origin, Meaning, Use and Abuse of a Phrase', *Middle Eastern Studies* 27 (1991), 539–50; Diana Muir, 'A Land without a People for a People without a Land', *Middle East Quarterly* 15, no. 2 (2008), 55–62.

have been surprised to encounter were nonetheless dispossessed. Thus we should avoid the guesswork of voluntarism in favour of an approach that relates historical outcomes to the practical logic of the human activities that produce them.[6]

Referring to the messianic brand of eliminationist logic espoused by Gush Emunim, the group that spearheaded the building of Jewish colonies ('settlements') in post-1967 occupied Palestine, the late dissident Israeli sociologist Baruch Kimmerling discerned a reawakening of 'the dormant codes of the immigrant-settler political culture'.[7] The rupture implied in the image of dormancy belies settler colonialism's discursive continuity, its status as structure rather than event.[8] In his lament for the country he had volunteered to defend, Bernard Avishai took a deeper historical view:

> Settlements were made in the territories beyond the Green Line so effortlessly after 1967 because the Zionist institutions that built them and the laws that drove them ... had all been going full throttle within the Green Line before 1967. To focus merely on West Bank settlers was always to beg the question.[9]

Though appreciably less episodic than Kimmerling's account, Avishai's 'laws that drove them' are restricted to the formal domain – referring, literally, to explicit legislative enactments. Purged of their dormancy, Kimmerling's 'codes' would come closer to the versatility and pervasiveness of settler discourse. Writing of Zionism's ideological beginnings, the staunchly Zionist writer Yosef Gorny was more rigorous:

> The fact that a people which was not resident in the country was laying claim to it by reason of historical rights in itself undermined the exclusive right of the country's Arab residents to voice the same claim. In other words, the trend to territorial concentration [of Jews], even if it did not entail the

---

6 Evasion of the criterion of outcomes underpins Derek Penslar's convoluted attempt to absolve Zionism of its settler-colonial essence. Penslar's apologia consists predominantly in a rehearsal of Zionists' putative mentality and intentions, with sparse acknowledgement of the consequences of their practical activities: 'Yet colonialist elements were present as well [as anti- and post-colonial ones] in the treatment of Israel's Arab minority and state confiscation of its land', Derek J. Penslar, 'Is Zionism a Colonial Movement?', chapter 5 of his *Israel in History: The Jewish State in Comparative Perspective* (London: Routledge, 2007), 91. With the exception of cursory references to Israel's foundational reliance on Palestinian dispossession (airily dismissed as 'an existential conflict between two nationalities', 95), Penslar's discussion proceeds solipsistically, as if Europeans' internal discourse were all that colonialism involved.

7 Baruch Kimmerling, *Politicide: The Real Legacy of Ariel Sharon* (2nd ed., London: Verso, 2006), 38.

8 Wolfe, *Settler Colonialism and the Transformation of Anthropology*, 2.

9 Bernard Avishai, 'Saving Israel from Itself: A Secular Future for the Jewish State', *Harper's Magazine* (January 2005), 37.

return to Zion of the majority of the Jewish people, was aimed at a fundamental transformation of the status quo as regards proprietorship of the country.[10]

Gorny's formulation absolves early Zionist theorists, many of whom had not set foot in Palestine, of the requirement for clairvoyance. The 'fundamental transformation' – Palestinian expropriation – inhered in the very nature of their enterprise.

With Gorny's account, then, we have the beginnings of a practical logic. True, it remains ideational rather than smelted through empirical practice, but, in its historical depth, it shows that Palestinian dispossession was no randomly seized opportunity. That dispossession followed from Zionist history as a systematic outcome, not as a fortuitous by-product. This historical depth is especially necessary when we consider the events of 1948, where the evidence of immediate intent is so overwhelming that it can divert us from tracing the deeper historical preconditions whereby the seizure of Palestine had been immanent in earlier practice.

The Logic of Zionism

The sudden catastrophe (al-nakba) that overtook Palestinians from late 1947 onwards did indeed bear the marks of a planned operation. Engulfed by fighting between Jewish[11] and Arab League forces – or, in many cases, on the mere approach of Jewish forces whose reputation for indiscriminate massacring had preceded them[12] – Palestinian households generally preferred discretion to valour and took to their heels. On attempting to return home once the threat had passed, however, most of them found that the familiar path was now barred to them. If they managed to slip through Jewish lines – many being shot in the attempt – they found, often as not, that home had vanished overnight, razed to the ground, its crops burned and fruit trees uprooted. Or perhaps Jewish strangers, many of them Holocaust survivors recently arrived from Europe, had already been moved into their home although they themselves had not moved out. It all happened suspiciously quickly. As Israeli journalist Tom Segev has described it, on an instant,

---

10 Yosef Gorny, *Zionism and the Arabs, 1882–1948: A Study of Ideology* (Oxford: Clarendon Press, 1987), 2.

11 'Jewish', rather than 'Israeli', as this process preceded the formation of the Israeli Defence Forces, which consolidated the pre-independence Zionist militias, Palmach, Haganah, Irgun and Lehi (the Stern Gang).

12 'This Arab propaganda [concerning Deir Yasin, the most infamous of Zionist massacres] spread a legend of terror amongst Arabs and Arab troops, who were seized with panic at the mention of Irgun soldiers. The legend was worth half a dozen battalions to the forces of Israel.' Menachem Begin, *The Revolt* (revised ed., Samuel Katz, trans., London: W. H. Allen, 1979 [1952]), 164, n.

free people – Arabs – had gone into exile and become destitute refugees; destitute refugees – Jews – took the exiles' places as the first step in their lives as free people. One group lost all they had, while the other found everything they needed – tables, chairs, closets, pots, pans, plates, sometimes clothes, family albums, books, radios, and pets.[13]

By 1961, after more than a decade of massive immigration, the proportion of Israeli Jews living in Palestinian people's houses was still as high as one third.[14] The temporary sojourn down the road had turned into refugee-camp banishment in a foreign country or exile further overseas. It is so to this day. As it transpired, this lightning takeover, with its still-fresh East European resonances,[15] was part of (or, at the very least, consistent with) a plan: the Zionist militia's notorious Plan Dalet, which provided a range of measures for ensuring that Palestinians who had been driven from their homes would be prevented from returning.[16] As the Israeli 'New Historians' have documented, between late 1947 and early 1949, Zionist militias, eventually consolidated as the Israeli Defence Forces, forcibly expelled many thousands of Palestinians from their homes and prevented others who had fled the fighting from returning home. In the event, some three-quarters of a million Palestinians were driven into exile, their homes being either destroyed or expropriated by Jewish immigrants. By the 1949 Armistice, the Jewish population – which two years earlier had constituted 26 per cent of the population of Mandate Palestine and had owned around 7 per cent of the total land – had seized 77 per cent of the land and come to constitute 80 per cent of the population.[17] As settler

---

13 Tom Segev, *The Seventh Million: The Israelis and the Holocaust* (Haim Watzman, trans., New York: Owl Books, 1993), 161.

14 Erskine Childers's figure quoted by D. K. Fieldhouse, *Western Imperialism in the Middle East, 1914–1958* (Oxford: Oxford UP, 2006), 194. 'Of the 370 new Jewish settlements established between 1948 and the beginning of 1953, 350 were on absentee property. In 1954, more than one third of Israel's Jewish population lived on absentee property and nearly a third of the new immigrants (250,000 people) settled in urban areas abandoned by Arabs.' Don Peretz, *Israel and the Palestine Arabs* (Washington: Middle East Institute, 1958), 143, citing official Israeli sources (for Custodian of Absentee Property figures, see 143–53). See also Shira Robinson, *Citizen Strangers: Palestinians and the Birth of Israel's Liberal Settler State* (Stanford: Stanford UP, 2013), 47.

15 'Jewish shops, houses, flats and personal belongings were seized by Poles, Rumanians and Hungarians.' Isaac Deutscher, *The Non-Jewish Jew and Other Essays* (London: Oxford UP, 1968), 88.

16 Walid Khalidi (ed.), *From Haven to Conquest: Readings in Zionism and the Palestinian Problem until 1948* (Beirut: Institute for Palestine Studies, 1971), 755–60. For divergent Israeli perspectives on Plan Dalet, the existence of which neither question, see Benny Morris, *The Birth of the Palestinian Refugee Problem Revisited* (Cambridge: Cambridge UP, 2004), 163–6, 263–6; cf. Pappe, *Making of the Arab-Israeli Conflict*, 89–93.

17 Ilan Pappe, *The Ethnic Cleansing of Palestine* (Oxford: Oneworld, 2006); Ilan Pappe, *A History of Modern Palestine* (2nd ed., Cambridge: Cambridge UP, 2006),

takeovers go, this lightning dispossession outpaces even the late-1830s seizure of Australia's Port Phillip grasslands or the postbellum invasion of the US Plains. Whether in Palestinian memory, as the Great Catastrophe, or in Zionist memory, as the War of Independence, these events truly constitute a watershed. On this at least, there is no disagreement.

From a historian's point of view, however, the problem with watersheds is that they tend to obscure preconditions, continuities, the deep groundwork of historical possibility. This is not to discount the existence of watersheds: the booms and busts, the revolutionary transformations or, for that matter, the seemingly miraculous flukes.[18] But it is to say that they did not rest on thin air. Rome is not alone in having taken more than a day to build. To be dazzled by a watershed is to miss the structure subtending the event. Thus the Nakba figures as a point of origin, as if it had no preconditions – apart, perhaps, from the Nazi Holocaust, itself a watershed. But just as the Holocaust presupposed and drew sustenance from a preceding history of European antisemitism, so did the Nakba rest on a well-established legacy of Zionist settler colonisation. Thus the fact that Jewish military planners recognised an opportunity when they saw one is not ultimately the point. If Plan Dalet had not existed, or if there were merit in Benny Morris's claim that the irregular violence of the Nakba sprang spontaneously from the heat of battle, this could not alter

---

122–40. Other standard references include Morris, *Palestinian Refugee Problem Revisited*; Benny Morris, *Righteous Victims: A History of the Zionist-Arab Conflict, 1881–2001* (New York: Vintage, 2001), 161–258. As these sources illustrate, what was new about the 'New Historians' was that they *were* historians, as distinct from the state propagandists who had previously provided Israeli Jews with their national narrative. For what was lost, Walid Khalidi's *All That Remains: The Palestinian Villages Occupied and Depopulated by Israel in 1948* (Washington: Institute for Palestine Studies, 1992) remains, along with photographic collections such as Khalidi's *Before Their Diaspora: A Photographic History of the Palestinians, 1876–1948* (Washington: Institute for Palestine Studies, 1984) and the evocative photographs by Khalil Raad in *Palestine Before 1948: Not Just Memory* (Beirut: Institute for Palestine Studies, 2013). According to official Israeli estimates, over 85 per cent of Palestinian villages were 'abandoned' in the Nakba, 218 villages being listed as destroyed. Figures summarised in Baruch Kimmerling, *Zionism and Territory: The Socio-Territorial Dimensions of Zionist Politics* (Berkeley: U.C. Berkeley Institute of International Studies no. 51, 1983), 122–5.

18   The idea that the Nakba was a miracle (biblical overtones included) has furnished grounds for its justification, as in Avraham Granott's assertion that, 'Since the Arabs surprisingly fled from the territory of the State', restitution was out of the question because 'mistakes may be corrected but not miracles.' Granott, *Agrarian Reform and the Record of Israel* (London: Eyre & Spottiswood, 1956), 96. Granott was here echoing the description of the Nakba by Israel's first president, Chaim Weizmann, as 'a miraculous simplification of Israel's tasks', quoted in Ian Lustick, *Arabs in the Jewish State: Israel's Control of a National Minority* (Austin: Texas UP, 1980), 28. As Erik Cohen notes, Israel's 1967 seizure of the balance of Mandate Palestine could also be depicted in 'miraculous or providential terms': Cohen, 'The Changing Legitimations of the State of Israel', in Peter Y. Medding (ed.), *Israel, State and Society, 1948–1988* (Oxford: Oxford UP, 1989), 157.

the preceding accumulation of purposive human activity that had placed
the Zionist forces in the Palestinian field and equipped them to do what
they did.[19]

The cumulative dimension is critical. The problem with voluntarism,
conceived as it is in individual terms, is that it elides accumulation in
its social aspect, as collectivity. Complementarily, the watershed view of
history elides accumulation in its temporal aspect, as continuity. Aspiring
to a fuller history, this chapter seeks to identify some of the structural
preconditions that enabled the Nakba event to occur, revealing it as a
consolidation rather than a point of origin. Continuing this history into
the post-Nakba era, the following chapter will then explore how the will
to eliminate Palestine became racialised within the Israeli nation-state.

The focus on practical logic cuts across a perspectival difference that
separates two of the most seminal works to have been written on the
Zionist seizure of Palestine. Maxime Rodinson's *Israel: A Colonial-Settler
State?*, the virtues of which include its early formulation,[20] sought to
demonstrate that Israel is part and parcel of what we might call project
Europe: the Zionism on which it is founded was organic to, and shaped
by, European imperialism. As such – and despite its English title –
Rodinson's book failed to specify what it is about the Zionist colonial
formation that makes it a specifically *settler*-colonial one. Thus it does
not provide a basis for distinguishing between, say, British India and
Australia, let alone for deciding whether Israel resembles either. Rather,
for Rodinson, Israel was generically colonial because it was scripted
within Europe and projected onto the world outside Europe.

By contrast, in his groundbreaking *Land, Labor, and the Origins of
the Israeli-Palestinian Conflict*, Gershon Shafir stressed immediate local
factors, arising from concrete settler/Native interchanges on the ground
in Palestine, to the effective exclusion of European-inspired ideology.
Shafir's insistence on distinguishing theory from practice, or Europe
from Palestine, justly restores practical contingency to Rodinson's ideal-
ist account, but it promotes the moment of encounter as itself a kind of
watershed (or recurring series of watersheds), implausibly bereft of the
ideological groundwork that had inspired the founding Zionists to leave
for Palestine in the first place.

In its initial enunciation, Zionism proposed a positive alternative to
a history of antisemitism and pogroms that was specifically and entirely
European. As such, it was not so much a projection as a rejection of
Europe – in Australian terms, it was as if the convicts had decided that they

---

19 Morris, *Palestinian Refugee Problem Revisited*, 341–413.

20 Rodinson published *Israël, fait colonial?* in 1967. He was preceded by Fayez
Sayegh, *The Zionist Colonization of Palestine* (Beirut: Institute of Palestine Studies,
1965).

wanted to go. This metropolitan motivation has provided Zionism with one of its central justifications for dispossessing Palestinians: Zionism was intended to rescue Jews, not to hurt anybody else. It had nothing against the Natives of Palestine. Jews were compelled to flee Europe – it was entirely legitimate that they should do so – and Native people just happened to get in their way. In Isaac Deutscher's apologia, which could hardly have dispensed more summarily with human outcomes, Zionists were no more responsible for harming Palestinians than a man leaping from the roof of a burning building would be responsible for harming the passer-by on whom he happened to land.[21]

It is to Shafir's credit that his carefully detailed research has comprehensively invalidated the Eurocentric negation of Palestinian existence that is entailed in the appeal to victimhood. Nonetheless, the suggestion that Zionists arrived in Palestine innocent of the invasive praxis that climaxed in the Nakba not only naturalises that praxis as arising spontaneously. It thereby casts those arriving Zionists as merely refugees rather than also colonists. Thus we need Rodinson as well as Shafir, lest we forget that the Jewish Colonisation Association, which funded the activities of Zionist settlers in Palestine, was a creation of European theorising.[22] Whatever Israeli apologists may say about Zionism being an anticolonial movement (since it resisted the British), founding Zionists were in no doubt as to their colonising aspirations, aspirations that would be abundantly realised, if not to the letter, in Palestine.

To rehearse a dialectical truism, theory is a form of practice. In their local interplay, as in that between metropole and colony, theory and practice condition one another. Each case is different. Thus it is not enough simply to classify Israel as settler-colonial on the basis of its manifest instantiation of the logic of elimination. We also need to trace the distinctive ways in which this logic acquired life and form through practical hostilities conducted between invaders and Natives on the colonial ground in Palestine. Settler colonialism's essential feature, its sustained institutional tendency to supplant the Indigenous population, reconciles a range of historical practices that might otherwise seem distinct. It is important to stress this multiplicity because the techniques of dispossession whereby settlers supplanted the Natives of Palestine differ significantly from the kindred sets of practices whereby settlers dispossessed the Natives of Australia and of North America. Nonetheless, the eliminatory outcome has remained constant, so the situation

---

21 'One cannot in fairness blame the Jews for this. People pursued by a monster and running to save their lives cannot help injuring those who are in the way.' Deutscher, *The Non-Jewish Jew*, 116; see also 136–7.

22 For the colonising activities of the Jewish Colonisation Association's companion organisation the Jewish National Fund (Keren Kayemet LeYisrael), see Walter Lehn (with Uri Davis), *The Jewish National Fund* (London: Kegan Paul International, 1988).

provides an opportunity to explore settler colonialism's strategic versatility. To explain a settler-colonial invasion, it can never be enough simply to invoke the global potency of capital, mighty though that is. Rather, in each case, settler ascendancy rests on a particular contextual mobilisation of Europe's preaccumulated colonial resources. We need to go behind the frontier to the historical preconditions that equipped the invaders for settlement before they set foot in Native country.

Two major differences have been held out as distinguishing the Zionist acquisition of Palestine from the settler colonisations of Australia and of the USA. In the first instance, Zionism originated as an international movement that consciously avoided confinement to a single metropolis in favour of a supportive transnational umbrella that Rodinson termed the 'collective mother country'.[23] Second, prior to the end of 1947, Zionism was conspicuous for its policy of purchasing Native land in at least notional conformity with the domestic laws of the current local power.[24] In these two important respects, Zionist policy in Palestine differed strikingly from settler policies in Australia or the United States. On examination, however, Zionist policy in Palestine constitutes an intensification of, rather than a departure from, earlier settler-colonial models.

In stark contrast to the Australian or US cases, for instance, Zionism rigorously refused, as it continues to refuse, any suggestion of Native assimilation. In this and other ways that will be discussed below, Zionism constitutes a more exclusive exercise of the settler logic of elimination than we encounter in the Australian and US examples. This conclusion only seems surprising if one concentrates on features that are extraneous to the Indigenous experience, as Zionist apologists understandably do. By way of correction, we will examine these two features that have frequently been cited as distinguishing Zionism from settler colonialism (the lack of a unitary metropole and the policy of purchase) not in isolation but in the wider historical context within which they were strategically conjoined. As will emerge, the two constitute integrated aspects of a uniquely developed programme of Indigenous dispossession.

The basic link between Zionism's diffuse metropole and Jewish land purchases in Palestine consists in the fact that the former financed the latter. As the joke of the time went, Zionism meant one Jew using another Jew's money to send a third Jew to Palestine. In common with much racist discourse, however, this joke represented a displacement, since there was nothing particular to Zionism about settler colonialism's metropolitan funding. Rather, in much the same way as antisemitism

---

23 Maxime Rodinson, *Israel: A Colonial-Settler State?* (David Thorstad trans., New York: Monad, 1973), 76.

24 This consideration has been argued, more with force than with cogency, by Alan Dershowitz, *The Case for Israel* (New York: Wiley & Sons, 2003), 22–8.

furnished a surrogate for capitalism to talk about itself, this joke might equally well have referred to the colonisation of Australia or the United States. As we saw earlier, the frontier was led from behind, typically by speculators – speculators, moreover, who tended not to be limited by nationality. So far as the creation of transnational networks for exporting metropolitan capital in order to place and maintain settlers in Palestine is concerned, therefore, there is nothing exceptional about Zionism. Rather, Zionism's peculiarity concerns the distinctive quality of the capital involved. This, in turn, reflects the fact that, in the case of Palestine, the Natives were already incorporated into – and to that extent, protected by – extensive (albeit moribund) colonial empires, first Ottoman then British, a factor that encouraged settler conformity to domestic property law.

In this context, the resources that Zionism was able to coordinate distinguished the capital transmitted to Palestine from the general run of speculative investment whereby capital was exported to other European colonies. With the possible (and early) exception of Baron Rothschild, the capital that Zionists garnered for investment in Palestine, as Barbara Smith has pointed out, was not conditional on the return of a financial profit.[25] As the Russian Zionist Jakob Klatzkin in 1915 answered the question of what would happen to the diaspora (*Galut*) on the founding of the Jewish state:

> Its function will be to serve as a source of supply for the renaissance of our people in its homeland. Eretz Israel will need the Galut for many generations to come ... Galut Jewry cannot survive ... But [its] temporary life has a great function, if it serves the purpose of a lasting life, of the upbuilding of our nation in its homeland.[26]

In this crucial regard, donors who funded the world Zionist project differed from the speculators who had financed territorial expansion in Australia and North America. Unencumbered by the requirement to return a profit, subsidised Zionist settlers enjoyed the easiest of imported advantages in relation to the local population, a confounding of capitalist rationality that overwhelmed the finite Native stock.

For a sustained colonising programme that was to achieve such enormous successes, the Zionist plan for Palestine displays a consistent set of features whose effectiveness has not been hampered by its remarkable simplicity. Ostensibly operating within established imperial frameworks, but always with an eye to eventually supplanting them, Zionists have

---

25 Barbara J. Smith, *The Roots of Separatism in Palestine: British Economic Policy, 1920–1929* (Syracuse: Syracuse UP, 1993), 11.

26 From Jakob Klatzkin, 'The Galut Must Be Preserved Long Enough to Be Transcended', in Hertzberg, *Zionist Idea*, 324.

secured international support, both from regnant imperial powers and from private sources, for two overriding purposes: to convert an ever-expanding contiguous wedge of Palestine from Native ownership into an irreversibly Jewish endowment, and to procure the import from overseas of funding and Jewish personnel at a level sufficient to maintain the continued expansion of this ethnocratically consolidated zone by whatever means should prove available and viable.[27] This strikingly simple plan has been pursued with a sleepless organisational tenacity that remains apparent in Israel's ongoing disinclination to specify its borders. To follow the broad outlines of this process, we shall start with its Ottoman origins.

Ottoman Origins

When the Zionist (or, more strictly, proto-Zionist) Bilu group landed in Palestine in the early 1880s, they can hardly have had the foundation of an exclusively Jewish nation-state in mind. At least, if any of them had such ambitions, they would have been hubristic in the extreme. Moreover, unlike their Second Aliya successors, who would begin to arrive in the early years of the twentieth century, this group did not object to employing local Palestinian labour on the agricultural cooperatives that, after a false start, it established with funding from Baron Rothschild.[28] As Shafir has shown, Zionist settlements in Palestine were modelled on European colonial experiments elsewhere, initially the French colonisation of Algeria and subsequently Bismarck's Germanisation of East Prussia.[29] When Rothschild came to the aid of the failing Bilu group, or First Aliya, he instituted an Algerian colon-style system in which Jewish settlers relied on a predominantly Native labour force to produce their crops (mainly grapevines). When viable returns remained unforthcoming, Rothschild precipitately withdrew his support, leaving the First Aliya in a crisis. By contrast, the Second Aliya firmly repudiated the Bilu group's reliance on Native collaboration, devoting its energies – again, with diasporan financial support – to establishing Jewish-only enclaves, the rigorously ethnocratic *kibbutzim* and modified *moshavot* agricultural collectives.

Despite this substantial difference, the Second Aliya chose to name itself as such – thereby retrospectively dubbing the Bilu group the 'First

27 The term 'ethnocracy' has been coined by Oren Yiftachel, *Ethnocracy: Land and Identity Politics in Israel/Palestine* (Philadelphia: Pennsylvania UP, 2006).

28 Gershon Shafir, *Land, Labor and the Origins of the Israeli-Palestinian Conflict, 1882–1914* (2nd ed., Berkeley: California UP, 1996), 52–63, 73–9; Neville J. Mandel, 'Ottoman Policy and Restrictions on Jewish Settlement in Palestine: 1881–1908. Part I', *Middle Eastern Studies* 10 (1974), 321–8; Mandel, *Arabs and Zionism*, 31–6. 'Aliya' (literally, ascent – i.e., to the Holy Land) is a term used to refer to the successive waves of Zionist emigration to Palestine, the second of which extended from early in the twentieth century to World War I.

29 Shafir, *Land, Labor and the Origins*, 50–1, 152–4.

Aliya' – in the interest of establishing both a historical continuity and a historical rupture. The continuity consisted in a colonial entity termed the 'New Yishuv', a mode of Jewish settlement in Palestine that was held to differ fundamentally from earlier Ashkenazi (European-Jewish) in-migrations, whose inspiration had been emphatically religious. Accordingly, these earlier Ashkeni arrivals, along with various non-European Jewish groups who had in some cases been in the region even longer, became in their turn the 'Old Yishuv', disparaged and orientalised by the Zionists as lethargic rabbinical misfits. Thus the rupture that Second-Aliya theorists ordained in co-opting the Bilu group's legacy as a settler point of origin provided, as Yehouda Shenhav has put it, 'an epistemological break, a point of discontinuity, which ma[de] possible the separation between the ethno-religious past and the ethno-national present'.[30] Ideologically, as we saw in chapter four, Zionism was organic to the nineteenth century, a European secular-colonial-nationalist movement.

As a tiny group of new arrivals, the New Yishuv was both constrained and protected by the Sublime Porte (the Ottoman administration). Natives recognised the incoming colonists' territorial agenda very early in the piece. The first Palestinian protest against modern Jewish settlement in Palestine came in 1891, in the form of a telegram asking the Grand Vizir to curb further immigration to and land purchases in Palestine on the part of Russian Jews. This protest, as Neville Mandel noted, 'was lodged less than a decade after modern Jewish immigration into Palestine began and several years before the Zionist Movement was founded'.[31] Mandel and others have documented the ways in which opposition to Jewish immigration and land purchases in Palestine gathered among Palestinian and other Arabs in the period leading up to World War I.[32] The Porte was sensitive to this opposition, not least because of its established enmity with Russia, the pogrom-plagued source of most of the Jewish immigration. Moreover, the 'sick man of Europe' had no desire to encourage large numbers of immigrants who, as Europeans, would be entitled to special privileges, including tax exemptions, under the system of capitulations.[33] Nor did it wish to incubate yet another nationalist problem in its midst. This last consideration prompted the Porte to place a selective ban on Jewish immigration into Palestine, which constituted a potential focus for the development of an unruly Jewish nationalism.[34]

Faced with these constraints, Zionist colonisers devised a range of strategic responses. The Ottoman administration was badly coordinated

30   Shenhav, *Arab Jews*, 90.
31   Mandel, *Arabs and Zionism*, 40.
32   Ibid., 207.
33   Mandel, 'Ottoman Policy and Restrictions', 315.
34   Ibid., 313.

and inefficient, with the result that many of the regulations designed to restrict Jewish immigration and land purchasing were inconsistently applied. Temporary visas for the purpose of religious pilgrimage were routinely used by Jews to enter Palestine, whereupon they might simply vanish into the local population or bribe corrupt officials to allow them to stay, while the capitulation system enabled Jews who encountered problems to enlist consular support from their European nations of citizenship. With regard to land purchases, Jews who were already resident Ottoman citizens, and even on occasion non-Jewish Arabs, could be used to buy land on behalf of the newcomers.[35] In 1901, taking advantage of a concession granted under an Ottoman land code dating from 1867, the Jewish Colonisation Association was able to acquire a very large tract of land in Tiberias from the Greek-Orthodox Sursuq landowning family, who were based in Beirut.[36] This purchase formed a territorial core around which further purchasing would subsequently enable a contiguous block of Jewish-owned land to be established. Though Jewish numbers remained a minute proportion of the population of Palestine as a whole, with landholdings to match, their rate of expansion (a tenfold increase over two decades) was dramatic.

A number of key features of Zionist settler colonialism that will figure importantly in the analysis to come are already apparent at this early stage. In particular, as noted, the acquisition of Native territory was initially carried out in conformity with the existing legal system. True, an appreciable level of friction between settlers and Natives developed once the settlers had moved onto the land they had purchased, friction arising principally from the settlers' disregard for local protocols concerning access to and use of land.[37] Nonetheless, the procedures whereby Zionists had obtained title to that land in the first place were more or less in accordance with Ottoman law, a situation that contrasts sharply with the lawless (from the Native point of view) violence that had characterised the acquisition of Native territory in Australia and the United States.

Lawless violence was simply not an option for a small group of European settlers who were trying to establish a colonial beachhead within a powerful, albeit decadent, established empire. The conventional settler technique of violent expropriation only became available to Zionism in 1948, when the ethnic purging of Native territory heralding national independence occurred in response to metropolitan withdrawal. Up to that point, however, the Yishuv had largely confined itself to

---

35 Ibid., 324.

36 William R. Polk, 'The Arabs and Palestine', in Polk, David M. Stamler and Edmund Asfour, *Backdrop to Tragedy: The Struggle for Palestine* (Boston: Beacon, 1957), 236–8.

37 Shafir, *Land, Labor and the Origins*, 40–1, 199–202.

operating within the framework of successive imperial umbrellas, first the Ottomans and then, eventually under the League of Nations' Palestine Mandate, the British. In addition to constraining the Zionist enterprise, these empires (in particular the British) also provided protection for it, together with a legal system that enabled the purchase of land and immigration regulations that were susceptible to strategic manipulation. Still lacking a colonial state, Zionism did not seek to end imperialism but to harness it. In this regard, a major success came about in 1917, when the Balfour Declaration anticipated the shift from Ottoman to British rule.

Ottoman to British

One of the biggest of the many big breaks that Zionism was to enjoy in the twentieth century came about in 1914, when the Ottomans not only chose to participate in World War I but picked the wrong side. In the wake of the Great War, Turkey, in common with Germany, was obliged to submit to its empire being dismembered and parcelled out among its victorious European rivals under the aegis of the newly established League of Nations' Wilsonian mandate system. In this division of imperial spoils, in which Australia's colonial coming of age was marked with a mandate over German New Guinea, Britain secured Iraq, and France secured Syria, only with Palestine excised from the south-west portion. Britain not only gained a mandate over the Palestine part of the Ottoman Empire but, fatefully, succeeded in having an extended version of the Balfour Declaration inserted into what thereby became a unique form of mandate, providing as it did for the preferential intrusion of a third party into the relationship between a European authority and the local population it was to administer.[38]

The Balfour Declaration had been issued in 1917, while General Allenby was advancing on Jerusalem, at that point still an Ottoman possession. It expressed a favourable view of the 'establishment in Palestine of a National Home for the Jewish people', an object whose achievement the British government would 'use their best endeavours to facilitate'. Strengthening these words four years after the defeat of Turkey, Article 6 of the 1922 Mandate charged the British to 'facilitate Jewish immigration under suitable conditions and [to] encourage, in co-operation with the Jewish Agency ... close settlement by Jews on the land, including State lands and waste lands not required for public purposes'.

---

38 For a penetrating critique of the wording of the Balfour Declaration that partly anticipates my comments here, see Erskine B. Childers, 'The Wordless Wish: From Citizens to Refugees', in Ibrahim Abu-Lughod (ed.), *The Transformation of Palestine: Essays on the Origin and Development of the Arab-Israeli Conflict* (Evanston: Northwestern UP, 1971), 170–1.

Lest the implications of 'close' Jewish settlement on state and 'waste' lands – which, under the continuing Ottoman system of tenure, were scheduled as public property rather than as abandoned or ownerless – were not clear enough, Article 11 of the Mandate went on to provide that, 'in connection with the development' of Palestine, the British administration would have

> full power to provide for public ownership or control of any of the natural resources of the country or of the public works, services and utilities established or to be established therein. It shall introduce a land system appropriate to the needs of the country, having regard ... to the desirability of promoting the close settlement and intensive cultivation of the land.

Thus did John Locke become an unlikely champion of Judaeocracy, the terms 'development' and 'intensive cultivation' invoking the classic liberal formula linking agricultural efficiency to population increase, while the repetition of Article 6's 'close settlement' – an outcome to be achieved through cooperation between the Mandate authorities and the Jewish Agency – left no doubt as to which population was scheduled to increase as a result of its progressive (read 'European') development of the land. This form of words represented a triumph for Zionist lobbying in both Britain and the United States, where Felix Frankfurter and Louis Brandeis secured President Woodrow Wilson's endorsement of the Balfour Declaration – itself in large part the result of the influence of Chaim Weizmann on British politicians, notably Arthur Balfour, David Lloyd George and Winston Churchill: Christian statesmen whose distaste for Jews was matched by their fondness for Zionism.[39]

In this and other decisive ways, the Yishuv's influence on Whitehall did not suffer from the lack of a delegated governmental structure. Indeed, the absence of a formal metropolitan relationship enhanced Zionism's capacity to mobilise a transatlantic network of support that was relatively independent of colonial rivalries between Western nations. In the years between the two world wars, the British Mandate provided an incubator within which international Zionism could make crucial progress towards assembling the demographic and territorial prerequisites for a European settler state in Palestine. To this end, with formidable organisational zeal, Zionist institutions secured the importation of Jewish people and capital into Palestine and maximised the efficiency of their distribution once

---

39 For discussion and examples of the well-known antisemitic sentiments harboured by Lloyd George, Balfour, Joseph Chamberlain, Churchill and others, see, e.g., Atran, 'Surrogate Colonization of Palestine', 721–2, 737–8, n. 2; W. T. Mallison, Jr., 'The Balfour Declaration: An Appraisal in International Law' (in Abhu-Lughod, *Transformation*), 67–9; Leonard Stein, *The Balfour Declaration* (London: Vallentine-Mitchell, 1961), 143.

they got there. This agenda was personified in the career and writings of colonial master-strategist Arthur Ruppin, whose incisive pragmatism informed the designs of central Zionist planners, including David Ben-Gurion and key removal planner Yosef Weitz.

The context in which this was made possible was the British Mandate. The harmony between Zionism and the British reflected a substantial convergence of interests.[40] In the absence of the Ottomans, the Yishuv needed an imperial protector to shield it from the resentment that its intrusive activities were bound to provoke among the Native majority. Support from the United States was effectively informal. Having only recently taken over from Turkey, Britain had the requisite administrative capacity without being compromised by long-standing affiliations (possession of which gave the Yishuv a local advantage), and Zionists had high-level connections within the British government. Correspondingly, Palestine's situation at the eastern end of the Mediterranean had major long- and short-term implications for British imperial strategy. In the long term, the region as a whole, especially the Suez Canal, was vital to traffic between Britain and its imperial holdings in India and beyond. A Jewish state there could provide a reliable regional ally without the need to overcome French resistance.[41]

This convergence of interests extended back to the Great War years, when British support for Zionist aspirations in Palestine had been intended to encourage Jews in both the United States and Russia to influence their governments to back Britain's war effort, not only against the Ottomans, whose defeat would make Palestine available, but against imperial Germany – who, in waging war on the Tsar, had taken on the instigator of the pogroms.[42] Jewish support for the British war effort could by no means be taken for granted, a consideration heightened by the occurrence of anti-war agitation on the part of some Jewish organisations in Britain, significantly composed of Russian refugees who, despite being denied British citizenship, were also threatened with the alternatives of conscription or repatriation to Russia.[43]

---

40   Frank Hardie and Irwin Herrman, *Britain and Zion: The Fateful Entanglement* (Belfast: Blackstaff Press, 1980), 19.

41   Fieldhouse, *Western Imperialism in the Middle East*, 138–48.

42   See, e.g., Victor Kattan, *From Coexistence to Conflict: International Law and the Origins of the Arab-Israeli Conflict, 1891–1949* (London: Pluto, 2009), 64–5. Laqueur (*History of Zionism*, 172–3) notes Zionist leaders' concern at pro-German sentiment among rank-and-file Zionists.

43   In particular the Foreign Jews' Protection Committee against Deportation [to Russia] and Compulsion. As one of their pamphlets put it, 'We can forgive [anti-Jewish and anti-immigrant activities in Britain] but to participate in a war in which one of your Allies is bathing in the blood of our brethren is unnatural and inhuman.' I. Wassilevsky, *Jewish Refugees and Military Service: The Ethical Aspect of Compulsion under Threat of Deportation* (London: The National Labour Press, 1916), 3.

Moreover, there was no saying that, after the war, the tripartite alliance of Britain, France and Russia would hold. A Jewish Palestine might provide a buffer zone capable of insulating British interests in Egypt from threats to the north and the east (a potentiality that Britain's most influential Zionist, Weizmann, promoted as an 'Asiatic Belgium').[44] It could even enable the Mediterranean and the Persian Gulf to be linked by rail, through an ideally British Mesopotamia/Iraq. In the event, as Kenneth Stein observed, once the Mandate had been established, Britain would come to devote an 'overwhelming predominance' of administrative expenditure to strategic purposes, 'while only small amounts of governmental revenue were made available to ameliorate the economic and social conditions of either the Arab or Jewish communities'[45] – an allocation that worked to the advantage of the one community that was receiving international contributions. In this regard, the Yishuv stood to gain from the metropole's neglect as much as from its support.[46]

The preference for Zionism that Britain had built into the League of Nations Mandate reflected these strategic interests. The Mandate's preamble included a safeguard clause protecting the rights of 'existing non-Jewish communities'. This clause is significant on a number of counts, not least the transience implied in the term 'existing', whose suggestion of temporariness was reinforced by the designation of 91 per cent of the population as 'non-Jewish'. The implications of this terminology resonated through the concept of 'national home', which the Mandate adopted from the Balfour Declaration. The term *Heimstätte* had originated as a Zionist codeword for the exclusively Jewish state that the movement actually desired, Herzl's second in command Nordau having suggested a formula that could 'deceive by its mildness' so long as there was a need to 'dissimulate our real aim'.[47] Understood as a euphemism for the Jewish state, the 'national home' commitment conflicted with the safeguards afforded the so-called 'non-Jewish' population – the national

---

44 Michael Haag, *Alexandria: City of Memory* (New Haven: Yale UP, 2004), 141, n. 72; Hardie and Herrman, *Britain and Zion*, 33.

45 Kenneth W. Stein, 'Legal Protection and Circumvention of Rights for Cultivators in Mandatory Palestine', in Joel S. Migdal (ed.), *Palestinian Society and Politics* (Princeton: Princeton UP, 1980), 234.

46 Ilan Pappe has picked up on Barbara Smith's identification of this factor. Pappe, 'Zionism as Colonialism: A Comparative View of Diluted Colonialism in Asia and Africa', *South Atlantic Quarterly* 107 (2008), 630; cf. Smith, *Roots of Separatism*, 135–58.

47 Quoted from Nordau's unpublished 'The Prosperity of His Servant' in Christopher Sykes [son of Mark Sykes, of Sykes-Picot fame], *Two Studies in Virtue* (New York: Knopf, 1953), 160, n. 1. 'Zionists knew that *Heimstätte* was a circumlocution for *Judenstaat*; so did the War Cabinet of 1917': John Ruedy, 'Dynamics of Land Alienation' (in Abu-Lughod, *Transformation*, 127), instancing Lloyd George's testimony before the Peel Commission.

home, as Stein again observed, being a statement of right; the safeguards 'a statement of sufferance'.[48]

This asymmetrical duality received official justification in Britain's pledge to encourage Jewish immigration into Palestine to the extent that 'the economy', significantly expressed in the singular, was capable of absorbing it. This formula overlooked, and thereby strengthened, Zionists' untiring efforts to effect a separation between two conflicting economies in Palestine (the policy that Ruppin termed 'economic segregation'[49]). The Mandate administration abetted these efforts by treating the Jewish economy's capacity to absorb immigrants as if it were the absorptive capacity of the whole of Palestine, ignoring the fact that the growth of the Jewish sector was taking place not in a vacuum but in a zero-sum relationship whereby its growth took place at the expense of the Indigenous sector.[50]

Even during a period of global recession, settler-colonial expansion, especially in the construction industry in the new Jewish city of Tel Aviv, enabled the sheltered Jewish economy to grow at the same time as the predominantly agrarian Native economy was placed under increasing strain.[51] The inflow of financial capital that sustained the Yishuv was beyond official control. So far as the companion inflow of human capital was concerned, Britain's administration of the Mandate provided the conditions that enabled world Zionism to continue building its state-to-be, a state that would ultimately exist instead of, rather than in, Palestine.[52]

Within Britain, the preferential treatment that the Yishuv was to enjoy under the Mandate did not pass unopposed. There was significant resistance to the idea that Palestine's Arab population should be betrayed, while prominent Jewish public figures under the leadership of Edwin Montagu opposed Zionism's allying itself with antisemitism for the purpose of encouraging Jewish emigration from Europe. Even Herbert Samuel – Britain's first Jewish cabinet minister who, as the first high commissioner to Palestine, was foremost among a number of Zionists appointed to senior positions in the administration – frustrated other leading Zionists by his adoption of ostensibly even-handed policies. In 1921, in a huge blow to Zionist ambitions that has been oddly

---

48   Kenneth W. Stein, *The Land Question in Palestine, 1917–1939* (Chapel Hill: North Carolina UP, 1984), 213.

49   Simha Flapan, *Zionism and the Palestinians* (London: Croom Helm, 1979), 173.

50   Smith, *Roots of Separatism*, 84–5.

51   Ibid., 77–81, citing Robert Szereszewski.

52   I have adapted this poignant distinction, which encapsulates Zionism's settler-colonial character, from Victor Kattan's observation that the Balfour Declaration 'provided that it [a Jewish national home] would be established in Palestine, not instead of Palestine.' Kattan, *Coexistence to Conflict*, 60.

downplayed in much scholarly literature, the British (through the office of Churchill) created the Amirate of Transjordan in the two thirds of future Mandate Palestine that lay east of the Jordan River.

This concession to Arab expectations had major unresolved implications that continue into the present day. In particular, Ze'ev Jabotinsky's formation in 1925 of Revisionist Zionism, which was committed to revising the Mandate to reincorporate the 'partitioned' section of the Jewish national home (the transplanted 'moral boundaries of Europe' that Nordau had envisioned extending to the Euphrates), inscribed a still-extant ambition to take over the East Bank that is prudently ignored in contemporary Western diplomacy.[53]

With regard to Britain's international obligations under the Mandate itself, official concern at the emergence of a sub-proletarian class of dispossessed Natives rendered landless by Zionist purchases led, in the 1930s, to the introduction of measures designed to restrain the transfer of land into Jewish hands. As World War II loomed, British concern that Arabs should not be attracted to side with the Germans led, as in World War I, to significant concessions, including restrictions on Jewish immigration that the 1937 Peel Commission recommended despite the ascendancy of Nazism. Sharpening such imperial considerations, Native resistance was maintained throughout the Mandate period, recurrently peaking in violent opposition, often directed against Jewish immigrants, that prompted a number of British policy shifts away from the pro-Zionist norm.[54] Typically, Zionist influence in Whitehall succeeded in having the new policies changed or, at least, in frustrating their restrictive provisions. Events surrounding the Shaw Commission and Hope Simpson reports, both published in 1930, provide a major case in point.

In the wake of homicidal street-fighting between Muslims and Jews that had started around the Western Wall in Jerusalem over access to holy places, the British established a commission of enquiry under Walter Shaw, which reported that the religious issue was symptomatic of wider Arab political and economic grievances stemming from British authorities' implementation of the Mandate's commitment to the Jewish national home. On this basis, the report recommended that Jewish immigration

---

53 This commitment has never been exclusive to the Revisionists, with whom Labour Zionism has disagreed on timing and means rather than ends. 'The entire world … considered the land of Israel on both sides of the Jordan one country and hoped it would be restored as promised by the Torah and the Prophets': David Ben-Gurion, *Israel: A Personal History* (Nechemia Meyers and Uzy Nystar, trans., London: New English Library, 1972), 802. For the moral extension of Europe to the Euphrates, see Nordau, *Ketavim tsioniyim*, vol. 2, 113, quoted in Atran, 'Surrogate Colonization', 720.

54 For the 'original intifada', or Arab Revolt of 1936–39, see Baruch Kimmerling and Joseph S. Migdal, *The Palestinian People: A History* (rev. ed., Cambridge, MA: Harvard UP, 2003), 102–31; Ted Swedenburg, *Memories of Revolt: The 1936–1939 Rebellion and the Palestinian National Past* (Fayetteville: Arkansas UP, 2003).

into Palestine be restricted and that 'a scientific enquiry should be held into land cultivation and settlement possibilities'.[55] Pending this second enquiry, the eviction of peasant cultivators, by which Shaw meant further Jewish land purchases, was to be checked.

The head of the second enquiry, John Hope Simpson, asserted that the Mandate's objectives required that the encouragement of close settlement and intensive cultivation should apply to Arabs as well as to Jews. To Zionist consternation, he recommended that, for Arab Natives of Palestine to be able to maintain their existing standard of living, Jewish immigration should be summarily curtailed. These recommendations found their way into a government white paper that was presented by Colonial Secretary Baron Passfield (the British Labour Party luminary, Sidney Webb).

The objections that Zionists raised in response to the Passfield White Paper were revealing in regard to the dual economy that the Shaw and Hope Simpson reports had both problematised. In response to Hope Simpson's assertion that Arab health was suffering as a result of the Jewish influx, Zionists argued that the immigration of more Jewish doctors could only alleviate the problem, an argument that denied the bifurcation of the two communities. At the same time, however, in response to Hope Simpson's related assertion that, in view of the level of unemployment among Arab workers, the Palestinian economy was incapable of absorbing any more immigrants, Zionists argued that Jewish immigrants were joining the industrial sector and would not impact on employment in the Arab agricultural sector, an argument that relied on mutual separation.[56]

In the event, it was not argumentation, consistent or otherwise, that won the day. Labour Zionism, under the leadership of David Ben-Gurion, secured its dominance of Yishuv politics at around the same time as British Labour first succeeded, by a vulnerably slender majority, in gaining government in Westminster. While the Zionist labour organisation Histadrut, in the person of their London representative Dov Hoz, lobbied Trades Union Congress leader Ernest Bevin, Weizmann was involved in a mysterious meeting with Prime Minister Ramsay MacDonald and his son Malcolm, from which emerged a memorandum that would, predictably enough, be dubbed 'the Black Letter' by Palestinian Arabs. Penned by Malcolm MacDonald, signed by his father, and addressed, Balfour Declaration-style, to Weizmann, the Black Letter, published on St Valentine's Day 1931, 'clarified' the Passfield White Paper out of meaningful existence, negating the material that the Zionists

---

55 Quoted in *Peel Commission Report* (*Palestine Royal Commission Report Presented by the Secretary of State for the Colonies to Parliament by Command of His Majesty*, London: H.M. Stationery Office, July 1937), 71.

56 The arguments and factors are summarised in Smith, *Roots of Separatism*, 66–76.

had found objectionable.[57] As Segev has crisply noted, 'The Passfield White Paper never went into effect; indeed, it is notable only because the Zionist movement was able to get it revoked.'[58]

Thus the absence of a formal hierarchy actually meant more metropole rather than less. The composite transnational network whereby Zionist organisations secured sponsorship without reciprocal commitment not only enabled them to draw on multiple sources of support. Even within the formal Mandate relationship, Zionists' capacity to influence British policy was hardly less than that enjoyed by colonial administrations elsewhere. In the outcome, Britain provided the military protection necessary for world Zionism to coordinate its importation into Palestine of international finance and East European immigrants, an arrangement that enabled the would-be Jewish nation to marshal its preaccumulated combination of capital, culture and labour with unparallelled effectiveness.[59]

Boycott and Conquer

The Jewish nation imagined in Zionism constituted a relationship between people and land that mutually realised both. The Yishuv was not merely a demographic unit. Indissolubly, and to no lesser extent, it was also territorial. As such, the Yishuv was not so much a state in waiting as an agenda, an end to be realised in the fusion of people and land. Such were the requirements of state-building, however, that this was to be a very particular fusion. The random purchasing of as much land as possible, which would have scattered islands of Jewish ownership across a multicultural Palestine, may have made room for more Jews but it would not have consolidated the Yishuv. Rather, the isolated Jewish groups that resulted would have had to participate in the local economy. For the Jews in Palestine to become a nation, they had first to be gathered together, a requirement that dictated contiguous land holdings.[60] In Zionism's

---

57 For a well-documented account of the events leading up to the Black Letter, see Atran, 'Surrogate Colonization', 730–1. See also *Peel Commission Report*, 70–8; Tom Segev, *One Palestine, Complete: Jews and Arabs under the British Mandate* (Haim Watzman, trans., New York: Metropolitan/Henry Holt, 2000), 335–8; Paul Kelemen, *The British Left and Zionism: History of a Divorce* (Manchester: Manchester UP, 2012), 19–24. For a Zionist version of events, see Yosef Gorny, *The British Labour Movement and Zionism, 1917–1948* (London: Frank Cass, 1983), 96–108.

58 Segev, *One Palestine, Complete*, 336.

59 The reasoning behind Zionist writers' claim that the lack of a unitary metropole renders the expropriation and elimination of Palestinians incommensurable with settler colonialism is baffling. Consider, for instance, Penslar's 'European colonialism was fostered by a colonizing state, a key factor missing in the early Zionist movement … the Zionist movement lacked a "mother country" and so defies simplistic association with European settlement-colonialism.' Penslar, *Israel in History*, 93–4.

60 As Anita Shapira has pointed out, this policy not only limited the extent of

obsession with contiguous Jewish ownership, we see how the strategic combination of metropolitan funding and the policy of purchase made possible the institutional practice known as the Conquest of Labour (or Hebrew Labour, *Avoda Ivrit*), the thoroughgoing system of ethno-racial exclusion on which the Jewish nation was to be built. This takes us back to the problems of the First Aliya.

When Rothschild suddenly withdrew his funding, the First Aliya was left in a crisis that was not at first resolved by the Second Aliya, who arrived early in the twentieth century in response to the fresh round of pogroms that had been unleashed in Kishinev. Initially, these refugees from antisemitism sought to compete with Natives on their own terms, attempting to survive at the subsistence level of surrounding agricultural-ists (*fellaheen*). Like their First Aliya predecessors, however, they found themselves unequal to the task, defeated by what Shafir has termed 'the contradiction between market-based colonisation and Jewish national aspirations'.[61] The level playing field was not an option for the Second Aliya. In 1905, however, the Jewish workers' organisation Hapoel Hatzair resolved to abandon market rationality in favour of a Jewish-only isolate in Palestine that would reject any labour that was not Jewish.[62] Thus began the Conquest of Labour. From the outset, it was not a strat-egy that made any pretence of competing with Palestinian labour on the open market. Rather, it depended on the provision and maintenance of a closed, protected and autonomously reproduced circuit of production, consumption and exchange – which is to say, on an exclusive and prefer-entially subsidised economy. As such, in a kind of wishful *corpus nullius*, its proponents sought to conduct their affairs as if nobody else was around.

There might the scheme have rested, had not the internationally con-stituted World Zionist Organisation taken it up, inspired in large part by Ruppin's admiration for Bismarck's colonisation scheme in East Prussia, under which the government had bought up failed Junker estates and broken them down into private allotments for subsidised sale to exclu-sively German smallholders, the idea being to rid the region of Poles. In the event, the WZO wholeheartedly adopted the Conquest of Labour, funding Jewish-only initiatives through the Jewish National Fund, which it had established in 1901 for the purpose of extending Jewish ownership of land in Palestine. Ideologically, the Conquest of Labour would find expression in the figure of the New Jew, whose distinctive

---

Jewish landholding; it also paved the way for partition. Shapira, *Land and Power: The Zionist Resort to Force, 1881–1948* (Stanford: Stanford UP, 1999), 176.

61 Gershon Shafir, talk presented at the 'Past Is Present: Settler Colonialism in Palestine' conference, SOAS, 5 March 2011.

62 Laqueur, *History of Zionism*, 284–8; Charles D. Smith, *Palestine and the Arab-Israeli Conflict* (Boston: Bedford/St. Martin's, 2007), 38–40.

iconography bore the marks of the extreme nationalisms that were emerging in Europe.[63] The ideal of the New Jew required incoming Zionists to remake themselves through the Conquest of Labour, not only clearing Natives from the land but boycotting Native labour and produce, a repudiation of dependency on others that progressively deprived them of their means of subsistence.[64]

In settler-colonial ideology, as we have seen, expropriation is routinely justified on the Lockean claim that the Native is unproductive. The New Jew was no exception. Its Palestinian Other, iconically a rootless nomadic Bedouin rather than a settled *fellah*, mirrored the unproductiveness of the rejected European Jew. In excluding Natives from its productive economy, Zionism replicated the exclusion of Jews from the productive economies of Eastern Europe, a displaced revenge whereby Sabras (Jews born in Palestine) made Hebrew-speaking substitute Gentiles of themselves and, correspondingly, Arabised European Jews of the Natives.[65] In quickening colonial discourse with metropolitan grievance, the campaign for the Conquest of Labour underpinned core Zionist institutions such as the kibbutz and the labour organisation Histadrut, striving for a totally insulated Jewish-only capsule that really would conduct its affairs (at least, its non-military ones) as if nobody else were around – a posture that exceeded the exclusiveness that settlers attained in Australia or the United States. Israel was founded on a boycott.

For analytical purposes, the Conquest of Labour exemplifies the dialectic between theory and practice, as well as between metropole and colony, that made Zionism a settler-colonial project at the same time as it distinguished it from others. Conventional Israeli histories trace the Conquest of Labour back to the concept of productivisation that had been promulgated by Zionist theorists in Eastern Europe. Productivisation had been championed in response to the self-loathing that discriminatory exclusions from productive industry, particularly agriculture, encouraged in East European Jewry (in this sense, as Shafir notes, Zionism mirrored European antisemitism[66]). As initially conceived in late-nineteenth-century Europe, productivisation was not designed to disempower

---

63 For example, see the Zionist recruitment poster calling on Jews to colonise the Galilee, Tom Segev, *One Palestine Complete: Jews and Arabs Under the British Mandate* (Haim Watzman, trans., New York: Henry Holt/Metropolitan Books, 2000), facing p. 374.

64 Clause 23 of the lease that Jewish settlers signed before taking up land purchased by the JNF required lessees to 'execute all works connected with cultivation of the holding, only with Jewish labour.' Quoted in M. F. Abcarius, *Palestine: Through the Fog of Propaganda* (London: Hutchinson, 1946), 131.

65 In so doing, as Massad has noted, they also made European Gentiles – and, accordingly, antisemites – of themselves. Massad, *Persistence of the Palestinian Question*, *passim*.

66 Shafir, *Land, Labor, and the Origins*, 81.

non-Jews. It was rather designed, autarchically as it were, to inculcate productive self-sufficiency in a Jewish population that had been relegated to the urban (principally financial) occupations stigmatised as parasitic by the surrounding Gentile population – a prejudice that those who sought to build the 'New Jew' endorsed insofar as they resisted its internalisation. Once the aggressive young Zionists of the Second Aliya had settled in Palestine, however, the doctrine evolved into a weapon of ethnic conflict, as Jewish industries were actively discouraged from employing non-Jewish labour, even though Natives worked for lower wages and, in many cases, more efficiently:

'Hebrew labor,' or 'conquest of labor' ... was born of Palestinian circumstances, and advocated a struggle against Palestinian Arab workers. This fundamental difference demonstrates the confusion created by referring 'Hebrew labor' back to the productivization movement and anachronistically describing it as evolving in a direct line from Eastern European origins.[67]

In this connection, we might, however, note that the settlers of the Second and Third Aliyot were not Nordau-style elite theorists but, in the main, pogrom-hardened East European refugees, fellows of those crossing Germany under the transit controls, whose strategic preaccumulation included the applied lesson in the efficacy of violence that they had received before setting off for Palestine. Financially, moreover, the Conquest of Labour derived directly from European sources, without which it could not have functioned, so we should adjust Shafir's emphasis. Left to their own devices, as Shafir himself demonstrates, the founding colonists of the Second Aliya were unequal to the task of supplanting Palestinians on their own terms. Their ethnocratic isolate could only be achieved with the backing of donors motivated by ideals, including productivisation, which had initially been coined in response to European conditions.

Relieved of the requirement to generate a surplus (the Jewish National Fund was able to run up large debts[68]), the Yishuv could prioritise ethnicity over efficiency. It was this backing that enabled the Conquest of Labour, as it was forged on the colonial ground, to subordinate economic efficiency to the demands of building the self-sufficient proto-national Yishuv at the expense of the surrounding Arab population. This subsidised local struggle produced the New Jew as subject of the labour that

---

67 Ibid., 81–2.

68 Confronting probable restrictions on its land purchases in the wake of the Peel Commission Report, the JNF resolved to adopt any measures, including deficit financing, to buy as much land as it could, a policy whereby, as the JNF reported in 1939, its 'indebtedness has been much enlarged'. JNF report quoted in Lehn, *Jewish National Fund*, 72–3.

it conquered. In the words of Zionist architect Julius Posner, reprising a folk song, 'We have come to the homeland to build and be rebuilt in it ... the creation of the new Jew [is also] the creator of that Jew.'[69] As such, the Conquest of Labour was central both to the institutional imagining of a *goyim rein* (Gentile-free) zone and to the continued stigmatisation of Jews who remained unredeemed in the Galut.[70]

The Conquest of Society

This would remain a core theme of the settler nation-state. By way of introduction to his terrorist memoir, for instance, future Israeli prime minister Menachem Begin announced that, in addition to his Jewish readers, he had also written the book for Gentiles: 'lest they be unwilling to realise, or all too ready to overlook, the fact that out of blood and fire and tears and ashes a new specimen of human being was born, a specimen completely unknown to the world for over eighteen hundred years, "the FIGHTING JEW."'[71]

It is important to note that the fighting Jew's opponents were not only Arabs. They conspicuously included the British, whose ignominious retreat from the Palestine Mandate had in no small measure been an achievement of Begin's Irgun fighters. More significantly, in harking back 1,800 years – which is to say, to the fighting Jews of Masada – Begin was also rejecting the fallen Jews of the diasporan interim. When this rejection was redirected from the diaspora to Palestine, however, Natives came to take the place of the fallen Jews. It is important not to make the mistake of viewing Zionism's adversaries as simply Gentiles (European Gentiles in Europe; Arabs ones in Palestine). If anything, Zionism's principal adversary was the old Jew – the unreconstructed, self-identifying parasite that, in so identifying, was the shameful collaborator of European antisemitism (in this respect, again, Zionism endorsed antisemitism). In forging the New Jew on the ground of dispossession in Palestine, Zionism was exorcising the diaspora (Begin's 'eighteen hundred years') from the Jewish soul.

A kind of self-hatred was preconditional to this transformation. Ascent (aliya) was not merely a matter of leaving behind Gentile others, who, as goyim, did not ultimately count. Much more importantly, it was a matter of leaving behind a strenuously rejected self. Extirpating Europe from the

69 Quoted in Mark LeVine, *Overthrowing Geography: Jaffa, Tel Aviv, and the Struggle for Palestine, 1880–1948* (Berkeley: California UP, 2005), 167.

70 Moshe Menuhin (father of Yehudi, Hepsibah and Yaltah) recalled of his Zionist schooling in Mandate Palestine that 'It was drummed into our young hearts that the fatherland must become ours, *"goyim rein"* (clear of Gentiles-Arabs).' Menuhin, *The Decadence of Judaism in Our Time* (New York: Exposition Press, 1965), 52.

71 Begin, *Revolt*, xxv, capitals in original.

old-Jewish self was the inseparable obverse of extirpating Arabs from the new-Jewish self. Herzl's metaphor of a building referred as much to this internal demolition/rebuilding as it did to the effacement/replacement of the Natives of Palestine. As such, it casts light on the zeal with which Zionists have prosecuted the cause of Palestinian extirpation.

The advocates of the New Jew would have agreed with Shafir. The New Jew could not exist in Europe. He (and it surely was he) would be a creation of a future that could only take place in Zion.[72] Their protestations notwithstanding, however, Zionist settlers did not stand alone. For the land that they purchased, and for their subsequent capacity to derive viable returns from their indifferent use of it, they relied on a transnational metropole that provided funding without requiring a return. Metropolitan capital, in short, was Zionism's indispensible preaccumulation.

In this, as observed, it hardly differed from other settler projects. But freedom from the discipline of the bottom line set Zionism apart from other colonial projects, for all their routine protectionism. Without this freedom, there could have been no Conquest of Labour – and, accordingly, no kibbutzim, no Histadrut and, ultimately, no Jewish state. Accordingly, the profound outcomes of this creative subversion of market principles are poorly characterised in terms of labour alone. The premise that it was more important that labour be Hebrew than that it be productive was the centrepiece of an all-encompassing conquest of society, enabled by Zionism's diffusely integrated metropole.

But society is not the state, which monopolises the legitimate exercise of violence. Funding alone could not relieve Zionism of the need for military support, even though the acquisition of Native territory was being conducted in at least notional conformity with the imperial legal system. As observed, the Yishuv's land-acquisition tactics were bound to provoke Native hostility. Thus military force was never far away, in the form of the colonial policing provided by British forces or, locally, by unofficial Zionist militias (the Haganah, forerunner to the Israeli army, was formed by Jabotinsky in 1920).[73] Here, however, in contrast to Australia and North America, violence or the threat of violence was deployed to secure territorial gains that had already been made by other means, rather than to gain territory in the first place. Eventually, of course – in 1948 – violence would become a viable way to gain territory, whereupon it would be used as such.

The relative restraint that Zionists displayed in the Ottoman and

---

72 Herzl only viewed the option of Uganda, which the British had suggested, as a possible 'shelter for a night.' Boas Evron, *Jewish State or Israeli Nation?* (Bloomington: Indiana UP, 1995), 56.

73 Morris, *Righteous Victims*, 96–7.

Mandate periods did not mean that they had yet to formulate the goal of replacing Palestinians in Palestine. The initial restraint was pragmatic; the later Nakba, to adapt Carl von Clausewitz, being a continuation of purchase by other means.[74] Moreover, the purchases were prerequisite to Zionism's attainment of these other means: a disciplined population with a contained territorial base, and an adequately funded state apparatus, possessed of military resources and a functioning hierarchy of command. Without Zionism's strategic coordination of human and capital imports, whereby a contiguous land base was secured and populated with Ashkenazi immigrants, none of these things would have been possible. When we contemplate this remarkably disciplined and systematic programme of settler-state formation, the complementarity between the creation of the Jewish state and the ethnic cleansing of Palestine – settler colonialism's positive and negative dimensions respectively – emerges with particular clarity, the two being inseparable features of a unified programme. Thus we turn to the land, the contested setting over which all of this took place.

Zionism's State in Waiting

In their ceaseless deliberations as to the best ways to tailor Jewish immigration to the goal of transferring Palestinian land into exclusively and irreversibly Jewish ownership, Zionist planners were aiming to build a fully formed ethnocratic parallel to the existing apparatus of government. To this end, they sought to modulate Jewish demographics so as to take maximum advantage of the Palestinian-owned land that became available for acquisition. Moreover, as noted, they did not simply acquire land wherever it could be bought. Nor did they limit their purchasing to agriculturally valuable land. Rather, they sought to create unbroken expanses of Jewish ownership.

Crucially, this ownership was not individual but collective. Once transferred into Jewish hands, parcels of land would cease being commodities in the general-alienability sense. Prior to leasing land out to Jewish tenants, the Zionist organisations that had purchased it imposed conditions preventing it from ever returning to Gentile ownership. On the basis of this plan, every inch of acquired Palestinian land would become forever Jewish. Which Jews took it over, and how – efficiently, inefficiently or otherwise – was not the point. What mattered was that they

---

74 Carl von Clausewitz, *On War* (Michael Howard and Peter Paret trans., Eaglewood Cliffs: Princeton UP, 1984). 'The whole of Palestine, or at least most of it, must belong to the Jewish people ... this can be achieved by three means: by force, but we do not have it, governmental coercion or purchase'. Menachem Ussishkin, *The Ussishkin Book* (Jerusalem: Ussishkin Publications, 1934), 105, translated and quoted in Pappe, 'Zionism as Colonialism', 616.

– and, whether or not they flourished, their successors in perpetuity – be Jewish.

Conceptually, the idea of collective ownership on behalf of the Jewish nation diametrically reversed the US ideology of private property, which, as we have seen, demonised Native ownership on the basis of its collective nature. In practical terms, however, the Zionist strategy shared characteristics with US Indian policy, where the collectivity – in that case, the US government – acquired Native land and transferred it into ethnically non-Indian hands. In the Zionist case, however, the acquiring had to be effected within the terms of an imperial legal system that could not be swept aside or imposed on in the way that settlers had dealt with Indigenous legal systems in the USA or Australia.[75] This legal system was based on the Ottoman *tanzimat* land reforms of the mid-nineteenth century, which were largely inherited and maintained by the British during the Mandate era and even, to a significant extent, by the post-Nakba Israeli state.

Operating within the continuing framework of Ottoman land law, abetted by the British penchant for property settlements, Zionist purchasers sought to convert nexuses of overlapping entitlements (a Levantine analogue to E. P. Thompson's 'messy complexities of coincident use-right'[76]) into an exclusive form of ownership that compressed discontinuous sets of rights into consolidated units of Jewish property.[77] So far as fellaheen 'tenants' were concerned, however, what mattered was not who had ultimate title to the land on which they made their livelihoods but the scope of that ownership. In general (there were exceptions[78]), large-scale effendi landowners under the Ottoman tanzimat system, who were often resident elsewhere,[79] owned, bought and sold their holdings subject to the

75   Early in the First Aliya, before Rothschild's intervention, Eliezer Ben-Yehuda was already writing, from Jerusalem, that: 'The thing we must do now is to ... conquer the country, covertly, bit by bit ... we shall act like silent spies, we shall buy, buy, buy.' Quoted in Morris, *Righteous Victims*, 49.

76   E. P. Thompson, *Whigs and Hunters: The Origin of the Black Act* (London: Allen Lane, 1975), 241.

77   In Ottoman terminology, this typically involved converting *masha'a* (collectively held land allocated to individual cultivators in rotation) into *mafruz* (Dawes-style individual allotments).

78   'Arab landowners before World War I could and did evict tenants without offering them compensation': Stein (citing 'Mr. Bennett of the [British] Palestine Lands Department'), 'Legal Protection and Circumvention of Rights', 238. See also Stein, *Land Question in Palestine*, 19.

79   According to Ruppin's testimony to the Shaw Commission, 90 per cent of vendors were absentees: *Report of the Commission on the Palestine Disturbances of August 1929, Command paper Cmd. 3530* (Shaw Commission report), 114. Granott's figures showed a drop from 86 per cent in 1923–27 to 14.9 per cent in 1933–36, the bulk of the difference being provided by 'large resident landowners': A. [Avraham] Granott, *The Land System in Palestine: History and Structure* (London: Eyre & Spottiswood, 1952), 277.

continuing use-rights of fellaheen, whose rent or other forms of tribute provided the return on the effendi's investment. To this extent, Ottoman land transactions were comparable to capitalist business takeovers, which do not generally involve the automatic replacement of employees.

Much has been made of these absentee landowners, whom Zionists were fond of characterising as unscrupulous Orientals bearing responsibility for their humbler countrymen's misfortunes.[80] No doubt in some cases the Zionists had a point. In others, though, landowners had only become absentees because their homes had been separated from their landholdings in the post-war Anglo-French carve-up of the Ottoman Empire.[81] Regardless of effendis' locations or motivations, however, the crucial factor for settler expansion was the attachment of usufruct to title. As observed, settler colonialism takes place at the level of usufruct. On its own, buying and selling between landlords, absent or present, does not depopulate, even if the rent collector changes. In the political realm, a change of ruler may occasion a change of tax collector, or even of the tax itself, without affecting proprietorship. Dispossession only takes place – Natives only become replaced – at the level of usufruct. The methods that Zionists used to attach usufruct to title, so that vendors might sell a consolidated right that would not otherwise have been theirs to sell, exploited the variety of social relationship that together constituted property under the Mandate regime.

Walter Lehn has charted how shifts in the acquisition policies of the Jewish National Fund reflected changing circumstances on the ground.[82] While large landholdings were the consistent preference, the JNF initially targeted absentee landowners because they were relatively immune from local pressure not to sell.[83] When British policy became more restrictive in response to Native insurgency in the later 1930s, however, 'it became JNF policy to buy any land from any owner, large or small, who was willing or could be persuaded or forced (e.g. through mortgage foreclosure) to sell'.[84] As Lehn's 'persuaded or forced' formulation suggests,

---

80 Atran has argued that some scholars, including Stein, have been influenced by orientalist stereotypes into disparaging the traditional style of land distribution, in particular the *masha'a* system of circulating tenure, which Atran sees as having protected fellaheen landholdings from alienation. Atran, 'Surrogate Colonization', 738–9.

81 See, e.g., Abcarius, *Fog of Propaganda*, 128.

82 Lehn, *Jewish National Fund*, 79. Strictly, the land was purchased for the JNF by Zionist land-purchasing agencies, principally Ruppin's Palestine Land Development Company. See Smith, *Roots of Separatism*, 89; Kenneth W. Stein, 'The Jewish National Fund: Land Purchase Methods and Priorities, 1924–1939', *Middle Eastern Studies* 20 (1984), 190–205.

83 Arthur Ruppin, *The Agricultural Colonisation of the Zionist Organisation in Palestine* (J. W. Feiwel trans., London: Martin Hopkinson, 1926), 69–70.

84 Lehn, *Jewish National Fund*, 79. See also Stein, 'Legal Protection and Circumvention of Rights', 246–7.

Zionist purchasing agencies used all available methods to acquire suitable land. In the early years of British rule, effendi who had enlarged their holdings by informal means under the Ottomans found themselves hamstrung by British regulations, and in many cases proved willing to sell.[85] Absentee landholders had been unable to collect rent during the war, so they were often responsive to the offer of cash.[86] After World War I, smallholding cultivators found themselves deep in debt, and many pledged their land as security for loans they could not service – eventually forfeiting their security to moneylenders, who amassed substantial holdings that they could sell on to Zionist purchasers.[87] Under a plan of Ruppin's (which Mandate assistant treasurer Michel Abcarius termed 'a vile use to which money can be put'), Zionists bought up land before there were enough Jewish immigrants to cultivate it, expelling the fellaheen and keeping the land in reserve and unused – the 'dead hand' of mortmain – until such time as Jewish tenants should become available.[88]

When the British introduced regulations to restrain such practices, ways were found around them.[89] As in the Ottoman period, proxy buyers could be arranged, or sales could be made into a future time when the regulations had been relaxed.[90] The widespread practice of under-registering landholdings so as to avoid taxation and military conscription enabled much larger parcels of land to change hands than the deeds indicated (by the same token, purchasers paid less tax[91]). Once again, however, the crucial factor was not so much the sale itself as the prior clearing of cultivators from the land. Given collusion between a Native landlord and a Jewish purchaser, this could be achieved in a number of ways. The requirement that tenants had a right of first refusal when land was sold could be evaded by having it publicly auctioned in satisfaction of mortgage debts 'collusively arrived-at' between a landlord and a purchaser.[92] Alternatively, tenants could be moved around, the targeted

---

85   Stein, *Land Question in Palestine*, 5.

86   Ibid., 40.

87   Polk, 'Arabs and Palestine', 234–6; Stein, *Land Question in Palestine*, 14–15, 19–21; Stein, 'Legal Protection and Circumvention of Rights', 238.

88   Abcarius, *Fog of Propaganda*, 156. See also Lehn, *Jewish National Fund*, 54, 72–3. 'The result of the purchase of land in Palestine by the Jewish National Fund has been that land has been extra-territorialised … The land is in mort-main and inalienable', *Hope Simpson Report* (Cmd. 5479), vol. 1, 54. *Cf.* 'The land shall not be sold for ever: for the land *is* mine; for ye *are* strangers and sojourners with me', Leviticus, 25:23.

89   Revealingly, however, 'the corporation tax imposed by the Turkish Government on such lands [held in mortmain] was practically the only fiscal measure which the Palestine [Mandate] Government failed to reinstate.' Abcarius, *Fog of Propaganda*, 137.

90   Smith, *Roots of Separatism*, 94; Stein, 'Legal Protection and Circumvention of Rights', 238–9.

91   Stein, 'Jewish National Fund', 201.

92   'In "forcing" a sale through the courts, the Arab seller blamed the British for

portion of land being let to incoming tenants who then let it on as agents of the landlord, tenants of tenants not being protected against eviction.[93] Landlords could apply duress to induce tenants to sign undertakings that they did not wish to purchase the land themselves, as they had been adequately compensated with land elsewhere.[94]

To these ends, Zionist organisations were careful to protect the anonymity of Native vendors, who could also be leaders of the emergent Palestine national movement. Stein, who painstakingly tracked these multifarious ruses, has described various ways whereby debts to Zionist purchasers could be contrived in order to obtain court orders for the land to be sold in satisfaction: 'this entire process was pre-planned so that the Jewish National Fund would obtain the land, the prestige of the seller would be protected, the rights of cultivators would be summarily circumvented, and the seller would obtain a price for the land well above the price set by the court.'[95]

A further, key component of Palestinians' expropriation was an assimilation of public land to the category of state land, which reflected the deeper penetration of the realm of property exercised by the industrial-capitalist British state in comparison to its Ottoman predecessor. Under the reformed Ottoman system, types of land tenure had been divided up into a mix of private and public categories.[96] Public forms of ownership could be state, religious, or local-collective based. Private ownership generally fell under the heading of the *mulk* form of tenure, which covered dwellings and private plots accompanying them, and which could be inherited. *Waqf* land was set aside for religious purposes, the revenue generally going to the upkeep of Muslim institutions. *Metruke* land was public in the widest sense, encompassing rivers, lakes, roads, public grazing areas and the like. Most of the land in Palestine was, however, classified as *miri*, a system under which ownership was vested in the state but usufructuary rights were assigned to fellaheen. In the event of miri land not being tilled for a period of five years, usufructuary rights reverted to the state, which could redistribute them to other fellaheen.

---

forcing him to sell his land to the Zionists': Stein, 'Jewish National Fund', 201. See also Atran, 'Surrogate Colonization', 733.

93   Stein, 'Legal Protection and Circumvention or Rights', 247.

94   Ibid., 258–9 (including specimen undertaking).

95   Stein, *Land Question in Palestine*, 72. For a general survey of these ruses, together with loopholes that Natives were able temporarily to exploit (for squatting, opportunistic grazing, etc.), see Anglo-American Committee of Inquiry, *A Survey of Palestine*, vol. 1 (reprint of 1946–47 original, Washington: Institute for Palestine Studies, 1991), 289–94.

96   For overviews of the Ottoman tenure system and its land classifications, see, e.g., *Survey of Palestine*, 225–37; George E. Bisharat, 'Land, Law, and Legitimacy in Israel and the Occupied Territories', *The American University Law Review* 43 (1994), 491–5.

By introducing the notion of state land, which had not existed as an Ottoman category, the British provided for such land as had not been assigned to particular owners – including common pasturage and hunting or wood-collecting grounds, as well as land that remained unregistered in the post-Ottoman confusion – to be treated as unclaimed.[97] In effect, land that was everybody's became land that was nobody's, which meant that it reverted to the state. Under the preferential provision whereby Mandate authorities were to encourage close Jewish settlement of 'state land and waste land not needed for public purposes', land thus reclassified could then be sold (or, in some cases, indefinitely leased) to Zionist purchasers.[98] The wide distribution of state land made it particularly suitable for filling in strategic gaps in the Zionists' overall land-acquisition programme, premised as this was on contiguity. Where fellaheen held land that was contiguous with existing Zionist holdings, for instance, state land could be purchased elsewhere as compensation for their displacement.[99] By such means, not only was the Yishuv consolidated but Palestinian communities were further fragmented.

For Palestinians, the continuing effects of the Ottoman land-tenure system, itself an imperial imposition, did not end with the Mandate. Various key tanzimat reforms were to survive the Nakba to provide ongoing pretexts for Israel's expropriation of Palestinian land. The preponderance of non-private forms of ownership became susceptible to interpretation as state ownership, which would come to mean collective Jewish ownership in the post-1948 era.[100] A further pretext was provided by the five-year reversion rule, which meant that Palestinians who had been driven from their land in 1948 could be made subject to forfeiture through having failed to cultivate it. Another resulted from the fact that, in 1858, fellaheen had become obliged to register their interest in particular tracts of land, an obligation that had become more thoroughly bureaucratised by the British in the Mandate period. A major disincentive to registration under the Ottomans had been that it rendered the

---

97 Rajah Shehadeh, *Occupier's Law: Israel and the West Bank* (rev. ed., Washington: Institute of Palestine Studies, 1985), 25. Under the Land (Settlement of Title) Ordinance of 1928, land not established as privately owned was to be registered in the name of the state: David Kretzmer, *The Legal Status of Arabs in Israel* (Boulder: Westview Press, 1990), 52.

98 Lehn, *Jewish National Fund*, 77.

99 Ibid., 76.

100 As one of the architects of Israel's post-Nakba campaign of expropriation expressed this pretext: 'On the day that the sovereignty of the New State was proclaimed, it inherited automatically and legally all real property previously belonging to the Mandatory Government. Under international law the State is the heir to the rights of the former Government, including ownership of land ... The Palestine Government had certain rural and urban lands registered in its name, according to law, in the Land Registry.' Granott, *Agrarian Reform*, 90.

person registering liable both to taxation and to the much-feared military conscription, prompting large numbers of fellaheen to avoid registration or to register the land in fictional or absentee names.[101] Eventually, this led many fellaheen to resort to urban-based moneylenders, to compensate both for their increased tax burden and for the loss of labour that they sustained as a result of increased military conscription. Subsequently, when they had fallen behind with their payments, the moneylenders could claim the land as collateral and sell it to Zionist purchasers, as occurred in the case of the Sursuq family's large sale.[102] In terms of future implications, however, the chaotically disordered record of local land tenure that resulted from this situation led to numerous fellaheen being unable to establish their entitlement to their land under the more demanding administrative requirements imposed by the British and, subsequently, under the punitive conditions of the Israeli legal system. The recitation could be continued indefinitely.[103] It is a litany of dispossession.

The Invasion Continues

It may seem contrary to offer a narrative of Palestinian dispossession that dwells so obliquely on the Nakba. My intention has not been to understate the repeated enormities that the nascent Jewish state perpetrated in the Nakba. Rather, it has been to situate it in the context of the ongoing (in Saree Makdisi's term, 'slow-motion') enormity that Zionists, with imperial and comprador connivance, had been conducting incrementally, day by day, for over half a century before the Nakba.[104] In the absence of that context, the Nakba would make no sense. We might even endorse Morris's assertion that ethnic cleansing was a spontaneous aberration that took place in the heat of warfare.[105] In the preceding context

---

101   Ruedy, 'Dynamics of Land Alienation', 124.

102   Polk, 'Existing Non-Jewish Communities', 236–8.

103   Hussein Abu Hussein and Fiona McKay, *Access Denied: Palestinian Land Rights in Israel* (London: Zed Books, 2003), 69–171; Bisharat, 'Land, Law, and Legitimacy', 512–17; Kretzmer, *Legal Status of the Arabs in Israel*, 50–61; Sabri Jiryis, 'The Legal Structure of the Expropriation and Absorption of Arab Lands in Israel', *Journal of Palestine Studies* 2 (1973), 82–103. For a select list of salient Israeli statutes, see Oren Yiftachel, *Planning a Mixed Region in Israel: The Political Geography of Arab-Jewish Relations in the Galilee* (Avebury: Ashgate, 1992), 313.

104   'Hebron is living evidence of what it means for Palestinians to be inexorably forced out of their homes and pushed off their land. It is a slow-motion "portrait" of Palestine being turned inside out.' Saree Makdisi, *Palestine Inside Out: An Everyday Occupation* (New York: Norton, 2008), 212.

105   That is, so long as we overlook the calculated system with which Zionist forces prevented Palestinians who had fled their homes from returning. See Morris, *Palestinian Refugee Problem Revisited*, 341–413. In Ben Gurion's view, 'I don't accept the formulation that we should not encourage their return. Their return must be prevented … at all costs', quoted in Simha Flapan, 'The Palestinian Exodus of 1948', *Journal of Palestine Studies* 16 (1987), 17.

of Zionism's conquest of society, however, the Nakba makes only too plain sense. There was no change of ends. The Nakba simply accelerated, very radically, the slow-motion means to those ends that had been the only means available to Zionists while they were still building their colonial state. If, in the 1930s, Palestinians had fled their homes instead of rising up against British rule, there would not have been enough Jews to fill them. By 1947, an adequate contingent of Jews was on hand, but the Zionists had failed to purchase enough land.

The same can be said for the dream of transfer (the Zionist euphemism for removing the Natives from Palestine). Though there had been much talk of transfer before World War II,[106] the practical exigencies of the mid-Mandate years meant that it could be no more than that – talk. To understand the Nakba, therefore, we have to keep in mind the crucial fact that it was Zionism's *first opportunity*. That the emergent Jewish state seized this opportunity with such devastating effectiveness was both a testament to and a legacy of its preparedness. As we have seen, the creation of the Jewish state and the ethnic cleansing of Palestine were two sides of the same coin. The conquest of society was a Nakba in waiting.

As historians, then, we should approach events carefully, recording them at face value but also looking behind them to their enabling contexts, the historical conditions that made them possible. This, I think, is also the reason why the scientist Israel Shahak refrained from discussing the infamous April 1948 massacre that Zionist troops carried out at Deir Yassin (the Jerusalem suburb since renamed Kfar Sha'ul): 'Accurate and detailed knowledge of Zionist thought as expressed by its leaders led to many incidents like Dayr Yasin [sic] and, more importantly, can yet again lead to similar or worse events.'[107]

Shahak's prescient warning brings us to the most urgent reason of all for attending to historical structures. It is in the nature of structures that, often as not, the deep-seated regularities subtending individual events can be traced forwards as well as backwards in time. For there to be any hope that the study of history might help us to escape being collectively condemned to repeat it, we should not submit to the tyranny of detail. This is not, of course, to jettison rigour. Rather, as Ted Carr retorted to the implacable G. R. Elton, 'Accuracy is a duty, not a virtue.'[108] The details do not speak for themselves. They speak in context. Four decades after the Nakba, for example, Israeli economist Ira Sharkansky was astounded to

---

106 For the genealogy of the Zionist dream of transfer, see, e.g., Morris, 'Yosef Weitz and the Transfer Committees'. See also chapter 2, 'The Idea of "Transfer" in Zionist Thinking before 1948', in Morris, *Palestinian Refugee Problem Revisited*, 39–64. Compare Masalha, *Expulsion of the Palestinians*, 94–101 and *passim*.

107 Shahak, 'History of the Concept of "Transfer"', 33.

108 E. H. Carr, *What Is History?* (2nd ed., R. W. Davies ed., London: Penguin, 1987), 11, crediting A. E. Housman.

find that the Israeli government's expenditure exceeded the gross national product (not government revenue, GNP!). On investigation, Sharkansky discovered that the government received revenues that did not emanate from productive activity, so they were not counted for GNP purposes: 'grants from overseas governments and private contributors, plus loans from overseas and domestic sources'.[109] Sharkansky found all this surprising. Aware of the historical background to Israel's diasporan funding, we should not be surprised.

As I write, Israeli authorities are engaged in forcibly evicting Palestinian residents from Wadi Hilweh (Silwan) in occupied al-Quds (East Jerusalem). 50,000 Palestinians live there. There is no saying how many will be driven from their homes. The pretext for this ongoing post-Nakba removal has been provided by a highly dubious archaeology according to which King David built a Jewish-only city there in the third millennium BCE.[110] The City of David Archaeological Park, which is replacing the Palestinian homes, is being financed by, among others, Ron Lauder of Estée Lauder perfume fame, who currently chairs the Jewish National Fund. Lauder is one of numerous plutocrats who are supporting this contemporary exercise in ethnic cleansing. We should not be surprised. It is no random event.

The purchases were only one element in the overall construction of the Zionist state in waiting in Palestine. To appreciate the whole, they need to be viewed in conjunction with the myriad associated ingredients that go into the formation of a settler-colonial state: the establishment, training and equipping of Zionist militias; the build-up of a Jewish-owned and controlled industrial infrastructure (including the acquisition of concessions to drain swampland and produce electricity); the creation of a formidable financial and administrative infrastructure through key institutions such as the Histadrut and the World Zionist Organisation; the scripting and consolidation of a highly distinctive settler culture, epitomised in the remarkable resuscitation of biblical Hebrew as a dynamic modern language; the recruitment and socialisation of a suitably pioneering group of Jewish immigrants, and numerous other achievements. The purchases constitute a representative feature of this whole complex process.

By any standards, Zionism has succeeded spectacularly. Correspondingly, and in inverse proportion, Palestinians have been spectacularly immiser-

---

109 Ira Sharkansky, *The Political Economy of Israel* (Oxford: Transaction Books, 1987), 24.

110 For website, go to cityofdavid.org/il. For the politically compromised career of the established tradition of Israeli archaeology, see Nadia Abu El-Haj, *Facts on the Ground: Archaeological Practice and Territorial Self-Fashioning in Israeli Society* (Chicago: Chicago UP, 2002); Piterberg, *Returns of Zionism*, 258–67. For updates on Wadi Hilweh (Silwan), go to silwanic.net.

ated. These are two sides of the same coin. Nonetheless, in the wake of
the Nakba, Palestinians were by no means completely eliminated, even
within the internationally recognised boundaries of the nascent settler
state. As in the cases of the other settler societies that we have considered,
race acquired new forms and meanings in the context of this unfinished
demographic business. Thus we turn now to the demographic profile of
the post-Nakba Israeli state. In the chapter to come, we shall consider
some of the distinctively Israeli ways in which the problems presented by
the presence of surviving Palestinians within the Jewish state came to be
translated into the language of race.

CHAPTER EIGHT

New Jews for Old

Racialising the Jewish State

In 2001, the American Society for Histocompatibility and Immuno-genetics found itself embroiled in a political controversy concerning racial origins. The controversy had arisen after the editors of the society's journal, *Human Immunology*, retrospectively expunged an article questioning the genetic exclusivity of Jewish people from the journal's Internet version.[1] The ensuing interchange was rancorous. 'Someone evil', a scientist involved in the controversy declared, 'has interpreted the withdrawal of the article by the Editor as a pressure because it contradicts Jewish ideology'.[2]

The heat generated by the issue should not come as a surprise to anyone conversant with the history of racial discourse. After all, as the continuing half-life of the so-called 'bell curve' brouhaha illustrates, science and race have always enjoyed the most intimate of mutualities. Though the scientists concerned have hardly been able to deny their respective disciplines' involvement in past racisms, their progressive ethic has encouraged them to reject any suggestion that contemporary science might be sustaining the supremacist germ that animated the practice of their acknowledged predecessors. 'Let's keep [!] science and politics apart,' as another of the

---

1 The article, entitled 'The Origin of Palestinians and Their Genetic Relatedness With Other Mediterranean Populations', by Antonio Arnaiz-Villena and eight others, originally appeared in *Human Immunology* 62 (2001), 889–900. These pages subsequently disappeared from the journal's Internet version. For an account, see Raphael Falk, 'Zionism, Race, and Eugenics', in Geoffrey Cantor and Marc Swetlitz (eds), *Jewish Tradition and the Challenge of Darwinism* (Chicago: Chicago UP, 2006, 137–62), 160–2. Those interested can contact me by email for a PDF of the original hard-copy article. In addition to the expunging of the article, the American Society for Histocompatibility and Immunogenetics also removed Arnaiz-Villena from the journal's editorial board.

2 Ariella Oppenheim, 'Letter to Dr. Moien Kanaan', *The Ambassadors Online Magazine* 5, no. 1 (January 2002), part 4.

parties to this controversy urged, 'otherwise I can see the end of good science at the beginning of this century.'[3]

The article in question, dedicated 'to all Palestinians and Jews who are suffering war', was appreciably more candid as to its political implications than comparable studies, in particular an article on the same topic by a team of Israeli scientists that had earlier been published in the same journal and remains available on its Internet version.[4] A comparison of the two articles reveals a high level of agreement concerning the empirical data, together with a significant disagreement concerning the interpretation of these results. The papers concur that Palestinians (whom the earlier paper limited to Palestinians living in Israel) are genetically closer to Mizrahim (in this case, Jews from Libya and Yemen) than either are to Ashkenazim (Jews from Europe) though all three share distinctive genetic characteristics. The two papers also agree that Ethiopian Jews are genetically remote from either Palestinians or the two other Jewish populations studied. Unsurprisingly, in short, the two Arab populations (Mizrahim and Palestinians) constitute a relatively integrated genetic category compared to the European Ashkenazi population, while these three combined are relatively integrated in comparison to the remoter Ethiopian population.

To this extent, the two papers' findings are consistent. The harmony was broken, however, when it came to the conclusions that the two papers drew from their convergent results. Whereas the Israeli scientists (who had omitted data on the relationship between Ashkenazi Jews and other Europeans) found that the results showed 'that Jews share common features, a fact that points to a common ancestry',[5] Arnaiz-Villena and his Spanish/Palestinian team grouped populations into three branches, the first of which, encompassing both eastern and western Mediterranean populations, contained both Jews and Palestinians and the third of which

---

3   Mazin Qumsiyeh, 'Letter to Dr. Oppenheim through Dr. Moien Kanaan', *The Ambassadors Online Magazine* 5, no. 1 (January 2002), part 2.

4   A. Amar et al., 'Molecular analysis of HLA class II Polymorphisms among Different Ethnic Groups in Israel', *Human Immunology* 60 (1999), 723–30. The article's population tree (p. 728) brackets together Ashkenazi Jews and Moroccan Jews (whom one presumes to be Sephardim of European – which is to say, Andalusian – ancestry), both being distinct from a same-order category containing Libyan Jews, Yemenite Jews and 'Israeli Arabs' (Palestinians within Israel). A lower-order category links Libyan and Yemenite Jews in contradistinction to Palestinians. In other words, the closest categories of all are the Libyan and the Yemenite Jews, but these two are closer to Palestinians than any of these three are to Ashkenazi or Moroccan Jews. At this level, Ashkenazi and Moroccan Jews together occupy a category distinct from the category containing Libyan Jews, Yemenite Jews and Palestinians.

5   Amar, 'Molecular Analysis', Abstract. Ultimately, of course, all humans share a common ancestry. The Amar paper failed to point out that, according to its own data, the common ancestry that some Jews share with Palestinians is closer than the common ancestry that these same Jews share with Ashkenazi or Moroccan Jews.

contained Greek and Ethiopian/sub-Saharan populations,[6] concluding that 'Palestinians are genetically very close to Jews and other Middle East populations, including Turks (Anatolians), Lebanese, Egyptians, Armenians, and Iranians.' On this basis they asserted that 'Palestinian–Jewish rivalry is based in cultural and religious, but not in genetic, differences.'[7]

The passion generated by this otherwise abstruse discussion recalled an earlier controversy that the Hungarian Jewish writer Arthur Koestler, one-time Zionist resident in Palestine, had triggered when he published his investigations into the mysterious, and long-lost, Jewish empire of the Khazars (located in the area between the Black and the Caspian Seas and extending to the north), which inexplicably disappeared around the end of the eighth century CE. On the other side of the *Human Immunology* imbroglio, Koestler's thesis would resurface virtually unchanged in the form of Shlomo Sand's *The Invention of the Jewish People*, which duly reignited the acrimony that had earlier greeted Koestler's publication.[8] For our purposes, the significance of this durable controversy lies not in its scientific merits but in the light that it casts on Zionism's racial ideology. It is hard to imagine that Koestler can have failed to appreciate the potential damage that his findings threatened for Zionism's racially-based claim to another people's land. It was this implication, rather than questions of historical procedure, that motivated his opponents' virulence. For our purposes, therefore, the significant question is not whether Koestler and Sand were right or wrong. The significant question is what the fuss was about.

Koestler contended that, rather than disappearing, the Khazars had actually become the Ashkenazi population of the Pale of Settlement – those, in other words, who would eventually become the Ostjuden.[9] Noting the coincidence between 'the disappearance of the Khazar nation from its historic habitat, and the simultaneous appearance in adjacent regions to the north-west of the greatest concentration of Jews since the beginnings of the Diaspora',[10] Koestler argued that, rather than being distinct, these phenomena were but opposing sides of the single coin of Khazar migration. This explanation, he insisted, fitted the known

---

6 The second group was restricted to the 'Mediterranean outgroups' of 'African Negroid and Japanese' populations, which presumably include Sudanese Jews. Arnaiz-Villena, 'Origin of Palestinians', 893.

7 Ibid., 889 (Abstract).

8 Shlomo Sand, *The Invention of the Jewish People* (Yael Lotan, trans., London: Verso, 2009).

9 Koestler cited A. N. Poliak, professor of Mediaeval Jewish History at Tel Aviv University, as a precursor ('one of the most radical propounders of the hypothesis concerning the Khazar origins of Jewry'). Arthur Koestler, *The Thirteenth Tribe: The Khazar Empire and Its Heritage* (London: Hutchinson, 1972), 16.

10 Ibid., 159.

facts much more satisfactorily than 'the traditional idea of a mass-exodus of western Jewry from the Rhineland to Poland all across Germany' ('a hostile, Jewless glacis'), an idea that he dismissed as historically untenable.[11]

The controversial aspect of Koestler's claim was not, however, the direction in which Ashkenazi Jews were held to have migrated but the manner in which they had become Jewish in the first place. Koestler asserted that, rather than inheriting their Judaism from the Hebrew prophets by way of the diasporan scattering that had allegedly followed the destruction of the second temple in 70 CE, the Khazars had converted to Judaism for strategic political reasons. Sandwiched between the decadent Roman Empire on one side and the expanding Islamic Caliphate on the other, the polytheistic Khazars realised that their lack of monotheism deprived them of the centralisation that these rival superpowers both enjoyed. Nonetheless, adopting the religion of either would have entailed submission and a resulting loss of independence. Under these circumstances, asked Koestler, 'What could have been more logical than to embrace a third creed, which was uncommitted towards either of the two, yet represented the venerable foundation of both?'[12]

However much the logic of this embrace may once have appealed to Khazars, in the present it could hardly have conflicted more subversively with Zionist logic, whose primary ideological justification for the colonisation of Palestine was that it constituted a return – to a place where converted Khazars had manifestly never been.[13] Moreover, Koestler's Khazars were by no means insignificant. On the contrary, even after the Holocaust, 'the large majority of surviving Jews in the world' was of Eastern European – 'and thus perhaps mainly of Khazar' – descent. The implications of this demographic possibility took Koestler directly into the scientific question that would subsequently prompt Yale geneticist Mazin Qumsiyeh to point out that the Israeli team's *Human Immunology* study had failed to include non-Jewish Slavic and other European populations, whose ancestral relationship to their Ashkenazi neighbours would have been revealed to be close – in all likelihood closer than

11 Ibid., 168.

12 Ibid., 59.

13 For examples of the Zionist vitriol that swiftly greeted the publication of Koestler's book, see, e.g., Chimen Abramsky, 'The Khazar Myth', *Jewish Chronicle*, 9 April 1976, 19; Hyam Maccoby, 'Koestler's Racism', *Midstream: A Monthly Jewish Review* 23, no. 3 (March 1977), 31–40, where Koestler figures, on p. 37, as 'a prodigy of wrongheadedness and incomprehension'. In his 2009 review of the Hebrew version of Sand's *Invention of the Jewish People*, Evan Goldstein was still pursuing the theme: 'Koestler and the Khazar theory he advanced lives [*sic*] on in the fever swamps of the white nationalist movement.' *Tablet Magazine: A New Read on Jewish Life*, 13 October 2009. Go to: tabletmag.com.

the Ashkenazis' relationship to Mizrahi Jews.[14] This was territory that Koestler had already entered. If, as Koestler reasoned, most of the Jews in the world were indeed descended from the Khazars, then it would follow that

> their ancestors came not from the Jordan but from the Volga, not from Canaan but from the Caucasus, once believed to be the cradle of the Aryan race; and that genetically they are more closely related to the Hun, Uigur and Magyar tribes than to the seed of Abraham, Isaac and Jacob.[15]

Ostensibly, Koestler's rhetorical agenda was to show that the Nazis had been mistaken in separating out Jews from the general European stock, a consequence that made the story of the Khazar empire begin to look like 'the most cruel hoax which history has ever perpetrated'.[16] By 1976, however, the political movement that stood to lose most from the suggestion that Ashkenazi Jews were of internally European provenance was not Nazism but Zionism. Lacking the core premise of return, which furnished its transcendent linkage of Jews to Palestine, Zionism would have been left as just another European colonial enterprise, a status hardly congenial to the anticolonial international climate in which, in 1947, the United Nations had given its qualified blessing to the establishment of the state of Israel.[17]

The Ideology of 'Return'

Among settler-colonial discourses, Zionism is distinguished by its claim to be returning to a land that it already owned rather than to be surpassing a prior, albeit inferior, Native mode of occupancy. The concept of return ('to Zion') is inseparable from that of origin, which in turn implies continuity. The raw nerve that both Koestler and the Spanish/Palestinian geneticists inflamed was the spectre of Jewish discontinuity. For Zionism to maintain its claim to Palestine, Jews had to be continuous both demographically – as a coherent and bounded human category – and historically, as an entity that had emanated from the region of the Jordan River. Regardless of the protagonists' scientific virtues or lack of them, therefore, the anxieties precipitated by Koestler and the geneticists

14 Mazin Qumsiyeh, 'Who Are the Palestinians?' *The Ambassadors Online Magazine* 5, no. 1 (January 2002). Qumsiyeh is Palestinian.

15 Koestler, *Thirteenth Tribe*, 17.

16 Ibid.

17 The United Nations Partition Plan (or 'General Assembly Resolution 181 [II] Future Government of Palestine'), which constituted a 'Plan of Partition with Economic Union', provided in part 3 for 'Independent Arab and Jewish States and [a] Special International Regime for the City of Jerusalem'.

are significant for the light that they cast on the Zionist brand of settler colonialism.

Settler colonialism's twin aspects, the goals of eliminating Native territoriality and constructing a new society in its place, are merged in the concept of return, which reverses the standard settler-colonial schedule whereby the physical expropriation of territory prepares the way for the ideological construction of a settler polity. In the Zionist case, the ideological construction of a settler polity ('the Jewish nation') was prerequisite to the physical expropriation of territory.[18] Despite this reversal, however, Zionism systematically combined the two aspects, seeking both the territorial dispossession of Palestinian society and its replacement by a Jewish alternative. Indeed, the settler polity's ideological prefabrication underlay Zionism's distinctively exclusive mode of settlement, which was (as it remains) maximally resistant to Native assimilation. 'Australians' and 'Americans' did not commence the process of Native dispossession as ready-made categories. Rather, the names 'Australian' and 'American' were initially applied to Natives rather than to settlers. The Australian and US nations were made in the settling, a relatively open-ended historical production that, as we have seen, was amenable to assimilation.

By contrast, premised on the concept of return, the new/old Sabra society that Zionism sought to construct would necessarily be atavistic, at least in part. Whereas Natives might merge (albeit in manageable quantities) into Euro-Australian or Euro-American futures, there was no place for Palestinians in Ashkenazi Zionism's renovated past. In the case of Palestinians, therefore, Zionism's racialisation strategy can be expressed with maximal simplicity: it is one of outright exclusion. As Israeli historian Gabriel Piterberg has noted of the endemically fissured Israeli-Jewish polity: 'The only facet of Jewish Israeli identity that is not fragmented is the agreement upon the sine qua non principle of distancing the Palestinians from the collective and, where possible, from the land.'[19]

The crucial codependence of demographic and historical continuities became consolidated in the course of Zionism's early development. In its late-nineteenth-century infancy, the Zionist movement had entertained the possibility of a Jewish colony in Argentina or in 'Uganda' (which included modern Kenya).[20] Indeed, the shift to an exclusive focus on Palestine (then an adjunct of Ottoman Western Syria) signified an ambivalent concession to a religious dimension that, as we saw

---

18 'The first [Jewish] Nationalists instead of producing an idea in order to satisfy a need were looking for a need which would correspond to their ideas.' Jacob Katz, 'The Jewish National Movement: A Sociological Analysis', *Cahiers d'Histoire Mondiale* 11, nos 1/2 (1968), 279.

19 Piterberg, *Returns of Zionism*, 200.

20 Laqueur, *History of Zionism*, 95, 122–3, 126–30.

in chapter three, was anathema to Theodor Herzl and his co-founders of political Zionism, who rejected a religious criterion for Jewishness in favour of a nineteenth-century concept of race.[21] Their Jewish nationalism, in keeping with the contemporary European nationalisms in the midst and likeness of which it grew, was secular, modernising and colonial. In harnessing this nationalism to Palestine, however, a project that rendered a biblical component inescapable, political Zionism incurred a founding contradiction that would continue to unsettle its colonisation of Palestine. As will emerge below, the religious contradiction would crucially determine the ways Jews come to be racialised in the Jewish state that Zionism eventually created.

On the one hand, Zionism sought to be internal to Europe. It aimed to build a civilised, territorially defined nation-state that would be thoroughly European in culture and allegiance. On the other hand, however, as a project that laid claim to a Palestinian inheritance, Zionism situated itself outside Europe, an exteriority that found expression in the diasporan narrative of temple-destruction and ensuing exile. Culturally, in other words, Zionism sought to belong to Europe while, ancestrally, it laid claim to an Oriental provenance. It was this contradictory need to be simultaneously both internal and external to Europe that Koestler, Sand and the censored geneticists would render unavoidable. In assigning a Khazar lineage to Ashkenazi Jews, Koestler and Sand were threatening the Jewish nation's externality to Europe, while, in rendering Mizrahim closer to Palestinians than they were to Ashkenazim, the censored geneticists were threatening its internality to Europe. In jeopardising Jewish demographic continuity, both jeopardised the historical continuity linking all Jews – as Jews – to Palestine.

The great lack that defined life in the European diaspora for Zionists was a territorial basis with which their pre-existing 'Jewish nation' could combine to form a state, understood as a demo-territorial unity. This is the point at which we can appreciate the full utility of the notion of return. Jews were by no means the only identifiable community in Europe that lacked a territory of its own, nor the only one to claim a primordial inheritance (as we know from Benedict Anderson, such narratives are endemic to nationalism[22]). Why, then, should Jews be intrinsically entitled to colonise Palestine? The answer that Zionism provided was that the Jewish lack was different to those of other communities, since it had

---

21   In basing Zionism on land and language, the Zionist intellectual Jakob Klatzkin made this rejection of religion explicit: 'Zionism began a new era, not only for the purpose of making an end to the Diaspora but also in order to establish a new definition of Jewish identity – *a secular definition.*' Klatzkin, 'A Nation Must Have Its Own Land and Language' (1914), in Hertzberg, *Zionist Idea*, 319.

22   Benedict Anderson, *Imagined Communities: The Origin and Spread of Nationalism* (London: Verso, 1983).

come to pass not by happenstance but through the unredeemed injustice of expulsion (at the hands, moreover, of the Romans, from whom Western European nations claimed succession).

This fateful distinction commended Palestine to political Zionism with a force that alternative venues could not command. There could be no 'returning' to Uganda, Angola or other options that colonial powers might offer. For Jews to migrate to places such as these (or, for that matter, to Western Europe or the United States) was an individual undertaking. Return, by contrast, was an irreducibly collective noun, converting individual destination into national destiny. On this count too, political Zionism found itself ensnared in religious apologetics, even Christian ones. As Amnon Raz-Krakotzkin has pointed out, the premise that the exilic condition is inherently inferior (Zionism's 'negation of exile') recapitulates the very Christian narrative 'upon whose rejection Jewish consciousness was previously established': 'Just as Christianity criticized Judaism as a historical anachronism, so did Zionism criticize the Jews in exile as having been left behind by history. Zionism came to "supersede" exilic Judaism just as Christianity purported to supersede Judaism.'[23]

The yield on this embarrassment was, however, incalculable: given the notion of return, Jews could be represented not just as a people without a base but as a nation which, through the loss of its land, had been deprived of its statehood, a situation that called for redress. The full implications of this construction become clear when one considers the situation of other stateless peoples within Europe, who did not lay claim to extra-European homelands. Europe was already comprehensively owned, by peoples whose acknowledged level of civilisation unquestionably qualified them for ownership. Palestine, by contrast, was merely occupied – even its sovereign was Muslim. In keeping with the discourse of conquest informing the doctrine of discovery, its Natives' credentials for property ownership were axiomatically diminished.[24] Here, then, is the genius

---

23   Amnon Raz-Krakotzkin, 'The Zionist Return to the West and the Mizrahi Perspective', in Ivan Davidson Kalmar and Derek J. Penslar (eds), *Orientalism and the Jews* (Waltham: Brandeis UP, 2005), 167. As Yakov Rabkin commented, 'Zionism casts itself as a replacement for Judaism, which it recognizes as a respected but by now obsolete predecessor. The analogy with Christianity is clear ... Christianity emerged from a Greek reading of the Torah and, over time, split off from Judaism, which remained in a minority position. Zionism reflects a nationalist, romantic reading of the Torah and, like Christianity before it, has been able to impose its vision upon the majority.' Rabkin, *Threat from Within*, 50, 227. For a sustained and insightful critique of the negation of exile, which has influenced my own account, see Piterberg, *Returns of Zionism*, especially 93–101.

24   Thus what was missing from the 'land without a people' was not human beings but, in strict conformity with the doctrine of discovery, Europeans. The non-European status of Palestine's population exacerbated the anomaly of there being Europeans ('a people') without a land. As Israel Zangwill put it, 'If Lord Shaftesbury was literally

of return: it allowed a non-state, a diffuse transnational metropole, to colonise.

Colonialism and Exclusion

But not just any kind of colonisation. Rather, the atavistic structuring of Zionism's Jewish nation subtended a particularly rigorous form of settler colonialism that comprehensively excluded non-Jews, defined as being incapable of returning. This thoroughgoing exclusiveness, which continues to inform Israeli resistance to anything resembling a policy of Native assimilation, was not effectively tested until 1967, when Israel came to occupy the balance of Mandate Palestine west of the Jordan River. Prior to this development, within the borders specified in the 1949 Armistice, Israeli Jews had reaped the demographic harvest of the Nakba, coming to comprise around 80 per cent of the resident population of the new state.[25] In 1967, however, though Israeli forces carried out some significant ethnic cleansing, Palestinians had learned the lesson of the Nakba and, in the main, proved less susceptible to intimidation.[26] In the event, the occupation presented Israel with a demographic problem that it had not had to confront within its post-1949 borders.

During the Nakba, Israel had been able to depopulate as it seized, with the result that it could claim the territory thus gained for inclusion within its borders on the same basis as the rest. After 1967, however, when the Zionist colony itself became a metropole, Israel could not formally annex the Occupied Territories, however much it may have wished to do so, without incorporating a resident Native population whose numbers would confound the Jewishness of the Jewish state. As is well known, the Zionist solution to this conundrum has consisted in a familiar settler strategy: an informal style of annexation-in-denial, spearheaded by maverick settlers and backed up by state force, a strategy that, as we have seen, is a regular feature of frontier expansion.[27]

Thus we should not confuse 'post-Nakba' with 'post-frontier'. In the Israeli case, as in that of the nineteenth-century USA, national independence took place during the frontier era. In regard to racial classifications,

---

inexact in describing Palestine as a country without a people, he was essentially correct ... there is at best an Arab encampment.' Zangwill, *Voice of Jerusalem*, 104.

25 See previous chapter, n. 17.

26 Nur Masalha, *A Land Without a People: Israel, Transfer and the Palestinians, 1949–96* (London: Faber & Faber, 1997), 111.

27 For the premeditation that went into Israel's 1967 invasion, plans for which were being drawn up in the politics department at the Hebrew University of Jerusalem as early as 1963, see Ilan Pappe, 'Revisiting 1967: The False Paradigm of Peace, Partition and Parity', *Settler Colonial Studies* 3(2013), 341–51.

therefore, it is consistent that Israel should continue to reject policies of Native assimilation, which, as we have seen, are characteristic of post-frontier societies. In infra-continental societies like those of mainland Europe, the frontier designates a national boundary as opposed to a mobile index of expansion. Israel's borders partake of both qualities. Despite Zionism's chronic addiction to territorial expansion, Israel's borders do not preclude the option of removal (in this connection, it is hardly surprising that a nation that has driven so many of its original inhabitants into the sand should express an abiding fear of itself being driven into the sea). Moreover, as in other settler societies, the continuing tendency to Native expulsion has not been limited to the unelaborated exercise of force. For instance, as Baruch Kimmerling and Joel Migdal have observed, Israeli officials only permit Palestinian family unifications 'in one direction – out of Israel'.[28]

Thus Israeli state endorsement of frontier expansion extends well beyond military protection for religious colonisers. In the wake of 1967, so handsome were the tax breaks and subsidies for West Bank 'economic settlers' (suburban commuters living in established West Bank colonies) that, 'on 26 November 1979, the newspaper *Yedi'ot Aharonot* reported that 85 per cent of Ashkenazi settlers owned two homes – one in Israel and one in the occupied territories'.[29] In the case of Israelis in the Occupied Palestinian Territories, no hard and fast distinction between 'military' and 'civilian' statuses can be maintained. Not only are commuter families subsidised to consolidate the invasion of occupied Palestinian territory (the transfer of one's own citizens into occupied territory being proscribed under Article 49 of the 4th Geneva Convention[30]). As Eyal Weizman and his colleagues have graphically demonstrated, even the architecture of

---

28　Kimmerling and Migdal, *Palestinian People*, 172.

29　G. N. Giladi, *Discord in Zion: Conflict between Ashkenazi and Sephardi Jews in Israel* (London: Scorpion, 1990), 134. 'Amana [a Yesha Council religio-militant off-shoot of Gush Emunim] is not responsible for settlement on the urban centers that have evolved in the territories; these are controlled by public authorities and most of their inhabitants do not necessarily share an idealistic calling': Eliezer Ben-Rafael and Yochanan Peres, *Is Israel One? Religion, Nationalism, and Multiculturalism Confounded* (Leiden: Brill, 2005), 93. In a section aptly entitled 'Suburban sprawl on the frontier', Gershon Shafir and Yoav Peled provide figures detailing how government grants to colonies in the Occupied Territories are higher than those to Israeli municipalities. Shafir and Peled, *Being Israeli: The Dynamics of Multiple Citizenship* (Cambridge: Cambridge UP, 2002), 174–83. My discussion generally refers to the occupied West Bank, including East Jerusalem. Gaza, which had been under Egyptian control from 1948 until the Israeli seizure of 1967, is different in various respects, including its very high proportion of post-Nakba Palestinian refugees, a factor that discouraged (but did not preclude) the establishment of Israeli colonies.

30　'The Occupying Power shall not deport or transfer parts of its own civilian population into the territory it occupies', *Convention (IV) relative to the Protection of Civilian Persons in Time of War* (The Fourth Geneva Convention, 12 August 1949, Israel as signatory), Art. 49.

West Bank settlements makes every Jewish householder an agent of colonial surveillance:

> According to the regional plans of politicians, suburban homes, industrial zones, infrastructure and roads are designed and built with the self-proclaimed aim of bisecting, disturbing and squeezing out Palestinian communities. Israeli civilians are placed in positions where they can supervise vital national interests just like plain-clothes security personnel ... Planning and building in the West Bank is effectively executing a political agenda through spatial manipulations.[31]

Among Israelis in the Palestinian territories, it is more appropriate to assign gradations of military status than to distinguish between military and civilian occupiers.

The differential militarisation of Israeli citizens combines settler colonialism's negative and positive aspects, simultaneously contributing to Palestinian suppression and to the building of Israeli social bonds. The positive aspect, settler state-formation, is no less crucial than the negative one. This is because the settler ideology of a pre-existent Jewish nation that had been marking time in the wings of history pending reunion with its ancestral territory is just that, an ideology. In practice, as Shafir has illustrated, Israeli-Jewish society, like any other settler society, has to be made and remade on the ground of conquest.

Moreover, there are degrees within the Jewish nation as well as within the Israeli state. Since the primary requirement of an expanding frontier society is the attraction of immigrants, the definition of Jewishness that applies for Law of Return purposes is maximally inclusive.[32] Consistently enough, given its ostensible role of shielding Jews from persecution, this definition approximates to the catch-all Nuremberg definition that the Nazis used during the Holocaust. Once inside Israel, however, Jewish migrants find their Jewishness subject to Halachic discriminations whose rabbinical imposition would have horrified the founding Zionists. Moreover, as we shall see, the religious/secular division intersects and overlaps with equally profound ethnic divisions. All this is a far cry from the 'normal state' that the founding Zionists intended their Jewish nation to become.

From the beginning, the Jewish nation was to become normalised as one among other European states, as Jewish as France was French.

---

31 Rafi Segal and Eyal Weizman, 'Introduction' to Segal and Weizman (eds), *A Civilian Occupation: The Politics of Israeli Architecture* (London: Verso, 2003), 19. See also Weizman's monumental *Hollow Land: Israel's Architecture of Occupation* (London: Verso, 2007).

32 Akiva Orr, *The UnJewish State: The Politics of Jewish Identity in Israel* (London: Ithaca Press, 1983), 27–31.

The New Jew was a way of talking about the practical realisation of this aim. Just as Englishmen became Americans or Australians through the practical minutiae of conquest, dispossession and replacement, so did Jews from Europe become Sabras in Zion through consolidating their takeover of Palestine. Ironically, therefore, by escaping from Europe, New Jews became like European Gentiles, whose alienation from their putative fellow-nationals left languishing in the diaspora continues to be apparent in Israeli Jews' reactions to encounters with Jewish communities overseas.[33] Moreover, the migratory transition at the heart of the concept of return continues to structure Israeli-Jewish identity, in which the collective (phylogenetic?) redemption from exile is recapitulated within the life cycle of individual settlers. Even Jews born in Israel are deemed to have in-migrated (the term 'oleh', plural 'olim', being conventionally rendered in English as 'settler'). Thus section 4 of the Law of Return provides that:

> Every Jew who has immigrated into this country before the coming into force of this Law, and every Jew who was born in this country, whether before or after the coming into force of this Law, shall be deemed to be a person who has come to this country as an oleh under this Law.

As David Kretzmer has noted, the implications of this provision were critically clarified in the notes to Israel's Nationality Law of 1952, which explained that the provision grants: 'the absolute right of Israeli nationality to an oleh under the Law of Return, that is to every Jew who comes to settle in Israel, and to every Jew who was born there'.[34] There could hardly be a clearer example of settler colonialism's replacement of Natives by immigrants. Under this foundational provision, the conferral of racial privilege on Palestine-born Jews was achieved by means of the poker-faced contrivance of converting them into honorary immigrants. In direct contrast to Koestler's Khazars, they were 'returning' to somewhere they had never left.

In the outcome, as Shira Robinson concisely notes, 'Israel would grant automatic citizenship to all Jews in the country, by virtue of their "immigrant" status, but only to 63,000 Palestinian Arabs, by virtue of their residence'[35] – to which we might add that the law thereby granted immigrant status to every Jew on earth, at the same time as it excluded

---

33   'Many [Israeli-Jewish] students told me, "We feel closer to Gentiles in the Diaspora than to Jews in the Diaspora".' Baruch Kurzweil, quoted in Orr, *UnJewish State*, 215.

34   Quoted in Kretzmer, *Legal Status of the Arabs in Israel*, 18. See also Shabtai Rosenne, 'The Israeli Nationality Law 5712 (1952) and the Law of Return (1950)', *Journal du Droit International* 81 (1954), 4–63.

35   Robinson, *Citizen Strangers*, 100.

Native-born Palestinian citizens of Israel from membership of the Jewish nation. References to Israeli nationality are rare in official Israeli discourse, since the national category is Jewish. There are no citizens of the Jewish nation.[36] Conversely, Israeli citizenship is not exclusively Jewish, there being Palestinian citizens of the Israeli state – a consequence, to use Robinson's words again, of 'the unprecedented colonial bargain that [Israel's] government believed it had to strike in order to gain international recognition in 1949 – to grant Palestinians the right to vote in the midst of its ongoing quest for their land'.[37]

But the priority of the nation is absolute. There are no Palestinians among 'Israeli nationals', either born or returned, an embarrassment that has encouraged official avoidance of the term. This avoidance underlies Israel's continuing failure to pass the constitution that was required under the terms of the UN Partition Resolution of November 1947. To secure the country's foundation on racial discrimination, an Israeli constitution would have to spell out the operative discrepancy between Jewish nation and Israeli state, a disparity that could not withstand international scrutiny.[38] As an internal corollary to the missing constitution, a citizen was not initially allowed to be described as an 'Israeli national' for the fledgling state's identity-card purposes.[39] Thus the exceptional use of the term 'Israeli national' in the legislation that consecrated judaeocracy is an index of the ultimate priority of the settler logic of elimination, manifest politically as the desire for the nation to exhaust the state.

---

36   The state of Israel relies on normal states' conflation of the categories 'state' and 'nation' to blur these categories in its international publicity. '*Over 90 per cent of all the Arabs resident in Israel today are Israeli nationals*': State of Israel, *The Arabs in Israel* (Tel Aviv: Government of Israel, 1955, 76, italics in original). As Mazin Qumsiyeh has pointed out, the rendering of the basic laws of the state of Israel that is to be found on the website of the Israeli Ministry of Foreign Affairs in both Hebrew and English versions systematically mistranslates between the Hebrew words *ezrahut* (citizenship) and *le'om* (national), so as 'to obfuscate the separation in the Hebrew text between ... citizenship ... and membership of Am Yisrael (the people of Israel, referring to all Jews anywhere).' Qumsiyeh, *Sharing the Land of Canaan: Human Rights and the Israeli-Palestinian Struggle* (London: Pluto, 2004), 87. For insightful discussion, see Robinson, *Citizen Strangers*, 108.

37   Robinson, *Citizen Strangers*, 55.

38   As an Israeli dissident has put it, 'If there existed an "Israeli" nationality it would, in theory, not be possible to legally differentiate between citizens.' Ronnie Barkan, 'Demanding equality – how is that illegal?' *Aljazeera.net*, 14 December 2012.

39   Prior to 2002, residents of Israel aged over sixteen were obliged to carry identity cards that specified their nationality. 'For Jewish residents, nationality [was] defined as "Jewish" and not "Israeli". The term 'Israeli' appears only in passports, where it defines citizenship [i.e., state, rather than national, membership]'. Benjamin Beit-Hallahmi, 'Back to the Fold: The Return to Judaism', in Zvi Sobel and Beit-Hallahmi (eds), *Tradition, Innovation, Conflict: Jewishness and Judaism in Contemporary Israel* (Albany: SUNY UP, 1991), 153.

The Bounds of Jewishness

Here again, however, the occupation brought about a change of priorities. In 1991, the Law of Return was significantly relaxed to allow the admission of non-Jewish (in the main, nominally Christian) relatives of immigrant Russian Jews.[40] Such a development would have been as unthinkable as it was unnecessary prior to 1967. Within its 1949 borders, Israel had succeeded in reducing the Palestinian population to a level that did not unduly hinder the positive process of nation-building, a task to which the rigorous application of the Law of Return was central. Confronted with the radically different demographic scenario that resulted from its occupying so much more of Mandate Palestine without effectively dispersing the Natives, however, Israel found itself back at the pre-Nakba conundrum of how to reduce the Native population to manageable proportions.

This situation was aggravated by a striking discrepancy between the respective birth rates of the Jewish and Palestinian populations, a predicament that has lent itself to memorable metaphors ('the war of the cradles', 'the demographic time-bomb', etc.).[41] Self-evidently, there are only three positive ways to increase the proportion of Jewish nationals: births to Jewish mothers, conversions to Judaism,[42] or immigration. Of these, conversion is somewhat unwieldy and has not received a significant level of official attention. Judaism is not an evangelical religion. Moreover, few would risk raising the theoretical possibility, no matter how outlandish, of a Palestinian mass-conversion.[43] Campaigns to increase the birth rate have, however, been energetically championed, though these have on occasion proved counterproductive, as when Ben-Gurion quietly dropped a baby bonus awarded to mothers who gave birth to their tenth child since a majority of the qualifying mothers were Palestinian.[44]

---

40 Naomi Shepherd, *The Russians in Israel: The Ordeal of Freedom* (New York: Simon & Schuster, 1993), 11–12. For comment, see Sand, *Invention of the Jewish People*, 291.

41 'The Israeli Arabs are a time bomb ... They are a potential fifth column ... If the threat to Israel is existential, expulsion will be justified.' Benny Morris, *Ha'aretz* interview with Ari Shavit, English version reproduced in *Counterpunch*, Weekend Ed., 16–18 January 2004, and at: logosjournal.com/morris. See also Youssef Courbage, 'Reshuffling the Demographic Cards in Israel/Palestine', *Journal of Palestine Studies* 28, no. 4 (Summer 1999), 25–6 ('borders are negotiated with babies'); Rhoda Ann Kanaaneh, *Birthing the Nation: Strategies of Palestinian Women in Israel* (Berkeley: California UP, 2002), 38–9.

42 Shepherd overlooks conversion in her reference to 'Halacha, or rabbinical law, which regards only the child of a Jewish mother as Jewish.' Shepherd, *Russians in Israel*, 12.

43 Though Ben-Gurion would seem to have at least toyed with the idea: 'In 1951, for instance, the army immediately shot down the prime minister's proposal to convert the population forcibly to Judaism en masse.' Robinson, *Citizen Strangers*, 134.

44 Masalha, *Land Without a People*, 144; Reinhard Weimer, 'Zionism and the Arabs

Nonetheless, fertility programmes have been encouraged, contraception has been discouraged, and family-planning clinics have been reported to be disproportionately distributed in Palestinian areas.[45] Far and away the most effective and immediate way to increase a population, however, is through immigration.[46]

In this regard, the relaxation of emigration restrictions that the Soviet Union had imposed on Jews in a more confident era promised a massive demographic windfall to Israel – so long, that is, as the Jews concerned could be discouraged from going elsewhere. In particular, as on previous occasions, emigrating Jews had to be diverted from a preference for the United States.[47] In the event, the US government obliged with more rigorous immigration restrictions that excluded Jews,[48] while every effort was made to welcome Russian Jews to Israel – a programme that occasioned complaints from earlier arrivals that the Russians were being allowed to jump the queues for housing and employment.[49] In this expanded demographic context, crucially different from that in which the Nationality Law had been passed, settler colonialism's negative dimension prevailed over its positive one. The need to reduce the proportion of Palestinians trumped the desire to build an exclusively Jewish state.

The Russians are not the only anomaly. In addition to people whose capacity to return is at best questionable, there are Jews who never left.

---

after the Establishment of the State of Israel', in Alexander Schölch (ed.), *Palestinians over the Green Line: Studies on the Relations between Palestinians on both sides of the 1949 Armistice Line since 1967* (London: Ithaca, 1983), 46.

45   Nira Yuval-Davis, 'The Jewish Collectivity and National Reproduction in Israel', in Khamsin Collective, *Women in the Middle East* (London: Zed Books, 1987), 80, 85 (no source cited). 'Despite the ministry's reluctance to start family planning programs in Jewish communities, it was eager to do so among Arabs. It was widely known among ministry employees that approval for a general clinic in an Arab [i.e., Palestinian] area was difficult to get, but approval was all but guaranteed if the proposed clinic included a family planning unit.' Kanaaneh, *Birthing the Nation*, 37.

46   Yossi Yonah, 'Israel's Immigration Policies: The Twofold Face of the "Demographic Threat"', *Social Identities* 10 (2004), 195–218.

47   For Zionist wartime pressure on President Franklin D. Roosevelt to discourage Jewish immigration to the USA in order to divert it to Palestine, see Hirst, *Gun and Olive Branch*, 114–15. 'From the end of the war in Europe to October 21st 1946, only 4,767 "displaced persons" had been permitted to immigrate to the United States', Nathan Weinstock, *Zionism: False Messiah* (Alan Adler, trans., London: Ink Links, 1979), 226.

48   As of 1 October 1991, the number of Soviet Jews allowed into the US as refugees was limited to 40,000 per year. At the same time, Soviet Jews were prevented from using Israeli visas to enter the USA (i.e., they were prevented from using Israel as a staging post). For comment, see Shepherd, *Russians in Israel*, 13–14.

49   Giladi, *Discord in Zion*, 254–5; Shepherd, *Russians in Israel*, 5. For an openly racist preference for the Russians ('Hurry up brothers, hurry up, we are terribly in need for you') over the Mizrahim ('the Israeli public sphere has become more Levantine, in the bad sense of the word'), penned by senior Israeli journalist Amnon Danker in his national column, see Yonah, 'Israel's Immigration Policies', 208–9.

Zionist ideology is hard-pressed to accommodate the Old Yishuv, Jews who had managed to live in Palestine for centuries without becoming New Jews. The Old Yishuv significantly included Jewish Palestinians, part of an assortment of ethnicities (Ottoman millets) whose mutual disdain had no kinship with European antisemitism.[50] As Ella Shohat has observed, Zionist taxonomies have no place for Arab-Jews, let alone Palestinian ones.[51]

It is very significant that the categories 'Jew' and 'Arab' cannot share space in Zionist discourse. A corollary to Arabs' inability to share space with Jews is that the space for Arabs is elsewhere. To put it very simply, but the point has significant ramifications, the space for Arabs is outside Israel – not merely outside the bounds of the Jewish nation but, as befits a primal Other, immediately outside. This narrative structure is, of course, abundantly grounded in Ashkenazi discourse, only now displaced onto the eastern Mediterranean, with Israel substituted for the ghetto or stetl and 'Arabs' for the surrounding Gentiles.

Arabs are Israel's 'neighbours', either as a hostile sea in which the victim nation is beleaguered or as those alongside whom the peace-loving nation wishes to live in harmony. In the diplomats' refrain about Israel living in peace with its neighbours, 'neighbours' is a horizontal category. It refers to Arabs living outside the bounds of Israel, not, vertically, to Arabs living within the Jewish state. In other words, 'neighbours', in common with 'Arabs' and 'Jews', is a composite noun in Zionist thought. Within the Jewish nation, Arabs cannot be individual neighbours, Palestinian fellow-citizens in the next-door apartment. Rather, as surveys consistently show, Palestinian fellow-citizens are ubiquitously shunned as neighbours, a demotic exclusion that is amply echoed in official provisions for residential segregation.[52]

Thus even the category 'Arab' is not an undifferentiated alterity. Rather, just as the fundamental division within the Jewish nation is between those in Zion (in their place) and those unredeemed in the diaspora, so the fundamental division within the Arab category is between those in their place (the diaspora, which for them is not exile) and those anomalously

---

50   For a judicious comparative historical account of Jewish communities' respective fortunes among Christian and Muslim societies, see Mark Cohen, 'Islam and the Jews: Myth, Counter-Myth, History', in Shlomo Deshen and Walter P. Zenner (eds), *Jews Among Muslims: Communities in the Precolonial Middle East* (London: Macmillan, 1996), 50–63, expanded in Cohen, *Under Crescent and Cross: The Jews in the Middle Ages* (2nd ed., Princeton: Princeton UP, 2008).

51   Ella Shohat, 'Sephardim in Israel', 11; Shohat, *Taboo Memories*, 213–15.

52   Residential segregation follows automatically from the Jewish National Fund's blanket restriction of all the land that it owns to Jewish tenants. For an account of the diplomatic problems that arose when the first Egyptian ambassador to Israel wished to lease a mansion subject to such restrictions, see Uri Davis, *Apartheid Israel: Possibilities for the Struggle Within* (London: Zed Books, 2003), 119–23.

persisting within Zion, which remains unredeemed to the extent that they are still there. Switching between the two senses (Natives and neighbours) of the single homonym 'Arab' enables Israel to make counterfactual claims about its benign intentions towards Palestinians. Thus even the foundational division between Jews and Arabs does not stand up to inspection. Rather, just as the category 'Jew' turns out to be multiply differentiated, so is the category 'Arab' reciprocally differentiated, the most fundamental distinction being the one separating Arabs who are in their place – outside Israel – from those who are not.

The primary divide is not, therefore, between Jews and Arabs, but between settlers and Natives. For Zionism, as the Russian example demonstrates, the bottom line consists in not being Palestinian. In the end, what makes the Jewish nation is not religion but settlement, the continuing process of invasion. As Yakov Rabkin has noted, this process is obscured by religious rhetoric, especially in Christian Zionism, which represents colonial expropriation as an eternal clash of faiths.[53] Conspicuous by their absence from this narrative are Christian Palestinians, who are scrupulously overlooked in clash-of-faiths discourse. For Evangelical Christianity, the problem with Christian Palestinians is not their status as already ex-Jews (at least, in the congregational sense), which makes them ineligible for millennial conversion. Otherwise, they would not be so manifestly unqualified for Christian fellowship. The problem with Christian Palestinians is, rather, that they are Natives, whose Christianity is thereby diminished. Despite their seemingly irreconcilable doctrinal differences, those of the renovated dispensations – whether born again in Zion or in Jesus – can at least agree on colonialism's fundamental text.

Thus the contradictions attending Israel's importation of the Russians are not particular to the one group. Rather, they are generic to the project of settler-state formation, the inherent tension between the need to maximise immigration and the need to maintain demographic stability being especially acute where Native assimilation is not an option. Given this tension, Christian Russians – or, for that matter, Christian Palestinians – are not the only ones to disappear. Even more emphatically, so do Jewish Palestinians. Binary oppositions are high-maintenance. As Jacques Derrida never tired of pointing out, the poles incline to re-entanglement. A corollary to Shafir's recognition that the New Jew was produced through colonial struggle is that the Yishuv depended on the Natives' contrapuntal presence.

An ideology premised on exile is vulnerable to success, which cancels its motivating life-force. This predicament is relieved by Arab hostility,

---

53 Yakov Rabkin, 'Nakba in Narratives About Zionism', in *Commemoration of Nakba* (Kyoto: Kyoto Bulletin of Islamic Area Studies, 3: 1, Kyoto UP, 2009), 33.

which domesticates exile, re-estranging the nation at home. This is no mere abstraction, nor a matter of past history. Rather, as the fissures that the Jewish nation is obliged to encompass indicate, if Israel really were to complete the goal of Palestinian transfer ('No Arabs, no terror' read the posters in the highway underpasses[54]), it would lose the single diversion that has proved capable of reconciling the Jewish segment's own internal contradictions. Pre-eminent among these contradictions is the near-majority population that, in a supposedly exclusive polarity, is neither exclusively Jewish nor exclusively Arab, but both.

Arab-Jews

Considering their anomalousness, the Christian Russians have been quite easily digested. But this is not surprising since, well before their arrival, Israel had already confronted the challenge of digesting a much more refractory anomaly, one that could not be remedied by conversion or the discreet passage of a generation or two. Arab-Jews – Mizrahim from places such as Yemen or Iraq – merge in the dominant Ashkenazi consciousness with the Sephardic descendants of the Jewish community that was expelled, along with Muslim Moors, from the Iberian Peninsula around the end of the fifteenth century.[55] Taken together, Mizrahim and Sephardim ('Oriental Jews') test the boundaries of the European-colonial fragment that Ashkenazi Zionists have constructed in Palestine.[56]

Thus the question arises of why, or how, they came to be there. After all, these people had not experienced European antisemitism, let alone the Holocaust. Moreover, as Elie Kedourie observed, 'Zionism is a doctrine that had no appeal to oriental Jewries', while Zionists in their turn 'had nothing but contempt for the way of life of these Jewries which according to them was primitive, feudal and unprogressive'.[57] Mizrahim went to Israel for their own reasons, of course. Prime among these reasons, however, was a consideration that settlers invariably face: the need to avoid becoming dependent on the productive vitality of a population whose elimination they also require.

Settlers, as we have seen, typically import subaltern labour in order to

54   Avishai, 'Saving Israel from Itself', 40.

55   Mizrahim actually encompass a much more varied provenance, including liturgical divisions between Sephardi, Roman, Bavli and Yemeni traditions as well as smaller groupings including Moroccan, Kurdish, Iranian and South Indian Jews. My discussion concerns the unitary category that has been formed in Israeli discourse.

56   Gabriel Piterberg, 'Domestic Orientalism: The representation of "Oriental" Jews in Zionist/Israeli historiography', *Journal of Middle Eastern Studies* 23 (1996), 1–20.

57   Elie Kedourie, *The Chatham House Version and Other Middle-Eastern Studies* (rev. ed., London: New England UP, 1984), 309, 311.

avoid having to depend on the Natives. In the Zionist case, this preference was sharpened by the desire to build an exclusively Jewish state in waiting in Palestine, which made it more important that the labour be Hebrew than that it be economic. As we saw in the previous chapter, the problem of inefficiency was outweighed by the fact that those who financed the settler project in Palestine did not require a financial return on their investment. In a context of steady but not overwhelming immigration from Europe (which, with British compliance, Yishuv leaders carefully modulated),[58] this inefficient condition was just about viable.

The Holocaust changed all this. In Israel's first three years, despite an inflow of around four hundred million dollars raised in the United States alone, a stupendous sum at the time, the flood of traumatised immigrants was overwhelming. Moreover, these immigrants were not, in the main, the kind of human material that the Yishuv was seeking. In preference to labouring to redeem the land, they generally headed for the cities to pursue commercial callings. Unlike earlier Zionist *halutzim* ('pioneers'), they had not self-selected for the rigours of tilling the soil and becoming Sabras. Nor had they been put through the demanding training courses that the Yishuv had required of earlier immigrants. Rather, they tended to be the kind of unredeemed diasporan Jews that Zionism had execrated, a deficiency corroborated by their humiliating failure to defend themselves (as Yitzhak Laor would later, shockingly, recall: 'In our parents' pioneering ideology, those who did not come to Palestine on time were responsible for their own fate').[59]

In the wake of the Nakba, the pressing need of the day was for replacement Palestinians. Incongruously, however, these Palestinians should be Jewish – Canaanites, Hebrews who could work the land. Hence the apparent paradox of a country that had been thrust into an overpopulation crisis seeking to populate its way out of it. Earlier in the century,

---

58 Albert M. Hyamson, *Palestine under the Mandate, 1920–1948* (London: Methuen, 1950), 52–3, 55; Kimmerling, *Zionism and Territory*, 97.

59 Yitzhak Laor, *The Myths of Liberal Zionism* (London: Verso, 2009), xxiii. 'The murder of millions of Jews shocked the Yishuv, but feelings of compassion and empathy for the survivors were accompanied by an "I told you so" attitude. It was as if the Yishuv were reprimanding the survivors for remaining in the Diaspora and not answering the call of Zionism.' Oz Almog, *The Sabra: The Creation of the New Jew* (Berkeley: California UP, 2000), 82. 'The image of Holocaust victims who went "like sheep to the slaughter" was rife in the *yishuv*. According to one kibbutz *haggadah*, "Hitler alone is not responsible for the death of six million – but all of us and above all the six million. If they knew that the Jew had power, they would not have all been butchered"'. Avshalom Reich's PhD, quoted in Charles S. Liebman and Eliezer Don-Yehiya, 'The Dilemma of Reconciling Traditional Culture and Political Needs: Civil Religion in Israel', in Ernest Krausz and David Glanz (eds), *Politics and Society in Israel* (*Studies of Israeli Society*, vol. 3, Oxford: Transaction Books/Israeli Sociological Society, 1985), 207. See also Jacqueline Rose, *The Question of Zion* (Princeton: Princeton UP, 2005), 137–42.

the Yishuv had attempted to avoid reliance on Native labour by importing Yemeni Jews, but this had soon been abandoned, with the discarded
Yemenis lapsing into marginal distress.[60] In the wake of the Nakba, even
if the nascent state had wished to fall back on Native labour, most of the
Palestinian population had been driven away.[61]

As the enormity of the problems confronting Israel became apparent, Zionist activists were dispatched to Jewish communities in Arab
countries to encourage them to migrate to the fledgling state. These
communities – ethnically, culturally and linguistically Arab – had not previously figured in Zionism's scrupulously Eurocentric calculations, but
the Nazis had murdered the greater part of the Jewish state's intended
constituency. In the case of some of these Arab-Jewish communities, fair
means sufficed. Zionists had actively participated in British death squads
that had been unleashed on Arab Palestinians during their great 1936–39
uprising against the Mandate. This, together with the growing evidence
that Zionists intended to expel Arabs from their eventual state, prompted
a series of outrages against Jewish neighbourhoods in the Arab world
whose ferocity approached that of East European pogroms. In many
cases, therefore, Mizrahim were happy to avail themselves of the airlifts
that Israel provided.

In other cases, though – Iraq being the most well-known – Jews were
reluctant to leave. Incredible as it may seem today, Jews constituted the
largest community in Baghdad in 1950, comprising roughly half the population.[62] Even though Baghdad had witnessed a particularly vicious bout
of anti-Jewish rioting (*farhud*) in 1941, most Iraqi Jews had no desire to
exchange their age-old and generally prosperous position in multicultural
Arab society for the alien prospect that the visiting Zionists were urging
upon them. In the event, though the details remain somewhat hazy, foul
means seem to have become the order of the day. Exemplifying what
Ben-Gurion referred to as 'cruel Zionism', visiting Zionists bombed and
terrorised synagogues and other Jewish community targets. Following
hard on the heels of World War II, the whole situation degenerated so
threateningly that the trickle of Iraqi-Jewish applications to emigrate to

60 Shafir, *Land, Labor and the Origins*, 99, 101, 108, 115–16. For comment on the
Yemenis' plight, on the documentary *An Unpromised Land* that recounted it, and on the
Zionist historical establishment's response, see Gabriel Piterberg, 'Can the Subaltern
Remember? A Pessimistic View of the Victims of Zionism', in Ussama Makdisi and
Paul A. Silverstein (eds), *Memory and Violence in the Middle East and North Africa*
(Bloomington: Indiana UP, 2006), 177–200, 191–5.

61 Though the surreptitious resort to Native labour had long been an option.
Hyamson, *Palestine under the Mandate*, 55, 63, 75; LeVine, *Overthrowing Geography*,
71–2.

62 Elie Kedourie, 'The Break between Muslims and Jews in Iraq', in Mark R.
Cohen and Abraham L. Udovitch (eds), *Jews Among Arabs: Contacts and Boundaries*
(Princeton: Darwin Press, 1989), 21.

Israel swelled rapidly. Rising to the opportunity, the Iraqi government obliged by easing emigration restrictions and commandeering much of the emigrants' property.[63]

The conditions that greeted Mizrahim on their arrival in Israel were hardly redemptory. Their lot was one of sub-standard camps, arid frontier zones and relegation to menial expendability. Many objected – in some cases, their letters home seem to have stemmed the flow of emigration.[64] Over the years, their situation stabilised into a second-class citizenship that was compensated by sharing in their Ashkenazi superiors' colonial domination of the Palestinians. Significantly, things did not improve for them in the second generation. Rather, as Deborah Bernstein and Shlomo Swirski's figures showed, the gap between Israeli-born Mizrahim and Ashkenazim widened (by 1975, 42 per cent of Ashkenazim had professional jobs compared to 12.5 per cent of 'Orientals'[65]). Historically, the social costs of Mizrahi debasement have been considerable, leading to the formation of insurgent groups, in particular the Black Panthers (whose nomenclature deliberately asserted an African American parallel, redolent of slavery), and ultimately to the splenetic bigotry of the powerful Shas political party.

The entrenchment of Mizrahi disadvantage partakes more of the quality of a race or caste situation than of an immigration wave (theirs was hardly an aliya). As a settler-colonial labour force that is racialised in contradistinction to their Ashkenazi superiors, Mizrahim are more like American slaves than Australian convicts, their subordination being phenotypically encoded across generations. On the other hand, like Australian convicts, they share the settlers' common denominator vis-à-vis the Natives, only in their case it is religious rather than phenotypical. Phenotypically, their community is with the Palestinian sub-group (hence suicide bombers could merge into the Jewish crowd). This community is pre-empted by religion alone. In Israel, religion operates as a racial

---

63 Numerous authors have recounted these events. See, e.g., The Black Panther, 'The Iraqi Jews and Their Coming to Israel' (Hebrew original, 1972), translated in Uri Davis and Norton Mezvinsky (eds), *Documents from Israel, 1967–1973. Readings for a Critique of Zionism* (London: Ithaca, 1975), 126–33; Pappe, *History of Modern Palestine*, 175–82; Michael Palumbo, *The Palestinian Catastrophe: The 1948 Expulsion of a People from Their Homeland* (London: Faber & Faber, 1987), 198–201; Abbas Shiblak, *The Lure of Zion: The Case of Iraqi Jews* (London: Al Saqi, 1986), 119–27; Woolfson, *Prophets in Babylon*, 182–201 (phrase attributed to Ben-Gurion, p. 199).

64 Woolfson, *Prophets in Babylon*, 198–9. For discussion (albeit muted) of the condition of the Yemenis, see Herbert S. Lewis, *After the Eagles Landed: The Yemenites of Israel* (Boulder: Westview Press, 1989), especially 49; Yehuda Nini, 'Immigration and Assimilation: The Yemenite Jews', *Jerusalem Quarterly* 21 (1981), 86–93, *cf.* Shohat, 'Sephardim in Israel', 1–35.

65 Deborah Bernstein and Shlomo Swirski, 'The Rapid Economic Development of Israel and the Emergence of the Ethnic Division of Labour', *British Journal of Sociology* 33 (1982), 75.

amnesty – nobody has to be told that the Arabs in 'No Arabs, no terror' are not Jewish.

In sum, far from constituting some spontaneous avatar of an eternal 'Jewish nation', the new state required the most careful demographic fashioning, a task to which Mizrahim became unexpectedly central. Indeed, in creating a Jewish underclass, Zionism was not only building its own state. It was simultaneously creating the Mizrahim themselves out of the variegated plurality of Jewish communities in the Arab world – though these were not, of course, the kind of New Jews that the founders had had in mind. The outcome – again, unimaginable to the founding Zionists – was that an overlooked 20-per-cent minority within world Jewry came to constitute a 55-per-cent majority of Israeli-Jewish society.[66]

This is the point at which the Jewish/Arab opposition lost veridical reference.[67] During the Mandate years, with the numerically insignificant exception of the Yemenis and some of the older of the Old Yishuv, it had made some sense to counterpose Jews to Arabs – though only within Palestine – since most of the Jews were from Europe and the Natives were Arabs. In the wake of the Mizrahi airlifts, however, this opposition could only be maintained by dint of an ideological conjuring trick whereby the Arab-Jews became deracinated. In failing to chart the relationship between Ashkenazi Jews and neighbouring Gentile populations in Europe, the Israeli geneticists suppressed this deracination. As Shohat has pointed out, however, it was Zionism that forced Mizrahim to choose, for the first time in their history, between being Jewish and being Arab.[68]

In practice, this choice was often far removed from the standard colonial alternatives – between modernity and backwardness, progress and stagnation, democracy and despotism, and so on – that Zionism held out. Rather, many immigrants from the Arab world were unsuited to the manual tasks that were assigned to them for the simple reason that their backgrounds were considerably more sophisticated than those of their Ashkenazi taskmasters. After all, life in the Tzarist Pale of Settlement, where many Ashkenazim originated, had hardly been a training ground in democracy and progress. Yet even an Ashkenazi commentator with the worldliness of Hannah Arendt could not shrug off Zionism's tired racist

66   'If one takes the best estimates for the number of Jews in the world today (around 12 million), only about 15 per cent are of Sephardic origin, but the majority of this minority now live in Israel and in fact are a majority of the population!' Sobel and Beit-Hallahmi, 'Introduction', in Sobel and Beit-Hallahmi, *Tradition, Innovation, Conflict*, 5 (where 'the population' should, of course, have read 'the Jewish population').

67   In this context, it is as well to mention the numerically much less significant non-Arab members of the Palestinian population, including people also of Armenian, Circassian, Bosnian and other ancestries.

68   Shohat, 'Sephardim in Israel', 11; Shohat, *Taboo Memories*, 213–15.

polarities when it came to characterising the Mizrahi crowd that gathered on the occasion of Adolf Eichmann's trial in Jerusalem, whom she notoriously described to Karl Jaspers as an: 'oriental mob, as if one were in Istanbul or some other half-Asiatic country'.[69]

For civic purposes, religion – together with its linguistic reflex, a European-inflected Hebrew – was all that held Mizrahim and Ashkenazim together. It was not culture or civilisation: Mizrahim were not European, and, as we have seen, Ashkenazi political rhetoric made much of their backwardness. Nor could it be history: unlike Ashkenazim, Mizrahim had not suffered genocide as Jews. Moreover, though Zionism had incorporated nineteenth-century nationalism's disastrous fusion of race and nation, Arabs could not be incorporated on the basis of race. There was only religion (the national flag, after all, was taken from a prayer shawl). Israel is the Jewish state, which is to say – and the Law of Return does say – it is a state for Jews (wherever they may be) as opposed to its citizens (who are not all Jews).

And yet, from the outset, Zionism had held itself out as a secular modernising creed, whose Jewishness was not a theological category but a secular historical one. As we saw in chapter four, Herzl had striven to build a Jewish movement that excluded the most obvious criterion for Jewishness – religion – from its identity. Hence Rabkin's ironic observation that 'it was exactly those Jews farthest removed from Judaism who found in Israel their last hope to remain a part of the Jewish people'.[70] In practice, however, the only reliable criterion for Jewishness was the very criterion that Zionism repudiated.[71] The last thing that this group of modernising, colonising European nationalists wanted was the reproach of theocracy, which would have disqualified them from participating in a discourse of nationhood that defined itself as separating church from state. The Zion to which they sought to stage their return was not the land of prophets and priests but that of the Hebrew kings, the original fighting Jews. The problem that Mizrahim pose for Zionism is, therefore, that, sharing neither ethnicity, culture nor history with European Jews, their visibly Arab presence in Israel has necessitated the

---

69   Arendt to Jaspers, 13 April 1961, in *Hannah Arendt–Karl Jaspers: Correspondence, 1926–1969* (Lotte Köhler and Hans Saner, eds, Robert and Rita Kimber, trans., New York: Mariner, 1992), 435. My thanks to Dirk Moses for bringing this letter to my attention.

70   Rabkin, *Threat from Within*, 50.

71   For Yeshayahu Leibowitz, the Zionist repudiation of the criterion of religion has undone Jewishness: 'The appeal to national solidarity among all Jews is nowadays merely verbal and declaratory. It reflects no living reality. Even the legal halakhic [religious] criterion for inclusion in the Jewish people is inadequate at present, since only a minority among those who consider themselves Jews regard the Halakhah as binding.' Leibowitz, *Judaism, Human Values, and the Jewish State* (Eliezer Goldman, ed., Eliezer Goldman et al, trans., Cambridge, MA: Harvard UP, 1992), 83.

accommodation of a reactionary rabbinical discourse that would have been anathema to the founding Zionists. It is the last laugh of the Old Yishuv, and a hollow one at that. Hence it is fitting that Boas Evron, who captured this contradiction with terse brilliance, should himself have been a Jewish Palestinian of Old Yishuv stock:

> The inner contradiction in Zionism derived from the assumption that all the Jews in the world constitute a single entity, an exiled territorial nation. Religion was conceived as a manifestation of this essential national trait, not as the very essence of Jewishness. But any attempt to discover extrareligious traits typical of the Jews as a whole, as Jews, has failed. The very attempt to go beyond religion, for all Jews, was trapped again in religion. The general formula defeated itself.[72]

As Arabs, not to say Semitic people, Mizrahim and Palestinians share histories and cultural affinities that go back centuries. Hence the poignance of Joseph Massad's observation that, at a 1989 meeting between Mizrahi and Palestinian intellectuals, 'Many of the Mizrahi delegates addressed the meeting in their native tongue, Arabic.'[73] Given that, within Israel, the two Arab communities also share in economic deprivation (albeit to different extents), the weight of the ideological burden that religious differentiation is required to carry becomes apparent. It is all that keeps Israel's herrenvolk theocracy together. Hence it is not surprising that this overworked differentiation should find expression in extremist forms of rabbinical politics that rely on Mizrahi support.

Thus a further reversal is in order. It was not that Mizrahim's shared religious identification led to their incorporation into Israel. On the contrary, few groups can have been as consensually atheist as the halutzim, the early pioneers who took every opportunity to insist that the defining criterion for Jewishness was national rather than religious (they even preferred Tel Aviv to Jerusalem[74]). Zionism did not have a religious identification. Rather than the hegemony of religion encouraging the admission of the Mizrahim, it was the other way around: the admission of the Mizrahim encouraged the hegemony of religion.

This impulse was dramatically energised in 1967. In capturing the Wailing Wall in East Jerusalem together with sacred sites such as the Tomb of the Patriarchs elsewhere in the West Bank, the Israeli army was impressively realising biblical covenant. Even secular Israelis were moved. This military triumph powerfully validated the maximalist religious definition of the Jewish state (*Eretz Israel*), which includes the east bank of the Jordan and is transcendentally impervious to the pragmatic

---

72 Evron, *Jewish State or Israeli Nation?* 62.
73 Massad, *Persistence of the Palestinian Question*, 75.
74 Laqueur, *History of Zionism*, xxiii.

niceties of international relations. At the same time, for diplomatic purposes, 1967 rehabilitated the victims of the Holocaust, as the New-Jewish rejection of a victimhood seen as shameful was jettisoned in favour of an appeal to a victimhood whereby the occupying power sought to clothe its aggression in the trappings of self-defence.[75] Demographically, this development – which strongly militates against any withdrawal from the Occupied Palestinian Territories – has crucial consequences that are quite separate from the romantic possibility (which, whatever its appeal, does seem doomed) of Mizrahi–Palestinian solidarities being forged out of pan-Arabism. These consequences take us back to the Russians.

The Return of Religion

On the face of it, the case of the Russian Christians would seem to be antithetical to that of the Mizrahim. In the Russian case, religion was overlooked rather than prioritised. But the end was the same: decreasing the Palestinian proportion of the population. The qualification is important. The issue is not raw numbers but relative proportions, in regard to which Native decline and settler growth are synonymous. Both the Mizrahim and the Russians contributed to settler growth: the Mizrahim at the high cost of their Arabness; the Russians at the relatively low cost of their accompanying Christians. As previously observed, however, assimilation is not primarily a recruitment into the settler community. Rather, it is primarily an elimination of Indigeneity. Neither Mizrahim nor Russians were recruited as fellow Jews into Israeli society. They were recruited as not-Palestinians.

The other side of the equation, Native decline, has proved more difficult. As we have seen, encouraging differential birth rates is at best an incremental strategy, while conversion has not been a significant factor. In practical terms, the only real complement to mass immigration is ethnic cleansing. Since even Israel could not continue to rely on Western support if it embarked on a full-scale campaign of direct physical annihilation, we can understand why, since 1967, the prospect of repeating the Nakba has retained such persistent appeal at all levels of Israeli political discourse. The Palestinians affected by 1967 are not only those living in the areas occupied by Israel. After that date, Palestinians living either side of Israel's official border were reunited by the shared condition of Israeli control.[76] As a result, those living within the 1949 borders, up to then

---

75 Jerusalem, too, was rehabilitated: 'The idea that Jerusalem was the beginning and the end of Zionism, that Israel could not exist without having full sovereignty over the entire city, emerged only after 1967 and with the growth of a religious fanaticism and aggressive nationalism that had more in common with the ideology of the Muslim Brotherhood than the founding fathers of Zionism.' Ibid.
76 For Israeli concern over this phenomenon, see, e.g., Sammy Smooha, *The*

quite manageably contained, suddenly became part of a demographic threat. Thus they too have been mutedly scheduled for transfer.

The two-state 'solution' offers a way to achieve this without creating further problems with refugees. As Israeli foreign minister Tzipi Livni expressed this thinking in 2007, 'Our idea is to refer to two states for two peoples. Or two nation states. Palestine and Israel living side by side in peace and security with each state constituting the homeland for its people and the fulfillment of their national aspirations and self-determination' – proceeding, with ominous candour, to a crucial quali-fication: 'I would like to emphasise that the meaning of "its people" is the Jewish people'.[77] Thus the Israel that Livni would have living side by side with Palestine would constitute the homeland for the Jewish people, a covert suggestion of ethnic exclusiveness – which is to say, of transfer – that is amplified in the reference to the 'fulfillment' of 'national aspirations and self-determination'. As befits a diplomat, by Zionist standards Livni was speaking relatively discreetly (or, at least, ellipti-cally). As we have seen, however, from the Balfour Declaration on, the realisation of a Jewish national home has consistently become more geographically extensive at the same time as it has become less demo-graphically inclusive. In the context of this stark exclusivism, a further implication of the admission of the Russians is that it demonstrates – as if additional proof were necessary – that Israel has no intention of giving up the Occupied Territories, in the absence of which there would be no 'demographic threat'. Where, then, might the space be found for Palestinians to achieve their reciprocal national fulfillment? Removing them to quasi-state reserves, as in the case of Gaza, would realise the rhet-oric of neighbourliness by converting Israel's vertical relationship with its 'Arabs' into a horizontal one. Indeed, even before their removal, as denationalised 'Arabs' rather than Palestinians, the candidates for transfer are already discursively merged into their projected future.

Its disadvantages notwithstanding, religion was central to Israel's absorption of the Mizrahim. If the possibility of a pan-Arabism capable of uniting Palestinians and Mizrahim is indeed doomed, one is still left with the question of how this came to pass. After all, on the face of it, one

---

Orientation and Politicization of the Arab Minority in Israel (Haifa: Institute of Middle East Studies/Haifa UP, 1980); Mark A. Tessler, 'Israel's Arabs and the Palestinian Problem', Middle East Journal 31 (1977), 313–29.

77   Tzipi Livni, 'Minutes from 8th Negotiation Team Meeting (In Preparation for Annapolis), Tuesday, 13th November 2007', Aljazeera Transparency Unit, The Palestine Papers, 2011 (ajtransparency.com/en/projects). Livni was quoted by Army Radio as saying to students at a Tel Aviv high school: 'Once a Palestinian state is established, I can come to Palestinian citizens, whom we call Israeli Arabs, and say to them, "You are citizens with equal rights, but the national solution for you is elsewhere."' From 'Livni: National aspirations of Israel's Arabs can be met by Palestinian homeland', Ha'aretz, 11 December 2008.

group of Arabs who were being oppressed by Europeans might well have found common cause with another group of Arabs who were being even more oppressed by the same Europeans, especially when both groups were well acquainted with the historical ordeal of European domination. Moreover, neither group of Arabs had undergone the racial genocide that was consecrating the oppressor state's civil religion.[78] Under these circumstances, the ideological requirement to fend off the open possibility of Mizrahi-Palestinian solidarities was intense.

In the event, the requisite intensity was furnished by traditional modes of Mizrahi religiosity, which formed an unlikely partnership with a Latvian style of orthodoxy that promoted a stridently sectarian version of traditional religion. To speak in general terms – though the finding is not surprising – the most intense anti-Palestinian sentiment is to be found among Palestinians' closest ethnic counterparts (with the Russians, also not surprisingly, coming a fairly close second).[79] As in the case of Brazil – another White-minority context – race is conspicuous by its absence from this situation, an absence that is central to social control. In aligning Mizrahim to fellow-Jews rather than to fellow-Arabs, race operates in negation (or, perhaps, under erasure[80]). Mizrahi *de*-racination is a work of race.[81]

---

78 Avraham Burg has termed this civil religion 'shoah idolatry': Burg, *The Holocaust Is Over; We Must Rise from Its Ashes* (Israel Amrani, trans., Basingstoke: Palgrave Macmillan, 2008), 5, see also 13, 16. For the concept, see Charles S. Liebman and Eliezer Don-Yehiya, *Civil Religion in Israel: Traditional Judaism and Political Culture in the Jewish State* (Berkeley: California UP, 1983), especially 9. Mizrahi distancing from the Holocaust remains disruptive. When pro-Nazi Hebrew daubings appeared on the entrance of Yad Vashem, Israel's Holocaust memorial, on the morning of 11 June 2012, it was noticeable that the blame did not fall on Palestinians. Rather, suspicion turned instantly to Neturai Karta and Eda Haredit, two anti-Zionist ultra-Orthodox groups who assert that the state of Israel is an offence against God. This was despite the fact that, below the graffiti thanking Hitler for the Holocaust, a more likely – though, significantly, much more numerous – source of discontent announced itself in unmistakable terms: 'Israel is the secular Auschwitz of the Sephardic Jewry' (ynetnews.com, accessed 15 June 2013).

79 'In short, "hatred for Arabs" is not a "latent drive in Orientals", but rather the result of policies made by those in control of a non-egalitarian society.' Shlomo Swirski, *Israel: The Oriental Majority* (Barbara Swirski, trans., London: Zed Books, 1989), 55. Maurice Roumani drily notes the lack of comparable scholarly interest in Ashkenazi swings to the right, Roumani, 'The Sephardi Factor in Israeli Politics', *Middle East Journal* 42 (1988), 432. Nonetheless, the symptoms of this inequity can be demonic. As the Israeli missiles blasted Gaza in July 2014, an Israeli-flag-draped crowd gathered in Tel Aviv to exult in the deaths of Palestinian children, the chants including: 'In Gaza there's no studying/No children are left there/Olé, olé, olé!' On inspection, this crowd is visibly Mizrahi. Arabs themselves, they chant: 'I hate all the Arabs. Oh-oh-oh-oh. Gaza is a graveyard!' For a video of the event, published by Jewish-Israeli journalist Haim Har-Zahav, go to: electronicintifada.net/blogs (accessed 28 August 2014).

80 As Gabi Piterberg once put it to me, the deracination of the Mizrahim 'represents the ultimate Hegelian *Aufhebung*'.

81 'Deracination' does not, of course, imply a belief in a 'real Arab race' to which

The price of a Jewish solidarity founded on a manifestly incoherent 'Jewish–Arab opposition' has been religion. In 1977, Begin acquiesced in a distinctly un-Zionist mode of religiosity in order to recruit the Mizrahi vote to the Revisionist cause and effectively put traditional Labour Zionism out of business. Certainly, religion was not the only basis for Begin's stunning success. The Revisionists had not contributed to Labour Zionism's making of the Mizrahim, and could reasonably claim common cause with them vis-à-vis the Labour-Zionist establishment. Moreover, Begin crafted a kind of pan-Jewish populism that was widely inter-preted (however misguidedly) as standing up for the Mizrahim.[82] Yet the religious element was emphatic and irrepressible. With young Gush Emunim fanatics pushing into the West Bank to establish colonial beach-heads with explicitly biblical mission statements, the term 'Religious Zionism' became increasingly normalised. The xenophobic messianism of the Shas party, whose pay-off for participating in government would be control of the powerful religious ministries, was developing apace.[83] No wonder liberal Zionism was thrown into panic.

A commonality of sorts was periodically restored among Israeli-Jewish society through warfare and its attendant rhetoric of victimhood – in par-ticular, the shared fear engendered by the near-reversal of Yom Kippur in 1972, a Labour-Zionist humiliation that Begin's 1982 'War of Choice' on Lebanon was meant to redeem; Saddam Hussein's Scud missiles during the first Gulf War of 1991; the violent suppression of the First Intifada in 1993; and the current demonisation of a nuclear Iran. To the consternation of secular Israelis, however, the ascendancy of the religious element has continued unabated. What, then, if Zionism were actually to win its war of wars? What if Israel were to be finally cleansed of its 'Arabs'? What would be left? No longer held together by the containing malevolence that Palestinians provide, Israel would be left with a choice between theocracy and implosion.

Thus we come to the final truth contained in Shafir's insight that Israeli society was forged through and dependent on the practice of conquest. Israel cannot survive without its Palestinians. Without the Palestinians – which is to say, when everyone is Jewish – the Mizrahim once again become Arabs. The Russians once again become suspect – what Zionist

---

Mizrahim and Palestinians putatively belong. Rather, it distinguishes Israel's failure to racialise Mizrahim from its rigorously exclusive racialisation of other Arab people.

82 Laor, *Myths of Liberal Zionism*, 154. As members of a Mizrahi 'chorus' in the deprived suburb of Bet Shemesh allegedly stated to Amos Oz, 'If they give back the territories, the Arabs will stop coming to work, and then and there you'll put us back into the dead-end jobs, like before.' Oz, *In the Land of Israel* (Maurie Goldberg-Bartura, trans., Orlando: Harvest, 1983), 36.

83 For Ashkenazi responses to this phenomenon, see, e.g., Ben-Rafael and Peres, *Is Israel One?* 111–12; Cohen, 'Changing Legitimations of the State of Israel', 157–60.

limpieza de sangre will determine which of them are really Christians? And what of the Sudanese? When everything is Jewish, difference itself becomes Jewish – a return to the precise condition that Zionism sought to suppress in order to build a nation out of groups of people whose differences from one another were greater than their commonalities. These contradictions instantiate what I have termed the return of the Native repressed – in this case, to adapt Piterberg's mordant irony, the practical return of Zionism. Mizrahi immigration was encouraged in the face of the problems presented by the continued presence of the Palestinian minority, no matter how attenuated by the Nakba. The Russians, their attendant Christianity notwithstanding, were encouraged in response to the crisis occasioned by the additional Palestinians who had to be accommodated in the wake of 1967.

These shifting racial strategies reflect Zionism's inability to eliminate Palestinian territoriality. As observed, the quest to replace Native society only maintains the refractory imprint of the Native counter-claim. In the event, the demographic profile of Israeli society – its very make-up, let alone its military and religious overdetermination – constitutes a thoroughgoing travesty of the founding Zionists' vision of their Jewish nation-state. This transformed state of affairs constitutes the trace, or so many traces, of a history of resistance, of Palestinians' steadfast refusal to disappear.

For Zionism, then, the conundrum of transfer can be expressed as follows: the Jewish state cannot live with Palestinians and it cannot live without them. If transfer were to succeed, leaving an ethnically cleansed Palestine finally at Israel's disposal, there would only remain the fissures that Zionism was premised on suppressing, with religion as their remedy. The drive to transfer is at once a drive to theocracy. Yet Israel cannot abandon transfer without abandoning the Jewishness of the Jewish state. This, again, is the motivation for liberal Zionism's counterfactual prevarications about a two-state 'solution' – a subterfuge that the religious zealots reject with derision.[84]

This impasse exists in the present. It is not dependent on the execution of a mass transfer that is not going to happen. Even though Palestinians will stay where they are, we can still observe the remorseless unfolding of the impossible situation that Zionism's contradictory brand of settler colonialism has brought about. The more Native territory Israel managed to conquer, the more Natives came with it, and the fewer Jews there were

---

84 For discussion of various aspects of Zionist maximalism (about which, as Ian Lustick puts it, Zionists characteristically 'speak quietly'), see Lustick, *Arabs in the Jewish State*, 31, 33, 37, 39–40; Childers, 'Wordless Wish', 178, n. 48; Jon and David Kimche, *Both Sides of the Hill: Britain and the Palestine War* (London: Secker & Warburg, 1960), 267 (concerning Operation Shin-Tav-Shin).

in comparison. In consequence, in order to maximise the Jewish proportion of the Jewish nation that it was seeking to construct, Israel found
itself obliged to tamper with its own ethnic definition. In the process, it
exacerbated the fissures within its already discordant population. Further
conquest – completing the ethnic cleansing of Palestine – would only
further aggravate this divisive situation. Success would be failure. This,
then, is the full implication of the Mizrahi stopgap – not the romance of
pan-Arabism, but the impossibility of Zionism.

At every turn, Zionism has tripped over its reluctant accommodation
to its inescapably religious dimension. Even the concept of return, for all
its denigration of diasporan life, is inherently rabbinical.[85] 'Next year in
Jerusalem' only makes sense as a diasporan utterance. Here too, anomaly
surrounds the Old Yishuv, who, like Gentiles, were incapable of return –
at least, until legislatively born again as olim. Why, then, has Zionism
so struggled with religion? Why could its Jewish nation only ever be
as French as France and never as Catholic as the Vatican? The reason is
simple: Herzl and his secular-bourgeois Zionist colleagues had no desire
to trade modernity for theocracy, even if the community of nations were
to allow them to do so. Why, then, has Zionism not dispensed with religion entirely? The answer, as Evron pointed out, is that it has tried to do
so and has failed.

In its commonality with the rabbinification of Israel, the deracination of the Mizrahim emerges as a symptom of and a response to – in
this book's terminology, as a trace of – the core historical contradiction
whereby the Jewish state cannot exist without the very category, 'Arabs',
that it is premised on excluding. But the ideological return on the counter-
fact of a Jewish/Arab opposition can hardly be overstated. At the most
rudimentary level of Western discourse, 'Jewish', as Koestler appreciated, signifies a 'venerable foundation', a legacy whose intrinsically
religious potency was further sacralised by the transcendent enormity
of the Holocaust. By contrast, the negative connotations of the category 'Arab', always at least tacitly supplemented by Islamophobia, could
hardly be more pervasively sedimented in Western cultural traditions.
In the event, the mythico-cultural yield accruing from a primordial mis-
match between 'Jews' and 'Arabs' overwhelms the profane symmetry of
a quite recent territorial dispute between two modern nations, Israel
and Palestine.

---

85 'The Zionist paradox is that it rejects Judaism and its conception of Jewish
history and uniqueness, while claiming the desire to preserve Jewish identity.' Benjamin
Beit-Hallahmi, *Original Sins: Reflections on the History of Zionism and Israel* (London:
Pluto Press, 1992), 52–3. In Yosef Hayim Yerushalmi's poignant encapsulation: 'I live
within the ironic awareness that the very mode in which I delve into the Jewish past
represents a decisive break with that past.' Yerushalmi, *Zakhor: Jewish History and Jewish
Memory* (Seattle: Washington UP, 1996), 81.

In counterposing 'someone evil' to 'Jewish ideology', the geneticist Ariella Oppenheim was seeking to summon this primordial potency, however gauchely. Had Dr Oppenheim instead stated, accurately, that the ideology of Jewish genetic continuity was 'Zionist' or 'Israeli' rather than 'Jewish', her scientist's corrective would have lacked the mythic sanction on which it relied. This departure from disciplinary caution is all the more significant for the fact that Oppenheim was speaking as a geneticist. In genetic terms, there can be no necessary incongruity between someone like myself, who is descended from Jewish stock in only the paternal line (and is, therefore – at least by established rabbinical reckonings – not Jewish) and someone who, by virtue of being descended from Jewish stock in only the maternal line, is Jewish by all reckonings. Such a level of indeterminacy – which, in this case, really is a consequence of Jewish ideology – makes genetics a rather inconclusive index of Jewish continuity. Moreover, the possibility of religious conversion – explicitly sanctioned and regulated by Jewish ideology – compounds the indeterminacy of genetics. In sum, while Jewish ideology is relatively impervious to genetic considerations, Zionist ideology is critically dependent on them – no genetic continuity, no ideology of return. This, then, is what the fuss was about.

The storm in the *Human Immunology* teacup casts light on much wider issues. So far as the ideological influencing of scientific practice is concerned, the censoring of the offending article (the principal author being sacked from the journal's editorial board for good measure) is not the only noteworthy aspect. Methodologically, it is striking that the earlier article by the Israeli team should have been accepted for publication in a form that included the clumsy *découpage* whereby a community was asserted between European Jews, Arab-Jews and Palestinians without the European Jews' possibly closer relationship with their immediate historical neighbours being considered. One might also note that the Israeli study recapitulated the official vanishing of Palestinian Jews.

For our purposes, however, the important issue is not one journal's susceptibility to extraneous influences, but the reason why this particular topic was sensitive enough to warrant such lapses from scientific protocol. At stake in the need to suppress the continuity between Palestinian Arabs and Jewish Arabs is the primary imperative to assert an overriding continuity that binds all Jews everywhere to each other as Jews. The cost is theocracy. The return ('to Zion') is the Jewish Nation.

Looking back over the different relationships of inequality that we have surveyed, then, we come to the perhaps surprising conclusion that the system of racial classification that the Israeli system most closely resembles is the Brazilian one. Both rely on a deracination whereby an otherwise majority population is fragmented. This similarity exists

despite the plethora of differences that distinguish the two colonial societies. These differences need to be registered along with the distinctive
common denominator. Again, therefore, it is not enough simply to classify Israel – or, for that matter, anywhere else – as settler-colonial. In
each case, the site-specific workings of the varied local expressions of the
settler drive to eliminate Native territoriality have to be reconstructed in
context and on their own terms, as this book has tried to do. Only on this
basis can we begin to derive general principles on which to base cross-
colonial, cross-community, anti-racist solidarities.

Conclusion

The Unfinished Business of Race

It is not my place to instruct colonised people on how to resist their condition, let alone to impersonate their agency. In this book, I have tried to offer an analysis, in the hope that it may prove useful. A conclusion to be drawn from this analysis is that race, being historically contingent, can be overcome.

Race is not here to stay. As we have seen, it had a beginning – different beginnings, in different times and places – and it requires constant ideological maintenance. Rather than dissolving away, Native populations in Australia, Brazil and the United States have grown dramatically as people refuse assimilation and collectively assert Indigenous subjectivities. A strategic response to this assertiveness has been multiculturalism, whereby settler states have sought to depoliticise Indigenous difference by reducing it to the detoxified arena of cultural variety, a sovereignty-free zone. This more recent development ranks with historical shifts that we have noted, as colonialism has adjusted to apparent compromises such as emancipation, tribal recognition or Native citizenship.

Race is versatile, fluid and opportunistic. Thus we should not link particular modes of racialisation to particular human groups in perpetuity, a perspective that recapitulates race's own essentialism. As both Arab-Jews and African Brazilians have found, the same group can be excluded under some circumstances and included or assimilated under others, with the end – colonial domination – remaining constant all the while. Accordingly, when Whites were in a minority, Blackness became distinctly mutable in Georgia and South Carolina. On emancipation, moreover, Black people in the USA became surplus to some requirements and, to that extent, more like Indians. Thus it is highly significant that the barbarities of Jim Crow should be post-emancipation phenomena. As valuable commodities, slaves had only been destroyed *in extremis*. Today in the USA, the blatant racial zoning of the penal system and large industrial cities – where the commonality with the Jewish experience finds expression in the term 'ghetto' – suggests that, once exploited people outlive their utility, settler societies can fall back on the repertoire of strategies (in this case, spatial sequestration) whereby they have dealt with the Native (in the European case, Jewish) surplus. The reverse also applies: in the frontier era, as we have seen, Native removal was conducted on the basis of an incorrigibility that Whites ascribed to Indians with all the fixity of the traits they also ascribed to Blacks. Again, therefore, race is not merely a social construct. In constantly requiring re-construction, its incompleteness becomes exposed and vulnerable to complex and versatile solidarities that refuse the strategic divisions that race would impose. Anti-racist solidarities need to conjoin as wide a range of historical relationships as colonialism itself has created.

Race's incompleteness reflects the jurisdictional patchworks whereby, within settler states, sovereignties remain contested and unevenly distributed. In Australia, the current 'intervention' separates out Aboriginal communities in the Northern Territory for a kind of medium-intensity martial law, while, at a lower level of intensity, Native Title legislation discriminates between the proprietorial – and, accordingly, sovereign – capacities of Aboriginal societies. In the United States, the vagaries of registration and tribal enrolment provide for a plethora of differential statuses.

Such differences are not static. They represent balances, relative standings in continuing contestations over colonial domination. In addition to its manifest spatiality, invasion is intrinsically historical, being conducted in ever-shifting counterpoint to its reflex and constant companion, resistance. New England is more completely invaded than New Mexico. The Northern Territory is less completely invaded – less complacently held – than Melbourne. The same holds, only more visibly, for Gaza and Tel Aviv. Moreover, as observed, it holds across time as well as space. The Northern Territory is less securely invaded today, it would seem, than it was ten years ago; Gaza certainly so. Nowadays, Indigenous peoples in Australia themselves determine the make-up of their communities, while parts of the Coranderrk woods are once again in Wurundjeri hands. These are important advances. The incompleteness of racial domination is the trace and the achievement of resistance, a space of hope.

Acknowledgements

When someone really does seem to believe in your work, it's hard to express your feelings adequately. Here's trying, anyway: Cindy Franklin, Tsianina Lomawaima (who insisted I stick with the title), Saree Makdisi, Dirk Moses, Gabi Piterberg, Lynette Russell, Zora Simic, Haunani-Kay Trask, Lorenzo Veracini, Richard White – thank you. I don't know whether this book would ever have got written but for your encouragement.

Some have been kind enough to provide me with opportunities that have helped me greatly: David Stannard, Tadhg Foley, Lionel Pilkington, Pat Grimshaw, Walter Johnson, Vince Brown and, again, Richard White – thank you.

For friendship sharpened with critical challenge (for the latter of which I've sometimes managed to be grateful), I shall always be indebted to Peter Gartlan, Kim Blodgett, Robert Kenny, Giordano Nanni, Scott Hancock, Aziz Rana, Ilan Pappe, Kēhaulani Kauanui, Connie Atkinson, Al Kennedy, Madhu Bhushan, the late R. L. Kumar, Yakov Rabkin, Pamela Grieman, Tamar Blickstein, Gershon Shafir, Amanda Kearney, Liz Strakosch, Cyn Young, Suzanna Reiss, Njoroge Njoroge, Marisa Fuentes, Paul Kramer, Josh Guild, Ben Silverstein, David Yarrow, Penny Edmonds, Dale Howard, Beverly Purrington.

Then there are the more diffuse intellectual foundations: endlessly pitting my wits against my mother Margaret Wolfe's virtuosic religious argumentation; vainly trying to outsmart my exasperatingly smart brother and sister Mike and Mary; a debt, much harder to acknowledge, to the Jesuits of my boarding-school unhappiness, who blended their sadism with critical rigour; the contradictory jumble of selfishness and altruism, drugs and anti-racism, Hermann Hesse and *Black Dwarf*, that somehow started me off reading Marx, then Gramsci, Althusser, Arendt, Fanon, Lévi-Strauss and Foucault; all those eager discussions with Dipesh Chakrabarty in Melbourne and Canberra when we were young (*bondhu*, I still hear your 'Yes, but...'); Geoff Sharp lecturing on Durkheim; reading Tagore and M. N. Roy with Sibnarayan Ray and Atindra Majumdar; stumbling on Said's *Orientalism* in Readings bookshop on Lygon Street; being amazed by the questioning of my children, Luke, Sean and Maeve; the incomparable supervision I received from Johnny Parry and Maurice Bloch at the LSE; the Kooris who bore with my gaucheness and taught me to see with new eyes: the late, still missed Lisa Bellear, along with the recently deceased, greatly respected Uncle Albert Mullett; Tony Birch, Destiny Deacon, Gary Foley, Johnny Harding, Aunty Joy Murphy-Wandin, Sonia Smallacombe, Marjorie Thorpe. Thank you, everyone.

The research for and writing of this book have been enabled by funding from a number of institutions: an Australian Research Council Australian Fellowship with generous accompanying grant held at Victoria University in Melbourne, a Victoria Fellowship also at Victoria University, a Charles La Trobe Fellowship in History at La Trobe University, and a Charles Warren Fellowship in US History at Harvard University, together with shorter visiting research appointments at the Midlo Center at the University of New Orleans and in the Humanities Center at Stanford University. I am very grateful for this support.

In addition to new material, this book incorporates some revised and amended material from a number of articles I have previously published. Since I have changed, reordered and recombined the material from these articles, I cannot simply allocate them to individual chapters. An early trial version of the overall perspective I develop here was published as 'Land, Labor, and Difference: Elementary Structures of Race', *American Historical Review* (106, 2001, 866–905). Revised material from four earlier articles is distributed through this book: 'Settler Colonialism and the Elimination of the Native', *Journal of Genocide Research* (8, 2006, 387–409); 'Race and the Trace of History: For Henry Reynolds', in Fiona Bateman and Lionel Pilkington (eds), *Studies in Settler Colonialism: Politics, Identity, and Culture* (Palgrave MacMillan U.K., 2011, 272–96); 'Elementary Forms of Colonialism', in Corinne Kumar (ed.), *Asking We Walk: The South as New Political Imaginary* (Book 3, Streelekha Publications, Bangalore, 2012, 69–93); and 'Recuperating Binarism: A Heretical Introduction', *Settler Colonial Studies* (3/4, 2013, 257–79). Chapters 5 and 6 draw on material from the following articles: '*Corpus Nullius*: The Exception of Indians and Other Aliens in U.S. Constitutional Discourse', *Postcolonial Studies* (10, 2007, 127–51); 'After the Frontier: Separation and Absorption in U.S. Indian Policy', *Settler Colonial Studies* (1, 2011, 13–50); and 'Against the Intentional Fallacy: Legocentrism and Continuity in the Rhetoric of Indian Dispossession', *American Indian Culture and Research Journal* (36, 2012, 3–45). Chapter

7 makes changes to 'Purchase by Other Means: The Palestine *Nakba* and Zionism's Conquest of Economics', *Settler Colonial Studies* (2, 2012, 133–171). Chapter 8 makes more substantial changes to 'Palestine, Project Europe and the (Un-)Making of the New Jew', in Ned Curthoys and Debjani Ganguly (eds), *Edward Said: The Legacy of a Public Intellectual* (Melbourne UP web text, 2007, 312–37); and to 'New Jews for Old: Settler State Formation and the Impossibility of Zionism', *Arena Journal* (29, 2012, 285–321).

Select Bibliography

Abcarius, M.F. *Palestine: Through the Fog of Propaganda*. London: Hutchinson, 1946.

Abel, Annie H. 'The History of Events Resulting in Indian Consolidation West of the Mississippi River', *American Historical Association Annual Report for 1906*, vol. ii. Washington DC: US Government Printing Office, 1908.

Abu-Lughod, Ibrahim, ed. *The Transformation of Palestine: Essays on the Origin and Development of the Arab-Israeli Conflict*. Evanston: Northwestern UP, 1971.

Alencastro, Luiz Felipe De. 'The Apprenticeship of Colonization', in Solow, *Slavery and the Rise of the Atlantic System*.

Andrews, George Reid. *Blacks and Whites in São Paulo, Brazil, 1888–1988*. Madison: Wisconsin UP, 1991.

Arendt, Hannah. 'Antisemitism', in Arendt, *The Jewish Writings*.

———. *The Jewish Writings*, various translators, edited by Jerome Kohn and Ron H. Feldman. New York: Schocken, 2007.

———. 'RaceThinking Before Racism', *The Review of Politics*, 6, 1944.

———. *The Origins of Totalitarianism*. San Diego: Harvest/Harcourt, 1966.

Atran, Scott. 'The Surrogate Colonization of Palestine, 1917–1939', *American Ethnologist*, 16, 1989.

Commonwealth of Australia, 'Aboriginal Welfare. Initial Conference of Commonwealth and State Aboriginal Authorities, Held at Canberra, 21st to 23rd April, 1937'. Canberra: Government Printer, 1937.

Azevedo, Thales de. *Democracia Racial: ideologia e realidade*. Petrópolis: Editora Vozes, 1975.

Banivanua Mar, Tracey. *Violence and Colonial Dialogue: The Australia-Pacific Labor Trade*. Honolulu: Hawai'i UP, 2007.

Barwick, Diane E. *Rebellion at Coranderrk*, edited by Laura E. Barwick and Richard E. Barwick. Canberra: Aboriginal History Monograph 5, 1998 [1985].

Begin, Menachem. *The Revolt* (revised edition), translated by Samuel Katz. London: W.H. Allen, 1979 [1952].

Berlin, Ira. 'From Creole to African: Atlantic Creoles and the Origins of African-American Society in Mainland North America', *William and Mary Quarterly*, 3rd Series, 53, 1966.

——. *Many Thousands Gone: The First Two Centuries of Slavery in North America*. Cambridge, MA: Harvard UP, 1988.

Leslie Bethell ed. *The Cambridge History of Latin America*, vol. 3, Cambridge: Cambridge UP, 1984.

Blackburn, Robin. *The Making of New World Slavery: From the Baroque to the Modern, 1492–1800*. London: Verso, 1997.

Boyce, James. *1835: The Founding of Melbourne and the Conquest of Australia*. Collingwood: Black Inc, 2011.

Broome, Richard. *Aboriginal Victorians: A History Since 1800*. Crows Nest: Allen & Unwin, 2005.

Bruyneel, Kevin. *The Third Space of Sovereignty: The Postcolonial Politics of U.S.-Indigenous Relations*. Minnesota: Minneapolis UP, 2007.

Carter, Kent. *The Dawes Commission and the Allotment of the Five Civilized Tribes, 1893–1914*. Orem: Ancestry, 1999.

Christie, M.F. *Aborigines in Colonial Victoria, 1835–86*. Sydney: Sydney UP, 1979.

Clinton, Robert N. 'The Proclamation of 1763: Colonial Prelude to Two Centuries of Federal-State Conflict Over the Management of Indian Affairs', *Boston University Law Review*, 69, 1989.

Cohen, Felix S. *Handbook of Federal Indian Law*. Washington, DC: US Government Printing Office, 1945.

Conrad, Robert Edgar. *World of Sorrow: The African Slave Trade to Brazil*. Baton Rouge: Louisiana State UP, 1986.

Davis, David Brion. *The Problem of Slavery in the Age of Revolution*. Ithaca: Cornell UP, 1975.

Deloria, Philip J. *Indians in Unexpected Places*. Lawrence: Kansas UP, 2004.

Deloria, Jr., Vine & Clifford Lytle. *American Indians, American Justice*. Austin: Texas UP, 1983.

——. and Raymond J. DeMallie. *Documents of American Indian Diplomacy: Treaties, Agreements, and Conventions, 1775–1979*, 2 vols, Norman: Oklahoma UP, 1999.

Douglas, Mary. *Purity and Danger: An Analysis of the Concepts of Pollution and Taboo*. New York: Praeger, 1966.

Evron, Boas. *Jewish State or Israeli Nation?* Bloomington: Indiana UP, 1995.

Fields, Barbara Jeanne. 'Slavery, Race and Ideology in the United States of America', *New Left Review*, 181, 1990.

Fitzpatrick, Brian. *British Imperialism and Australia, 1783–1833: An Economic History of Australia*. Sydney: Sydney UP, 1939.

Gebara, Ademir. *O mercado de trabalho livre no Brasil, 1871–1888*. São Paulo: Brasiliense, 1986.

Giladi, G. N. *Discord in Zion: Conflict between Ashkenazi and Sephardi Jews in Israel*. London: Scorpion, 1990.

Gorny, Yosef. *Zionism and the Arabs, 1882–1948: A Study of Ideology*. Oxford: Clarendon Press, 1987.

Guzmán, Tracy Devine. *Native and National in Brazil: Indigeneity after Independence*. Chapel Hill: North Carolina UP, 2013.

Haebich, Anna. *Broken Circles: Fragmenting Indigenous Families, 1800–2000*. Fremantle: Fremantle Arts Centre Press, 2000.

Hertzberg, Arthur, ed. *The Zionist Idea: A Historical Analysis and Reader*. Philadelphia: Jewish Publication Society, 1997.

Jordan, Winthrop D. *White Over Black: American Attitudes Toward the Negro, 1550–1812*. Chapel Hill: North Carolina UP/Institute of Early American History and Culture, 1968.

Kappler, Charles J, ed. *Indian Treaties 1778–1883. Indian Affairs: Laws and Treaties*, vol. ii, Washington, DC: US Government Printing Office.

Kauanui, J. Kehaulani. *Hawaiian Blood: Colonialism and the Politics of Sovereignty and Indigeneity*. Durham: Duke UP, 2008.

Kenny, Robert. *Gardens of Fire: An Investigative Memoir*. Perth: Western Australia UP, 2013.

Khalidi, Walid. *All That Remains: The Palestinian Villages Occupied and Depopulated by Israel in 1948*. Washington, DC: Institute for Palestine Studies, 1992.

Koestler, Arthur. *The Thirteenth Tribe: The Khazar Empire and Its Heritage*. London: Hutchinson, 1972.

Kowarick, Lúcio. *The Subjugation of Labour: The Constitution of Capitalism in Brazil*, translated by Kevin Mundi, Amsterdam: CEDLA, 1987.

Kretzmer, David. *The Legal Status of Arabs in Israel*. Boulder: Westview Press, 1990.

Laor, Yitzhak. *The Myths of Liberal Zionism*. London: Verso, 2009.

Laqueur, Walter. *A History of Zionism: From the French Revolution to the Establishment of the State of Israel*. New York: Schocken, 2003.

Leibowitz, Yeshayahu. *Judaism, Human Values, and the Jewish State,* edited by Eliezer Goldman, translated by Eliezer Goldman et al., Cambridge, MA: Harvard UP, 1992.

Lemkin, Raphaël. *Axis Rule in Occupied Europe: Laws of Occupation, Analysis of Government, Proposals for Redress*. Washington, DC: Carnegie Endowment for International Peace, 1944.

Liebman Charles S., and Eliezer Don-Yehiya. *Civil Religion in Israel: Traditional Judaism and Political Culture in the Jewish State*. Berkeley: California UP, 1983.

Livni, Tsipi. 'Minutes from 8th Negotiation Team Meeting (in Preparation for Annapolis), 13th November 2007', Al Jazeera Transparency Unit, *The Palestine Papers*, 2011. Available at: www.ajtransparency.com/en/projects/thepalestinepapers/20121823740234656.html.

Makdisi, Saree. *Palestine Inside Out: An Everyday Occupation*. New York: Norton, 2008.

————. *Making England Western: Occidentalism, Race and Imperial Culture*. Chicago: Chicago UP, 2014.

Mandel, Neville J. 'Ottoman Policy and Restrictions on Jewish Settlement in Palestine: 1881–1908, Part I', *Middle Eastern Studies* 10, 1974.

————. *The Arabs and Zionism Before World War I*. Berkeley: California UP, 1976.

Masalha, Nur. *Expulsion of the Palestinians: The Concept of 'Transfer' in Zionist Political Thought, 1882–1948*. Washington, DC: Institute for Palestine Studies, 1992.

————. *A Land Without a People: Israel, Transfer and the Palestinians, 1949–96*. London: Faber & Faber, 1997.

Massad, Joseph A. *The Persistence of the Palestinian Question: Essays on Zionism and the Palestinians*. New York: Routledge, 2006.

Miller, Joseph C. *Way of Death: Merchant Capitalism and the Angolan Slave Trade, 1730–1830*. Madison: Wisconsin UP, 1988.

Morgan, Edmund S. 'Slavery and Freedom: the American Paradox', *Journal of American History*, 59, 1972.

————. *American Slavery, American Freedom: The Ordeal of Colonial Virginia*. New York: Norton, 1975.

Morgan, T. J. 'What Is an Indian?', in *Commissioner of Indian Affairs, Sixty-First Annual Report*. Washington DC, 1892.

Morris, Benny. 'Yosef Weitz and the Transfer Committees, 1948–1949', *Middle Eastern Studies* 22, 1986.

————. *The Birth of the Palestinian Refugee Problem Revisited*. Cambridge: Cambridge UP, 2004.

————. *Ha'aretz* interview with Ari Shavit, English version reproduced in *Counterpunch*, Weekend Ed., January 1–8, 2004, and at: www.logosjournal. com/morris.htm.

Moses, A. Dirk. 'An Antipodean Genocide? The Origins of the Genocidal Moment in the Colonization of Australia', *Journal of Genocide Research* 2, 2000.

Mosse, George L. *Toward the Final Solution: A History of European Racism*. Madison: Wisconsin UP, 1985.

Murray, Pauli, comp. and ed. *States' Laws on Race and Color*. Athens, GA: Women's Division of Christian Service, 1951.

Nanni, Giordano and Andrea James. *Coranderrk: We Will Show the Country*. Canberra: Aboriginal Studies Press, 2013.

National Inquiry into the Separation of Aboriginal and Torres Strait Islander Children from their Families (Australia). *Bringing Them Home: Report of the National Inquiry into the Separation of Aboriginal and Torres Strait Islander Children and their Families*. Canberra: Human Rights and Equal Opportunity Commission, 1997.

Nordau, Max. 'Speech to the first Zionist Congress', in Hertzberg, *Zionist Idea*.

Oliveira e Oliveira, Eduardo de. 'O mulato, um obstáculo epistemológico', *Argumento 1*, no. 3, 1974.

Oppenheim, Ariella. 'Letter to Dr. Moien Kanaan', *The Ambassadors Online Magazine* 5, i, January 2002, part 4.

Orr, Akiva. *The unJewish State: The Politics of Jewish Identity in Israel*. London: Ithaca Press, 1983.

Otis, D.S. *The Dawes Act and the Allotment of Indian Lands,* edited by Francis Paul Prucha. Norman: Oklahoma UP, 1973 [1934].

Pappe, Ilan. *The Making of the Arab–Israeli Conflict, 1947–1951*. London: I.B. Tauris, 2001.

———. *The Ethnic Cleansing of Palestine*. Oxford: Oneworld, 2006.

Penslar, Derek J. *Israel in History: The Jewish State in Comparative Perspective*. London: Routledge, 2007.

Perdue, Theda. *'Mixed Blood' Indians: Racial Construction in the Early South*. Athens, GA: Georgia UP, 2003.

First Australians: episode three, 'Freedom for Our Lifetime', directed by Rachel Perkins, produced by Darren Dale. On demand at: www.sbs.com.au/firstaustralians/index/index/epid/3

Pinsker, Leon. *Auto-Emancipation: An Appeal to His People by a Russian Jew,* 1882, in Hertzberg, *Zionist Idea*.

Piterberg, Gabriel. 'Domestic Orientalism: The representation of "Oriental" Jews in Zionist/Israeli historiography', *Journal of Middle Eastern Studies* 23, 1996.

———. *The Returns of Zionism: Myths, Politics and Scholarship in Israel*. London: Verso, 2008.

Prucha, Francis Paul. *American Indian Policy in the Formative Years: The Indian Trade and Intercourse Acts, 1790–1834*. Cambridge, MA: Harvard UP, 1962.

———. *Americanizing the American Indians: Writings by the 'Friends of the Indian', 1880–1900*. Cambridge, MA: Harvard UP, 1973.

Qumsiyeh, Mazin. 'Who Are the Palestinians?', *The Ambassadors Online Magazine*, 5, i, January 2002.

———. 'Letter to Dr. Oppenheim Through Dr. Moien Kanaan', *The Ambassadors Online Magazine*, 5, i, January 2002, part 2.

Raad, Khalil. *Palestine Before 1948: Not Just Memory*. Beirut: Institute for Palestine Studies, 2013.

Rabkin, Yakov M. *A Threat from Within: A Century of Jewish Opposition to Zionism*. London: Zed Books, 2006.

———. 'Nakba in Narratives about Zionism', in *Commemoration of Nakba*. Kyoto: Kyoto Bulletin of Islamic Area Studies, 3: 1, Kyoto UP, 2009.

Ramos, Alcida Rita. *Indigenism: Ethnic Politics in Brazil*. Madison: Wisconsin UP, 1998.

Rana, Aziz. *The Two Faces of American Freedom*. Cambridge, MA: Harvard UP, 2010.

Reis, João José. *Slave Rebellion in Brazil: The Muslim Uprising of 1835 in Bahia,* translated by Arthur Brakel. Baltimore: Johns Hopkins UP, 1993.

Reynolds, Henry. *Aboriginal Sovereignty: Reflections on Race, State and Nation*. Sydney: Allen & Unwin, 1996.

Robinson, Shira. *Citizen Strangers: Palestinians and the Birth of Israel's Liberal Settler State*. Stanford: Stanford UP, 2013.

Rodinson, Maxime. *Israel: A Colonial-Settler State?*, translated by David Thorstad. New York: Monad, 1973.

Rosenberg, Hans. 'AntiSemitism and the "Great Depression", 1873–1896', in Strauss, *Hostages of Modernization*.

Ruppin, Arthur. *The Agricultural Colonisation of the Zionist Organisation in Palestine*, translated by J.W. Feiwel. London: Martin Hopkinson, 1926.

Sand, Shlomo. *The Invention of the Jewish People*, translated by Yael Lotan. London: Verso, 2009.

Sayegh, Fayez. *The Zionist Colonization of Palestine*. Beirut: Institute of Palestine Studies, 1965.

Schmitt, Carl. *Political Theology: Four Chapters on the Concept of Sovereignty*, translated by George Schwab. Chicago: Chicago UP, 1985.

Schwartz, Stuart B. 'Indian Labor and New World Plantations: European Demand and Indian Responses in Northeastern Brazil', *American Historical Review*, 8, 1978.

———. *Sugar Plantations in the Formation of Brazilian Society: Bahia, 1550–1835*. Cambridge: Cambridge UP, 1985.

———. ed. *Tropical Babylons: Sugar and the Making of the Atlantic World, 1450–1680*. Chapel Hill: North Carolina UP, 2004.

Swirski, Shlomo. *Israel The Oriental Majority*, translated by Barbara Swirski. London: Zed Books, 1989.

Segev, Tom. *One Palestine, Complete: Jews and Arabs under the British Mandate*, translated by Haim Watzman. New York: Metropolitan/Holt, 2000.

———. *The Seventh Million: The Israelis and the Holocaust*, translated by Haim Watzman. New York: Owl Books, 1993.

Selzer, Michael. *The Aryanization of the Jewish State*. New York: Black Star, 1967.

Shafir, Gershon. *Land, Labor and the Origins of the Israeli-Palestinian Conflict, 1882–1914*, 2nd ed., Berkeley: California UP, 1996.

Shahak, Israel. 'A History of the Concept of "Transfer" in Zionism', *Journal of Palestine Studies*, 18, iii, 1989.

Shohat, Ella. 'Sephardim in Israel: Zionism from the Standpoint of Its Jewish Victims', *Social Text* 19/20, 1988.

———. *Taboo Memories, Diasporic Voices*. Durham: Duke University Press, 2006.

Smith, Andrea. *Conquest: Sexual Violence and American Indian Genocide*. Boston, MA: South End Press, 2005.

Smith, Barbara J. *The Roots of Separatism in Palestine: British Economic Policy, 1920–1929*. Syracuse: Syracuse UP, 1993.

Sobel, Zvi and Benjamin Beit-Halahmi, eds. *Tradition, Innovation, Conflict: Jewishness and Judaism in Contemporary Israel*. Albany: SUNY UP, 1991.

Solow, Barbara L, ed. *Slavery and the Rise of the Atlantic System*. Cambridge: Cambridge UP/Harvard Du Bois Institute, 1991.

Spickard, Paul R. *Mixed Blood: Intermarriage and Ethnic Identity in Twentieth-Century America*. Madison: Wisconsin UP, 1989.

Spruhan, Paul. 'A Legal History of Blood Quantum in Federal Indian Law to 1935', *South Dakota Law Review*, 51, 2006.

Stein, Kenneth W. 'Legal Protection and Circumvention of Rights for Cultivators in Mandatory Palestine', in Joel S. Migdal, ed., *Palestinian Society and Politics*. Princeton: Princeton UP, 1980.

———. 'The Jewish National Fund: Land Purchase Methods and Priorities, 1924–1939', *Middle Eastern Studies* 20, 1984.

———. *The Land Question in Palestine, 1917–1939*. Chapel Hill: North Carolina UP, 1984.

Strauss, Herbert A, ed. *Hostages of Modernization: Studies on Modern Anti-semitism, 1870–1933/39. Germany, Great Britain, France*. Berlin: Walter de Gruyter, 1993.

Traverso, Enzo. *The Jews and Germany: From the 'Judeo-German Symbiosis' to the Memory of Auschwitz*. Lincoln: Nebraska UP, 1995.

Utley, Robert M. *The Indian Frontier of the American West, 1846–1890*. Albuquerque: New Mexico UP, 1984.

Veracini, Lorenzo. *Settler Colonialism: A Theoretical Introduction*. London: Palgrave Macmillan, 2010.

Viotti da Costa, Emilia. *The Brazilian Empire: Myths and Histories*. Chicago: Chicago UP, 1985.

Warren, Charles. *The Supreme Court in United States History*, vol. 2: *1821–1855*, Boston: Little, Brown & Co, 1922.

Wassilevsky, I. *Jewish Refugees and Military Service: The Ethical Aspect of Compulsion under Threat of Deportation*. London: The National Labour Press, 1916.

Weizman, Eyal. *Hollow Land: Israel's Architecture of Occupation*. London: Verso, 2007.

Wertheimer, Jack. *Unwelcome Strangers: East European Jews in Imperial Germany*. Oxford: Oxford UP, 1987.

White, Richard. *The Roots of Dependency: Subsistence, Environment, and Social Change among the Choctaws, Pawnees, and Navajo*. Lincoln: Nebraska UP, 1983.

———. *The Middle Ground: Indians, Empires, and Republics in the Great Lakes Region, 1650–1815*. New York: Cambridge UP, 1991.

Williams, Eric. *Capitalism and Slavery*. Chapel Hill: North Carolina UP, 1994 [1944].

Williams, Jr., Robert A. *The American Indian in Western Legal Thought: The Discourses of Conquest*. New York: Oxford UP, 1990.

Wolfe, Patrick. *Settler Colonialism and the Transformation of Anthropology: The Politics and Poetics of an Ethnographic Event*. London: Cassell, 1999.

————. 'Settler Colonialism and the Elimination of the Native', *Journal of Genocide Research*, 8, 2006.

Woodward, C. Vann. *A History of the South, Volume 9: Origins of the New South, 1877–1913*. Baton Rouge: Louisiana State UP/Littlefield Fund, 1951.

————. *The Strange Career of Jim Crow*. New York: Oxford UP, 1955.

Woolfson, Marion. *Prophets in Babylon: Jews in the Arab World*. London: Faber & Faber, 1980.

Wunder, John R. *'Retained by the People': A History of American Indians and the Bill of Rights*. New York: Oxford UP, 1994.

Young, Mary E. *Redskins, Ruffleshirts, and Rednecks: Indian Allotments in Alabama and Mississippi, 1830–1860*. Norman: Oklahoma UP, 1961.

Index